History and Class

For external students enrolled in the courses
'Introduction to Marx and History' and
'The Development of Capitalism in England 1660–1850' at
the University of New England, New South Wales

History and Class

*Essential Readings
in Theory and Interpretation*

Edited by R. S. Neale

Basil Blackwell

Editorial matter and organization © R. S. Neale 1983

First published 1983
Reprinted 1984

Basil Blackwell Publisher Limited
108 Cowley Road, Oxford OX4 1JF, England

Basil Blackwell Inc.
432 Park Avenue South, Suite 1505,
New York, NY 10016, USA

British Library Cataloguing in Publication Data

History and class.
 1. Social classes – England – History – Historiography
 I. Neale, R. S.
 305.5′072042   HN400.S6

ISBN 0-631-13016-0
ISBN 0-631-13135-3 Pbk

Typesetting by Oxford Verbatim Limited
Printed in Great Britain by T. J. Press Padstow

Contents

Acknowledgements

An early version of this collection was produced by the Department of External Studies at the University of New England, NSW in 1977. It came out as a companion volume to a similarly produced edition of *Class in English History*, to meet the needs of external students of the university. Therefore, it owes its being to my work with external students, and I warmly acknowledge the part they played. But the book owes its revised format and its new title to the gentle prodding and advice of John Davey of Basil Blackwell, and my thanks go to him.

Although the book had its origins in my work with students, it owes its construction to opportunities to shrug off their pressing needs and to forget the general demands of the university. I acknowledge the initiative of Eugene Kamenka for one such occasion. His initiative and the subsequent grant of a Visiting Fellowship at the Australian National University enabled me to think and work in The History of Ideas Unit during the Australian summer of 1980–81. For a similar opportunity, during the Californian winter of 1982, I am indebted to the Trustees of the Huntington Library. Indeed, it was in 'retirement' at the Huntington that I finished the Afterword. In the faded italianate splendour of Caltech's Athenaeum. There holding my breath at the Gainsboroughs and Reynolds in the Huntington, and marvelling at the twentieth-century manor-houses, villas and mansions of all the great ages in the development of capitalism surrounding it, I felt the weight of Lukác's remark that the positions of dons, *littérateurs* and pundits in the 'free world' was '*ein behaglicher Leerlauf*', 'a comfortable cossetted emptiness'. And it concentrated my mind. I hope this book might prove Lukács wrong.

I thank, too, all those publishers and authors who gave permission for reproduction of the extracts in the collection: Associated Book Publishers Ltd. (Chapter 10); Basic Books Inc. (Chapter 12); Cambridge University Press (Chapter 2); Craig Calhoun and *Social History* (Chapter 6); Lawrence & Wishart Ltd. (Chapter 3); Macmillan & Co. Ltd. (Chapter 1); Oxford University Press (Chapter 4); Routledge & Kegan Paul Ltd. (Chapters 5 and 9); Victor Gollancz Ltd. (Chapter 7); *Victorian Studies* (Chapter 8); Weidenfeld & Nicolson Ltd. (Chapter 11).

As always I am in debt for the preparation of this book to the skill and patience of Jenny Weissel, who types and re-types, making sense and order, when frequently there is none, in the pages I give her. To her my thanks. Also my thanks to Graydon Henning, who held the fort in Armidale on numerous occasions in 1980–82, during my 'retirement'.

Finally, Margaret. I owe her beyond measure.

Introduction

This collection of readings is a companion volume to my *Class in English History 1680–1850* (Basil Blackwell, 1981). The collection has two parts: Theory and Interpretation. Readings included under the heading Theory raise important questions on the theme of the language of class, introduced by Asa Briggs in the opening chapter; and all are essays on vocabulary and are classic statements in their field. The essays by Marx are particularly important for identifying the content of the Marxian notion, *class* consciousness. Readings included under the heading Interpretation offer descriptions and accounts of changes in social structure in England in the period 1680–1850. All but one of the authors of these essays consciously set their histories within conceptual and sometimes theoretical frameworks, and all use a language of class in their explanations of events and of change. The one exception, Gertrude Himmelfarb, vehemently rejects all overt theorizing as irrelevant to the historians' task. Nevertheless, she, too, uses a vocabulary of class. Therefore, the link between all the readings in this collection is their interest in the use of a language of class within some larger theoretical framework for the purpose of describing social structure and changes in it.

In *Class in English History* I have already commented at length upon the essays in this collection, except for those by Gareth Stedman Jones and Craig Calhoun. Therefore, I will neither summarize nor comment upon them again in this Introduction. I include the essay by Stedman Jones, 'From Historical Sociology to Theoretical History', because in it Stedman Jones emphasizes the importance of theory *in* history, by which he means theory that is internal to the process of historical inquiry itself, not imported from another discipline, for example, sociology or economics, which some might like to think of as already theoretically sophisticated. As Stedman Jones writes, 'The criteria by which the construction of a problem will be judged of historical significance will ultimately be dependent upon some explicit or implicit theory of social causation. In this sense, there is no distinction in principle between history and any other of the "social sciences". The distinction is not that between theory and non-theory, but between the adequacy or inadequacy of the theory brought to bear.' The significance of this essay for the language of class is made clear by Stedman Jones himself.

I include Calhoun's essay, 'Community: Toward a Variable Conceptualisation for Comparative Research', because Calhoun does what Stedman Jones says historians ought not to do; he imports social-anthropological theory into history, and does so in a way which he claims to be relevant to the problem of class in English History, particularly as it relates to the existence of conditions favourable to violent protest during the process of industrialization. Whereas Briggs claims that the development of a language of class indicated real changes taking place in England in the early nineteenth century, Calhoun believes that 'the emergence of the concept community also referred to some real and important phenomena in the eighteenth and early nineteenth centuries.' He writes that it is important that we refine the concept community rather than abandon it. In his own book, *The Question of Class Struggle*, Calhoun uses the concept community to challenge the importance hitherto given to class in English history before 1820. I will consider the significance for class theory and class history of Calhoun's book when I discuss, in the Afterword, several other important and relevant books published since I wrote *Class in English History*.

I have chosen this method of proceeding because, as I have implied, *Class in English History 1680–1850* is itself an introduction to this collection – and that book, now, is part of the historiographical problem I discuss in it, and around which this collection is built. Furthermore, these recent books complement, expand or challenge aspects of my argument, and it is through the Afterword rather than this Introduction that I hope to take up some of the points they raise in order to develop the dialogue begun in *Class in English History* . I say 'develop the dialogue' deliberately, because it seems to me that the books to which I will refer and my comments upon them do take the argument beyond that contained in the readings in this collection, and beyond that contained in *Class in English History*.

Part I
THEORY

1

The Language of 'Class' in Early Nineteenth-Century England

ASA BRIGGS

The collection begins with this essay by Asa Briggs because of the originality of its central concern: the relationship between words and social movements, in an English context. Although the paper is sketchy and untheoretical it still stands, almost alone, as an attempt by an historian to study language as an indication of the emergence and characteristics of social movements. Above all it argues the importance of understanding the social meaning of the new language of class, which was developing at the turn of the eighteenth and nineteenth centuries. Key points in Briggs' discussion are: his location of the beginnings of a language of class in the growing self consciousness of a middle class as they measured themselves against the dominant landowning aristocracy, at least by the second decade of the nineteenth century; his identification of Charles Hall as the originator of a class theory of society in 1802; his emphasis on the crucial importance, for the formation of a working class language of class, of the idea that labour had a right to the whole of its product; his notion that the mood of social hostility and class antagonism carried within the language of class was identified early in the development of that language, and counteracted by the development of a language of sociology and social mobility. Several of these key points are critically discussed elsewhere, in *Class in English History* and in the Afterword to this collection. Their appearance in this essay, in the context of a discussion of the language of class, marked what might have been the starting point of a potentially fertile area in English social history. Unfortunately Briggs has

From A. Briggs and J. Saville (eds.), *Essays in Labour History* (Macmillan, London, 1967), pp. 154–77.

had few successors. Except, perhaps, for Raymond Williams' *Keywords* and Karel Williams' more recent, *From Pauperism to Poverty*, this essay is an original. I place it first, out of its chronological sequence, almost as an introduction. The other four essays in this section fall easily into a chronological sequence from Marx in 1843–44 to Calhoun in 1980, as well as into a sequence of argument about theory and history, and about class.

The concept of social 'class' with all its attendant terminology was a product of large-scale economic and social changes of the late eighteenth and early nineteenth centuries. Before the rise of modern industry[1] writers on society spoke of 'ranks', 'orders', and 'degrees' or, when they wished to direct attention to particular economic groupings, of 'interests'. The word 'class' was reserved for a number of people banded together for educational purposes[2] or more generally with reference to subdivisions in schemes of 'classification'.[3] Thus the 1824 edition of the *Encyclopædia Britannica* spoke of 'classes of quadrupeds, birds, fishes and so forth, which are again subdivided into series or orders and these last into genera'. It directed its readers to articles on 'Animal Kingdom' and 'Botany'. By 1824, however, the word 'class' had already established itself as a social label, and ten years later John Stuart Mill was to remark:

They revolve in their eternal circle of landlords, capitalists and labourers, until they seem to think of the distinction of society into those three classes as if it were one of God's ordinances not man's, and as little under human control as the division of day or night. Scarcely any one of them seems to have proposed to himself as a subject of inquiry, what changes the relations of those classes to one another are likely to undergo in the progress of society.[4]

The word 'class' has figured so prominently in the subsequent development of the socialist — and of other social — vocabularies that a

[1] In its modern sense the word 'industry', used with reference not to a particular human attribute, but to a complex of manufacturing and productive institutions, was itself a new word in the late eighteenth century. See R. Williams, *Culture and Society* (1958), p. xv. Adam Smith was one of the first writers to use the word in this way: he did not use the word 'class' in the sense discussed in this essay.

[2] It was later used by the Methodists to refer to 'class' meetings, a usage which was later borrowed by early nineteenth-century 'Political Protestants' and Chartists.

[3] Daniel Defoe, who usually wrote in terms of 'orders', 'ranks', and 'degrees', on a few occasions used 'class' in contexts where he was referring to social classification. See, for instance, *Review*, 14 Apr. 1705, 21 June 1709. Smith also referred (incidentally) to 'classes of people' in his account of 'the three great orders of society' in his *The Wealth of Nations*, bk. i, chap. 11.

[4] *Monthly Repository* (1834), p. 320.

study of the origins and early use of the term in Britain is not simply an academic exercise in semantics. There was no dearth of social conflicts in pre-industrial society, but they were not conceived of at the time in straight class terms. The change in nomenclature in the late eighteenth and early nineteenth centuries reflected a basic change not only in men's ways of viewing society but in society itself. It is with the relationship between words and movements – in an English context – that this essay is concerned.

I

Eighteenth-century English society was hierarchical, and was often conceived of in terms of a pyramid with the 'common people', those without rank or 'dignity' at the base. The 'meer labouring people who depend upon their hands', as Defoe called them, were never without defenders[5] but social othodoxy had little use for 'the gross and inconsistent notion' of equality.[6] Skilled artisans had their own grades of 'superiority' and 'inferiority'[7] while between the 'nobility' and the 'commonalty' were the growing numbers of 'middling people' or 'middling sorts' whose praises were frequently sung in an age of increasing wealth and mercantile expansion. The most successful of them were easily absorbed into the 'gentry', that most English of social groupings, and chapter 24 of Defoe's *Complete English Tradesman* (1726) was entitled 'Extracts from the genealogies of several illustrious families of our English nobility, some of which owe their rise to trade, and others their descent and fortunes to prudent alliances with the families of citizens.[8]

The element of mobility in the social system – based on what Adam Smith and Malthus after him called 'the natural effort of every indi-

[5] For one of the most important strands in the defence, see C. Hill, The Norman Yoke in J. Saville (ed.), *Democracy and the Labour Movement* (1954).
[6] For an early eighteenth-century criticism of it and an alternative analysis of society, see D. Defoe, *Of Royall Educacion* (written 1728–9).
[7] Francis Place complained in the early nineteenth century of the indiscriminate jumbling together of 'the most skilled and the most prudent workmen with the most ignorant and imprudent labourers and paupers' when the term 'lower orders' was used. 'The difference is great indeed,' he went on, 'and in many cases will scarce admit of comparison.' Place Papers, British Museum, Add. MSS. 27,834, f. 45.
[8] Cp. P. J. Grosley, *A Tour of London, II* (1772): 'The mixture and confusion . . . between the nobility and the mercantile part of the nation, is an inexhaustible source of wealth to the state, the nobility having acquired an accession of wealth by marriage, the tradesmen make up for their loss by their eager endeavours to make a fortune, and the gentry conspire to the same end by their efforts to raise such an estate as shall procure a peerage for themselves or their children.'

vidual to better his own condition'[9] – was often stressed by social commentators, particularly those who drew a sharp distinction between England and the continent. There were two other very different elements, however, which were given equal attention and were especially emphasized by the first generation of writers to condemn the social disintegration' consequent upon the rise of factory industry. The first of them was what Cobbett called 'the chain of connection' between the rich and the poor[10] and the second was what Southey described as 'the bond of attachment'.[11] The use of the nouns 'chain' and 'bond' is as eloquent (in retrospect) as the choice of 'connection' and 'attachment', but Cobbett and Southey in their different ways were praising the past in order to condemn the present. 'Connection' was associated not only with a network of social obligation but with gentle slopes of social gradation. It implied that every man had his place within an order, but that the order allowed for declensions of status as well as bold contrast. To those who were willing to disturb that order Cobbett exclaimed, 'You are for reducing the community to two classes: Masters and Slaves.'[12] 'Attachment' was directly associated both with 'duty' – the 'duty' to appropriate to 'rank' – and with dependence, and thereby with 'charity', 'deference', and 'subordination'. 'The bond of attachment is broken,' wrote Southey in 1829, 'there is no longer the generous bounty which calls forth a grateful and honest and confiding dependence.'[13]

Before the Industrial Revolution of the 1780s there were many signs of tension and contradiction both in society and in contemporary writings about it. The growth of population, the problem of 'indigence', the enclosure movement in the villages, the increase in home and foreign trade, and the emergence of 'radical' ideas in politics preceded the development of the steam-engine. It was the steam-engine, however, which was the 'principal factor in accelerating urban concentration' and 'generalizing' the labour force.[14] In was the steam-engine also which inspired both the optimistic panegyrics of man's 'conquest of Nature' and the critical analyses of the contradictions and conflicts of the new society. The extent of the contradictions and the

[9] *The Wealth of Nations* (1776), bk. iv, chap. 9.

[10] *Political Register*, 14 April 1821.

[11] R. Southey, *Sir Thomas More: or, Colloquies on the Progress and Prospects of Society* (1829), p. 47.

[12] *Political Register*, 14 April 1821.

[13] R. Southey, *Sir Thomas More*, p. 47.

[14] For the social impact of the change from water power to steam power, see G. D. H. Cole, *Studies in Class Structure* (1955), pp. 28–30. Marx, *Capital*, i, pt. IV, chap. 13 quoted A. Redgrave, a factory inspector, who argued that 'the steam-engine is the parent of manufacturing towns'. (Everyman edition, 1930, i. 398.)

conflicts was clearly appreciated before the term 'industrial revolution' was coined. John Wade, the author of the *History of the Middle and Working Classes* (1833), one of the first attempts to put the facts of the recent past into historical perspective, wrote as follows:

The physical order of communities, in which the production of the necessaries of subsistence is the first want and chief occupation, has in our case been rapidly inverted, and in lieu of agricultural supremacy, a vast and over-stopping superstructure of manufacturing wealth and population has been substituted. . . . To this extraordinary revolution, I doubt not, may be traced much of the bane and many of the blessings incidental to our condition – the growth of an opulent commercial and a numerous, restless and intelligent operative class; sudden alternations of prosperity and depression – of internal quiet and violent political excitement; extremes of opulence and destitution; the increase of crime; conflicting claims of capital and industry; the spread of an imperfect knowledge, that agitates and unsettles the old without having definitely settled the new foundations; clashing and independent opinions on most public questions, with other anomalies peculiar to our existing but changeful social existence.[15]

The use of the word 'class' and the sense of class that made the use increasingly meaningful must be related to what Wade called both 'the bane' and 'the blessings' of the new society. The development of factory industry often broke 'the bond of attachment', substituting for it what Carlyle was to call a 'cash nexus'.[16] The continued existence of factory paternalism checked but did not reverse this process. At the same time with the breaking of the bond there was increasing pressure to secure 'union' among the workers themselves. The demand not only for union at the factory or the local level but for 'general union', the story of which has been told by Professor Cole,[17] was directly related to the story of the emergence of a self-conscious 'working class'. Cobbett, who was one of the most forthright advocates of the old social system operating in an ideal form, saw clearly that once that system had been destroyed, 'classes' would be ranged against each other:

They [working men] combine to effect a rise in wages. The masters combine against them. One side complains of the other; but neither knows the *cause* of

[15] J. Wade, *History of the Middle and Working Classes* (1842 edn.), Preface, p. 1.

[16] This phrase, which was used by Disraeli, the authors of the *Communist Manifesto*, and many of the novelists and reviewers of the 1840s, was first used by Carlyle. As early as 1829 he wrote in his essay *Signs of the Times* that 'Cash Payment' was becoming the 'sole nexus' between man and man. Later, the shorter term became something of a slogan.

[17] *Attempts at General Union* (1953), originally published in 1939 in the *International Review for Social History*.

the turmoil, and the turmoil goes on. The different trades combine, and call the combination GENERAL UNION. So that here is one class of society united to oppose another class.[18]

The same consequence followed on the growth of industrial cities, where the 'masses' were segregated and left to their own devices. A few years before Disraeli used the phrase 'two nations', a distinguished preacher spoke in very similar terms at a chapel in Boston across the Atlantic:

It is the unhappiness of most large cities that, instead of inspiring union and sympathy among different 'conditions of men', they consist of different ranks, so widely separated indeed as to form different communities. In most large cities there may be said to be two nations, understanding as little of one another, having as little intercourse, as if they lived in different lands. . . . This estrangement of men from men, of class from class, is one of the saddest features of a great city.[19]

It was a theme which was to be taken up frequently in nineteenth-century argument, and which dominated Engels's picture of Manchester in the 1840s. 'We know well enough,' Engels wrote, 'that [the] isolation of the individual . . . is everywhere the fundamental principle of modern society. But nowhere is this selfish egotism so blatantly evident as in the frantic bustle of the great city.[20] But the 'disintegration of society into individuals' was accompanied by the carving out of classes. 'The cities first saw the rise of the workers and the middle classes into opposing social groups.'[21]

Forty years before Engels, Charles Hall had stressed the snapping of 'the chain of continuity' in society and stated clearly for the first time the central proposition of a class theory of society:

The people in a civilised state may be divided into different orders; but for the purpose of investigating the manner in which they enjoy or are deprived of the requisites to support the health of their bodies and minds, they need only be divided into two classes, viz. the rich and the poor.[22]

The sharp contrasts of industrialism encouraged the restatement of theories of society in these terms. In one sense 'class' was a more

[18] *Political Register*, 27 Aug. 1825.

[19] W. E. Channing, *A Discourse on the Life and Character of Rev. Joseph Tuckerman* (Boston, Mass., 1841), pp. 7–8.

[20] F. Engels, *The Condition of the Working Class in England* (tr. W. O. Henderson and W. H. Chaloner, 1958), p. 31.

[21] *Ibid.*, p. 203.

[22] C. Hall, *The Effects of Civilisation on the People in European States* (1805), p. 3.

indefinite word than 'rank' and this may have been among the reasons for its introduction.[23] In another sense, however, employment of the word 'class' allowed for a sharper and more generalized picture of society, which could be provided with a historical and economic underpinning. Conservatives continued to prefer to talk of 'ranks' and 'orders' – as they still did in the middle of the nineteenth century[24] – and the old language coexisted with the new, as it did in the words of the preacher quoted above, but analysts of the distribution of the national income[25] and social critics alike talked increasingly in class terms. So too did politicians, particularly as new social forces were given political expression. The stormiest political decade of early nineteenth-century English history, that which began with the financial crisis of 1836 and the economic crisis of 1837, was the decade when class terms were most generally used and 'middle classes' and 'working classes' alike did not hesitate to relate politics directly to class antagonisms.

There was, however, an influential social cross-current which directed attention not to the contrasting fortunes and purposes of 'middle-classes' and 'working classes' but to a different division in industrial society, that between 'the industrious classes' and the rest. Those writers who were more impressed by the productive possibilities of large-scale industry than afraid of social 'disintegration' dwelt on this second division. Saint-Simon's demand for unity of 'the productive classes' against parasitic 'non-producers'[26] had many parallels as well as echoes inside England. Patrick Colquhoun, whose statistical tables were used by Robert Owen and John Gray,[27] attempted to divide industrial society into a productive class whose labour increased

---

[23] R. Williams, *Culture and Society*, p. xv.

[24] The *Quarterly Review*, which continued to refer to 'attachment' and 'continuity' in many of its articles on the social system even in the second half of the nineteenth century, referred in 1869 (vol. 126, p. 450) to 'lower-middle class', adding hastily, 'We must apologize for using this painful nomenclature, but really there is no choice.'

[25] Writers on the national income were among the first to have to consider how best to describe the various sections of the population. 'Political arithmetic' and social classification went together.

[26] See G. D. H. Cole, *Socialist Thought, The Forerunners, 1789–1850*, pp. 42–3, for the distinction between *les industriels* and *le oisifs*. The word 'industry' itself had a special significance for Saint-Simon (see his *L'Industrie* (1817)), and there were socialist undertones beneath many of the words derived from it. See the fascinating, pioneer article by A. E. Bestor. The Evolution of the Socialist Vocabulary, in the *Journal of the History of Ideas*, 9 June 1948.

[27] Owen constructed visual aids to illustrate Colquhoun's tables, a set of eight cubes exhibiting a 'General View of Society', the working classes being represented at the base by a large cube whilst the apex was formed by a small cube, representing the royal family and the aristocracy. See F. Podmore, *Robert Owen* (1906), pp. 255–6. John Gray's *A Lecture on Human Happiness* (1825) set out the case that Labour received only one-fifth of its produce, the rest being appropriated by the 'unproductive' classes.

the national income and a 'diminishing class' which produced no 'new property'. When he argued that 'it is by the labour of the people, employed in various branches of industry, that all ranks of the community in every condition of life annually subsist',[28] he was not saying, as Gray later did, that manual labour created all wealth. Owen, who occasionally wrote in what were coming to be regarded as conventional terms of the 'upper', the 'middle' and the 'working classes', more usually conceived of society in the same terms as Colquhoun:

There will be, therefore, at no distant period, a union of the government, aristocracy, and non-producers on the one part and the Industrious Classes, the body of the people generally, on the other part; and the two most formidable powers for good or evil are thus forming.[29]

The same conception influenced radical politics. The *Extraordinary Black Book*, also borrowing from Colquhoun and mixing up the language of 'class' and 'orders', maintained that:

The industrious orders may be compared to the soil, out of which every thing is evolved and produced; the other classes to the trees, tares, weeds and vegetables drawing their nutriment, supported and maintained on its surface. . . . When mankind attain a state of greater perfectibility . . . [the useful classes] ought to exist in a perfect state. The other classes have mostly originated in our vices and ignorance . . . having no employment, their name and office will cease in the social state.[30]

Thomas Attwood, who in favourable social and economic circumstances in Birmingham, tried to unite 'middle' and 'working classes' in a single Political Union,[31] also believed that what he called 'the industrious classes' should secure political power. 'The ox is muzzled that

[28] *A Treatise on the Wealth, Power and Resources of the British Empire* (1814). Colquhoun's attempt – in his own words 'to show how . . . New Property . . . is distributed among the different Classes of the Community' – had socialist implications which he did not draw out. He believed that poverty was necessary in society, that Malthus's population doctrine was sound, and that improved 'social police' would hold society together. Yet just as Ricardian economics were used to develop a socialist theory of value, so Colquhoun's statistics were used to propound a socialist analysis of distribution, behind both Ricardo and Colquhoun was Adam Smith. For Smith's account of 'productive' and 'unproductive' labour, see *The Wealth of Nations*, bk. ii, chap. 3

[29] Address to the Sovereign, printed in *The Crisis*, 4 Aug. 1832.

[30] *The Extraordinary Black Book* (1831 edn.), pp. 217–18. Colquhoun was described as 'a bold, but, as experience had proved, a very shrewd calculator'. (*Ibid.*, p. 216.)

[31] For the significance of his thought and work against a European background, see my article, 'Social Structure and Politics in Birmingham and Lyons' (1825–48) in the *British Journal of Sociology*, i, Mar. 1950.

treadeth the corn.'[32] It was only after the Reform Bill of 1832 had failed
to satisfy his hopes – and only then for a short period of time – that he
claimed that 'in a great cause, he was content to stand or fall with the
workmen alone' even if the middle classes, to which he belonged,
were against him.[33]

II

Before turning to 'working-class' critics of both Owen and Attwood
and to the statement of class theory in specifically working-class
perspectives, the terms 'upper class' and 'middle class' require more
careful and detailed examination. The phrase 'higher classes' was used
for the first time by Burke in his *Thoughts on French Affairs* in 1791,
significantly only when the position of 'higher classes' seemed to be
threatened not only in France but in England. It was an exhortatory
phrase in much of the Evangelical literature of the last decade of the
century. When the French Revolution challeged the power of aristo-
cracies and in England traditional duties seemed to be in disrepair,
there was a need to re-define them. It was in this mood that Thomas
Gisborne, clergyman friend of Wilberforce, published his *Enquiry into
the Duties of Men in the Higher Rank and Middle Classes of Society in Great
Britain* in 1795. There was much literature of this kind in the 1790s.
Hannah More, Cobbett's 'old bishop in petticoats',[34] was an inde-
fatigable supporter of 'the old order', and here tracts, some of which
were specially addressed to 'Persons of the Middle Ranks', 'were
brought by the gentry and middling classes full as much as by the
common people'.[35]
    The phrase 'middle classes', which antedates the phrase 'working
classes',[36] was a product, however, not of exhortation but of conscious

[32] *Report of the Proceedings* of the *Birmingham Political Union*, 25 Jan. 1830. The Declaration of
the Union drawn up on this occasion claimed that the House of Commons 'in its present state'
was 'too far removed in habits, wealth and station, from the wants and interests of the lower and
middle classes of the people to have any just views respecting them, or any close identity of
feeling with them'. It went on to complain of the over-representation of the 'great aristocratical
interests', only nominally counter-balanced by the presence of a few 'rich and retired capitalists'.
The National Political Union, founded in London in 1831, also proclaimed as one of its
purposes, 'to watch over and promote the interests, and to better the condition of the
INDUSTRIOUS AND WORKING CLASSES'. (Place Papers, Add. MSS. 27,791, f. 184.)
    [33] *Birmingham Journal*, 17 Jan. 1836.
    [34] *Political Register*, 20 Apr. 1822.
    [35] Letter to Zachary Macaulay, 6 Jan. 1796, quoted by M. G. Jones, *Hannah More* (1952),
p. 144. These tracts were regarded as 'antidotes to Tom Paine', 'Burke for Beginners'.
    [36] Gisborne's *Enquiry* was certainly one of the first publications to use the term 'middle
classes'. In 1797 the *Monthly Magazine,* founded by Richard Phillips and John Aikin to 'propagate

pride. As early as the 1780s attempts had been made to create new organizations which would uphold the claims of the new manufacturers. Pitt's commercial policy goaded manufacturers to set up the General Chamber of Manufacturers in 1785:

Common danger having at length brought together a number of Manufacturers in various branches, and from various places, and their having felt the advantages resulting to each from unreserved conferences and mutual assistance, they are now persuaded, that the prosperity of the Manufacturers of this kingdom, and of course that of the kingdom itself, will be promoted by the formation of a general bond of union, whereby the influence and experience of the whole being collected at one common centre, they will be better enabled to effect any useful purposes for their general benefit.

In eighteenth-century terms this was the mobilization of a new economic 'interest', an interest which failed to maintain its unity in the immediate future. In was something more than that, however. 'The manufacturers of Great Britain', their statement began, 'constitute a very large, if not a principal part of the community; and their industry, ingenuity and wealth, have contributed no small share towards raising this kingdom to the distinguished and envied rank which she bears among the European nations.'[37] The word 'class' was not used, as it was used freely and unashamedly by the Anti-Corn Law League half a century later, but what was whispered in private in the 1780s was shouted on the platforms in the 1840s.

There were several factors encouraging the development of a sense of middle-class unity where hitherto there had been a recognition of (imperfect) mutual interst. First in time was the imposition of Pitt's income tax, which entailed the common treatment of a group of diverse 'interests' by the government. Second was the impact of the Napoleonic Wars as a whole, which laid emphasis on the incidence of 'burdens', burdens which seemed to be of unequal weight for the owners of land and the owners of capital. Adam Smith had already distinguished clearly between these two 'interests' or 'orders' as he called them (and, indeed, a third 'interest', that 'of those who live by

---

liberal principles', spoke of 'the middle and industrious classes of society' (p. 397). The phrase 'working classes' seems to have been used for the first time by Robert Owen in 1813 in his *Essays on the Formation of Character*, later reprinted under the more familiar title *A New View of Society*, but it was a descriptive rather than an analytical term ('the poor and working classes of Great Britain and Ireland have been found to exceed 12 millions of persons'). He used the term frequently in letters to the newspapers in 1817 and in 1818 he published *Two Memorials on Behalf of the Working Classes*.

[37] *Sketch of a Plan of the General Chamber of Manufacturers of Great Britain* (1785).

wages' as well), but he did not concede the claims of the merchants and 'master manufacturers': in his opinion they were more concerned with their own affairs than with the affairs of society as a whole. 'Their superiority over the country gentleman is, not so much in their knowledge of the public interest, as in their having a better knowledge of their own interest than he has of his.'[38] Between 1776 and 1815, however, the numbers and wealth of the 'owners of capital' increased, and both their public grievances and their public claims were advocated with energy and persistence.

It is not surprising that a sense of grievance stimulated talk of 'class', and there are many expressions of it in the periodicals of the day. 'Why rejoice in the midst of rivers of blood,' asked a writer in the *Monthly Repository* in 1809, 'while the burden of taxation presses so heavily on the middle classes of society, so as to leave the best part of the community little to hope and everything to fear?'[39] Four years later the same magazine demanded immediate peace 'for the relief of those privations and burdens, which now oppress every class in the community, including the poor and middle classes'.[40] The *Oxford English Dictionary* gives 1812 as the first occasion on which the phrase 'middle class' was used – in the *Examiner* of the August of that year – and in the twentieth century the example has a very familiar ring – 'such of the Middle Class of Society who have fallen upon evil days'.

By 1815, however, statements about the 'middle classes' or the still popular term 'middle ranks' often drew attention not to grievances but first to the special role of the middle classes in society as a strategic and 'progressive' group and second to their common economic interests.

As early as 1798 the *Monthly Magazine* sang the praises of 'the middle ranks' in whom 'the great mass of information, and of public and private virtues reside'.[41] In 1807 the *Athenaeum* eulogized 'those persons whom the wisest politicians have always counted the most valuable, because the least corrupted members of society, the middle ranks of people'.[42] Such magazine comments had an element of editorial flattery about them, but beneath the flattery was a keen awareness of social trends. The growing reading public included large numbers of people who belonged to the 'middle classes',[43] and their

[38] Smith's general account of the division of the 'annual produce' of land and labour is given at the end of the last chapter (11) of bk. i of *The Wealth of Nations*. For Smith's view of the 'labourer', see above, p. 165.
[39] *Monthly Repository* (1809), p. 501.
[40] *Ibid.*, (1813), p. 65.
[41] *Monthly Magazine* (1798), p. 1. It referred to the 'ignorant apathy' of the 'lowest classes'.
[42] *Athenaeum* (1807), p. 124.
[43] See R. D. Atlick, *The English Common Reader* (Chicago, 1957), p. 41.

views were considered to be the main expression of the new 'public opinion'. It was not difficult, indeed, to argue, as James Mill did in his *Essay on Government*, that 'the class which is universally described as both the most wise and the most virtuous part of the community, the middle rank' was the main opinion-making group in a dynamic society and would control politics 'if the basis of representation were extended'.[44] In the diffusion of Utilitarian ideas in the 1820s this case was frequently argued. The middle classes, 'the class who will really approve endeavours in favour of good government, and of the happiness and intelligence of men', had to unite to bring pressure upon the aristocracy. Their philosophy, like their wealth, depended on 'individualism', but their social action had to be concerted. 'Public opinion operates in various ways upon the aristocratical classes, partly by contagion, partly by conviction, and partly by intimidation: and the principal strength of that current is derived from the greatness of the mass by which it is swelled.'[45]

Politicians could not remain indifferent to this language, particularly when it was backed by wealth and increasing economic authority. One of the first to appreciate the need to win the support of the 'middle classes' was Henry Brougham. While the Luddites were engaged in what Engels later called 'the first organized resistance of the workers, as a class, to the bourgeoisie',[46] the 'middle classes' were being mobilized in a campaign to abolish the Orders-in-Council. Brougham, 'the life and soul' of the agitation, was later in his life to produce his celebrated equation of the 'middle classes' and 'the People'. 'By the people, I mean the middle classes, the wealth and intelligence of the country, the glory of the British name.'[47] During the Reform Bill agitation of 1830–2 many similar statements were made by Whig leaders who were anxious, in Durham's phrase, 'to attach numbers to property and good order'.[48] Even the aristocratic Grey, who feared the Political Unions with their propaganda for unity between the middle

---

[44] *An Essay on Government* (ed. E. Barker, 1937), pp. 71–2. The essay was completed in 1820. There is a remarkable and significant contrast between the method and style of Mill's argument and the form of his dogmatic and defiant concluding sentence. 'It is altogether futile with regard to the foundation of good government to say that this or the other portion of the people, may at this, or the other time, depart from the wisdom of the middle rank. It is enough that the great majority of the people never cease to be guided by that rank; and we may with some confidence, challenge the adversaries of the people to produce a single instance to the contrary in the history of the world' (*Ibid.*, 73.)

[45] James Mill in the *Westminster Review*, 1, Oct. 1824.

[36] Engels, *The Condition of the Working Class in England*, p. 243.

[47] This quotation is given in the *Oxford English Dictionary*. In introducing the Reform Bill Lord John Russell talked of changing the House of Commons from 'an assembly of representatives of small classes and particular interests' into 'a body of men who represent the people'.

[48] Quoted by N. Gash, *Politics in the Age of Peel* (1953), p. 16.

classes and the working classes, chose to appeal 'to the middle classes who form the real and efficient mass of public opinion and without whom the power of the gentry is nothing'.[49] The Whigs wished to hitch the middle classes to the constitution to prevent a revolution: a section of the extreme radicals wanted to associate them with the working classes to secure revolution. In the tense atmosphere of the years 1830–2 it was not surprising that advocates of cautious change insisted that 'any plan [of Reform] must be objectionable which, by keeping the Franchise very high and exclusive, fails to give satisfaction to the middle and respectable ranks of society, and drives them to a union, founded on dissatisfaction, with the lower orders. It is of the utmost importance to associate the middle with the higher orders of society in the love and support of the institutions and government of the country.'[50] The language as much as the content of this statement reflects a traditionalist view not only of politics but of society.

The relationship between 'public opinion' and the growing strength of the 'middle classes' was recognized even when there was an absence of political crisis. Sir James Graham, at that time an independent but later a member both of the Whig committee which drafted the Reform Bill and of the Conservative cabinet which proposed the repeal of the corn laws, remarked in 1826:

I know no bound but public opinion. The seat of public opinion is in the middle ranks of life – in that numerous class, removed from the wants of labour and the cravings of ambition, enjoying the advantages of leisure, and possessing intelligence sufficient for the formation of a sound judgement, neither warped by interest nor obscured by passion.[51]

The remark echoes Aristotle rather than Mill,[52] but it was one version of an extended argument. Another, more cogent, was set out in a historically important but neglected treatise. *On the Rise, Progress, and Present State of Public Opinion in Great Britain and Other Parts of the World* (1828). Its author, W. A. Mackinnon, generalized from recent ex-

---

[49] Grey made this remark outside Parliament. See Henry, Earl Grey (ed.), *The Correspondence of the Late Earl Grey with His Majesty King William IV* (1867), i. 376.

[50] H. Cockburn, *Letters on Affairs of Scotland*, quoted by Gash, op. cit. 15.

[51] Sir James Graham, *Corn and Currency* (1826), p. 9. Graham appealed to the landed proprietors to unite as 'the manufacturing and commercial body' had done, and to frame their actions in accordance with 'public opinion' and 'the interest of the community'.

[52] It also recalls a passage in Defoe's *Robinson Crusoe* – 'Mine was the middle state or what might be called the upper station of low life . . . not exposed to the Labour and sufferings of the Mechanick part of Mankind, and not embarrassed with the Pride, Luxury, Ambition and Envy of the Upper Part of Mankind.'

perience.[53] His book began with a 'definition' of the 'classes of society' and went on to describe how the rise of the 'middle classes' led to the growth of wealth and freedom:

The extent or power of public opinion . . . resolves itself into the question whether . . . a community is possessed of an extensive middle class society, when compared to a lower class; for the advantages called requisites for public opinion, cannot exist without forming a proportionate middle class. . . . In every community or state where public opinion becomes powerful or has influence, it appears that the form of government becomes liberal in the exact proportion as the power of public opinion increases.[54]

Mackinnon related the recent rise of the 'middle classes' to what was later called 'the industrial revolution':

Machinery creates wealth, which augments the middle class, which gives strength to public opinion; consequently, to allude to the extension of machinery is to account for the increase of the middle class of society.[55]

In a footnote to this passage he drew attention to the magnitude of the changes in his own lifetime:

That the results arising from the improvement of machinery and its increase, are almost beyond the grasp of the human mind to define, may seem probable from the change that has and is daily taking place in the world.

Finally, he pegged class divisions to the distribution of property:

The only means by which the classes of society can be defined, in a community where the laws are equal, is from the amount of property, either real or personal, possessed by individuals. As long as freedom and civilisation exist, property is so entirely the only power that no other means, or choice is left of distinguishing the several classes, than by the amount of property belonging to the individuals of which they are formed.[56]

Not only the amount of property was relevant in shaping class consciousness after 1815, but the kind. The prolonged but intermittent battle for the repeal of the corn laws encouraged social analysis in

---

[53] William Mackinnon was a Member of Parliament almost continuously from 1830 to 1865. His book on public opinion was rewritten in 1846 as a *History of Civilisation*. Mackinnon was one of the first writers to relate the rise of the 'middle classes' to the 'progress of civilization'.

[54] W. A. MacKinnon, *On the Rise, Progress, and Present State of Public Opinion* (1828), pp. 6–7.

[55] *Ibid.*, p. 10.

[56] *Ibid.*, p. 2.

class terms: at the same time, particularly in its last stages, it sharpened middle-class consciousness and gave it highly organized means of expression.

The kind of social analysis set out in T. Perronet Thompson's *Catechism on the Corn Laws* (1826) was immediately popular for its content as much as for its style of exposition. The theory of rent was used to drive a wedge between the 'landlords' and the rest of the community, often with as much force as the labour theory of value was used in working-class arguments. Rent was defined as 'the superfluity of price, or that part of it which is not necessary to pay for the production with a living profit'. Adam Smith's argument that 'the landed interest', unlike the manufacturing interest, had a direct concern in 'the affairs of society as a whole' was turned on its head. The landlords were described by the repealers as selfish monopolists, who used the corn laws to protect their own selfish interest against the interests of the community. No vituperation was spared. There were two other particular interesting questions and answers in the *Catechism*. 'Q. That we must reconcile conflicting interests. A. There can be no conflict on a wrong. When the question is of a purse unjustly given, it is a fallacy to say we must reconcile conflicting interests, and give the taker half. Q. That the relation between the landlords and others, arising out of the Corn Laws is a source of kindly feelings and mutual virtues. A. Exactly the same was said of slavery.'[57]

Between the publication of the *Catechism* and the formation of the Anti-Corn Law League in 1839 there was a lull in the agitation. The League, however, was a uniquely powerful instrument in the forging of middle-class consciousness. 'We were a middle-class set of agitators', Cobden admitted, and the League was admnistered 'by those means by which the middle class usually carries on its movements'.[58] When the battle for repeal had been won Cobden asked Peel directly – 'do you shrink from the post of governing through the *bona fide* representatives of the middle class? Look at the facts, and can the country be otherwise ruled at all? There must be an end of the juggle of parties, the mere representatives of tradition, and some man must of necessity rule the state through its governing class. The Reform Bill decreed it: the passing of the Corn Bill has realized it.'[59] Such a bold statement demonstrates that by 1846, not only had the phrase 'middle

---

[57] For the background of the *Catechism* and its importance in the struggle for repeal, see L. G. Johnson, *General T. Perronet Thompson* (1957), chap. 8, and D. G. Barnes, *A History of the English Corn Laws* (1930), pp. 210–12.

[58] J. Morley, *The Life of Richard Cobden* (1903 edn.), i, p. 249.

[59] *Ibid.*, pp. 390–7. In his reply Peel was careful to avoid all reference to 'class'.

class' established itself as a political concept, but those people who considered themselves as representatives of the middle classes were prepared to assert in the strongest possible language their claim to political leadership.

Behind the League was middle-class wealth and what Disraeli in *Coningsby* (1844) called 'the pride of an order'.[60] There was also what had recently been called 'a strong belief in the nobility and dignity of industry and commerce', a kind of businessmen's romantic movement: '. . . trade has now a chivalry of its own; a chivalry whose stars are radiant with the more benignant lustre of justice, happiness and religion, and whose titles will outlive the barbarous nomenclature of Charlemagne.'[61]

This kind of rhetoric was usually accompanied by attacks on 'aristocratic tyranny', 'hereditary opulence' and 'social injustice', and by the declaration that 'trade shall no longer pay a tribute to the soil'. At the same time, it was necessary to supplement it – for political purposes– by an appeal to the 'working classes' ('joint victims' of the 'monopolists') and by an attempt to win over tenant farmers and to draw 'a broad distinction . . . between the landed and the agricultural interest'.[62] The case for repeal had to be stated in different terms from those employed in Manchester in 1815, when the narrow economic interests of the manufacturers were the main staple of the published argument.[63] In Morley's famous words, 'class-interest widened into the consciousness of a commanding national interest'.[64] The argument was radically different in its tone and its implications from that advanced by the General Chamber of Manufacturers in the 1780s. Again Morley has caught the mood as the Leaguers themselves liked to interpret it:

Moral ideas of the relations of class to class in this country, and of the relations of country to country in the civilized world, lay behind the contention of the

[60] Disraeli also referred to 'classes'. When Coningsby went to Manchester, 'the great Metropolis of Labour', he 'perceived that [industrial] wealth was rapidly developing classes whose power was imperfectly recognized in the constitutional scheme, and whose duties in the social system seemed altogether omitted'. (bk. iv, chap. 2.) In conversing with Milbank he had already 'heard for the first time of influential classes in the country, who were not noble, and yet were determined to acquire power' (bk ii, chap. 6.) He referred to 'the various classes of this country [being] arrayed against each other'. (bk. iv, chap. 12.)

[61] H. Dunckley, *The Charter of the Nations* (1854), p. 25. Quoted by N. McCord, *The Anti-Corn Law League* (1958), p. 24.

[62] A phrase of Cobden, quoted *ibid.*, p. 145.

[63] The early advocates of free trade in 1815 'took the untenable and unpopular ground that it was necessary to have cheap bread in order to reduce the English rate of wages to the continental level, and so long as they persisted in this blunder, the cause of free trade made little progress'. W. Cooke Taylor, *The Life and Times of Sir Robert Peel* (1842), p. 111.

[64] J. Morley, *The Life of Richard Cobden*, i. p. 180.

hour, and in the course of that contention came into new light. The prompt-ings of a commercial shrewdness were gradually enlarged into enthusiasm for a far-reaching principle, and the hard-headed man of business gradually felt himself touched with the generous glow of the partriot and the de-liverer.[65]

III

The glow was not always infectious, and although the League had some success in attracting the support of 'the working classes of the more respectable sort',[66] it was confronted in the provinces with the first large-scale self-consciously 'working' movement, Chartism. Re-lations between Chartists and Leaguers often demonstrated straight class antagonism. Mark Hovell quotes the story of the relations be-tween the two groups in Sunderland. The Leaguers asked the Local Chartist leaders, moderate men who agreed that the corn laws were an intolerable evil, to join them in their agitation. They replied that they could not co-operate merely on the merits of the question:

What is our present relation to you as a section of the middle class? – they went on – It is one of violent opposition. You are the holders of power, participation in which you refuse us; for demanding which you persecute us with a malignity paralleled only by the ruffian Tories. We are therefore surprised that you should ask us to co-operate with you.[67]

This attitude was not shared by all Chartists in all parts of the country – actual class relations, as distinct from theories of class, varied from place to place – but it was strong enough and sufficiently persistent to ensure that Chartists and Leaguers were as violently opposed to each other as both were the government. Indeed, middle-class claims both of the rhetorical and of the economic kind helped to sharpen working-class consciousness, while fear of independent working-class action, tinged as it was with fear of violence, gave middle-class opinion a new edge. To men like Ebenezer Elliott, the Corn Law Rhymer, who believed – as part of the same programme – in repeal, suffrage exten-sion, and class conciliation, the 'middle classes' were being assailed on two sides. On the one side was 'the tyranny of aristocracy': on the

[65] *Ibid.*, p. 182.
[66] A phrase used in a letter from a repealer in Carlisle, quoted by N. McCord, *The Anti-Corn Law League*, p. 97. There was strong working-class support in Carlisle for Julian Harney, who preached a very different gospel to that of the League. See A. R. Schoyen, *The Chartist Challenge* (1958), p. 72.
[67] Quoted by M. Hovell, *The Chartist Movement* (1925 edn.), pp. 215–16.

other was 'the foolish insolence of the Chartists, which has exasperated into madness the un-natural hatred which the have-somethings bear to the have-nothings'.[68]

Chartist theories of class and expressions of class consciousness have recently been scrutinized.[69] In this essay more attention will be paid to the concept of a 'working class' before it was proclaimed in eloquent language by William Lovett and the London Working Men's Association in 1836.

Adam Smith often showed considerably sympathy in his writings for the 'workman', but the sympathy was frequently accompanied by statements about the workman's powerlessness. 'Many workmen could not subsist a week, few could subsist a month, and scarce any a year without employment.' Nor did their 'tumultuous combinations' do them much good. 'The interposition of the civil magistrate', 'the superior steadiness of the masters', and 'the necessity which the greater part of the workmen are under of submitting for the sake of the present subsistence' were handicaps to concerted action.[70] In addition Smith was impressed by the limitations on the effectiveness of political action on the part of the 'labourer':

Though the interest of the labourer is strictly connected with that of the society, he is incapable either of comprehending that interest, or of understanding its connection with his own. His condition leaves him no time to receive the necessary information, and his education and habits are commonly such as to render him unfit to judge even though he was fully informed. In the public deliberations, therefore, his voice is little heard and less regarded, except upon some particular occasions, when his clamour is animated, set on, and supported by his employers, not for his, but their own particular purposes.[71]

Between 1776 and 1836 such a diagnosis, warmed as it was by human sympathy, began to be increasingly unrealistic. The combined effect of the French and industrial revolutions was to direct attention not to the powerlessness of the labourer but to the potential power of the 'working clases', whether hitched to the 'middle classes' or, more ominously, relying on their own leaders. In the early 1830s, when political radicalism was often blended with labour economics in a lively brew, critics of 'working class' claims, like Peter Gaskell, talked of the dangers of the growth of a dual society hopelessly torn apart:

[68] Quoted by L. G. Johnson, *General T. Perronet Thompson*, p. 233.
[69] See A. R. Schoyen, *op. cit.*; A Briggs (ed.) *Chartist Studies* (1959), chap. 9.
[70] *Wealth of Nations*, bk. i, chap. 8.
[71] *Ibid.*, bk. i, chap. 9.

Since the Steam Engine has concentrated men into localities – has drawn together the population into dense masses – and since an imperfect education has enlarged, and to some degree distorted their views, union is become easy and from being so closely packed, simultaneous action is readily excited. The organisation these [working-class] societies is now so complete that they form an 'imperium in imperio' of the most obnoxious description. . . . Labour and Capital are coming into collision – the operative and the master are at issue, and the peace, and well-being of the Kingdom are at stake.[72]

The same case was argued in Henry Tufnell's extremely interesting study, *The Character, Objects and Effects of Trades Unions* (1834), which expressed horrified alarm at the ramifications of a secret and hidden system of trade-union authority, based on its own laws with 'no reference to the laws of the land'. Like Gaskell, Tufnell argued that:

Where combinations have been most frequent and powerful, a complete separation of feeling seems to have taken place between masters and men. Each party looks upon the other as an enemy, and suspicion and distrust have driven out the mutual sentiments of kindness and goodwill, by which their intercourse was previously marked.[73]

Leaving on one side the merits of Tufnell's assessment of earlier industrial relations,[74] there has been a marked shift of emphasis since *The Wealth of Nations*. The shift was marked even in the far shorter period between the end of the Napoleonic Wars and the Reform Bill crisis. James Mill, who in his *Essay on Government* stated categorically that 'the opinions of that class of the people, who are below the middle rank, are formed, and their minds are directed by that intelligent and virtuous rank, who come the most immediately in contact with them . . . to whom they fly for advice and assistance in all their numerous difficulties, upon whom they feel an immediate and daily dependence',[75] was bemoaning in 1831 the spread of 'dangerous doctrines'

[72] Gaskell to Lord Melbourne, 16 April 1834 (Home Office Papers 40/32). Gaskell, whose book *The Manufacturing Population of England* (1833) was freely used by Engels, had a diametrically opposed view of the correct answer to the 'social problem'.

[73] H. Tufnell, *The Character, Objects and Effects of Trades Unions* (1834), pp. 2, 97.

[74] Gaskell shared his tendency to idealize social relations before the industrial revolution. 'The distinctions of rank, which are the safest guarantee for the performance of the relative duties of classes, were at this time in full force' (Gaskell, *The Manufacturing Population of England*, p. 20). Engels, who did not make use of this sentence, borrowed direct from Gaskell in the 'Historical Introduction' which forms the first chapter of his book, and thereby over-rated 'patriarchal relationships' and 'idyllic simplicity'. He broke sharply with Gaskell, however, in his conclusion. Workers before the rise of steam-power 'know nothing of the great events that were taking place in the outside world. . . . The Industrial revolution . . . forced the workers to think for themselves and to demand a fuller life in human society' (*Ibid.*, p. 12).

[75] James Mill, *Esssay on Government*, p. 72. He added the words 'to whom their children look up as models for their imitation, whose opinions they hear daily repeated, and account it their honour to adopt'.

among 'the common people' which would lead to a 'subversion of civilised society, worse than the overwhelming deluge of Huns and Tartars'. In a letter to Brougham he exclaimed:

Nothing can be conceived more mischievous that the doctrines which have been preached to the common people. The illicit cheap publications, in which the doctrine of the right of the labouring people, who say they are the only producers, to all that is produced, is very generally preached, are superseding the Sunday newspapers and every other channel through which the people might get better information.[76]

A pamphlet published by an 'approved source', the Society for the Diffusion of Useful Knowledge, warned that such doctrines, apparently 'harmless as abstract propositions', would end in 'maddening passion, drunken frenzy, unappeasable tumult, plunder, fire, and blood'.[77]

While James Mill was finishing off his *Essay on Government*, there had already been published what seems to be one of the first English working-class manifestos to talk straight language of 'class'. *The Gorgon*, published in London in November 1818, set out a series of four objections to an argument which was being frequently employed at that time that 'workmen must be expected to share the difficulties of their employers and the general distress of the times'. The language of the eighteenth and nineteenth centuries overlaps in the statement of their second objection, as it does in much of the socialist literature of the 1820s:

To abridge the necessary means of subsistence of the working classes, is to degrade, consequently to demoralise them; and when the largest and most valuable portion of any community is thus degraded and demoralised, ages may pass away before society recovers its former character of virtue and happiness.[78]

Their other objections – the last of them related to the lack of political representation – were frequently reiterated by later working-class organizations. What Mill most complained of in 1831 – the spread of the doctrine of the right of the labouring people to the whole produce of labour – still needs a more systematic examination than historians have given it. The story of the development of formal labour econo-

---

[76] Quoted by A. Bain, *James Mill* (1882), p. 365.
[77] The Rights of Industry (1831), *passim*.
[78] The statement in *The Gorgon* (28 Nov. 1818) is printed in full in G. D. H. Cole and A. W. Filson, *British Working-Class Movements, Select Documents, 1789–1875* (1951), p. 159.

mics in the 1820s is relatively well charted,[79] but the story of popular social radicalism is as yet only partly explored. The two stories are related, but they are not the same. Cobbett's post-war demand for the restoration of the dignity of labour in a changing society[80] merged with Owen's demand for an end to 'the depreciation of human labour',[81] and theories of radical reform of parliament and economic co-operation were often seen not as alternative ways to working-class emancipation but as pointers to complementary areas of working-class action. As early as 1826 a speaker in Manchester claimed that 'the purpose of parliamentary reform was to secure to the labourer the fruits of his own labour . . . and to every British subject a full participation in all the privileges and advantages of British citizens.'[82] John Doherty and his supporters in industrial Lancashire continued to argue that 'universal suffrage means nothing more than a power given to every man to protect his own labour from being devoured by others' and urged that parliamentary reform would be of little value to the masses of the population unless it was accompanied by social action to guarantee to the workmen 'the whole produce of their labour'.[83] The same views were being canvassed in the London Rotunda in 1831 and 1832 and were often expressed in the pages of the *Poor Man's Guardian*.[84] During the agitation for the Reform Bill the National Union of the Working Classes, founded in 1831, identified political oppression and social injustice:

Why were the laws not made to protect industry, but property or capital? Because the law-makers were compounded of fund and landholders, possessors of property, and the laws were made to suit their own purposes, being

[79] The road leads back before Adam Smith, but Ricardo's *Principles of Economics* (1817) was the greatest single milestone. Smith used the phrase 'the whole produce of labour' (bk. i, chap. 8), but claimed that the labourer had only been able to secure it in a primitive society and economy, 'the original state of things'. Ricardo (with important qualifications) based his general theory of value on 'the quantity of labour realised in commodities'. William Thompson (*An Inquiry into the Principles of the Distribution of Wealth, most Conducive to Human Happiness* [1824]) and Thomas Hodgskin (*Labour Defended* [1825]) anticipated Marx in using the theory as part of a socialist analysis.

[80] *Political Register*, 2 Nov. 1816. 'The real strength and all the resources of a country, ever have sprung and ever must spring, from the *labour* of its people'.

[81] See 'Labour, the Source of All Value' in *A Report to the County of Lanark* (1820). Owenism has been studied far less than Owen.

[82] *Wheeler's Manchester Chronicle*, 28 Oct. 1826.

[83] Home Office 52/18. A letter from a Preston correspondent to the Home Secretary encloses a pamphlet, *A Letter from one of the 3730 Electors of Preston to his Fellow Countrymen*. See also Doherty's pamphlet, *A Letter to the Members of the National Association for the Protection of Labour* (1831).

[84] E.g. 16 Feb. 1833. 'Universal suffrage would give the power to those who produce the wealth to enjoy it.'

utterly regardless of the sources from which the property arose. . . . Had the producers of wealth been the makers of laws, would they have left those who made the country rich to perish by starvation?[85]

As far as the leaders and members of the National Union of the Working Classes were concerned – numerically they were extremely small, and on many points they were divided[86] – it did not need disillusionment with the results of the Reform Bill of 1832 to make them distinguish clearly between the interests of the 'middle classes' and the 'working classes'. The distinction was made on economic grounds before 1832. The 'working classes', the argument ran, were victims of the industrial system, yet they constituted a majority in society. They did not receive that to which they were legitimately entitled: the rights of property were the wrongs of the poor.[87] They could only secure their proper place in society, however, by concerted action, what was called in the language of the day – with both economic and political reference – 'union'. History could be employed to support their claims,[88] but the claims could be understood without difficulty in their immediate context, an industrial system founded on 'competition' instead of co-operation'. There was an urgent need for 'the elite of the working classes'[89] to communicate their ideas and solutions to the rest. As one popular lecturer on co-operation in Lancashire put it:

About one third of our working population . . . consists of weavers and labourers, whose average earnings do not amount to a sum sufficient to bring up and maintain their families without parochial assistance. . . . It is to this class of poor fellow creatures in particular, that I desire to recommend the system of co-operation, as the only means which at present, seem calculated to diminish the evils under which they live.[90]

Owen might be suspicious of the mixing of his doctrines with those of

[85] *Ibid.*, 24 Dec. 1831.
[86] For the division between 'Huntites' and 'Owenites', see *ibid.*, 4 Feb. 1832.
[87] *Ibid.*, 26 Jan. 1833.
[88] The old Saxon/Norman theme (see note 5 above) was still raised. In a London debate in 1833 on the notion that 'until the laws of property are properly discussed, explored, and understood by the producers of all property the wretched condition of the working classes can never be improved', more than one spectator referred to 'the misappropriation' of the Norman Conquest and its aftermath. (*Ibid.*, 18 May 1833.)
[89] This phrase, which has often been used with reference to the London Working Men's Association, was employed in the *Poor Man's Guardian*. Describing the fourth Co-operative Congress, the newspaper reporter said that it was comprised of 'plain but intelligent workmen . . . the very elite of the working classes'. (*Ibid.*, 19 Oct. 1833.)
[90] F. Baker, *First Lecture on Co-operation* (Bolton, 1830), p. 2.

popular radical reformers[91] and continue to talk of the need to create an ideal class of 'producers' which included both workmen and employers, but the social and political situation was beyond his control. It was not only the National Union of Working Classes which talked in class terms. As the third Co-operative Congress held at the Institution of the Industrious Classes in London 1832 several speakers described operative and employers as separate and hostile forces,[92] while in the pages of *Pioneer*, which first appeared in September 1833, there were many signs of differences of opinion between the editor, James Morrison, and Owen on questions of class. The first number of the *Pioneer* had a 'correct' Owenite editorial,[93] but Morrison soon proclaimed the independence of the 'working class' from the 'middle men'.[94] In one striking passage he declared:

Trust none who is a grade above our class, and does not back us in the hour of trial. . . . Orphans we are, and bastards of society.[95]

In writing the detailed history of working-class movements of the 1830s, culminating in Chartism, it is necessary to separate out different strands.[96] For the purposes of this essay, however, emphasis must be placed on the element of class consciousness which in various forms was common to them all. Bronterre O'Brien, who was identified with three of the main movements – the struggle for Reform in 1831 and 1832, trade unionism, and Chartism – described this element as follows:

A spirit of combination had grown up among the working classes, of which there has been no example in former times. . . . The object of it is the sublimest that can be conceived, namely – to establish for the productive classes a complete dominion over the fruits of their own industry. . . . Reports show that an entire change in society – a change amounting to a complete sub-

[91] He sharply condemned 'a party of Owenites of the Rotunda or desperadoes' and said that he had never been to the London Rotunda (*Union,* 17 Dec. 1831).

[92] See *the Crisis*, 28 Apr. 1832.

[93] 'The Union [The Grand National Consolidated Trade Union] is a well-organized body of working men, bound together by wise and discreet laws, and by one common interest. Its object is to affect the general amelioration of the producers of wealth, and the welfare of the whole community. Its members do not desire to be at war with any class, neither will they suffer any class to usurp their rights.' *Pioneer*, 7 Sept. 1833.

[94] *Ibid.*, 21 June 1834. 'The capitalist,' he wrote (21 Dec. 1833), 'merely as a property man, has no power at all, and labour . . . regulated by intelligence, will in a very few years, be the only existent power in this and in all highly civilized countries.'

[95] *Ibid.*, 22 Mar. 1834.

[96] See for the various strands, *Chartist Studies*, especially chap. 1, 'The Local Background of Chartism'. It is important to note that at the local level many working-class activists joined several movements, caring less about doctrinal differences than leaders or writers.

version of the existing 'order of the world' – is contemplated by the working classes. They aspire to be at the top instead of at the bottom of society – or rather that there should be no bottom or top at all.[97]

In the bitter rivalry between Chartists and Leaguers there was class consciousness on both sides, although a section of the Chartists came to the conclusion that they would be able to accomplish nothing without middle-class support and the Leaguers were always compelled to look for working-class allies. Tory traditionalists disliked the language of 'class' from whichever quarter of society it came. Peel, prime minister in the critical years of the century, would have nothing to do with it. During the middle years of the century, the language class was softened as much as social antagonisms themselves, but it burst out again in many different places in the years which led up to the second Reform Bill of 1867.

IV

There were some affinities, on the surface at least, between eithteenth-century views of society and those most frequently canvassed in the 1850s and 1860s. Attention was paid not to the broad contours of class division, but to an almost endless series of social gradations. The role of deference even in an industrial society was stressed, and the idea of a 'gentleman', one of the most powerful of mid-Victorian ideas but an extremely complicated one both to define and to disentangle, was scrutinized by novelists as much as by pamphleteers. The case for inequality was as much a part of social orthodoxy as it had been a hundred years before. 'Almost everybody in England has a hard word for social equality', wrote Matthew Arnold in 1878.[98] The language of 'interests' enjoyed a new vogue both in the world of politics and outside. It was perhaps a sign of the times that the Amalgamated Society of Engineers, founded in 1851, did not claim that it was its duty to secure the objects of a 'class' but rather 'to exercise the same control over that in which we have a vested interest, as the physician who holds his diploma, or the author who is protected by his copyright'.[99] The term 'labour interest' figured prominently in political discussion at all levels. A distinction was drawn even by radical politicians between the articulate 'labour interest' and the 'residuum',

[97] *Poor Man's Guardian*, 19 Oct. 1833.
[98] Essay on 'Equality' in *Mixed Essays* (1878), p. 49.
[99] Quoted in J. B. Jefferys (ed.), *Labour's Formative Years* (1948), p. 30.

the great mass of the working-class population. The concept of the 'residuum', indeed, was useful to writers who wished to write off the 'condition of England question' of the 1840s as something dead and done with.

Against this background, 'class' came to be though of as a rather naughty word with unpleasant associations. *The Times* in 1861 remarked that 'the word "class", when employed as an adjective, is too often intended to convey some reproach. We speak of "class prejudices" and "class legislation", and inveigh agaiht the selfishness of class interest.'[100] One of the most influential of the people who inveighed was Herbert Spencer. In a chapter with the significant title 'The Class Bias' he wrote:

The egoism of individuals leads to an egoism of the class they form; and besides the separate efforts, generates a joint effort to get an undue share of the aggregate proceeds of social activity. The aggressive tendency of each class thus produced has to be balanced by like aggressive tendencies of other classes.[101]

The word 'balance' was one of the key words of the period both in relation to politics and to society.

It is not surprising that during these years three main points were made about 'class' in England. First, England was a country where there was a marked degree of individual mobility and this made class divisions tolerable. Second, the dividing lines between classes were extremely difficult to draw. Third, there were significant divisions *inside* what were conventionally regarded as classes, and these divisions were often more significant than divisions *between* the classes. Taken together these three points constituted a description rather than an analysis. The description was compared, however, with descriptions of the state of affairs in other countries, the United States or France, for example, or even India.[102] Whereas during the 1840s both middle-class and working-class politicians (and most writers on society) had urged about 'class' in general terms, relating what was happening in England to what was happening in other countries,[103]

---

[100] *The Times*, 10 Aug. 1861.   [101] H. Spencer, *Principles of Sociology* (1873), p. 242.

[102] See, for instance, Walter Bagehot's essay on Sterne and Thackeray reprinted in *Literary Studies* (1873), where he distinguished between social systems founded upon caste and those founded upon equality. The English system of 'removable inequalities' was preferable to both.

[103] The leaders of the London Working Men's Association, for example, had clearly stated in addresses to working men in America, Belgium, and Poland that there were common interests among 'the productive millions' in all parts of the world and that it was 'our ignorance of society and of government – our prejudices, our disunion and distrust' which was one of the biggest obstacles to the dissolution of the 'unholy compact of despotism'. See W. Lovett, *Life and Struggles* (1876), p. 152.

during the middle years of the century most of the arguments were designed to show that England was a favoured special case.

The 'facts' of individual mobility were stated eloquently and forcefully by Palmerston in his famous speech during the Don Pacifico debate in the House of Commons in 1850:

We have shown the example of a nation, in which every class in society accepts with cheerfulness the lot which Providence has assigned to it; while at the same time every individual of each class is constantly striving to raise himself in the social scale – not by injustice and wrong, not by violence and illegality, but by preserving good conduct, and by the steady and energetic execution of the moral and intellectual faculties with which his Creator endowed him.[104]

Only two years after the revolutions of 1848 and the waning of Chartism the language of politics was changing. The values were the same as those described by Beatrice Webb at the beginning of *My Apprenticeship*:

It was the bounden duty of every citizen to better his social status; to ignore those beneath him, and to aim steadily at the top rung of the ladder. Only by this persistent pursuits by each individual of his own and his family's interest would the highest general level of civilisation be attained.[105]

The rungs of the ladder did not move: it was individuals who were expected to do so. 'Individuals may rise and fall by special excellence or defects', wrote Edward Thring, the famous public school headmaster, 'but the classes cannot change places.'[106]

The metaphor of 'ladders' and 'rungs' proved inadequate for the many writers who wished to emphasize the blurring of class dividing-lines in mid-Victorian England. 'Take any class of Englishmen, from the highest to the lowest', wrote the young Dicey in a stimulating essay, 'and it will be found to mix, by imperceptible degrees, with the class below it. Who can say where the upper class ends, or where the middle class begins?'[107] Arnold, who was quick to catch the 'stock

---

[104] Quoted in J. Joll (ed.), *Britain and Europe, Pitt to Churchill* (1950), pp. 124–5.

[105] B. Webb, *My Apprenticeship* (1950 edn.), p. 13.

[106] Rev. E. Thring, *Education and School* (1864), p. 5.

[107] *Essays on Reform* (1867), p. 74. Dicey added that 'in criticizing a theory of class representation, the words "classes", "orders", or "interests", must be constantly employed.' Such employment, in his view, gave an undue advantage to the view criticized, for 'the very basis on which this view rests is not firm enough to support the conclusions grounded upon it.' For a parallel question of a later date about the social position of 'working men' see C. Booth, *Life and Labour of the People, East London* (1889), p. 99.

notions' of his age, some of which he believed in himself, referred in *Friendship's Garland* to 'the rich diversity of our English life . . . the happy blending of classes and character.'[108] Other writers described 'intermediate classes' bridging the chasms of class antagonism.

Finally, divisions within classes – the presence of what were sometimes called 'sub-classes' – were stressed. The 'middle classes', which Cobden had struggled to pull together during the 1840s, separated out into diverging elements after 1846, and the plans of the more daring spirits of the Manchester School to carry through a 'middle-class revolution' were never realized.[109] To cross the 'moral and intellectual' gulf between the skilled workers and unskilled, wrote Henry Mayhew, was to reach 'a new level . . . among another race'.[110] In some respects, at least, dividing lines seemed to be sharper at the base of the social pyramid than towards the apex.

The political debate which followed the death of Palmerston in 1865 and ended with the passing of the Second Reform Bill two years later led to a revival of interest in the problems and terminology of 'class'.[111] It was the change in economic circumstances in the 1870s and 1880s, however, and the disturbance of the mid-Victorian social balance which shifted the debate on to a wider front. An understanding of the new phase which was opening during the late Victorian years depends on a thorough examination of the phrase 'working classes' in a context of socialism. Whatever else may be said of the new phase, one development is incontrovertible. The language of 'ranks', 'orders', and 'degrees', which has survived the Industrial Revolution,[112] was

[108] *Friendship's Garland* (1897 edn.), pp. 49–50. One aspect of the blending, which deserves an essay to itself, was the association of the industrial and agricultural 'interests'. 'Protection,' wrote a shrewd observer, Bernard Cracroft, 'was the only wall of separation between land and trade. That wall removed, the material interests of the two classes have become and tend to become every day more indissolubly connected and inseparably blended.' (*Essays on Reform*, p. 110.)

[109] Cobden himself came to believe in the 1860s that 'feudalism is every day more and more in the ascendant in political and social life. . . . Manufacturers and merchants as a rule seem only to desire riches that they may be enable to prostitute themselves at the feet of feudalism.' (Quoted by Morley, *The Life of Richard Cobden*, ii, chap. 25.) He was very critical of the alliance of the industrial and the landed 'interest', and on one occasion in 1861 wrote to a friend, 'I wonder the working people are so quiet under the taunts and insults offered to them. Have they no Spartacus among them to head a revolt of the slave class against their political tormentors?' (quoted *ibid.*, ii, chap. 30).

[110] H. Mayhew, *London Labour and the London Poor,* i (1862), 6–7. Cp. T. Wright, *Our New Masters* (1873): 'Between the artisan and the unskilled a gulf is fixed. While the former resents the spirit in which he believes the followers of "genteel occupations" look down upon him, he in his turn looks down upon the labourers' (p. 5).

[111] A. Briggs and J. Saville (eds.), *Essays in Labour History* (1959) p. 220. See the remarkable letter writted by Professor Beesly on the day Palmerston died.

[112] Traditionalists employed the old language in some of the mid-century debates about education, e.g., P. Peace, *An Address on the Improvement of the Condition of the Labouring Poor* (Shaftesbury, 1852), p. 15. 'Children must be instructed according to their different ranks and

finally cast into limbo. The language of class, like the facts of class, remained.

---

the station they will probably fill in the graduated scale of society.' A similar thought was expressed quite differently by Sir Charles Adderley in 1874. 'The educating by the artificial stimulus of large public expenditure, a particular class, out of instead of in the condition of life in which they naturally fill an important part of the community, must upset the social equilibrium.' (*A Few Thoughts on National Education and Punishment*, p. 11.)

2

Introduction to A Contribution to the Critique of Hegel's 'Philosophy of Right'

KARL MARX

The first of these two extracts from Marx, his Introduction to *A Contribution to the Critique of Hegel's 'Philosophy of Right'*, was probably written in the period September 1843 to January 1844, well before Marx set foot in England. I include it in this collection for two reasons. First, because the Introduction, in its entirety, is Marx's early attempt to formulate a class analysis of society – German society. And, secondly, because, at the same time, it shows so well the Hegelian image reservoirs in Marx's language of class.

In the extract Marx argues that material force must be overthrown by material force, but that theory, once it seizes the masses, also becomes a material force available for their use. And Marx claims that among the material forces already at work in the 1840s was the proletariat, 'already beginning its struggle against the bourgeoisie' – presumably, so far, without the benefit of thought. Marx is also clear, that although the German proletariat was weak, it *was* the product of industrialization and the creation of an industrial, property-owning, middle class. Therefore, its experience was not to be confused with that of the 'mass of men mechanically oppressed by the weight of society' nor with that of the, 'victims of natural poverty and Christian-Germanic serfdom,' although the latter were also to join the proletariat. Such, then, was the proletariat; a product of the production process, even if not explicity located in it.

But, the proletariat was also something like a universal class, suf-

From Karl Marx, *A Contribution to the Critique of Hegel's 'Philosophy of Right'*, edited with an Introduction by Joseph O'Malley (Cambridge University Press, 1970) pp. 137–42.

fering, through the abolition of property, univesal wrong, and thereby, charged with the task of achieving the redemption of mankind through the abolition of *all* private property. Thus, 'This dissolution of society existing as a particular class is the proletariat'.

To help the already struggling proletarians to arrive at a true consciousness of their place in society and their role in history, there was also the lightning of thought – Marx's writings.

Thirty years later, in 1875, Marx, still driven by a need to bring the lightning of thought to the German proletariat, but clearer in his own mind about the conditions necessary for the determination of the proletariat, wrote his criticism of the Gotha Programme, shortly before the Gotha Unity Congress. The Social-Democratic Workers' Party was about to enter into negotiations with the Lassallean General Association of German Workers, and Marx, believing the proposed 'programme is no good altogether', sought to influence the discussions. He sent his critique to the leaders of the Social-Democratic Workers' Party, but his efforts failed. However, in 1890, the Halle Party Congress had again put discussion of the Gotha Programme on the agenda of the party, and Engels published Marx's *Critique* for the first time in 1891. On this occasion, at Erfurt, the party adopted a programme rather more in accord with it.

In *Class in English History* I read the *Critique* for what it has to say about Marx's notion of *class* consciousness. Yet I do not pretend to have set out systematically the conditions and relationships necessary for the passage from *class* to *class* consciousness, whether the conditions be one or all of, position in the production process, lightning of thought, act of revolution. *Class* consciousness *is* a problem in Marx. The *Critique* is the second extract from Marx.

The question arises. can Germany attain a praxis *à la hauteur des principes*, that is to say, a revolution that will raise it not only to the official level of modern nations, but to the human level which will be the immediate future of these nations?

The weapon of criticism certainly cannot replace the criticism of weapons; material force must be overthrown by material force; but theory, too, becomes a material force once it seizes the masses. Theory is capable of seizing the masses once it demonstrates *ad hominem*, and it demonstrates *ad hominem* once it becomes radical. To be radical is to grasp matters at the root. But for many the root is man himself. The manifest proof of the radicalism of German theory, and thus of its practical energy, is the fact of its issuing from a resolute positive transcendence [*Aufhebung*] of religion. The critique of religion ends in the doctrine that man is the supreme being for man; thus it ends with the categorical imperative to overthrow all conditions in which man is a debased, enslaved, neglected, contemptible being – conditions which cannot be better described than by the Frenchman's exclamation about a proposed tax on dogs: 'Poor dogs! They want to treat you like men!'

Even from the historical point of view, theoretical emancipation has a specific practical importance for Germany. Germany's revolutionary past is precisely theoretical: it is the Reformation. As at that time it was a monk, so now it is the philosopher in whose brain the revolution begins.

Luther, to be sure, overcame servitude based on devotion, but by replacing it with servitude based on conviction. He shattered faith in authority by restoring the authority of faith. He transformed the priests into laymen by changing the laymen into priests. He liberated man from external religiosity by making religiosity that which is innermost to man. He freed the body of chains by putting the heart in chains.

But if Protestantism was not the real solution it at least posed the problem correctly. Thereafter it was no longer a question of the laymen's struggle with the priest outside of him, but of his struggle with his own inner priest, his priestly nature. And if the Protestant transformation of the German laity into priests emancipated the lay popes – the princes together with their clergy, the privileged and the philistines – so the philosophical transformation of the priestly Germans into men will emancipate the people. But just as emancipation is not limited to the princes, so the secularization of property will not be limited to the confiscation of church property, which as practiced especially by hypocritical Prussia. At that time, the Peasant War, the most radical event in German history, foundered because of theology. Today, when theology itself has foundered, the most unfree thing in German history, our *status quo*, will be shattered by philosophy. On the eve of the Reformation official Germany was the most abject servant of Rome. On the eve of its revolution Germany is the abject servant of those who are inferior to Rome, of Prussia and Austria, of petty squires and philistines.

However, a major difficulty appears to stand in the way of a radical German revolution.

Revolutions require a passive element, a material basis. Theory will be realized in a people only in so far as it is the realization of their needs. Will the enormous discrepancy between the demands of German thought and the answers of German actuality be matched by a similar discrepancy between civil society and the state, and within civil society itself? Will theoretical needs be directly practical needs? It is not enough that thought strive to actualize itself; actuality must itself strive toward thought.

But Germany has not passed through the middle state of political emancipation at the same time as the modern nations. The very stages it has surpassed in theory it has not yet reached in practice. How is Germany, with a *salto mortale*, to surmount not only its own limitations, but also those of the modern nations, limitations which it must actually experience and strive for as the liberation from its own actual limitations? A radical revolution can only be a revolution of radical needs, whose preconditions and birthplaces appear to be lacking.

But if Germany accompanied the development of modern nations only with the abstract activity of thought, without taking an active part in the actual struggles of this development, it has still shared the pains of this development without sharing its pleasures or its partial satisfaction. The abstract activity on the one hand corresponds to the abstract pain on the other. One day Germany will find itself at the level of European decadence before it has ever achieved the level of European emancipation. It will be like a fetishist suffering from the illnesses of Christianity.

If we examine the German governments we find that the circumstances of the time, the situation in Gemany, the viewpoint of German culture, and finally their own lucky instinct, all drive them to combine the civilized deficiencies of the modern political world, whose advantages we do not enjoy, with the barbaric deficiencies of the *ancien régime*, which we enjoy in full measure; so that Germany must participate more and more, if not in the rationality, at least in the irrationality of the political forms that transcend its *status quo*. For example, is there any country in the world which shares as naively as so-called constitutional Germany all the illusions of the constitutional régime without any of its realities? Wasn't it somehow necessarily a German government brain-wave to combine the torments of censorship with those of the French September Laws [of 1835], which presuppose the freedom of the press! Just as the gods of all nations were found in the Roman Pantheon, so the sins of all state-forms are to be found in the Holy Roman German Empire. That this eclecticism will attain an unprecedented level is assured by the politico-aesthetic *gourmanderie* of a German king [Frederick William IV], who intends to play all the roles of royalty – the feudal as well as the bureaucratic, absolute as well as constitutional, autocratic as well as democratic – if not in the person of the people at least in his own person, if not for the people at least for himself. Germany, as the deficiency of the political present constituted into an individual system, will be unable to demolish the specific German limitations without demolishing the general limitations of the political present.

It is not a radical revolution, universal human emancipation, that is a utopian dream for Germany, but rather a partial, merely political revolution, a revolution that leaves the pillars of the edifice standing. What is the basis of a partial, merely political revolution? It is this: a section of civil society emancipates itself and achieves universal dominance; a determinate class undertakes from its particular situation the universal emancipation of society. This class emancipates the whole society, but only on the condition that the whole society shares its situation; for example, that it has or can obtain money and education.

No class of civil society can play this role unless it arouses in itself and in the masses a moment of enthusiasm, a moment in which it associates, fuses, and identifies itself with society in general, and is felt and recognized to be society's general representative, a moment in which its demands and rights are truly those of society itself, of which it is the social head and heart. Only in the name of the universal rights of society can a particular class lay claim to universal dominance. To take over this liberating position, and therewith the political exploitation of all the spheres of society in the interest of its own sphere, revolutionary energy and spiritual self-confidence do not suffice. For a popular revolution and the emancipation of a particular class to coincide, for one class to stand for the whole of society, another class must, on the other hand, concentrate in itself all the defects of society, must be the class of universal offence and the embodiment of universal limits. A particular social sphere must stand for the notorious crime of the whole society, so that liberation from this sphere appears to be universal liberation. For one class to be the class *par excellence* of liberation, another class must, on the other hand, be openly the subjugating class. The negative general significance of the French nobility and clergy determined the positive general significance of the bourgeoisie, the class standing next to and opposing them.

But every class in Germany lacks the consistency, the keenness, the courage, and the ruthlessness which would mark it as the negative representative of society. Moreover, every class lacks the breadth of soul which identifies it, if only for a moment, with the soul of the people; that genius which animates material force into political power; that revolutionary boldness which flings at its adversary the defiant phrase: I am nothing and I should be everything. The principal feature of German morality and honour, not only in individuals but in classes as well, is that modest egoism which asserts its narrowness and allows narrowness to be asserted against it. The relationship of the different spheres of German society is, therefore, not dramatic, but epic. Each of them begins to be aware of itself and to establish itself with its particular claims beside the others, not as soon as it is oppressed, but as soon as circumstances independent of its actions create a lower social stratum against which it can in turn exert pressure. Even the moral self-esteem of the German middle class is based merely on the consciousness of being the general representative of the philistine mediocrity of all the other classes. It is, therefore, not only the German kings who ascend the throne *mal à propos*. Each sphere of civil society suffers its defeat before it celebrates its victory, erects its own barrier before it overthrows its opposing barrier, asserts its narrow-minded nature before it can assert its generosity, so that the opportunity of playing a great role has passed before it ever actually existed, and each class, at the moment it begins to struggle with the class above it, is involved in the struggle with the class beneath. Hence, the princes are in conflict with the king, the bureaucracy with the nobility, the bourgeoisie with all of them, while the proletariat is already beginning its struggle against the bourgeoisie. The middle class hardly dares to conceive of the idea of emancipation from its own point of view, and already the development of social conditions and the progress of political theory show that this point of view itself is antiquated, or at least questionable.

In France it is enough to be something in order to desire to be everything. In Germany no one may be anything unless he renounces everything. In France partial emancipation is the basis of universal emancipation. In Germany universal emancipation is the *conditio sine qua non* for any partial emancipation. In France it is the actuality, in Germany the impossibility, of gradual emancipation which must give birth to full freedom. In France every national class is politically idealistic and considers itself above all to be not a particular class but the representative of the needs of society overall. The role of the emancipator thus passes in a dramatic movement to the different classes of the French nation, until it finally reaches the class which actualizes social freedom no longer on the basis of presupposed conditions which are at once external to man yet created by human society, but rather organizing all the conditions of human existence on the basis of social freedom. In Germany, on the other hand, where practical life is as little intellectual as intellectual life is practical, no class of civil society has the need and the capacity for universal emancipation until it is forced to it by its immediate situation, material necessity, and its very chains.

Where, then, is the positive possibility of German emancipation?

Our answer: in the formation of a class with radical chains, a class in civil society that is not of civil society, a class that is the dissolution of all classes, a sphere of society having a universal character because of its universal suffering and claiming no particular right because no particular wrong but unqualified wrong is perpetrated on it; a sphere that can claim no traditional title but only a human title; a sphere that does not stand partially opposed to the consequences, but totally opposed to the premises of the German political system; a sphere, finally, that cannot emancipate itself without emancipating itself from all the other spheres of society, thereby emancipating them; a sphere, in short, that is the complete loss of humanity and can only redeem itself through the total redemption of humanity. This dissolution of society existing as a particular class is the proletariat.

The proletariat is only beginning to appear in Germany as a result of the industrial development taking place. For it is not naturally existing poverty but artificially produced poverty, not the mass of men mechanically oppressed by the weight of society but the mass of men resulting from society's, and especially the middle class', acute dissolution that constitutes the proletariat – though at the same time, needless to say, victims of natural poverty and Christian–Germanic serfdom also become members.

When the proletariat announces the dissolution of the existing order of things it merely declares the secret of its own existence, for it *is* the *de facto* dissolution of this order of things. When the proletariat demands the negation of private property it merely elevates into a principle of society what society has advanced as the principle of the proletariat, and what the proletariat already involuntarily embodies as the negative result of society. The proletariat thus has the same right relative to the new world which is coming into being as the German king relative to the existing world, when he calls the people his people and a horse his horse. In calling the prople his private property the king merely expresses the fact that the owner of private property is king.

Just as philosophy finds its material weapons in the proletariat, so the proletariat finds its spiritual weapons in philosophy; and once the lightning of thought has struck deeply into this naive soil of the people the emancipation of Germans into men will be accomplished.

Let us summarize:

The only practically possible emancipation of Germany is the emancipation based on the unique theory which holds that man is the supreme being for man. In Germany emancipation from the Middle Ages is possible only as the simultaneous emancipation from the partial victories over the Middle Ages. In Germany no form of bondage can be broken unless every form of bondage is broken. Germany, enamored of fundamentals, can have nothing less than a fundamental revolution. The emancipation of Germany is the emancipation of man. The head of this emancipation is philosophy, its heart is the proletariat. Philosophy cannot be actualized without the abolition [Aufhebung] of the proletariat; the proletariat cannot be abolished without the actualization of philosophy.

When all the intrinsic conditions are fulfilled, the day of German resurrection will be announced by the growing of the Gallic cock.

3

Critique of the Gotha Programme

KARL MARX

I

1 Labour is the source of all wealth and all culture, *and since* useful labour is possible only in society and through society, the proceeds of labour belong undiminished with equal right to all members of society.

First Part of the Paragraph: 'Labour is the source of all wealth and all culture.'

Labour is *not the source* of all wealth. *Nature* is just as much the source of use values (and it is surely of such that material wealth consists!) as labour, which itself is only the manifestation of a force of nature, human labour power. The above phrase is to be found in all children's primers and is correct is so far as it is *implied* that labour is performed with the appurtenant subjects and instruments. But a socialist programme cannot allow such bourgeois phrases to pass over in silence the *conditions* that alone give them meaning. And in so far as man from the beginning behaves towards nature, the primary source of all instruments and subjects of labour, as an owner, treats her as belonging to him, his labour becomes the source of use values, therefore also of wealth. The bourgeois have very good grounds for falsely ascribing *supernatural creative power* to labour; since precisely from the fact that labour depends on nature it follows that the man who possesses no other property than his labour power must, in all conditions of society and culture, be the slave of other men who have made themselves the owners of the material conditions of labour. He can work only with their permission, hence live only with their permission.

'Marginal Notes to the Programme of the German Workers' Party' (written by Marx in 1875, first published by Engels in 1891), from Karl Marx and Frederick Engels, *Selected Works in Two Volumes*, Vol. II (Foreign Languages Publishing House, Moscow, 1958), pp. 15–37. All footnotes are additions by the editor of that volume.

Let us now leave the sentence as it stands, or rather limps. What would one have expected in conclusion? Obviously this:

'Since labour is the source of all wealth, no one in society can appropriate wealth except as the product of labour. Therefore, if he himself does not work, he lives by the labour of others and also acquires his culture at the expense of the labour of others.'

Instead of this, by means of the verbal rivet '*and since*' a second proposition is added in order to draw a conclusion from this and not from the first one.

Second Part of the Paragraph: 'Useful labour is possible only in society and through society.'

According to the first proposition, labour was the source of all wealth and all culture; therefore no society is possible without labour. Now we learn, conversely, that no 'useful' labour is possible without society.

One could just as well have said that only in society can useless and even socially harmful labour become a branch of gainful occupation, that only in society can one live by being idle, etc., etc. – in short, one could just as well have copied the whole of Rousseau.

And what is 'useful' labour? Surely only labour which produces the intended useful result. A savage – and man was a savage after he had ceased to be an ape – who kills an animal with a stone, who collects fruits, etc., performs 'useful' labour.

Thirdly. The Conclusion: 'And since useful labour is possible only in society and through society, the proceeds of labour belong undiminished with equal right to all members of society.'

A fine conclusion! If useful labour is possible only in society and through society, the proceeds of labour belong to society – and only so much therefrom accrues to the individual worker as is not required to maintain the 'condition' of labour, society.

In fact, this proposition has at all times been made use of by the champions of the *state of society prevailing at any given time*. First come the claims of the government and everything that sticks to it, since it is the social organ for the maintenance of the social order; then comes the claims of the various kinds of private property, for the various kinds of private property are the foundations of society, etc. One sees that such hollow phrases can be twisted and turned as desired.

The first and second parts of the paragraph have some intelligible connection only in the following wording:

'Labour becomes the source of wealth and culture only as social labour,' or, what is the same thing, 'in and through society'.

This proposition is incontestably correct, for although isolated labour (its material conditions presupposed) can create use values, it can create neither wealth nor culture.

But equally incontestable is this other proposition:

'In proportion as labour develops socially, and becomes thereby a source of wealth and culture, poverty and destitution develop among the workers, and wealth and culture among the non-workers.'

This is the law of all history hitherto. What, therefore, had to be done here, instead of setting down general phrases about 'labour' and 'society', was to prove concretely how in present capitalist society the material, etc., conditions have at last been created which enable and compel the workers to lift this social curse.

In fact, however, the whole paragraph, bungled in style and content, is only there in order to inscribe the Lassallean catchword of the 'undiminished proceeds of labour' as a slogan at the top of the party banner. I shall return later to the 'proceeds of labour', 'equal right', etc., since the same thing recurs in a somewhat different form further on.

2 In present-day society, the instruments of labour are the monopoly of the capitalist class; the resulting dependence of the working class is the cause of misery and servitude in all its forms.

This sentence, borrowed from the Rules of the International, is incorrect in this 'improved' edition.

In present-day society the instruments of labour are the monopoly of the landowners (the monopoly of property in land is even the basis of the monopoly of capital) *and* the capitalists. In the passage in question, the Rules of the International do not mention either the one or the other class of monopolists. They speak of the '*monopolizer of the means of labour*, that is, *the sources of life*'. The addition, '*sources of life*', makes it sufficiently clear that land is included in the instruments of labour.

The correction was introduced because Lassalle, for reasons now generally known, attacked *only* the capitalist class and not the landowners. In England, the capitalist is usually not even the owner of the land on which his factory stands.

3 The emancipation of labour demands the promotion of the instruments of labour to the common property of society and the co-operative regulation of the total labour with a fair distribution of the proceeds of labour.

'Promotion of the instruments of labour to the common property' ought obviously to read their 'conversion into the common property'; but this only in passing.

What are 'proceeds of labour'? The product of labour or its value? And in the latter case, is it the total value of the product or only that part of the value which labour has newly added to the value of the means of production consumed?

'Proceeds of labour' is a loose notion which Lassalle has put in the place of definite economic conceptions.

What is 'a fair distribution'?

Do not the bourgeois assert that the present-day distribution is 'fair'? And is it not, in fact, the only 'fair' distribution on the basis of the present-day mode of production? Are economic relations regulated by legal conceptions or do not, on the contrary, legal relation arise from economic ones? Have not also the socialist sectarians the most varied notions about 'fair' distribution?

To understand what is implied in this connection by the phrase 'fair distribution', we must take the first paragraph and this one together. The latter presupposes a society wherein 'the instruments of labour are common property and the total labour is co-operatively regulated', and from the first paragraph we learn that 'the proceeds of labour belong undiminished with equal right to all members of society'.

'To all members of society'? To those who do not work as well? What remains then of the 'undiminished proceeds of labour'? Only to those member of society who work? What remains then of the 'equal right' of all members of society?

But 'all members of society' and 'equal rights' are obviously mere phrases. The kernel consists in this, that in this communist society every worker must receive the 'undiminished' Lassallean 'proceeds of labour'.

Let us take first of all the words 'proceeds of labour' in the sense of the product of labour, then the co-operative proceeds of labour are the *total social product*.

From this must now be deducted:

First, cover for replacement of the means of production used up.

Secondly, additional portion for expansion of production.

Thirdly, reserve or insurance funds to provide against accidents, dislocations cause by natural calamities, etc.

These deductions from the 'undiminished proceeds of labour' are an economic necessity and their magnitude is to be determined according to available means and forces, and partly by computation of probabilities, but they are in no way calculable by equity.

There remains the other part of the total product, intended to serve as means of consumption.

Before this is divided among the individuals, there has to be deducted again, from it:

First, the general costs of administration not belonging to production.

This part will, from the outset, be very considerably restricted in comparison with present-day society and it diminishes in proportion as the new society develops.

Secondly, that which is intended for the common satisfaction of needs, such as schools, health services, etc.

From the outset this part grows considerably in comparison with present-day society and it grows in proportion as the new society develops.

Thirdly, funds for those unable to work, etc., in short, for what is included under so-called official poor relief today.

Only now do we come to the 'distribution' which the programme, under Lassallean influence, alone has in view in its narrow fashion, namely, to that part of the means of consumption which is divided among the individual producers of the co-operative society.

The 'undiminished proceeds of labour' have already unnoticeably become converted in the 'diminished' proceeds, although what the producer is deprived of in his capacity as a private individual benefits him directly or indirectly in his capacity as a member of society.

Just as the phrase of the 'undiminished proceeds of labour' has disappeared, so now does the phrase of the 'proceeds of labour' disappear altogether.

Within the co-operative society based on common ownership of the means of production, the producers do not exchange their products; just as little does the labour employed on the products appear here *as the value* of these products, as a material quality possessed by them, since now, in contrast to capitalist society, individual labour no longer exists in an indirect fashion but directly as a component part of the total labour. The phrase 'proceeds of labour', objectionable also today on account of its ambiguity, thus loses all meaning.

What we have to deal with here is a communist society, not as it has *developed* on its own foundations, but, on the contrary, just as it *emerges* from capitalist society; which is thus in every respect, economically, morally and intellectually, still stamped with the birth marks of the old society from whose womb it emerges. Accordingly, the individual producer receives back from society – after the deductions have been made – exactly what he gives to it. What he has given to it is his individual quantum of labour. For example, the social working day consists of the sum of the individual hours of work; the individual labour time of the individual producer is the part of the social working day contributed by him, his share in it. He receives a certificate from society that he has furnished such and such an amount of labour (after deducting his labour for the common funds), and with this certificate he draws from the social stock of means of consumption as much as costs the same amount of labour. The same amount of labour which he has given to society in one form he receives back in another.

Here obviously the same principle prevails as that which regulated the exchange of commodities, as far as this is exchange of equal values. Content and form are changed, because under the altered circumstances no one can give anything except his labour, and because, on the other hand, nothing can pass to the ownership of individuals except individual means of consumption. But, as far as the distribution of the latter among the individual producers is concerned, the same principle prevails as in the exchange of commodity-equivalents: a given amount of labour in one form is exchanged for an equal amount of labour in another form.

Hence, *equal right* here is still in principle – *bourgeois right*, although principle and practice are no longer at loggerheads, while the exchange of equivalents in commodity exchange only exists *on the average* and not in the individual case.

In spite of this advance, this *equal right* is still constantly stigmatized by a bourgeois limitation. The right of the producers is *proportional* to the labour they supply; the equality consists in the fact that measurement is made with an *equal standard*, labour.

But one man is superior to another physically or mentally and so supplies more labour in the same time, or can labour for a longer time; and labour, to serve as a measure, must be defined by its duration or intensity, otherwise it ceases to be a standard of measurement. This *equal* right is an unequal right for unequal labour. It recognizes no class differences, because everyone is only a worker like everyone else; but it tacitly recognizes unequal individual endowment and thus productive capacity as natural privileges. *It is, therefore, a right of inequality, in its content, like every right.* Right by its very nature can consist only in the application of an equal standard; but unequal individuals (and they would not be different individuals if they were not unequal) are measurable only by an equal standard in so far as they are brought under an equal point of view, are taken from one *definite* side only, for instance, in the present case, are regarded *only as workers* and nothing more is seen in them, everything else being ignored. Further, one worker is married, another not; one has more children than another, and so on and so forth. Thus, with an equal performance of labour, and hence an equal share in the social consumption fund, one will in fact receive more than another, one will be richer than another, and so on. To avoid all these defects, right instead of being equal would have to be unequal.

But these defects are inevitable in the first phase of communist society as it is when it has just emerged after prolonged birth pangs from capitalist society. Right can never be higher than the economic structure of society and its cultural development conditioned thereby.

In a higher phase of communist society, after the enslaving subordination of the individual to the division of labour, and therewith also the antithesis between mental and physical labour, has vanished; after labour has become not only a means of life but life's prime want; after the productive forces have also increased with the all-round development of the individual, and all the springs of co-operative wealth flow more abundantly – only then can the narrow horizon of bourgeois right be crossed in its entirety and society inscribe on its banners: From each according to his ability, to each according to his needs!

I have dealt more at length with the 'undiminished proceeds of labour', on the one hand, and with 'equal right' and 'fair distribution', on the other, in order to show what a crime it is to attempt, on the one hand, to force on our Party again, as dogmas, ideas which in a certain period had some meaning but have now become obsolete verbal rubbish, while again perverting, on the other, the realistic outlook, which it cost so much effort to instil into the Party but which has now taken root in it, by means of ideological nonsense about right and other trash so common among the democrats and French Socialists.

Quite apart from the analysis so far given, it was in general a mistake to make a fuss about so-called *distribution* and put the principal stress on it.

Any distribution whatever of the means of consumption is only a consequence of the distribution of the conditions of production themselves. The latter distribution, however, is a feature of the mode of production itself. The capitalist mode of production, for example, rests on the fact that the material conditions of production are in the hands of non-workers in the form of property in capital and land, while the masses are only owners of the personal condition of production, of labour power. If the elements of production are so distributed, then the present-day distribution of the means of consumption results automatically. If the material conditions of production are the co-operative property of the workers themselves, then there likewise results a distribution of the means of consumption different from the present one. Vulgar socialism (and from it in turn a section of democracy) has taken over from the bourgeois economists the consideration and treatment of distribution as independent of the mode of production and hence the presentation of socialism as turning principally on distribution. After the real relation has long been made clear, why retrogress again?

4 The emancipation of labour must be the work of the working class, relatively to which all other classes are *only one reactionary mass.*

The first strophe is taken from the introductory words of the Rules of the International, but 'improved'. There it is said: 'The emancipation, of the working class must be the act of the workers themselves'; here, on the contrary, the 'working class' has to emancipate – what? 'Labour'. Let him understand who can.

In compensation, the antistrophe, on the other hand, is a Lassallean quotation of the first water: 'relatively to which (the working class) all other classes are *only one reactionary mass*'.

In the *Communist Manifesto* it is said: 'Of all the classes that stand face to face with the bourgeoisie today, the proletariat alone is a *really revolutionary class*. The other classes decay and finally disappear in the face of modern industry; the proletariat is its special and essential product.[1]

The bourgeoisie is here conceived as a revolutionary class – as the bearer of large scale industry – relatively to the feudal lords and the lower middle class, who desire to maintain all social positions that are the creation of obsolete modes of production. Thus they do not form *together* with the *bourgeoisie* only one reactionary mass.

On the other hand, the proletariat is revolutionary relatively to the bourgeoisis because, having itself grown up on the basis of large-scale industry, it strives to strip off from production the capitalist character that the bourgeoisis seeks to perpetuate. But the *Manifesto* adds that the 'lower middle class' is becoming revolutionary 'in view of [its] impending transfer into the proletariat'.

From this point of view, therefore, it is again nonsense to say that it, together with the bourgeoisie, and with the feudal lords into the bargain, 'form only one reactionary mass' relatively to the working class.

Has one proclaimed to the artisans, small manufacturers, etc., and

---

[1] See *Selected Works in Two Volumes*, Vol. I, p. 43.

peasants during the last elections: Relatively to us you, together with the bourgeoisie and feudal lords, form only one reactionary mass?

Lasselle knew the *Communist Manifesto* by heart, as his faithful followers know the gospels written by him. If, therefore, he has falsified it so grossly, this has occurred only to put a good colour on his alliance with absolutist and feudal opponents against the bourgeoisie.

In the above paragraph, moreover, his oracular saying is dragged in by main force without any connection with the botched quotation from the Rules of the International. Thus is it here simply an impertinence, and indeed not at all displeasing to Herr Bismarck, one of those cheap pieces of insolence in which the Marat of Berlin[2] deals.

5 The working class strives for its emancipation first of all *within the framework of the present-day national state*, conscious that the necessary result of its efforts, which are common to the workers of all civilized countries, will be the international brotherhood of peoples.

Lassalle, in opposition to the *Communist Manifesto* and to all earlier socialism, conceived the workers' movement from the narrowest national standpoint. He is being followed in this – and that after the work of the International!

It is altogether self-evident that, to be able to fight at all, the working class must organize itself at home *as a class* and that its own country is the immediate arena of its struggle. In so far its class struggle is national, not in substance, but, as the *Communist Manifesto* says, 'in form'. But the 'framework of the present-day national state', for instance, the German Empire, is itself in its turn economically 'within the framework' of the world market, politically 'within the framework' of the system of states. Every businessman knows that German trade is at the same time foreign trade, and the greatness of Herr Bismarck consists, to be sure, precisely in his pursuing a kind of *international* policy.

And to what does the German workers' party reduce its internationalism? To the consciousness that the result of its efforts will be *'the international brotherhood of peoples'* – a phrase borrowed from the bourgeois League of Peace and Freedom,[3] which is intended to pass as equivalent to the international brotherhood of the working classes

---

[2] The 'Marat of Berlin' is obviously an ironical reference to Hasselmann, the chief editor of the *Neuer Social-Demokrat*, the central organ of the Lassalleans.

[3] The *International League of Peace and Freedom* was organized in Geneva in 1867 by bourgeois democrats and pacifists. On the insistence of Marx and under his direction, the First International resolutely fought against the League's demagogic slogans, which diverted the proletariat from the class struggle.

in the joint struggle against the ruling classes and their governments. Not a word, therefore, *about the international functions* of the German working class! And it is thus that it is to challenge its own bourgeoisie – which is already linked up in brotherhood against it with the bourgeois of all other countries – Herr Bismarck's international policy of conspiracy!

In fact, the internationalism of the programme stands *even infinitely below* that of the Free Trade Party. The latter also asserts that the result of its efforts will be 'the international brotherhood of peoples'. But it also *does* something to make trade international and by no means contents itself with the consciousness – that all peoples are carrying on trade at home.

The international activity of the working classes does not in any way depend on the existence of the *International Working Men's Association*. This was only the first attempt to create a central organ for that activity; an attempt which was a lasting success on account of the impulse which it gave but which was no longer realizable in its *first historical form* after the fall of the Paris Commune.

Bismarck's *Norddeutsche* was absolutely right when it announced, to the satisfaction of its master, that the German workers' party had sworn off internationalism in the new programme.[4]

II

Starting from these basic principles, the German workers' party strives by all legal means for the *free state – and* – socialist society: the abolition of the wage system *together with* the *iron law of wages* – and – exploitation in every form; the elimination of all social and political inequality.

I shall return to the 'free' state later.

So, in future, the German workers' party has got to believe in Lassalle's 'iron law of wages'! That this may not be lost, the nonsense is perpetrated of speaking of the 'abolition of the wage system' (it should read: system of wage labour) '*together with* the iron law of wages'. If I abolish wage labour, then naturally I abolish its laws also, whether thay are of 'iron' or sponge. But Lassalle's attack on wage labour turns almost solely on this so-called law. In order, therefore, to

---

[4] Marx refers to the editorial which appeared in No. 67 of the *Norddeutsche Allgemeine Zeitung* [*North German General Newspaper*] of 20 March 1875. It stated with regard to Article 5 of the Social-Democratic Programme that 'Social-Democratic agitation had in many respects become more prudent' and that it was 'repudiating the International.'

prove that Lassalle's sect has conquered, the 'wage system' must be abolished '*together with* the iron law of wages' and not without it.

It is well known that nothing of the 'iron law of wages' is Lassalle's except the word 'iron' borrowed from Goethe's 'great eternal iron laws'. The word *iron* is a label by which the true believers recognize one another. But if I take the law with Lassalle's stamp on it and, consequently, in his sense, the I must also take it with his substantiation for it. And what is that? As Lange already showed, shortly after Lassalle's death, it is the Malthusian theory of population (preached by Lange himself). But if this theory is correct, then again I *cannot* abolish the law even if I abolish wage labour a hundred times over, because the law then governs not only the system of wage labour but *every* social system. Basing themselves directly on this, the economists have been proving for fifty years and more that socialism cannot abolish poverty, *which has its basis in nature*, but can only make it *general*, distribute it simultaneously over the whole surface of society!

But all this is not the main thing. *Quite apart* from the *false* Lassallean formulation of the law, the truly outrageous retrogression consists in the following:

Since Lassalle's death there has asserted itself in *our* Party the scientific understanding that wages are not what they *appear* to be, namely, the *value*, or *price*, of *labour*, but only a masked form for the *value*, or *price*, of *labour power*. Thereby the whole bourgeois conception of wages hitherto, as well as all the criticism hitherto directed against this conception, was thrown overboard once for all and it was made clear that the wage-worker has permission to work for his own subsistence, that is, *to live*, only in so far as he works for a certain time gratis for the capitalist (and hence also for the latter's co-consumers of surplus value); that the whole capitalist system of production turns on the increase of this gratis labour by extending the working day or by developing the productivity, that is, increasing the intensity of labour power, etc.; that, consequently, the system of wage labour is a system of slavery, and indeed of a slavery which becomes most severe in proportion as the social productive forces of labour develop, whether the worker receives better or worse payment. And after this understanding has gained more and more ground in our Party, one returns to Lassalle's dogmas, although one must have known that Lassalle *did not know* what wages were, but following in the wake of the bourgeois economists took the appearance for the essence of the matter.

It is as if, among slaves who have at last got behind the secret of slavery and broken out in rebellion, a slave still in thrall to obsolete notions were to inscribe on the programme of the rebellion: Slavery must be abolished because the feeding of slaves in the system of slavery cannot exceed a certain low minimum!

Does not the mere fact that the representatives of our Party were capable of perpetrating such a monstrous attack on the understanding that has spread among the mass of our Party prove by itself with what criminal levity and with what lack of conscience they set to work in drawing up this compromise programme!

Instead of the indefinite concluding phrase of the paragraph, 'the elimination of all social and political inequality', it ought to have been said that with the abolition of class distinctions all social and political inequality arising from them would disappear of itself.

III

The German workers' party, in order *to pave the way to the solution of the social question*, demands the establishment of producers' co-operative societies *with state aid under the democratic control of the toiling people*. The producers' co-operative societies *are to be called into being* for industry and agriculture on such a scale *that the socialist organization of the total labour will arise from them*.

After the Lassallean 'iron law of wages', the physic of the prophet. The way to it is 'paved' in worthy fashion. In place of the existing class struggle appears a newspaper scribbler's phrase: 'the social *question*', to the '*solution*' of which one 'paves the way'. Instead of arising from the revolutionary process of transformation of society, the 'socialist organization of the total labour' 'arises' from the 'state aid' that the state gives to the producers' co-operative societies and which the state, not the worker, 'calls into being'. It is worthy of Lassalle's imagination that with state loans one can build a new society just as well as a new railway!

From the remnants of a sense of shame, 'state aid' has been put – under the democratic control of the 'toiling people'.

In the first place, the majority of the 'toiling people' in Germany consists of peasants, and not of proletarians.

Secondly, 'democratic' means in German '*volksherrschaftlich*' ['by the rule of the people']. But what does 'control by the rule of the people of the toiling people' mean? And particularly in the case of a toiling people which, through these demands that it puts to the state, expresses its full consciousness that it neither rules nor is ripe for ruling!

It would be superfluous to deal here with the criticism of the recipe prescribed by Buchez in the reign of Louis Philippe in *oppostion* to the French Socialists and accepted by the reactionary workers of the *Atelier*.[5] The chief offence does not lie in having inscribed this specific nostrum in the programme, but in taking, in general, a retrograde step from the standpoint of a class movement to that of a sectarian movement.

That the workers desire to establish the conditions for co-operative production on a social scale, and first of all on a national scale, in their own country, only means that they are working to revolutionize the present conditions of production, and it has nothing in common with the foundation of co-operative societies with state aid. But as far as the present co-operative societies are concerned, they are of value *only* in so far as they are the independent creations of the workers and not protégés either of the governments or of the bourgeois.

IV

I come now to the democratic section.

A   *The free basis of the state.*

First of all, according to II, the German workers' party strives for 'the free state'.

Free state – what is this?

It is by no means the aim of the workers, who have got rid of the narrow mentality of humble subjects, to set the state free. In the German Empire the 'state' is almost as 'free' as in Russia. Freedom consists in converting the state from an organ superimposed upon society into one completely subordinate to it, and today, too, the forms of state are more free or less free to the extent that they restrict the 'freedom of the state'.

The German workers' party – at least if it adopts the programme – shows that its socialist ideas are not even skin-deep; in that, instead of treating existing society (and this holds good for any future one) as the *basis* of the existing state (or of the future state in the case of future society), it treats the state rather as an independent entity that possesses its own *intellectual, ethical and libertarian bases.*

And what of the riotous misuse which the programme makes of the

---

[5] *Atelier* [Workshop]. A workers' monthly which appeared in Paris in 1840–50. It was under the influence of the Catholic socialism of Buchez.

words '*present-day state*', '*present-day society*', and of the still more riotous misconception it creates in regard to the state to which it addresses its demands?

'Present-day society' is capitalist society, which exists in all civilized countries, more or less free from medieval admixture, more or less modified by the special historical development of each country, more or less developed. On the other hand, the 'present-day state' changes with a country's frontier. It is different in the Prusso-German Empire from what it is in Switzerland, it is different in England from what it is in the United States. The 'present-day state' is, therefore, a fiction.

Nevertheless, the different states of the different civilized countries, in spite of their manifold diversity of form, all have this in common, that they are based on modern bourgeois society, only one more or less capitalistically developed. They have, therefore, also certain essential features in common. In this sense it is possible to speak of the 'present-day state', in contrast with the future, in which its present root, bourgeois society, will have died off.

The question then arises: what transformation will the state undergo in communist society? In other words, what social functions will remain in existence there that are analogous to present functions of the state? This question can only be answered scientifically, and one does not get a flea-hop nearer to the problem by a thousandfold combination of the word people with the word state.

Between capitalist and communist society lies the period of the revolutionary transformation of the one into the other. There corresponds to this also a political transition period in which the state can be nothing but *the revolutionary dictatorship of the proletariat*.

Now the programme does not deal with this nor with the future state of communist society.

Its political demands contain nothing beyond the old democratic litany familiar to all: universal suffrage, direct legislation, popular rights, a people's militia, etc. They are a mere echo of the bourgeois People's Party, of the League of Peace and Freedom. They are all demands which, in so far as they are not exaggerated in fantastic presentation, have already been *realized*. Only the state to which they belong does not lie within the borders of the German Empire, but in Switzerland, the United States, etc. This sort of 'state of the future' is a present-day state, although existing outside the 'framework' of the German Empire.

But one thing has been forgotten. Since the German workers' party expressly declares that it acts within 'the present-day national state', hence within *its own* state, the Prusso-German Empire – its demands

would indeed otherwise be largely meaningless, since one only demands what one has not got – it should not have forgotten the chief
thing, namely, that all those pretty little gewgaws rest on the recognition of the so-called sovereignty of the people and hence are appropriate only in a *democratic republic*.

Since one has not the courage – and wisely so, for the circumstances
demand caution – to demand the democratic republic, as the French
workers' programmes under Louis Philippe and under Louis Napoleon
did, one should not have resorted, either, to the subterfuge, neither
'honest'[6] nor decent, of demanding things which have meaning only
in a democratic republic from a state which is nothing but a police-
guarded military despotism, embellished with parliamentary forms,
alloyed with a feudal admixture, already influenced by the bourgeoisie
and bureaucratically carpentered, and then to assure this state into
the bargain that one imagines one will be able to force such things
upon it 'by legal means'.

Even vulgar democracy, which sees the millennium in the democratic republic and has no suspicion that it is precisly in this last form
of state of bourgeois society that the class struggle has to be fought out
to a conclusion – even it towers mountains above this kind of demo-
cratism which keeps within the limits of what is permitted by the
police and not permitted by logic.

That, in fact, by the word 'state' is meant the government machine,
or the state in so far as it forms a special organism separated from
society through division of labour, is shown by the words 'the German
worker's party demands *as the economic basis of the state*: a single
progressive income tax,' etc. Taxes are the conomic basis of the
government machinery and of nothing else. In the state of the future,
existing in Switzerland, this demand has been pretty well fulfilled.
Income tax presupposes various sources of income of the various
social classes, and hence capitalist society. It is, therefore, nothing
remarkable that the Liverpool financial reformers, bourgeois headed
by Gladstone's brother, are putting forward the same demand as the
programme.

B   The German workers' party demands as the intellectual and ethical basis
of the state:
1   Universal and *equal elementary education* by the state. Universal compulsory
school attendance. Free instruction.

Equal elementary education? What idea lies behind these words? Is
it believed that in present-day society (and it is only with this one has

---

[6] *'Honest'* was the epithet applied to the Eisenachers. Here a play upon words.

to deal) education can be *equal* for all classes? Or is it demanded that the upper classes also shall be compulsorily reduced to the modicum of education – the elementary school – that alone is compatible with the economic conditions not only of the wage-workers but of the peasants as well?

'Universal compulsory school attendance. Free instruction.' The former exists even in Germany, the second in Switzerland and in the United States in the case of elementary schools. If in some states of the latter country higher educational institutions are also 'free' that only means in fact defraying the cost of the education of the upper classes from the general tax receipts. Incidentally, the same holds good for 'free administration of justice' demanded under A, 5. The administration of criminal justice is to be had free everywhere; that of civil justice is concerned almost exclusively with conflicts over property and hence affects almost exclusively the possessing classes. Are they to carry on their litigation at the expense of the national coffers?

The paragraph on the schools should at least have demanded technical schools (theoretical and practical) in combination with the elementary school.

'*Elementary education by the state*' is altogether objectionable. Defining by a general law the expenditures on the elementary schools, the qualifications of the teaching staff, the branches of instruction, etc., and, as is done in the United States, supervising the fulfilment of these legal specifications by state inspectors, is a very different thing from appointing the state as the educator of the people! Government and Church should rather be equally excluded from an influence on the school. Particularly, indeed, in the Prusso-German Empire (and one should not take refuge in the rotten subterfuge that one is speaking of a 'state of the future'; we have seen how matters stand in this respect) the state has need, on the contrary, of a very stern education by the people.

But the whole programme, for all its democratic clang, is tainted through and through by the Lassallean sect's servile belief in the state, or, what is no better, by a democratic belief in miracles, or rather it is a compromise between these two kinds of belief in miracles, both equally remote from socialism.

'*Freedom of science*' says a paragraph of the Prussian Constitution. Why, then, here?

'*Freedom of conscience*'! If one desired at this time of the *Kulturkampf*[7] to remind liberalism of its old catchwords, it surely could

---

[7] *Kulturkampf* [Struggle for culture]: Bismarck's struggle in the seventies against the German Catholic Party, the Party of the 'Centre', by means of police persecution of Catholicism.

have been done only in the following form: Everyone should be able to attend to his religious as well as his bodily needs without the police sticking their noses in. But the workers' party ought at any rate in this connection to have expressed its awareness of the fact that bourgeois 'freedom of conscience' is nothing but the toleration of all possible kinds of *religious freedom of conscience*, and that for its part it endeavours rather to liberate the conscience from the witchery of religion. But one chooses not to transgress the 'bourgeois' level.

I have now come to the end, for the appendix that now follows in the programme does not constitute a characteristic component part of it. Hence I can be very brief here.

2 *Normal working day.*

In no other country has the workers' party limited itself to such an indefinite demand, but has always fixed the length of the working day that it considers normal under the given circumstances.

3 Restriction of female labour and prohibition of child labour

The standardization of the working day must include the restriction of female labour, in so far as it relates to the duration, intermissions, etc., of the working day; otherwise it could only mean the exclusion of female labour from branches of industry that are especially unhealthy for the female body or are objectionable morally for the female sex. If that is what was meant, it should have been said so.

'*Prohibiton of child labour.*' Here it was absolutely essential to state the age limit.

A *general prohibition* of child labour is incompatible with the existence of large-scale industry and hence an empty, pious wish. Its realization – if it were possible – would be reactionary, since, with a strict regulation of the working time according to the different age groups and other safety measures for the protection of children, an early combination of productive labour with education is one of the most potent means for the transformation of present-day society.

4 State supervision of factory, workshop and domestic industry.

In consideration of the Prusso-German state it should definitely have been demanded that the inspectors are to be removable only by a court of law; that any worker can have them prosecuted for neglect of duty; that they must belong to the medical profession.

5 Regulation of prison labour.

A petty demand in a general worker's programme. In any case, it should have been clearly stated that there is no intention from fear of competition to allow ordinary criminals to be treated like beasts, and especially that there is no desire to deprive them of their sole means of betterment, productive labour. This was surely the least one might have expected from Socialists.

6 An effective liability law.

It should have been stated what is meant by an 'effective' liability law.

Be it noted, incidentally, that in speaking of the normal working day the part of factory legislation that deals with health regulations and safety measures, etc., has been overlooked. The liability law only comes into operation when these regulations are infringed.

In short, this appendix also is distinguished by slovenly editing.

Dixi et salvavi animam meam.[8]

[8] I have spoken and saved my soul.

4

Class, Status, Party

MAX WEBER

This essay was published posthumously in 1944, and may be accepted as a mature, albeit a brief formulation of Max Weber's views on class, status and party. Many of the points he makes have been 're-discovered' by a recent generation of social historians who, in their search for a non-Marxist theory to tie their histories together, have clutched at the arguments in this essay. Sometimes these historians have arrived at Weber through the writing of W. G. Runciman who refers to class, status and power, rather than to class, status and party, and it is for that reason I discuss Weber in *Class in English History* under the first rather than the second trio. In any case, as Weber writes, '"parties" live in a house of "power".' And his thoughts are random rather than well organized.

Weber's exploration of the language of class seems to challenge Marx by noticing also the languages of community, status, caste and party (power). Yet he cannot escape from Marx. Thus '"Property" and "lack of property" are, therefore, the basic categories of all class situations.' And, 'Property as such is not always recognized as a status qualification, but in the long run it is, and with extraordinary regularity.' Moreover, Weber himself recognizes the over-simplification of his view, 'that "classes" are stratified according to their relations to the production and acquisition of goods; whereas "status groups" are stratified according to the principles of their *consumption* of goods as represented by special "styles of life".' The over-simplification lies in not recognizing the importance of Weber's own claim about the long

From H. H. Gerth and C. Wright Mills (translated, edited and introduction) *From Max Weber: Essays in Sociology* (Oxford University Press, London 1970) pp. 180–95. All footnotes are additions by the editors of that volume.

run relationship between property and status, in divorcing the production and acquisition of goods from consumption, in not exploring relationships between these elements, law and power, and in avoiding rather than analysing the significance of all these elements and their relationships for the unresolved problem of class consciousness. Nevertheless, students of history should read this essay by Weber, if only to become aware of these problems rather than to jump at the solutions the essay seems to offer.

---

1 ECONOMICALLY DETERMINED POWER AND THE SOCIAL ORDER

Law exists when there is a probability that an order will be upheld by a specific staff of men who will use physical or psychical compulsion with the intention of obtaining conformity with the order, or of inflicting sanctions for infringement of it.[1] The structure of every legal order directly influences the distribution of power, economic or otherwise, within its respective community. This is true of all legal orders and not only that of the state. In general, we understand by 'power' the chance of a man or of a number of men to realize their own will in a communal action even against the resistance of others who are participating in the action.

'Economically conditioned' power is not, of course, identical with 'power' as such. On the contrary, the emergence of economic power may be the consequence of power existing on other grounds. Man does not strive for power only in order to enrich himself economically. Power, including economic power, may be valued 'for its own sake.' Very frequently the striving for power is also conditioned by the social 'honour' it entails. Not all power, however, entails social honour: The typical American Boss, as well as the typical big speculator, deliberately relinquishes social honour. Quite generally, 'mere economic' power, and especially 'naked' money power, is by no means a recognized basis of social honour. Nor is power the only basis of social honour. Indeed, social honour, or prestige, may even be the basis of political or economic power, and very frequently has been. Power, as well as honour, may be guaranteed by the legal order, but, at least normally, it is not their primary source. The legal order is

[1] *Wirtschaft und Gesellschaft*, part III, chap. 4, pp. 631–40. The first sentence in paragraph one and the several definitions in this chapter which are in brackets do not appear in the original text. They have been taken from other contexts of *Wirtschaft und Gesellschaft*.

rather an additional factor that enhances the chance to hold power or honour; but it cannot always secure them.

The way in which social honour is distributed in a community between typical groups participating in this distribution we may call the 'social order'. The social order and the economic order are, of course, similarly related to the 'legal order'. However, the social and the economic order are not identical. The economic order is for us merely the way in which economic goods and services are distributed and used. The social order is of course conditioned by the economic order to a high degree, and in its turn reacts upon it.

Now: 'classes', 'status groups', and 'parties' are phenomena of the distribution of power within a community.

2 DETERMINATION OF CLASS-SITUATION BY MARKET-SITUATION

In our teminology, 'classes' are not communities; they merely represent possible, and frequent, bases for communal action. We may speak of a 'class' when (1) a number of people have in common a specific causal component of their life chances, in so far as (2) this component is represented exclusively by economic interests in the possession of goods and opportunities for income, and (3) is represented under the conditions of the commodity or labour markets. [These points refer to 'class situation', which we may express more briefly as the typical chance for a supply of goods, external living conditions, and personal life experiences, in so far as this chance is determined by the amount and kind of power, or lack of such, to dispose of goods or skills for the sake of income in a given economic order. The term 'class' refers to any group of people that is found in the same class situation.]

It is the most elemental economic fact that the way in which the disposition over material property is distributed among a plurality of people, meeting competitively in the market for the purpose of exchange, in itself creates specific life chances. According to the law of marginal utility this mode of distribution excludes the non-owners from competing for highly valued goods; it favours the owners and, in fact, gives to them a monopoly to acquire such goods. Other things being equal, this mode of distribution monopolizes the opportunities for profitable deals for all those who, provided with goods, do not necessarily have to exchange them. It increases, at least generally, their power in price wars with those who, being propertyless, have nothing to offer but their services in native form or goods in a form constituted through their own labour, and who above all are compelled to get rid of these products in order barely to subsist. This mode of distribution gives to the propertied a monopoly on the possibility of transferring property from the sphere of use as a 'fortune,' to the sphere of 'capital goods'; that is, it gives them the entrepreneurial function and all chances to share directly or indirectly in returns on capital. All this holds true within the area in which pure market conditions prevail. 'Property' and 'lack of property' are, therefore, the basic categories of all class situations. It does not matter whether these two categories become effective in price wars or in competitive struggles.

Within these categories, however, class situations are further differentiated; on the one hand, according to the kind of property that is usable for returns; and, on the other hand, according to the kind of services that can be offered in the market. Ownership of domestic buildings; productive establishments; warehouses; stores; agriculturally usable land, large and small holding – quantitative differences with possibly qualitative consequences –; ownership of mines; cattle; men (slaves); disposition over mobile instruments of production, or capital goods of all sorts, especially money or objects that can be exchanged for money easily and at any time; disposition over products of one's own labour or of others' labour differing according to their various distances from consumability; disposition over transferable monopolies of any kind – all these distinctions differentiate the class situations of the propertied just as does the 'meaning' which they can and do give to the utilization of property, especially to property which has money equivalence. Accordingly, the propertied, for instance, may belong to the class of rentiers or to the class of entrepreneurs.

Those who have no property but who offer services are differentiated just as much according to their kinds of services as according to the way in which they make use of these services, in a continuous or discontinuous relation to a recipient. But always this is the generic connotation of the concept of class: that the kind of chance in the *market* is the decisive moment which presents a common condition for the individual's fate. 'Class situation' is, in this sense, ultimately 'market situation'. The effect of naked possession *per se*, which among cattle breeders gives the non-owning slave or serf into the power of the cattle owner, is only a fore-runner of real 'class' formation. However, in the cattle loan and in the naked severity of the law of debts in such communities, for the first time mere 'possession' as such emerges as decisive for the fate of the individual. This is very much in contrast to the agricultural communities based on labour. The creditor-debtor relation becomes the basis of 'class situations' only in those cities where a 'credit market', however primitive, with rates of interest increasing according to the extent of dearth and a factual monopolization of credits, is developed by a plutocracy. Therewith 'class struggles' begin.

Those men whose fate is not determined by the chance of using goods or services for themselves on the market, e.g. slaves, are not, however, a 'class' in the technical sense of the term. They are, rather, a 'status group'.

3 COMMUNAL ACTION FLOWING FROM CLASS INTEREST

According to our terminology, the factor that creates 'class' is un-ambiguously economic interest, and indeed, only those interests involved in the existence of the 'market'. Nevertheless, the concept of 'class-interest' is an ambiguous one; even as an empirical concept it is ambiguous as soon as one understands by it something other than the factual direction of interests following with a certain probability from the class situation for a certain 'average' of those people subjected to the class situation. The class situation and other circumstances remaining the same, the direction in which the individual worker, for instance, is likely to pursue his interests may vary widely, according to whether he is constitutionally qualified for the task at hand to a high, to an average, or to a low degree. In the same way, the direction of interests may vary according to whether or not a *communal* action of a larger or smaller portion of those commonly affected by the 'class situation', or even an association among them, e.g. a 'trade union', has grown out of the class situation from which the individual may or may not expect promising results. (Communal action refers to that action which is oriented to the feeling of the actors that they belong together. Societal action, on the other hand, is oriented to a rationally motivated adjustment of interests). The rise of societal or even of communal action from a common class situation is by no means a universal phenomenon.

The class situation may be restricted in its effects to the generation of essentially *similar* reactions, that is to say, within our teminology, of 'mass actions'. However, it may not have even this result. Furthermore, often merely an amorphous communal action emerges. For example, the 'murmuring' of the workers known in ancient oriental ethics: the moral disapproval of the work-master's conduct, which in its practical significance was probably equivalent to an increasingly typical phenomenon of precisely the latest industrial development, namely, the 'slow down' (the deliberate limiting of work effort) of laborers by virtue of tacit agreement. The degree in which 'communal action' and possibly 'societal action', emerges from the 'mass actions' of the members of a class is linked to general cultural conditions, especially to those of an intellectual sort. It is also linked to the extent of the contrasts that have already evolved, and is especially linked to the *transparency* of the connections between the causes and the consequences of the 'class situation'. For however different life chances may be, this fact in itself, according to all experience, by no means gives birth to 'class action' (communal action by the members of a class). The fact of being conditioned and the results of the class situation must be distinctly recognizable. For only then the contrast of life chances can be felt not as an absolutely given fact to be accepted, but as a resultant from either (1) the given distribution of property, or (2) the structure of the concrete economic order. It is only then that people may react against the class structure not only through acts of an intermittent and irrational protest, but in the form of rational association. There have been 'class situations' of the first category (1), of a specifically naked and transparent sort, in the urban centres of Antiquity and during the Middle Ages; especially then, when great fortunes were accumulated by factually monopolized trading in industrial products of these localities or in foodstuffs. Furthermore, under certain circumstances, in the rural economy of the most diverse periods, when agriculture was increasingly exploited in a profit-making manner. The most important historical example of the second category (2) is the class situation of the modern 'proletariat'.

4 TYPES OF 'CLASS STRUGGLE'

Thus every class may be the carrier of any one of the possibly innumerable forms of 'class action', but this is not necessarily so. In any case, a class does not in itself constitute a community. To treat 'class' conceptually as having the same value as 'community' leads to distortion. That men in the same class situation regularly react in mass actions to such tangible situations as economic ones in the direction of those interests that are the most adequate to the average number is an important and after all simple fact for the understanding of historical events. Above all, this fact must not lead to that kind of pseudo-scientific operation with the concepts of 'class' and 'class interests' so frequently found these days, and which has found its most classic expression in the statement of a talented author, that the individual may be in error concerning his interests but that the 'class' is 'infallible' about its interests. Yet, if classes as such are not communities, nevertheless class situations emerge only on the basis of communalization. The communal action that brings forth class situations, however, is not basically action between members of the identical class; it is an action between members of different classes. Communal actions that directly determine the class situation of the worker and the entrepreneur are: the labour market, the commodities market, and the capitalistic enterprise. But, in its turn, the existence of a capitalistic enterprise presupposes that a very specific communal action exists and that it is specifically structured to protect the possession of goods *per se*, and especially the power of individuals to dispose, in principle freely, over the means of production. The existence of a capitalistic enterprise is preconditioned by a specific kind of 'legal order'. Each kind of class situation, and above all when it rests upon the power of property *per se*, will become most clearly efficacious when all other determinants of reciprocal relations are, as far as possible, eliminated in their significance. It is in this way that the utilization of the power of property in the market obtains its most sovereign importance.

Now 'status groups' hinder the strict carrying through of the sheer market principle. In the present context they are of interest to us only from this one point of view. Before we briefly consider them, note that not much of a general nature can be said about the more specific kinds of antagonism between 'classes' (in our meaning of the term). The great shift, which has been going on continuously in the past, and up to our times, may be summarized although at the cost of some precision: the struggle in which class situations are effective has progressively shifted from consumption credit toward, first, competitive struggles in the commodity market and, then, toward price wars on the labour market. The 'class struggles' of antiquity – to the extent that they were genuine class struggles and not struggles between status groups – were initially carried on by indebted peasants, and perhaps also by artisans threatened by debt bondage and struggling against urban creditors. For debt bondage is the normal result of the differentiation of wealth in commercial cities, especially in seaport cities. A similar situation has existed among cattle breeders. Debt relationships as such produced class action up to the time of Cataline. Along with this, and with an increase in provision of grain for the city by transporting it from the outside, the struggle over the means of sustenance emerged. It centred in the first place around the provision of bread and the determination of the price of bread. It lasted throughout antiquity and the entire Middle Ages. The propertyless as such flocked together against those who actually and supposedly were interested in the dearth of bread. This fight spread until it involved all those commodities essential to the way of life and to handicraft production. There were only incipient discussions of wage disputes in antiquity and in the Middle Ages. But they have been slowly increasing up into modern times. In the earlier periods they were completely secondary to slave rebellions as well as to fights in the commodity market.

The propertyless of antiquity and of the Middle Ages protested against monopolies, pre-emption, forestalling, and the withholding of goods from the market in order to raise prices. Today the central issue is the determination of the price of labour.

This transition is respresented by the fight for access to the market and for the determination of the price of products. Such fights went on between merchants and workers in the putting-out system of domestic handicraft during the transition to modern times. Since it is quite a general phenomenon we must mention here that the class antagonisms that are conditioned through the market situation are usually most bitter between those who actually and directly participate as opponents in price wars. It is not the rentier, the share-holder, and the banker who suffer the ill will of the worker, but almost exclusively the manufacturere and the business executives who are the direct opponents of workers in price wars. This is so in spite of the fact that it is precisely the cash boxes of the rentier, the share-holder, and the banker into which the more or less 'unearned' gains flow, rather than into the pockets of the manufacturers or of the business executives. This simple state of affairs has very frequently been decisive for the role the class situation has played in the formation of political parties. For example, it has made possible the varieties of partriarchal socialism and the frequent attempts – formerly, at least – of threatened status groups to form alliances with the proletariat against the 'bourgeoisie'.

5 STATUS HONOUR

In contrast to classes, *status groups* are normally communities. They are, however, often of an amorphous kind. In contrast to the purely economically determined 'class situation' we wish to designate as 'status situation' every typical component of the life fate of men that is determined by a specific, positive or negative, social estimation of *honour*. This honour may be connected with any quality shared by a plurality, and, of course, it can be knit to a class situation: class distinctions are linked in the most varied ways with status distinctions. Property as such is not always recognized as a status qualification, but in the long run it is, and with extraordinary regularity. In the subsistence economy of the organized neighborhood, very often the richest man is simply the chieftain. However, this often means only an honorific preference. For example, in the so-called pure modern 'democracy', that is, one devoid of any expressly ordered status privileges for individuals, it may be that only the families coming under approximately the same tax class dance with one another. This example is reported of certain smaller Swiss cities. But status honour need not necessarily be linked with a 'class situation'. On the contrary, it normally stands in sharp opposition to the pretensions of sheer property.

Both propertied and propertyless people can belong to the same status group, and frequently they do with very tangible consequences. This 'equality' of social esteem may, however, in the long run become quite precarious. The 'equality' of status among the American 'gentlemen', for instance, is expressed by the fact that outside the subordination determined by the different functions of 'business', it would be considered strictly repugnant – wherever the old tradition still prevails – if even the richest 'chief', while playing billiards or cards in his club in the evening, would not treat his 'clerk' as in every sense fully his equal in birthright. It would be repugnant if the American 'chief' would bestow upon his 'clerk' the condescending 'benevolence' marking a distinction of 'position', which the German chief can never dissever from his attitude. This is one of the most important reasons why in America the German 'clubby-ness' has never been able to attain the attraction that the American clubs have.

6 GUARANTEES OF STATUS STRATIFICATION

In content, status honour is normally expressed by the fact that above all else a specific *style of life* can be expected from all those who wish to belong to the circle. Linked with this expectation are restrictions on 'social' intercourse (that is, intercourse which is not subservient to economic or any other of business's 'functional' purposes). These restrictions may confine normal marriages to within the status circle and may lead to complete endogamous closure. As soon as there is not a mere individual and socially irrelevant imitation of another style of life, but an agreed-upon communal action of this closing character, the 'status' development is under way.

In its characteristic form, stratification by 'status groups' on the basis of conventional styles of life evolves at the present time in the United States out of the traditional democracy. For example, only the resident of a certain street ('the street') is considered as belonging to 'society', is qualified for social intercourse, and is visited and invited. Above all, this differentiation evolves in such a way as to make for strict submission to the fashion that is dominant at a given time in society. This submission to fashion also exists among men in America to a degree unknown in Germany. Such submission is considered to be an indication of the fact that a given man *pretends* to qualify as a gentleman. This submission decides, at least *prima facie*, that he will be treated as such. And this recognition becomes just as important for his employment chances in 'swank' establishments, and above all, for social intercourse and marriage with 'esteemed' families, as the qualification for dueling among Germans in the Kaiser's day. As for the rest: certain families resident for a long time, and, of course, correspondingly wealthy, e.g. FFV, i.e. 'First Families of Virginia', or the actual or alleged descendants of the 'Indian Princess' Pocahontas, of the Pilgrim fathers, or of the Knickerbockers, the members of almost inaccessible sects and all sorts of circles setting themselves apart by means of any other characteristics and badges . . . all these elements usurp 'status' honour. The development of status is essentially a question of stratification resting upon usurpation. Such usurpation is the normal origin of almost all status honour. But the road from this purely conventional situation to legal privilege, positive or negative, is easily traveled as soon as a certain stratification of the social order has in fact been 'lived in' and has achieved stability by virtue of a stable distribution of economic power.

7 'ETHNIC' SEGREGATION AND 'CASTE'

Where the consequences have been realized to their full extent, the status group evolves into a closed 'caste'. Status distinctions are then guaranteed not merely by conventions and laws, but also by *rituals*. This occurs in such a way that every physical contact with a member of any caste that is considered to be 'lower' by the members of a 'higher' caste is considered as making for a ritualistic impurity and to be a stigma which must be expiated by a religious act. Individual castes develop quite distinct cults and gods.

In general, however, the status structure reaches such extreme consequences only where there are underlying differences which are held to be 'ethnic'. The 'caste' is, indeed, the normal form in which ethnic communities usually live side by side in a 'societalized' manner. These ethnic communities believe in blood relationship and exclude exogamous marriage and social intercourse. Such a caste situation is part of the phenomenon of 'pariah' peoples and is found all over the world. These people form communities, acquire specific occupational traditions of handicrafts or of other arts, and cultivate a belief in their ethnic community. They live in a 'diaspora' strictly segregated from all personal intercourse, except that of an unavoidable sort, and their situation is legally precarious. Yet, by virtue of their economic indispensability, they are tolerated, indeed, frequently privileged, and they live in interspersed political communities. The Jews are the most impressive historical example.

A 'status' segregation grown into a 'caste' differs in its structure from a mere 'ethnic' segregation: the caste structure transforms the horizontal and unconnected coexistences of ethnically segregated groups into a vertical social system of super- and subordination. Correctly formulated: a comprehensive societalization integrates the ethnically divided communities into specific political and communal action. In their consequences they differ precisely in this way: ethnic coexistences condition a mutual repulsion and disdain but allow each ethnic community to consider its own honour as the highest one; the caste structure brings about a social subordination and an acknowledgment of 'more honour' in favour of the privileged caste and status groups. This is due to the fact that in the caste structure ethnic distinctions as such have become 'functional' distinctions within the political societalization (warriors, priests, artisans that are politically important for war and building, and so on). But even pariah people who are most despised are usually apt to continue cultivating in some manner that which is equally peculiar to ethnic and to status communities: the belief in their own specific 'honour'. This is the case with the Jews.

Only with the negatively privileged status groups does the 'sense of dignity' take a specific deviation. A sense of dignity is the precipitation in individuals of social honour and of conventional demands which a positively privileged status group raises for the deportment of its members. The sense of dignity that characterizes positively privileged status groups is naturally related to their 'being' which does not transcend itself, that is, it is to their 'beauty and excellence' ($\chi\alpha\lambda o$-$\chi\grave{\alpha}\gamma\alpha\theta\iota\alpha$). Their kingdom is 'of this world'. They live for the present and by exploiting their great past. The sense of dignity of the negatively privileged strata naturally refers to a future lying beyond the present, whether it is of this life or of another. In other words, it must be nurtured by the belief in a providential 'mission' and by a belief in a specific honour before God. The 'chosen people's' dignity is nurtured by a belief either that in the beyond 'the last will be the first,' or that in this life a Messiah will appear to bring forth into the light of the world which has cast them out the hidden honour of the pariah people. This simple state of affairs, and not the 'resentment' which is so strongly emphasized in Nietzsche's much admired construction in the *Genealogy of Morals*, is the source of the religiosity cultivated by pariah status groups. In passing, we may note that resentment may be accurately applied only to a limited extent; for one of Nietzsche's main examples, Buddhism, it is not at all applicable.

Incidentally, the development of status groups from ethnic segregations is by no means the normal phenomenon. On the contrary, since objective 'racial differences' are by no means basic to every subjective sentiment of an ethnic community, the ultimately racial foundation of status structure is rightly and absolutely a question of the concrete individual case. Very frequently a status group is instrumental in the production of a thoroughbred anthropological type. Certainly a status group is to a high degree effective in producing extreme types, for they select personally qualified individuals (e.g. the Knighthood selects those who are fit for warfare, physically and psychically). But selection is far from being the only, or the predominant, way in which status groups are formed: Political membership or class situation has at all times been at least as frequently decisive. And today the class situation is by far the predominant factor, for of course the possibility of a style of life expected for members of a status group is usually conditioned economically.

8 STATUS PRIVILEGES

For all practical purposes, stratification by status goes hand in had with a monopolization of ideal and material goods or opportunities, in a manner we have come to know as typical. Besides the specific status honour, which always rests upon distance and exclusiveness, we find all sorts of material monopolies. Such honorific preferences may consist of the privilege of wearing special costumes, of eating special dishes taboo to others, of carrying arms – which is most obvious in its consequences – the right to pursue certain non-professional dilettante artistic practices, e.g. to play certain musical instruments. Of couse, material monopolies provide the most effective motives for the exclusiveness of a status group; although, in themselves, they are rarely sufficient, almost always they come into play to some extent. Within a status circle there is the question of intermarriage: the interest of the families in the monopolization of potential bridegrooms is at least of equal importance and is parallel to the interest in the monopolization of daughters. The daughters of the circle must be provided for. With an increased inclosure of the status group, the conventional preferential opportunities for special employment grow into a legal monopoly of special offices for the members. Certain goods become objects for monopolization by status groups. In the typical fashion these include 'entailed estates' and frequently also the possessions of serfs or bondsmen and, finally, special trades. This monopolization occurs positively when the status group is exclusively entitled to own and to manage them; and negatively when, in order to maintain its specific way of life, the status group must *not* own and manage them.

The decisive role of a 'style of life' in status 'honour' means that status groups are the specific bearers of all 'conventions'. In whatever way it may be manifest, all 'stylization' of life either originates in status groups or is at least conserved by them. Even if the principles of status conventions differ greatly, they reveal certain typical traits, especially among those strata which are most privileged. Quite generally, among privileged status groups there is a status disqualification that operates against the performance of common physical labour. This disqualification is now 'setting in' in America against the old tradition of esteem for labour. Very frequently every rational economic pursuit, and especially 'entrepreneurial activity', is looked upon as a disqualification of status. Artistic and literary activity is also considered as degrading work as soon as it is exploited for income, or at least when it is connected with hard physical exertion. An example is the sculptor working like a mason in his dusty smock as over against the painter in his salon-like 'studio' and those forms of musical practice that are acceptable to the status group.

9 ECONOMIC CONDITIONS AND EFFECTS OF STATUS STRATIFICATION

The frequent disqualification of the gainfully employed as such is a direct result of the principle of status stratification peculiar to the social order, and of course, of this principle's opposition to a distribution of power which is regulated exclusively through the market. These two factors operate along with various individual ones, which will be touched upon below.

We have seen above that the market and its processes 'knows no personal distinctions': 'functional' interests dominate it. It knows nothing of 'honour'. The status order means precisely the reverse, viz.: stratification in terms of 'honour' and of styles of life peculiar to status groups as such. If mere economic acquisition and naked economic power still bearing the stigma of its extra-status origin could bestow upon anyone who has won it the same honour as those who are interested in status by virtue of style of life claim for themselves, the status order would be threatened at its very root. This is the more so as, given equality of status honour, property *per se* represents an addition even if it is not overtly acknowledged to be such. Yet if such economic acquisition and power gave the agent any honour at all, his wealth would result in his attaining more honour than those who successfully claim honour by virtue of style of life. Therefore all groups having interests in the status order react with special sharpness precisely against the pretensions of purely economic acquisition. In most cases they react the more vigorously the more they feel themselves threatened. Calderon's respectful treatment of the peasant, for instance, as opposed to Shakespeare's simultaneous and ostensible disdain of the *canaille* illustrates the different way in which a firmly structured status order reacts as compared with a status order that has become economically precarious. This is an example of a state of affairs that recurs everywhere. Precisely because of the rigorous reactions against the claims of property *per se*, the 'parvenu' is never accepted, personally and without reservation, by the privileged status groups, no matter how completely his style of life has been adjusted to theirs. They will only accept his descendants who have been educated in the conventions of their status group and who have never besmirched its honour by their own economic labour.

As to the general *effect* of the status order, only one consequence can be stated, but it is a very important one: the hindrance of the free development of the market occurs first for those goods which status groups directly withheld from free exchange by monopolization. This monopolization may be affected either legally or conventionally. For example, in many Hellenic cities during the epoch of status groups, and also originally in Rome, the inherited estate (as is shown by the old formula for indiction against spendthrifts) was monopolized just as were the estates of the knights, peasants, priests, and especially the clientele of the craft and merchant guilds. The market is restricted, and the power of naked property *per se*, which gives its stamp to 'class formation', is pushed into the background. The results of this process can be most varied. Of course, they do not necessarily weaken the contrasts in the economic situation. Frequently they strengthen these contrasts, and in any case, where stratification by status permeates a community as strongly as was the case in all political communities of antiquity and of the Middle Ages, one can never speak of a genuinely free market competition as we understand it today. There are wider effects than this direct exclusion of special goods from the market. From the contrariety between the status order and the purely economic order mentioned above, it follows that in most instances the notion of honour peculiar to status absolutely abhors that which is essential to the market: higgling. Honour abhors higgling among peers and occasionally it taboos higgling for the members of a status group in general. Therefore, everywhere some status groups, and usually the most influential, consider almost any kind of overt participation in economic acquisition as absolutely stigmatizing.

With some over-simplification, one might thus say that 'classes' are stratified according to their relations to the production and acquisition of goods; whereas 'status groups' are stratified according to the principles of their *consumption* of goods as represented by special 'styles of life'.

An 'occupational group' is also a status group. For normally, it successfully claims social honour only by virtue of the special style of life which may be determined by it. The differences between classes and status groups frequently overlap. It is precisely those status communities most strictly segregated in terms of honour (viz. the Indian castes) who today show, although within very rigid limits, a relatively high degree of indifference to pecuniary income. However, the Brahmins seek such income in many different ways.

As to the general economic conditions making for the predominance of stratification by 'status', only very little can be said. When the bases of the acquisition and distribution of goods are relatively stable, stratification by status is favoured. Every technological repercussion and economic transformation threatens stratification by status and pushes the class situation into the foreground. Epochs and countries in which the naked class situation is of predominant significance are regularly the periods of technical and economic transformations. And every slowing down of the shifting of economic stratifications leads, in due course, to the growth of status structures and makes for a resuscitation of the important role of social honour.

10 PARTIES

Whereas the genuine place of 'classes' is within the economic order, the place of 'status groups' is within the social order, that is, within the sphere of the distribution of 'honour'. From within these spheres, classes and status groups influence one another and they influence the legal order and are in turn influenced by it. But 'parties' live in a house of 'power'.

Their action is oriented toward the acquisition of social 'power', that is to say, toward influencing a communal action no matter what its content may be. In principle, parties exist in a social 'club' as well as in a 'state'. As over against the actions of classes and status groups, for which this is not necessarily the case, the communal actions of 'parties' always mean a societalization. For party actions are always directed toward a goal which is striven for in planned manner. This goal may be a 'cause' (the party may aim at realizing a programme for ideal or material purposes), or the goal may be 'personal' (sinecures, power, and from these, honour for the leader and the followers of the party). Usually the party action aims at all these simultaneously. Parties are, therefore, only possible within communities that are societalized, that is, which have some rational order and a staff of persons available who are ready to enforce it. For parties aim precisely at influencing this staff, and if possible, to recruit it from party followers.

In any individual case, parties may represent interests determined through 'class situation' or 'status situation', and they may recruit their following respectively from one or the other. But they need be neither purely 'class' nor purely 'status' parties. In most cases they are partly class parties and partly status parties, but sometimes they are neither. They may represent ephemeral or enduring structures. Their means of attaining power may be quite varied, ranging from naked violence of any sort to canvassing for votes with coarse or subtle means: money, social influence, the force of speech suggestion, clumsy hoax, and so on to the rougher or more artful tactics of obstruction in parliamentary bodies.

The sociological structure of parties differs in a basic way according to the kind of communal action which they struggle to influence. Parties also differ according to whether or not the community is stratified by status or by classes. Above all else, they vary according to the structure of domination within the community. For their leaders normally deal with the conquest of a community. They are, in the general concept which is maintained here, not only products of specially modern forms of domination. We shall also designate as parties the ancient and medieval 'parties', despite the fact that their structure differs basically from the structure of modern parties. By virtue of these structural differences of domination it is impossible to say anything about the structure of parties without discussing the structural forms of social domination *per se*. Parties, which are always structures struggling for domination are very frequently organized in a very strict 'authoritarian' fashion.

Concerning 'classes', 'status groups', and 'parties', it must be said in general that they necessarily presuppose a comprehensive societalization, and especially a political framework of communal action, within which they operate. This does not mean that parties would be confined by the frontiers of any individual political community. On the contrary, at all times it has been the order of the day that the societalization (even when it aims at the use of military force in common) reaches beyond the frontiers of politics. This has been the case in the solidarity of interests among the Oligarchs and among the democrats in Hellas, among the Guelfs and among Ghibellines in the Middle Ages, and within the Calvinist party during the period of religious struggles. It has been the case up to the solidarity of the landlords (international congress of agrarian landlords), and has continued among princes (holy alliance, Karlsbad decrees), socialist workers, conservatives (the longing of Prussian conservatives for Russian intervention in 1850). But their aim is not necessarily the establishment of new international political, i.e. *territorial*, dominion. In the main they aim to influence the existing dominion.[2]

[2] The posthumously published text breaks off here. We omit an incomplete sketch of types of 'warrior estates.'

5

From Historical Sociology
to Theoretical History

GARETH STEDMAN JONES

In this essay, first published in 1976, Gareth Stedman Jones, in raising
the question of the relationship of sociology to history, refers in
general to the way recent historians have used the concept 'class', and
specifically to their preference for some usage based on Weber's notion
of 'class, status and power'. He writes, 'the most noticeable phenomenon has been the importation of sociological notions of class and
social structure' into the work of modern historians. He is wholly
critical of this development because it means that, 'classes are not tied
to the relations of production within their modes of production and no
distinction is made between a mode of production and a social formation'. In fact Stedman Jones's criticism of historians' Weberian
language of class, although mildly expressed – he finds its effects
'disconcerting' – is devastating. Thus, 'The word "class" has been
domesticated into the historians' vocabulary', resulting in 'a form of
discussion which is pre- rather than post-Marxist'. Yet his criticism
may well have passed unnoticed, at least if R. J. Morris's 1979 booklet
for the Economic History Society is anything to go by. Morris does
not refer his readers to Stedman Jones's essay and deplores the fact that
Weber's ideas have been so little used by historians! Therefore it
appears timely to reprint the essay in this collection.

The essay is also important because it discusses the merits of the
Weberian language of class within a wider discourse on the use of
theory in history, and on this question Stedman Jones argues a position similar to that in Class in English History and in the Afterword to
this collection. However, I do not share Stedman Jones's urgent desire

From *British Journal of Sociology*, 27(3) (1976), pp. 295–305.

to construct an historical science. His emphasis on the importance of understanding history as a science could be misleading; it could suggest a deficiency in history compared with some other 'hard' disciplines, perpetuate the notion that history *is* theoretically empty, unless it adopts the methods of natural science, and revive the sterile debate on the relationship of history to science, when what really matters is an assessment of the status of the truth claims made by historians and of the procedures they employ in making them. In this task the methods of the natural sciences can claim no priority.

During the last fifteen years, the relationship between history and sociology, at least at a formal level, has been closer than at any time in the past. Not only have there been frequent discussions about the desirability of breaking down boundaries between the two subjects, but, at a practical level, a tendency towards convergence has been encouraged by the SSRC, by mixed degree courses at universities and polytechnics and by the emergence of sociology alongside history as a secondary school subject. Leaving aside pious statements of good intent and the polite diplomacy of academic conferences and scholarly foot-notage, it is remarkable how little serious attention this shift has provoked. A few conservative historians, notably G. R. Elton,[1] have cogently defended a traditional case for the autonomy of history against the encroachments of 'social science', but the prevailing view appears to take it for granted that in principle it is desirable that history and sociology should achieve some painless form of symbiosis.

The latter has generally been regarded as the progressive solution to the problem. But much of its apparent radicalism is in reality spurious. Its vision of historically-informed sociologists and sociologically-informed historians leaves the conventional demarcation between the subjects intact. It challenges neither the traditional conception of history nor the theoretical credentials of sociology. It fails to question the standard assumption, common both to historians and their opponents, that history is a subject devoid of theory. An accepted division of labour continues, even if the builder is advised to read up some architecture, and the architect is invited to try his hand at laying bricks. History remains the scholarly investigation of past events – *wie es eigentlich gewesen* (simply, how it really happened) in Ranke's words – and once this investigation is completed, the task of the historian as such is over. Theory, on the other hand, remains the

---

[1] G. R. Elton, *The Practice of History* (London, 1967).

property of the 'social sciences', and if the historian is to situate his work in a theoretical context, it is to these non-historical disciplines that he must resort. The usual result of this approach is once again to elide history with the empirical, and sociology with the theoretical, and then to imagine a seamless synthesis between the two.

Such reasoning is based upon extremely questionable premises. The problem should be posed differently. It must first be asked why history has been regarded as theoretically empty and whether this assumption is justified. Secondly, if the possibility of a theoretically defined history is conceded, it should then further be asked whether sociological conceptions of historical and social causality could be adequate to the demands of such an historical science. The two problems are linked. It will be argued that it has been the non-resolution of the scientific content and status of history that has led historians to seek a short-cut theoretical salvation in sociology. On the other hand, it is the incoherence of much sociological reasoning when seriously applied to history that might finally convince the historian that theoretical work in history is too important to be subcontracted to others.

It is first necessary to question the Rankean identification of history with pre-given past events. It is generally upon this foundation that a plethora of distinctions have been constructed, all of which in one way or another identify history with the particular and sociology with the universal. Many historians have celebrated this definition of history, a few have bemoaned it. But it is in fact a misleading way of looking at the problem. For history, like any other 'social science', is an entirely intellectual operation which takes place in the present and in the head. The fact that the 'past' in some sensed 'happened' is not of primary significance since the past is in no sense synonomous with history. Firstly, the historian investigates or reconstructs not the past, but the residues of the past which have survived into the present (literary sources, price data, inscriptions, field systems, archaeological sites etc.). The proper evaluation and use of these residues in order to make historical statements are technical skills of the historian. Secondly, and more important, the work of the historian is an active intellectual exercise which designates which of these residues possess historical significance, and what significance they possess. The historian, in other words, constructs historical problems on the basis of an argued case for their relevance to historical analysis, and then, through the critical use of extant residues (or even a search for new ones), attempts to provide a solution to them. The criteria by which the construction of a problem will be judged of historical significance will ultimately be dependent upon some explicit or implicit theory of social causation. In this sense, there is no distinction in principle between history and any of the other 'social sciences'. The distinction is not that between theory and non-theory, but between the adequacy or inadequacy of the theory brought to bear.

Why then has history appeared so theoretically empty to so many of its practitioners? The answer may be easier if the technical and theoretical aspects of the historian's practice are for a moment considered apart. For advances are quite possible in one sector without concomitant advances in the other. History as a rigorous discipline in either sense is a comparatively recent innovation. It scarcely dates back to 1800. Its claim to scientific status rests on two intellectual revolutions which took place in the nineteenth century. The first was technical – involving the discovery of critical procedures for the evaluation of past residues, and some accepted criteria for the verification of certain (relatively simple) types of historical statement. This was associated initially with the work of Niebuhr and Mommsen. The second, and infinitely more contentious, was theoretical – involving the elaboration of a form of causality specific to human history. This was the unfinished achievement of Marx.

Clearly a technical revolution, however necessary as a precondition, cannot of itself produce a science (although historians have confused the technical with the theoretical in this way). It is also well known that Marx's writings scarcely impinged upon the work of other historians during the nineteenth century, and have only enjoyed partial and intermittent recognition since. Thus, when as a result of the spread of this technical revolution across Europe, there arose a generation of historians, claiming that their subject was a science, the resulting definitions of this science were inevitably unsatisfactory. There was no clear conception of the necessity of the construction of a form of causality, both concordant with the materialist nature of science and specific to human history. In the positivistic climate of the late nineteenth century, those most insistent upon the possibility of an exact historical science analagous to the natural sciences projected natural scientific causality, particularly that of classical mechanics, onto human history. On the one hand, those most insistent upon the specificity of human history – a central tenet of the neo-Kantian and neo-Hegelian movements – retreated into an explicitly anti-materialist emphasis upon hermeneutical intuition as the essence of historical understanding (history was not accidentally entitled a *Geistes*wissenschaft). But this second current made more impact upon philosophers and sociologists than upon historians, and in England, apart from the odd exception like Collingwood, the positivistic conception predominated. In this scenario, once all the 'facts' had been discovered and assembled (the really vital work of the historian), they would fall into place, as if of their own accord, in a chain of events, linked one to another in a mechanical fashion by relations of a simple transitive causality.

Such a chain might also be conceived as an evolutionary progress from a lower to a higher state. But despite its obvious ideological importance, it is misleading to imply that evolutionist assumptions were in any serious way essential to the working methods of positivistic historians. Ranke, the first major ideologist of the technical revolution in historical research, was determinedly anti-evolutionist. Every age, he wrote, 'was equal in the sight of God'. In the 1960s, Elton maintained a secularized version of the same proposition: 'no argument exists which successfully establishes a hierarchy of worth among historical periods or regions as such'.[2] In the meantime, the rise and fall of whig or progressive-evolutionist theories of history had made remarkably little impact upon the way in which history was actually written.

It is, therefore, not the changing fashions for evolutionist, relativist or empiricist philosophies of history, but the persistence of positivistic working assumptions about causality, which has been at the root of the embarrassed and defensive relationship between history and theory. The positivistic characterization of history was not self-evidently inadequate so long as professional historians confined their attention to the legal, constitutional, administrative and diplomatic spheres. It was moreover in these areas that the achievements of the technical revolution were most visible. The incoherence of mechanical conceptions of social causality only began to surface as a problem, once the issues posed by the economic and the social could not longer be evaded, and it became clear that the forms of causality necessary to comprehend changing social relations were infinitely more complex that anything which historical positivism could encompass. Such rethinking might have been expected to develop during the interwar period. But, apart from the isolated case of Namier who made an astonishing attempt to introduce psychoanalysis into historical explanation, it did not. There was impressive work in social and economic history, produced by Tawney, the Hammonds, Eileen Power, Clapham, Postan and the *Economic History Review* during its early years. But like the German generation of economic historians and sociologists of capitalism, which had preceded them, there was no profound or sustained break

[2] *Ibid.*, p. 13.

with traditional assumptions about historical causality. Selected insights from Marx might be taken over, even by his opponents, but no serious attention was paid to his form of historical reasoning. None of these writers were marxist, indeed most of them were determinedly anti-marxist, but the main reason why Marx was not studied as an historical theorist (as opposed to a prophet, or a serious but eccentric economic historian) was that his theory was also understood in positivist terms. Even his admirers generally misinterpreted him in a mechanistic fashion and the result, in practice, was often a dogmatic economic determinism, which antagonists could legitimately oppose as an *a priori* imposition of 'theory' on the 'facts'.

Had there been any generally felt intellectual impasse among historians, had the reulting confusion been such that further historical advance would be rendered impossible, the result might have been a more profound rethinking of the possible foundations of a historical science. But the relative autonomy of the technical component of historical work ensured that considerable advances could continue to be registered in specialized fields, while central epistomological problems remained in a state of limbo. In the face of the unanswered questions posed by historical materialism and psychoanalysis, most professional historians retreated to the one area about which they felt reasonably confident – the solid advances which their discipline had achieved in the technique of historical investigation.

It was not in fact until the end of the '50s that there developed a widespread if only half articulated discontent both about the state of history as a discipline and about the way in which it was taught. By that time, such intellectual stimulus as history had received during the interwar years seemed exhausted. The broad issues opened up in economic history had lost their generality. Questions in economic history had become increasingly specialized and technical, and this tendency had been reinforced by the growth of separate economic history departments, in which major questions of historical interpretation were often abandoned, and history simple employed as a testing ground for propositions derived from neo-classical or Keynesian economics. In modern political history, the general interpretative challenge represented by the work of Namier had become narrowed down to rather monotonous applications of a particular historiographical technique. At the conceptual level, theoretical experiment and all but the most innocuous forms of historical generalization had been inhibited by a sophisticated empiricism strenuously urged by Popper and his disciples. Questions posed by marxism or psychoanalysis were excluded from the outset, since they were alleged to be unamenable to Popperian criteria of falsification. Outside the dominant academic establishment, the picture was by no means so grey. Much of the most creative and pioneering historical work during the 1950s centred around the Marxist-inspired journal, *Past and Present*. But even here, there had developed a faltering of confidence in the ability of a marxist-based history to stand on its own feet, and around the end of the '50s, the subtitle, 'journal of scientific history', was dropped in favour of the more anodyne, 'journal of historical studies'.

It was the malaise in history around the end of the '50s which led historians towards a closer relationship with sociology. The discontent affected both liberal and socialist historian. Among left-inclined historians, the crisis of 1956 led some to a questioning of what had passed as marxism during the Stalinist era, and to the belief that a resort to sociology might help to resolve questions to which marxism apparently had no solution; the emergence of the 'third world' and the stability of advanced countries probably reinforced these feelings; and so, probably, did the claim of sociology to be a post- rather than anti-marxist pre-occupation. Among liberal historians, a different and more tentative path to sociology can be traced. The Suez crisis, the incontrovertible evidence of American hegemony and the rapid pace of decolonization all threw into relief the parochialism of prevalent approaches to history, whether of a whig or of a Namierite kind. In some cases, this led historians into the interdisciplinary zone of the economics and sociology of 'development' or the politics of 'modernization'. In other cases, it led from constitutional or party history to American electoral or political sociology. It should not be forgotten, of course, that the bulk of historians remained indifferent to sociology, and an articulate minority on the right, actively hostile. But among those, of whatever political persuasion, who felt the necessity of some change of approach, sociology appeared to promise a solution.

The relationship established between history and sociology at the end of the 1950s was very much a one-way affair, and it has largely remained so. There is little evidence that sociologists have become noticeably more 'historical', as E. H. Carr hoped in 1960.[3] If sociologists are no longer as confident about the solidity of sociology as they were in 1959, and if some even speak of a 'crisis' of sociology, it is not because of the intervention of historians. One the other hand, there is now much greater evidence of the influence of sociology on history than there was fifteen years ago. The most positive side of this influence has been the immense increase in the scope of history. It is hard to

[3] E. H. Carr, *What is History?* (1962), p. 60.

imagine the extent of current historical interest in magic, witchcraft, popular culture, family, urban, rural and oral history without at least the indirect spur of sociology and social anthropology. The old restriction of academic history to politics, church, constitution and diplomacy has largely disappeared, and it is probably the example of sociology which has emboldened historians to undertake comparative history. But the negative effects of the relationship have been at least equally prominent. Attitudes towards sociological theory among sociologically inclined historians, have often verged on the credulous, and although more critical sociologists might have rejected as naïvely positivist any distinction between history and sociology which sees the one as 'idiographic' and the other as 'nomothetic', many of these historians have behaved in practice as if they considered such a division of labour to be legitimate. Defensive about their own subject and repelled by an inadequately understood marxism which appeared to be the only other contender, they have looked uncritically to sociology as a theoretical storehouse from which they could simply select concepts most serviceable for their individual needs.

Even if sociology has possessed the theory which history required, it would be difficult to justify the eclectic manner in which historians have sometimes shopped around in it. But, in fact, academic sociology is no more a science or even the approximation of one than academic history. The vague and shifting character of its object, the inconstancy of its definitions, the non-cumulative character of much of its knowledge, its proneness to passing theoretical fashions and the triteness of some of its 'laws'[4] suggest that its theoretical foundations are contestable and insecure. Against the prevalent view, it must be emphasized that the problem of sociology is not simply that it is insufficiently 'historical'. It is certainly true that much sociological conceptualization is decidedly adverse to the detailed analysis of historical change. But it is also true that sociologists have made sincere calls for 'process' or a 'dynamic sociology'. Nevertheless, the practical results have generally been disappointing. Too often, all that is heard is the awkward grating noise which accompanies the driver's attempt to find first gear in a motor which has only been designed to run in neutral. The primitiveness of current historical categorizations in sociology is in effect a symptom, not a cause of its inadequacy. The problem is that in as far as sociology defines its object of investigation as 'society', 'the social system' or some such general unspecified synonym, it denies itself any

---

[4] For example, see the discussion of the proposition that social interaction, promotes friendliness (derived from Homans) in H. L. Zetterberg, *On Theory and Verification in Sociology* (1954), cited in W. G. Runciman, *Sociology in its Place* (Cambridge, 1970), pp. 32–3.

rigorous principle of historical periodization; hence, its persistent resort to loosely defined dyads – traditional/modern; pre-industrial/industrial; Gemeinschaft/Gesellschaft; status/contract, etc. *Society*, like Ranke's *wie es eigentlich gewesen*, is a descriptively pre-given rather than a theoretically constructed object. It thus imposes no limits in its application or interpretation, no consistent principles of classification or internal differentiation and no form of causality specific to its object. For these reasons, the type of discourse and method of proof characteristic of sociology cannot be said to have escaped the impasse confronted by late nineteenth century positivistic proponents of a historical science and their historicist opponents. The same antinomy remains. Hermeneutics disciplined by statistical tests, of probability (Weber's idea of *Verstehen* and his use of 'ideal types' for example) merges the two approaches, but does not transcend them. Once it is recognized that history and sociology are not divided by a fundamental scientific breakthrough, genuine collaboration between the two subjects will become easier.

There is no space here to range over the uses and limitations of sociology or to distinguish between the characteristic emphases of its different schools. But something may be said of its effect upon the work of modern historians in the last fifteen years. Here the most noticeable phenomenon has been the importation of sociological notions of class and social structure. Because of their own lack of theoretical self-confidence, historians have been prone to accept sociology's self-definition as 'post-marxist'. They have not attempted to investigate whether the Weberian incorporation of a 'marxian' notion of class within a schema of 'class, status and power' is in fact an accurate rendering of Marx's conception of classes, let alone their operation in relation to modes of production and social formations. The effect has been disconcerting. The word 'class' has been domesticated into the historian's vocabulary. But the result has been a subjectification of social relations and a form of discussion which is pre- rather than post-marxist. For sociological theories of stratification have been persistently characterized by the evasion or denial of objective economic relationships. At most what is substituted are differentials of income, and the ownership or non-ownership of property. Classes are not tied to the relations of production within modes of production, and no distinction is made between a mode of production and a social formation. They are only related to similarities of 'market chances' in a social system. Thus it is not surprising that the effects of a dichotomy between property and non-property in a stratification system can simply be viewed as one of possibly conflicting but generally subordinate economic 'interests' – these interests being understood not in a marxist but in a utilitarian sense. From there it is only a short step to show that 'class' in a 'marxian sense' possesses at most a secondary importance in the operation of a social structure, that it is secondary to the subjective assessment of actors in a social system, both of their place and of the place of others. Either 'class' is shown to be the only one of many forms of stratification, or, as in Dahrendorf,[5] it is considered to be only a 'special case' of a more general conflict concerning authority. Ever since Weber introduced his distinction between 'class, status and power', the majority of political sociologists, stratification theorists, and now in their wake, historians, have been concerned with 'status' – the relative position of actors or social groups in a subjectively defined hierarchy of honour and prestige. Once social relations are subjectivized in this fashion, the historical relationship between class disappears into a multiplicity of reciprocal perceptions possessed by hierarchically ordered strata in a social system, itself validated purely at the level of perception. Class becomes indistinguishable from class consciousness and it becomes meaningful for one historian to describe eighteenth century England as a 'classless hierarchy',[6] and for another to understand the late nineteenth century as a period in which class replaces religion as the politically salient reference group.[7]

It is the same kind of approach which has informed the growing pre-occupation of social historians with an analysis of 'social structure'. The phrase implies a theoretical promise. The reproduction of social relations within modes of production and social formations often exhibits long-term historical regularities and these are important and hitherto neglected objects of study for British historians. But it is extremely dubious whether the adoption of a sociological approach has really advanced the understanding of such phenomena. Here again, what is offered is not the theoretical construction of an object of study, but merely the systematization of predefined data, originally gathered

[5] R. Dahrendorf, *Class and Class Conflict in Industrial Society* (London, 1959), p. 139.

[6] H. Perkin, *The Origins of Modern English Society, 1780–1880* (1972), p. 13.

[7] P. F. Clarke, 'The Electoral Sociology of Modern Britain', *History* (1972), p. 42. This article provides a very useful survey of the various recent attempts to apply sociological theory to the analysis of nineteenth century voting behaviour, and a cogent critique of John Vincent's interesting attempt to apply a Dahrendorfian approach to mid-nineteenth century voting patterns in *Pollbooks: How the Victorians Voted*, (Cambridge, 1967). But his own approach based primarily on Weber, which defines class as material interests, while aligning consciousness with the immaterial 'cultural politics' of status – is precluded by this framework from providing a coherent explanation of the political significance of industrial conflict during the period. The formation by the bulk of the organised working class of a political party of its own is thus treated as a purely electoral phenomenon, which new liberalism but for World War I would have prevented.

primarily to answer demographic questions, i.e., decennial censuses of population. Such data can of course be used imaginatively to answer different questions.[8] But as far as it has been used to designate social structures, the result, so far, is not generally an anatomy of a complex system of class relationships at a given point in time, but a purely quantitative hierarchy of discrete groups who exist in no obvious relationship to one another. The only distinctions analysed are those deducible from census enumerators' books. Thus in studies of nineteenth century towns, we are likely to learn much less about relationships of employment, rent or credit, than about distinctions between servant-keeping and non-servant-keeping households or mere differences of family size (quite proper, of course, if the investigation were purely demographic), not because this information is vital to the solution of important historical questions, but simply because it lends itself more readily to quantification.

A parallel example of this phenomenon has been the growth of historical election studies. If sociology pioneered attitude surveys and opinion polls, historians have begun to poll the dead. Once more, when a problem is not constructed theoretically, the researcher is liable to remain at the mercy of his data, and discussions ostensibly about theoretical approach become in fact simply controversies about technique. It is as noticeable in the analysis of voting behaviour as in the elaboration of a census-defined social structure that, for all the valuable work that has been done, a symbiotic relationship exists between type of material and type of analysis. The confusion of theory and technique has resulted in a meaningless but harmful division between quantitative and non-quantitative historians, as if this marked the real boundary of historical progress and reaction. Quantitative history is obviously invaluable where important problems can be resolved by quantitative means. But it should scarcely need to be said that many historical problems are not amenable to quantification and that quantification itself will be no more significant than the questions which inform it. In nineteenth century political history, even though in 1911, only 60 per cent of adult males were entitled to vote, and even though, as one historian has acutely put it,[9] the parties selected the voters rather than the voters the parties, there has been an ever more unilateral concentration upon the act of voting. To have nineteenth century voting patterns systematized and codified is without question a major service – but of a technical rather than a theoretical kind. The study of

---

[8] See for example, H. J. Dyos and D. A. Reader, 'Slums and Suburbs', in H. J. Dyos and M. Wolff (eds.), *The Victorian City* (London, 1973).

[9] P. F. Clarke, 'The Electoral Sociology of Modern Britain' p. 33.

shifts in popular politics and the apparently successful 'liberalization' of the political system in the nineteenth century still abounds with unsolved problems. The place of elections in this complex of problems is not entirely clear, but given the complexities of class relations and the still as yet largely unexplored ideological shifts, it can by no means be assumed that the political behaviour of different social groups can be adequantly deduced from their voting patterns merely because this is the most obvious and easiest evidence to handle.

Once again, the intervention of a conventional sociological approach into this general political-ideological area begs more questions that it solves. Another effect of the application of Weber's trichotomy of class, status and power has been a confusing compartmentalization of 'class' and 'power' in recent historical discussion. Class relations, as Nicos Poulantzas has pointed out,[10] *are* relations of power. Once class relations are formally divorced from power relations, a host of falsely posed problems become the subject of inconclusive historical debate. Most common are those in which a subordinate group does not manifest any explicit or measurable collective consciousness of exploitation or oppression. In such a situation, a sociological approach is apt to imply that such groups collude in their subordinate position and then to provide psychologistic interpretations of their behaviour. Elkins' theory of slavery views the question in this way, and similar theories of deference (internalized acceptance of inferiority or dependence, rather than externally necessitated compliance) have been applied to servants, women, agricultural labourers and some groups of industrial workers. Such an approach is by no means confined to conservative social theorists and historians. Other historians have attempted to reach different answers within the same framework by resorting to some notion of social control.[11] But the result is conceptual confusion, since social control is an idea which is inseparable from its functionalist presuppositions. Occasionally, even the Gramscian notion of 'hegemony' has been misapplied in a similar fashion by writers genuinely anxious to discover reasons for a non-emergence of a proletariat possessing the revolutionary consciousness 'ascribed' to it by Lukács on the basis of an application of the Weberian theory of 'ideal types'. The lesson of these attempts is, once again, that historians, and for that matter sociologists, cannot afford to take theoretical propositions on trust. They must examine the conceptual provenance of an apparent problem requiring solution, to see whether there is not

[10] N. Poulantzas, *Political Power and Social Classes* (London, 1973), p. 99.
[11] For one ambiguous use of the term in this sense, see my own *Outcast London* (Oxford, 1971), p. 252.

something unsound in the theoretical foundations themselves.[12]

What then should finally be said of the relationship between history and sociology? How should that relationship develop? What is wrong with the present relationship is not its existence, which is in principle good, but its uncritical character. The belief in a theoretically empty history serviced by a theoretically proven sociology is now perhaps beginning to be undermined by sociologists themselves. But a recognition by historians of the need to engage in theoretical work themselves has still to make headway. The process will be considerably eased once the pretensions of sociology to be an already constituted science are given up. Once this is accepted, a more modest, but more equal and more genuinely fruitful, relationship between the two subjects can begin. Ultimately, of course, they are only different aspects of a single concern: the construction of a historical science. But a reformulation of their relationship and an elaboration of the theoretical problems common to both will not happen of its own accord. Joint work is necessary; not of a celebratory or diplomatic kind, but of a critical kind. The history of history and sociology as subjects must be treated as part of a single ideological terrain. If sociology is not to be treated as a cumulative science, then it plainly requires a different type of history from that which is currently provided. A start has already been made on this work. Under the aegis of the *History Workshop Journal*, a group of historians, sociologists and social anthropologists are preparing detailed research papers on the history of sociology in Britain.[13] To redraw the intellectual map in a satisfactory fashion, many such ventures will be necessary. The weight of positivistic assumptions both in history and sociology will not be removed without active and constant intellectual debate. But the gains could be enormous. Shadow boxing about demarcation between the 'social sciences' would be relegated to the shades where they belong, and the phantoms of Ranke and Comte who still haunt such proceedings would finally be accorded a decent burial.

[12] It appears to me that despite its considerable importance as a theoretically informed contribution to historical research, John Foster's *Class Struggle and the Industrial Revolution* (London, 1974), exemplifies the false problematic that is set up by an attempt to marry incompatible concepts. The Lukacsian Weberian notion of consciousness, the Leninist conception of trade union consciousness, the Engels–Lenin theory of labour aristocracy and the sociological notions of social structure and social control can only be tied together in a dogmatic way. The silences of the book on certain obvious points, despite a massive apparatus of empirical research, would also appear to be a result of the mistaken fashion in which the problem of the relation between history and theory was initially conceived. I have examined some of these problems in a review article, Class Struggle and the Industrial Revolution, *New Left Review*, 90 (1975).

[13] It is intended that these papers will be published, either in book form or as a special number of the *History Workshop Journal*. Also for an approach on similar lines, see Göran Therborn, *Science, Class and Society: On the Formation of Sociology and Historical Materialism* (London, 1976).

6

Community: Toward a Variable Conceptualization for Comparative Research

CRAIG CALHOUN

Craig Calhoun's recent essay is important because it seeks to move beyond or behind the language of class to reveal what its author believes to be the more significant language of community, at least for pre-industrial societies. In the essay Calhoun describes the content of the language of community and suggests the importance this language might have for the language of class, particularly in relation to earlier analysis of popular, radical protest movements. He argues that community provides a surer basis for mobilizing people for collective action than does class, and that an appreciation of this fact by historians would reshape the histories they write. In the Afterword I look in some detail at Calhoun's argument as it is expanded and elaborated in his book, *The Question of Class Struggle*. And I do not wish to repeat myself, except to say that in this essay, as in his book, Calhoun does import sociological theory into history in a way challenging to Stedman Jones's injunction against such a practice.

THE FOUNDATIONS OF THE CONCEPT OF COMMUNITY

As we have suggested, community may be conceived as both a sociological variable and a morally valued way of life. Nisbet notes:

Community begins as a moral value; only gradually does the secularization of this concept beome apparent in sociological thought in the nineteenth century.[1]

From *Social History* 5 (1980), pp. 107–27.

[1] R. A. Nisbet, *The Sociological Tradition* (London, 1970), p. 18.

Even as secularized, however, the concept has remained ambiguous. The relationship between community as a complex of social relationships and community as a complex of ideas and sentiments has been little explored. Nisbet tends to fuse the experiential quality of community with the social relationships on which it depends. In this, he is an accurate follower of the tradition of 'communal' criticism of modern society and human alienation:

By community I mean something that goes far beyond mere local community. The word, as we find it in much nineteenth- and twentieth-century thought encompasses all forms of relationship which are characterized by a high degree of personal intimacy, emotional depth, moral commitment, social cohesion, and continuity in time. Community is founded on man conceived in his wholeness rather than in one or another of the roles, taken separately, that he may hold in a social order. It draws its psychological strength from levels of motivation deeper than those of mere volition or interest, and it achieves its fulfilment in a submergence of individual will that is not possible in unions of mere convenience or rational assent.[2]

'Community', in such a usage, becomes more an evocative symbol than an analytic tool. We must ask what connection there is between 'personal intimacy, emotional depth, moral commitment, social cohesion, and continuity in time'. We must ask under what circumstances man is to be 'conceived in his wholeness' rather than in one or another of his roles, and why he should be motivated to submerge his individual will to the fulfilment of community. In order to answer these questions we need a more complex view of community in which we seek elements and relations among elements rather than listing attributes. In the pages which follow we shall develop such a view based on the structuring of social relations.

Even when one leaves such explicitly normative statements about community aside, there is still a variance in the proportion of attention given to 'experiential' vs. 'structural' aspects of community. In Tönnie's *Gemeinschaft/Gesellschaft* dichotomy, the emphasis is on the *a priori*, assumed nature of community in opposition to the optional nature of association.[3] The latter draws on the conscious choices of relatively independent individuals. *Gemeinschaft*, on the other hand, is a subjective community of 'inner' relations:

Being together, so to speak, is the vegetative heart and sole of *Gemeinschaft* — the very existence of *Gemeinschaft* rests in the consciousness of belonging

[2] Nisbet, *The Sociological Tradition*, p. 48.
[3] *Community and Association (Gemeinschaft and Gesellschaft)* is Tönnies's classic work, giving the widespread nineteenth-century dichotomy its most influential shape.

together with the affirmation of the condition of mutual dependence which is posed by that affirmation.[4]

Weber took up the same view, defining the communal relationship as based on subjective feeling, as opposed to the rationality of the associative relationship.[5]

Such an emphasis on the inner qualities of community life tends to discount the importance of the social bonds and political mechanisms which hold communities together and make them work. This discounting incidentally allows the proponents of idealized community frequently to underestimate the restraint which real community requires, the sacrifices that it demands, and the fears which enforce them. It is based in part on an artificial separation of rationality from irrationality, in which the individuality of actions is by assumption linked to a notion of effectiveness in the concept of rationality (in this case Weber's *Zweckrationalitat*). In other words, Weber opposes the subjective to the rational, rather than to the objective. He assumes a distinction between that communal orientation to action which is based on the feeling of actors that they belong together, and the societal orientation which is based on a rationally motivated adjustment of individual interests.[6] This distinction does not take account of the possibility that individuals pursuing their rational self-interests will not provide collective goods.[7] While it would be in the interests of each of the individuals to provide a share of the costs of the collective goods, characteristics of the collectivity may make it irrational for any of them to do so barring some from of selective incentive or coercion. A community may act as the source of the selective inducements to participate in collective action – quite without depending on the individual's sense of belonging. It may produce collectively rational (useful) results which individual rationality would not have done. But it does not seem meaningful to say that the provision of collective goods by a community is irrational from the point of view of the individuals.[8] We might better say that the significance of individual

---

[4] F. Tönnies, 'The Concept of *Gemeinschaft*' in W. T. Cahnman and R. Heberle (eds. and translators) *Ferdinand Töennies on Sociology: Pure, Applied and Empirical* (Chicago, 1971), p. 69.

[5] M. Weber, *The Theory of Social and Economic Organization* trans. by A. M. Henderson and T. Parsons (New York, 1964), p. 126. Weber was more optimistic than Tönnies about the possibilities for extreme rationality in social relationships. He also tended to focus on small, generally diadic, units of relationship.

[6] M. Weber, 'Class, Status and Party', from *Wirtschaft and Gesellschaft* in H. H. Gerth and C. W. Mills (eds.), *From Max Weber* (London, 1948), pp. 183–4.

[7] See M. Olson, *The Logic of Collective Action*, 2nd ed. (New York, 1971).

[8] It may well be considered *non*-rational from the point of view of the dynamics of individual decision-making. For extended discussion of these issues, see Talcott Parsons, *The Structure of Social Action*, 2 vols. (New York, 1968).

rationality varies depending on the extent to which the individual acts as a member of a community. It may be reasonable to separate the subjective from the objective, but it seems unreasonable to hold that 'rationality' is exclusively identified with the latter. The same is true of community: the experiential dimension is not independent of the structural; the sense of belonging to a community is directly founded on the social relationships through which one does belong to a community.

We can bring the significance of the above comments into clearer focus by emphasizing that community (and, for that matter, society) must be seen as variable. Organization is the crucial factor which may make a community (or a society) out of a mere aggregation of people.[9] Organization, further, comes through the social relationships of the people in question, and the relations among those relationships (a phrase on which we elaborate below). While everyday usage may allow us to oppose individuality to community as polar opposites, this cannot be admitted in theory or analysis. It stems in part from conservative objections to the increasing independence of individual actions from communal constraints, especially during the period of the Industrial Revolution. It suggests, misleadingly, the possibility of an asocial individual. Yet, in part, the opposition itself was coined to argue that man could not be properly human outside the bonds of community. The critique of alienation was that man, by attempting to act as a mere individual, was reduced to a sub-human existence as an appendage of an alien world, to which state he was reduced by his one-sided economic life. To be a full individual, one had to be both a part of the web of moral relations and multi-faceted.[10] It was not necessary that the human individual be an alienated or isolated individual: this was the essence of the critique which reached its fullness in Hegel and Marx, uniting elements of both the enlightenment and the conservative anti-enlightenment. What might better be held to be the

---

[9] It was in this sense that Sorokin distinguished integrated social units from mere spatial aggregations or congeries (P. S. Sorokin, *Social and Cultural Dynamics* (Boston, 1957), pp. 2–19). He was, perhaps, oversanguine in thinking that there was 'no need to stress that fact that the degree of functional interdependence is everywhere not the same' (p. 7). It has rather too often been taken as a postulate, or at least a 'functional imperative'. See also MacIver's repeated emphasis of the same idea in R. M. MacIver, *Community: A Sociological Study* (London, 1928), perhaps the most elaborate sociological treatment of the concept if, unfortunately, not on a secure organizational foundation itself.

[10] This two-sided treatment of individualism if prominent in Hegel, where the *Bildungsprozess* of the cultivation of full human individuality is the positive pole and the mere individuality of alienated economic life the negative. It is in personality, will, that immediate individuality is transcended. See paragraphs 39 and 40 of G. W. F. Hegel, *The Philosophy of Right*, trans. by T. M. Knox (Oxford, 1967). See also Georg Lukács, *The Young Hegel*, trans. by R. Livingstone (London, 1975), pp. 294–9.

opposite of community is de Maistre's '*l'espirit particulier*', which implies men wilfully opposing themselves to the community and to their social nature.[11]

We have argued against defining community in terms of the members' sense of belonging. This is not to suggest that such subjective attitudes are not important, but rather that they will not get us very far as analytic constructs. We need to ask what action the parties to communal relations will be likely to take. Will any given population aggregate be able to secure the cooperation of its members in some undertaking to secure a collective good? Will it require external coercion or do the relations of community act as a self-regulatory mechanism on the 'rational' decisions and actions of the members? People may feel that they belong in a wide variety of social contexts, but these self-identifications do not always modify their action, let alone produce collective action. What is important about 'sense of belonging' is not someones' identification of membership in a bounded collectivity, but his modification of his consideration of alternative courses of action on the basis of the communal relations to which he belongs. If he takes certain concrete relations for granted as immutable, then this consciousness does act to limit the range of options he considers, and to constrain his action in favour of the community. If, for example, a worker, unsure of whether or not to join his fellows in a strike, feels that he must necessarily live out the rest of his life among them (like it or not) then his decision will be far more constrained than if he regards these relationships as mere consequences of a coincidence of residence or employment which he might alter at any time.

When we study society or community it is with the relationships among social actors that we are concerned. Obviously, these relationships spread beyond the bounds of specific localities, polities, linguistic groups, and all the other devices which we impose to give limits to our studies. Thus, in Fortes's words:

For the concept of society as a closed unit . . . we must substitute the concept of society as a socio-geographic region, the elements of which are more closely knit together among themselves than any of them are knit together with social elements of the same kind outside that region. We must substitute a relative and dynamic concept for an absolute and static one.[12]

Behind this conception lies the segmentary lineage system with its sliding scale of identification by contraposition. Thus, two Tallensi,

---

[11] Joseph De Maistre, Du Pape, in *Oeuvres Complètes*, vol. II (Lyon, 1884–7). See also S. Lukes, *Individualism* (Oxford, 1973), esp. Part One on the semantic history of 'individualism'.

[12] M. Fortes, *The Dynamics of Clanship among the Tallensi* (Oxford, 1945), p. 231.

say, who meet may distinguish their respective identities primarily in terms of the largest descent categories into which they do not both fall. Conversely, they will emphasize their commonalty primarily at the lower level (smallest group) in which they share membership.[13] We do the same, though much less systematically. To the European I am an American; another American may express an interest in my state; if a fellow Kentuckian asks me where I am from, I will name the town in which I grew up. There are, however, many dimensions of possible identification by contraposition in modern society, one of the most important of which is class. This is a major way in which our society is 'less systemic' than societies whose organization is dominated by the single system of kinship. It should also be noted that there is choice in identification. I have, for example, lived in other places than Kentucky, but choose that to represent 'home'. There is room for such manipulation in kinship systems as well, though generally less. Much depends on the information available to actors, but not all. Known fictions are sometimes willingly maintained to the point where truth is difficult to judge.

The communal may be regarded as a specialized sub-set of the social. In the connotations of everyday usage, community suggests a greater 'closeness' of relations than does society.[14] This closeness seems to imply, though not rigidly, face to face contact, commonalty of purpose, familiarity and dependability. All these connotations are suggestive, and none is negated by our usage. We may gain greater incisiveness, however, by distinguishing community through the self-regulation of its patterns of organization, and then analysing how its constituent relations work to permit this freedom from specialized and/or external control. As the maintenance and functioning of a pattern of social organization either weakens, or comes to be enforced by external or specialized agency then the population aggregate so organized becomes less a community.[15] In other words, community

---

[13] Fortes also emphasized the evanescence of lineage segments, called into action as required by actors' motives and circumstances, well before the 'process theorists' who would sometimes claim and are often attributed with great innovation (see for example V. W. Turner's preface to the 1970 edition of *Schism and Continuity in an African Society*, (Manchester, 1970). See M. G. Smith, 'On Segmentary Lineage Systems', in *Corporations and Society* (London, 1956) on the political aspects of the contraposition of segments.

[14] See the quotation from Nisbet, *The Sociological Tradition*, pp. 3–4.

[15] Some similarity to Parsons's notion of a latency or pattern maintenance function will be noted. Making the distinction between community and society in this way, however, helps us to place attention on both integration and specialized coercion, and the contents in which they are respectively most important. Parsons tends to ignore much of the role of power in maintaining patterns of social organization. See Anthony Giddens, '"Power" in the recent writings of Talcott Parsons', *Sociology*, II (1968), pp. 257–72, and Steven Lukes, *Power: A Radical View* (London, 1974), esp. pp. 26–33.

may be stronger or weaker, and a pattern of sociation may be more or less communal. This usage allows us to integrate numerous assertions of everyday discourse. Thus, the need for police power is related to the inability of communities to maintain order. Towns fail to provide public goods because their citizens lack a sense of communal responsibility – i.e. either they view their membership of the collectivity as contingent, optional, or they perceive that it is to their advantage to attempt to be a free rider, even if everyone else will do the same and the goods will not be provided. The inefficiency of American bankruptcy laws is discovered as creditors become increasingly impersonal and social pressures cease to discourage default. Similarly, the law of contract proliferates in correspondence to the ineffectiveness of informal, but communally enforced agreements.

Collective goods, and collective responsibility are closely related in community organization. Many, and especially long-term, collective goods are only likely to be provided by communities, that is, by collectivities whose members are strongly tied into relationships which constrain them to act in the interests of the whole. Such members also bear a responsibility to and for the whole. The manner in which they are accountable is an indication of the extent to which the collectivity is communal. Thus, Moore distinguishes 'legal' and 'moral' obligations in terms of the nature of the normative response to violations: legal obligations are those in which specific performance or repair may be immediately achieved through physical force. Moral obligations are those in which the sanction of social pressure is used to obtain performance.[16] Legal obligations generally require a greater apparatus of collective decision making, as they involve consciously concerted and formalized penalties. They tend to give rise to specialized agencies of enforcement, or, in societies characterized by armed self-help, to elaborate and formalized feuds.[17] Moral obligations are essentially the stuff of community. Although in most societies legal sanctions may exist for repeated failure to conform to moral ones, it is impossible to enforce moral sanctions outside the realm of fairly dense and/or highly significant social relationships. As these disappear, legal sanctions must take the place of moral. During the late-eighteenth and early-nineteenth centuries, a great many public hostilities involved the

[16] S. F. Moore, 'Legal Liability and Evolutionary Interpretation: Some Aspects of Strict Liability, Self-help and Collective Responsibility', in M. Gluckman (ed.), *The Allocation of Responsibility* (Manchester, 1972), p. 91.

[17] In societies of the latter sort, groups must have clear boundaries and generally are likely to have strong mechanisms for ensuring responsibility on the part of their members – up to and including expulsion for bringing the hostilities to bear on the other members of a collectively responsible grouping. See S. F. Moore, 'Legal Liability . . .', pp.89–90.

attempt of local communities to enforce moral obligations with great traditional weight behind them on those who no longer felt the social pressure of community to be any sanction. Merchants and other middlemen, especially those trading in foodstuffs, were likely to be attacked for 'forestalling and engrossing' and other violations of communal norms of fair pricing. Local magistrates might sympathize with the moral claims of the crowd, but the law was to the advantage of the merchants. It did not, in any case, allow local authorities to be very active, though they could informally give licence to the actions of the crowd. Similarly, the 'immorality' of many a manufacturer was his withdrawal from a web of communal relationships which would have guaranteed his behaviour in accordance with communal norms and opinion. This is particularly evident, for example, in the Luddite risings of the 1810s.[18] Conversely, an illegal trade union was dependent on moral sanctions over its members.

The importance of self-regulation is evident in anthropological treatments of the difference between state and stateless societies. Hocart is a relatively early example:

We cannot go on without a central government because our society is so vast and complex that some coordinating system is needed, for each one has to cooperate with thousands whom he never sees, or even hears of. There are societies where everyone is related to everyone else; they have no need for a coordinating system. They work by mutual understanding. . . . As a matter of fact we vastly exaggerate the importance of government in our own society . . . the vast, silent, daily work of men and women . . . is the real life of a nation. That daily routine is self-organized.[19]

In this account, Hocart reflects on the contrast which has made the Industrial Revolution a key *animus* in sociological thought. The very terms of social action seem to have changed from the predictable and well-understood nexus of community life to the large-scale and uncertain affairs of political society. The interconnections of people and groups have become weaker (although this is partly due to the increasing size of population aggregates) and this has resulted in realtive social disorganization. The control of this less communal society has become the object of political power and formal government institutions.

[18] See for example Frank Reed, *The Risings of the Luddites* (New York, 1968), p. 127, noting that small masters might join in rebellion against larger ones who withdrew from the community. The decline in the 'normality' of family relationships can also be seen as largely a matter of communal constraints and the availability of options outside the bonds of moral relations. See M. Anderson, *Family Structure in Nineteenth Century Lancashire* (Cambridge, 1970), esp. pp. 172–9.

[19] A. M. Hocart, *Kings and Councillors* (Chicago, 1970), pp. 128–9.

We find here an echo of the debate which took place in varying forms and intensities from the fourteenth to the nineteenth centuries about the customary and in some cases formally legal rights of the vestiges of medieval corporations, of crafts and communities.[20] The defence of these traditional collectivities and organizations came to be identified with conservative ideology but this was not a necessary connection. There was as much of the 'radical' or 'populist' in some of the claims based upon communities and crafts. The 'attack' on the traditional institutions was largely the intellectual counterpart of the material growth of centralized state power; it would eventually include much of early 'liberal' thought. It was in the context of this debate that social theory began to be created out of political and moral philosophy.

The theory of the state which was developed during the rise of European absolutism was largely concerned with the question of how political authority was to be separated from the community. The absolutist states had to oppose local authorities and self-regulating communal systems. In this context, it was no longer possible to speak with much clarity of an undifferentiated 'political community'. Federalists, like Althusius, attempted to defend decentralized society from the growth of such absolutist state. In the course of their defence, they laid part of the groundwork for a theory of social relations and community in opposition to a more purely political theory focusing on power and conscious control. Though positive jurisprudence was the most direct heir to the legacy of Althusius and the other federalists, they left their mark also on social theory, especially in France, and on the popular imagination. The reality of the state helped to point attention to the very decentralized pattern of social organization it was disrupting.

An analysis in this vein was current during the Industrial Revolution. In England, writers from Cobbett to Coleridge recognized and bemoaned the loss of older self-regulatory mechanisms of community. Their historical perspective was telescoped, however, and they tended to attribute rather more, and more recent, vitality to the traditional English community than seems justified. Those who would use 'before and after' contrasts of community and dissociation need to have their perspectives broadened, in general, by an 'elsewhere' criterion. But even traditional or tribal societies do not form an ideal type exempli-

---

[20] For some partial outlines of this long debate and the early growth of social theory, a complete history of which remains to be written, see Gierke, *Political Theories of the Middle Age* and *Natural Law and the Theory of Society*. On the material growth of the states see Perry Anderson, *Lineages of the Absolutist State* (London, 1974).

fying total self-regulation. Beyond the most fleeting of communal experiences,[21] some regulatory mechanisms must be developed. In many tribal societies, kinship systems perform this function, and may knit together millions of people in some degree. The more concerted the action which a group attempts, however, the more elaborate must be its external or specialized regulatory mechanisms. Its communal nature will be proportionately sacrificed. A corollary of our definition of community, thus, is that new, ordered and directed actions will be difficult to sustain for any substantial period of time on the basis of communal bonds. Conversely, the ability to alter the order or direction of action is limited by the necessary conservatism of the communal bonds, if any, on which it is founded.

A community, in this usage, is able to pursue only implicit and/or traditional ends, or to respond to external threats to its ability to follow its traditional way of life. This is important, for from communal bonds comes a great deal of the potential strength of motivation for social action. Different types of social organization thus yield different capabilities for social action. On the one hand, there is the development of analytic capabilities and mechanisms for social decision making and intentional organization. On the other hand, there are the stronger, but less consciously directed, bonds of community, which may provide for much longer-term co-ordination of social activity. There is a partial contradiction between the focus with which a social aggregate can attack a problem, and the strenth and endurance of motivation which underpins its attention. In a community, the manifold immediate connections among people – social actors – may be quite conscious, but

this does not mean, of course, that each member of a society is conscious of such an abstract notion of unit. It means that he is absorbed in innumerable, specific relations and in the feeling and the knowledge of determining others and of being determined by them.[22]

It is largely in these specific relations and determinations that community exists. Clearly, such community cannot everywhere equally obtain, and other mechanisms for social integration must exist, if indeed there is to be any social integration. In a large or dispersed set of people, or one divided into relatively non-interacting sub-groups:

[21] Turner's 'Communitas' if one does not accept his wilder assertions of its maintenance over long periods of time. See U. W. Turner, *The Ritual Process* (Chicago, 1969), esp. chapters 3 and 4.

[22] George Simmel, 'How is Society Possible?', in D. Levine (ed.), *George Simmel on Individuality and Social Forms* (Chicago 1971), p. 7.

mechanisms of association must make up for the loss of community character; techniques of communication will make the wide-range coordination of behaviour possible; and administrative machinery will enforce it; and idea systems will sustain the awareness of belonging together which can no longer spring from proximity and familiarity.[23]

In many kin-based societies, the local community and the wider network of formal kin relations are counterposed. Thus, among the Nuer, villages on the borders of clan territories may interact much more frequently with, and develop strong ties to villages which are formally part of other clans. Each village still remains bound in formal terms to its own clan, but is tied in numerous specific relationships to its neighbour. Evans-Pritchard says the formal bonds must dominate, but we may assume, I think, that there is a considerable amount of play in the relationship.[24] Similarly, one kind of kinship tie may be counterposed to another. Among the Tallensi, patrilineal kinship groups are at alternate genealogical levels unified by common or distinguished by differing matrilateral kin. This is a key dynamic in the social individualization of young men, who usually receive their first personal property from a kinsman of their mother. A similar process works at the larger level of the fission of lineage segments.[25] Thus, even relatively stable societies provide for a considerable amoung of flexibility, and leave room for political manipulation.

The more distant and less frequently actualized the ties among actors are, the more important external reguations and political power become. Where people are only loosley connected to each other, they may choose to prolong a conflict or abandon the community which proposes a solution they do not like – unless prevented by material power. The self-regulation of community is dependent on dense, multiplex bonds.[26] These are bonds of many strands, so that actors linked in one context or through one institution are also linked in and through others. This makes it more difficult for one actor to cross another in any specific context than it would be if there were only that single dimension to their relationship. An effect of this is to force people to accept resolutions to conflicts and give weight to 'public opinion'. The pressure of community consensus can even be used, where community is strong, to violate formal ideological precepts,

[23] S. F. Nadel, *The Foundations of Social Anthropology* (London, 1951, p. 154.

[24] E. E. Evans-Pritchard, *The Nuer* (Oxford, 1940), esp. pp. 122–3.

[25] M. Fortes, *The Web of Kinship among the Tallensi* (Oxford, 1949); Fortes has developed a general statement of this in his (contested) notion of complementary filiation in *Kinship and the Social Order* (Chicago, 1969).

[26] The term is Gluckman's; there is further discussion below.

such as those of kinship systems. Thus, in response to scarcity of land and other resources, communities (and, within them, families) may find ways to expel members, and thus maintain themselves in spite of normative cultural constraints. Among the Chagga of Tanzania, for example, middle brothers suffer most often from witchcraft accusations (through the complaints of their brothers' wives against their own wives). Despite rituals of communal solidarity, the victims are forced – or at least made sufficiently uncomfortable that they choose – to leave.[27] The organization of community is based on particular ties among social actors, even in kin-dominated societies. There is always an imperfect fit between the narrower social field of community and both the formal and informal overall organization of society.

Community, as a pattern of social organization and as a culturally defined way of life, depends on a fairly high degree of stability. The bonds of community are indeed bonds: they tie social actors to each other and to their own pasts. Communal bonds are loaded with the expectations which both 'co-actors' and the interested public bring to their evaluations of social interaction. These expectations derive from broad cultural rules and both localized and widespread traditions. Thus each social actor develops a reputation as well as playing a role. 'Tradition', as anthropologists have often noted, is malleable and is not infrequently developed for or adapted to the demands of a new situation by enterprising persons.[28] In seeking this they draw upon both broader cultural patterns for the construction of traditions, and their own social resources (including, for example, obligations which their fellows may have toward them). The malleability of tradition is wholly relative. It can nowhere be totally absent, or the practices and ideas of communities and societies would become brittle and fail to adapt to changing conditions. On the other hand, where tradition's real links with the past become almost totally lost, it is unlikely to be the source of any enduring consensus. Actual social practice and

[27] This outcome depends, of course, on there being somewhere for them to go, and thus on the present growth of the urban Tanzanian economy. See S. F. Moore 'Selection for Failure in a Small Social Field: Ritual Concord and Fraternal Strife among the Chagga Kilimanjaro 1968–9, in S. F. Moore and B. G. Myerhoff (eds.), *Symbol and Politics in Communal Ideology* (Ithaca, 1975), pp. 109–43.

[28] This is in contrast to M. Weber's use of the term which assumes that real continuity with the past is critical: 'The Social Psychology of World Religions', in H. H. Gerth and L. W. Mills (eds.), *From Max Weber* (London, 1948), p. 296. Sociologists who devote much attention to tradition have generally followed Weber on this (cf. E. A. Shils, 'Tradition', *Comparative Studies in Society and History*, XIII (2) (1975), pp. 122–59. For the contrary view see N. Yalman 'Some Observations on Secularism in Islam: The Cultural Revolution in Turkey', *Daedalus: Post-Traditional Societies*, CII (1) (1973), p. 139 and E. Colson *Tradition and Contract: The Problem of Order* (London, 1974), p. 76.

tradition are constantly interrelated and mutually determining, though the weight of determination may vary.

In the preceding pages we have given an introduction to the concept of community, and considered some of its general characteristics. In the process, we have begun to elaborate a systematic view of community which ought now to be more systematically presented. This view sees community as made up of relationships among social actors, and relations among these relationships. That is, it focuses our attention on the ways in which specific social actors are linked to each other, and on the aggregate characteristics of these links within a bounded population. This relational level of analysis is the basic one at which we see community in operation. It is the foundation upon which our discussions of other characteristics of communities must be based; it is the objective aspect of community, which can be analysed more or less in and of itself, but without which the subjective aspect cannot be understood. We have now to spell out this conceptualization in greater detail.

THE CONCEPT SYSTEMATICALLY SUMMARIZED

Characteristics of relationships
There are three orders of communal bonds: those based on familiarity, specific obligations and diffuse obligations. A relationship may but need not be limited to one of the three orders of bond. All three are generally involved in making any particular community as communal as it may be, but in varying proportions. Taken by themselves, familiarity offers the least indication of community, diffuse obligation the most. The influence of familiarity is great, however, helping even to distinguish the strength of various diffuse obligations. We have a certain investment in the familiar, even when it is not what we might choose. Thus simple frequency of interaction and the built-up familiarity and predictablility which it entails can be a major factor in strengthening a social relationship.[29] A more significant, more binding, sort of relationship is that which carries specific obligations. At the first level, both economic interdependence and co-membership of formal organizations form this order of bond. Such relationships

[29] In Blau's primitive theory of social structure, differential rates of interaction are made the primary (almost exclusive) foundation of a conceptualization of social structure: P. M. Blau 'Parameters of Social Structure' *American Sociological Review*, XXXIX (1974), pp. 615–35, and *Inequality and Heterogeneity* (New York, 1977). The latter is considerably subtler, with the content of interaction allowed back into analysis, through the back door. It is summarized in 'A Macrosociological Theory of Social Structure', *American Journal of Sociology*, LXXXIII (1) (1977), pp. 26–54.

imply relatively clear and usually clearly stated and/or contractual obligations between or among their parties. Such relationships may, however, be either more or less a part of a broader system of moral, or in Parsonian language, 'diffuse' obligations. Contractual obligations are attendant on the social realtionships themselves.[30] Where community pressures enforce the 'sanctity of contract', it should be emphasized, this is not a characteristic of the contract but of the membership of its parties in the community. Thus, kinship, and in most societies, friendship, are relations identified and sanctioned by public opinion as well as the immediate investment and agreement of the parties.[31] Bonds of kinship and friendship not only link particular parties to each other, but involve each specific relationship and friendship in a wider network of social relations, in which the whole is governed by more or less commonly accepted principles. They thus provide for long-term social bonds which are not dependent on continuing reactivation for all of their binding force.[32] These are bonds of quite a different order from familiarity or immediate interest.

Characteristics of networks of relationships
Central to this increase in the strength of social bond is the embeddedness of the particular relationship in a set of relations among relationships. If the bond between individuals is taken as unitary, a network and not a population becomes the focus of analysis. The network, a set of social relationships, may be characterized by various properties: crucially, density, multiplexity and systematicity. The first two are essentially arithmetical properties; where appropriate boundaries can be drawn it is, at least in principle, possible to compute comparable measurements. Systematicity is a structural, essentially geometrical, property for which qualitative variations are apparent but quantitative measurements are difficult. The general phenomenon described by all

---

[30] There is a close, but not quite exact relationship between this distinction and that which Moore has drawn between legal and moral obligations. Her distinction is based, solely on the kinds of sanctions which can be used to enforce obligations, not on the content of the obligations themselves: See S. F. Moore 'Legal Liability . . .' in M. Gluckman (ed.), *The Allocation of Responsibility* (Manchester, 1972).

[31] This is dealt with, in Fortes's notion of the 'morality of kinship' (the fullest general discussion is in *Kinship and the Social Order*), for which some writers have unjustly taken him to task. P. Worsley, 'The Kinship system of the Tallensi. a revaluation', *Journal of the Royal Anthropological Institute*, LXXXVI (1) (1950), pp. 37–75 advocates a rather crudely materialist alternative view of Fortes's Tallensi data.

[32] Compare this with the entirely short-term and individualistic criteria of social interaction which P. M. Blau considers. A good discussion of the long-term importance of kinship relations, in particular as they are morally sanctioned is to be found in M. Bloch, 'The Long Term and the Short Term: The Economic and Political Significance of the Morality of Kinship', in J. Goody (ed.), *The Character of Kinship* (Cambridge, 1973), pp. 75–87.

three concepts is the implication of a relatively wide range of potential actors in the activities of a small number. Thus, it is impossible fully to account for or make sense of any particular kin relationship taken in isolation from the broader context of kin relations. The content and strength of the relationship between child and parent does not depend just on idiosyncratic factors and cultural definition. It also depends on the density, multiplexity and systematicity of the networks of which it forms one constituent link: family, kinship system, collection of friends, community. One may define a network by any mechanism which yields a set of relationships, just as one may bound a population by any arbitrary convention. What most matters analytically is the description of the network, not its mere existence.[33]

Density is the most elementary of such analytic description. It is simply the extent to which all possible links among the parties to a network are in fact present. Considering only dyadic relations, there are ten possible links in a five-person network. Obviously, in general, the smaller a population the more likely it is to have a relatively high density of social relationships. It becomes possible 'for everyone to know everyone else'. Thus, in the West Riding village of Cleckheaton in the early nineteenth century, children are reported to have relieved the monotony of repetitive tasks by reciting the name of every in-habitant of the village as they went along.[34] In some very small towns, one might not only *know* everyone else but be related by kinship to many or most. There are indeed still towns in England and America where three or four surnames account for a majority of the inhabi-tants. One of the effects of high density is to make it likely that each of those with whom one has a relationship will also be related to the others. One's friends are each other's friends. This clearly imposes certain constraints on – and grants certain strengths to – the friendship relation.

The second of the relations among bonds is that of multiplexity. This refers to the extent to which individuals who are linked in one type of relationship – say kinship – are also linked in other types, co-residence, co-religion and economic interdependence, for example.

---

[33] Bear in mind that we are concerned here not with an exhaustive list of concepts with which to analyse networks, but with the construction of a definition of community. Our treatment of community is linked to network analysis in taking social relationships as its fundamental unit. For one attempt to give an exhaustive list of criteria for comparing networks, see J. C. Mitchell, 'The Concept and Use of Social Networks', in J. C. Mitchell (ed.), *Social Networks in Urban Situations* (Manchester, 1969).

[34] Frank Reed 'Old Cleckheaton', *Cleckheaton Guardian*, 22 February 1884. P. M. Blau's recent work demonstrates the power which such matters of numerical analysis as size and relative density of relationships may have in sociological analysis.

Each kind of bond implies another social context in which the same parties are co-actors. The responsibility for meeting the claims of one relationship is enforced by the other strands which also tie its parties together. As Gluckman has noted:

Because men and women in tribal society play so many of their varied purposive roles with the same set of fellows, each action in addition is charged with high moral import.[35]

Such 'moral import' forces people to look beyond the immediate instrumental considerations which might otherwise determine their actions. The same is true of

...those many situations in modern life where we find 'pockets' of social relations which resemble those of tribal society in that there are 'groups' whose members live together in such a way that their relations in one set of roles directly influence their performance of other roles.[36]

We might alternatively say that the roles played by people in such multiplex social networks are not fragmented into so many separate social dramas as are those of most of us.[37]

The last important relationship among bonds may be called systematicity or corporateness. This involves the linkage of individuals to social groups, and the ordering of groups in some unifying system of incorporation. Thus, in a segmentary society, kinship will make a person a member of an entire hierarchy of corporate groups, the smaller of which are components of the larger. The actions of an individual member may implicate the whole; accordingly, the corporation has strong powers of coercion over the individual.[38] One effect of such systematicity is to provide social actors with determinate identities. Such identities are constraints on the range of possible actions open to either party in any interaction.

[35] M. Gluckman 'Les rites de passage', in M. Gluckman (ed.), *Essays on the Ritual of Social Relations* (Manchester, 1962), p. 28.

[36] *Ibid.*, p. 43.

[37] Thus it is an illusion to think as some modern social scientists and planners have done, that it is equally plausible to create community with or without propinquity (cf. M. M. Webber 'Order in Diversity: Community without Propinquity', in L. Wirigo (ed.), *Cities and Space* (Baltimore, 1963)) These writers neglect the importance of multiplexity and focus their attention actively on simple-purpose relationships.

[38] Corporations are 'publics' in M. G. Smith's sense: each is an enduring presumably perpetual group with determinate boundaries and membership, having an internal organization and a unitary set of external relations, an exclusive body of common affairs, and, autonomy and procedures adequate to regulate them; M. G. Smith, 'A Structural Approach to Comparative Politics', in *Corporation and Society* (London, 1974), p. 94.

In the small corporate groups of pre-industrial societies, and in their relationships with one another, disputes between individuals are far more likely to be disruptive to the social fabric than in impersonal, large-scale societies. In part, this is inherently so because of the small numbers, but it is the more so because of the way in which structurally determined partisan commitments spread the effects of what start as individual disputes.[39]

Corporateness thus increases the motivation of a population to settle its internal disputes. Systematicity also involves the existence of common principles which establish and order social relationships. It is thus guaranteed that as far as such a system is in operation, any set of social actors may readily establish their relationships to each other.

Through bonds and networks of these kinds, social actors are knit together into communities. They are not discrete and wholly independent individuals – *homo oeconomicus* – but social persons subject to innumerable constraints on their individual autonomy and in return receiving collective supports. As social persons, their behaviour can involve other social persons, involuntarily, in a stream of actions, either through interpersonal bonds or as members of corporate groups. For these reasons:

Communities . . . do not leave their members free to go their own way and explore every possible avenue of behaviour. They operate with a set of rules or standards which define appropriate action under a variety of circumstances. The rules, by and large, operate to eliminate conflict of interests by defining what it is people can expect from certain of their fellows. This has the healthy effect of limiting demands and allowing the public to judge performance.[40]

It is in this sense, as well as in that of accumulated esoterica and personal familiarity, that the community is a culturally defined way of life. It holds its members to a set of rules and standards which allows them the intensity of their interaction. These norms may also govern patterns of consumtpion and production in favour of longer-term continuity, like a far more effective 'invisible hand' than any which has ruled since *laissez-faire* became self-conscious theory or policy.

COMMUNITY AND AUTHORITY

A central question regarding community life is how obedience to rules and standards is enforced when social pressure proves inadequate. A

[39] S. F. Moore, 'Legal Liability . . .', p. 74.
[40] E. Colson, *Tradition and Contract* (London, 1974), p. 52.

corollary to this question is how changes in communal life and public opinion are collectively legitimated. We have stressed in our preceding discussion the relative absence of specialized agencies of coercion or regulation in communities. That is, there are no independent chiefs or bureaucracies capable of enforcing laws or announcing changes in them. In accordance as these are absent, however, there must be some method for expressing communal opinion. In tribal societies such mechanisms, particularly divination, are often bound up with ancestor worship. Reverence for ancestors expresses a reverence for the community, as ancestors symbolically represent lines of collective affiliation in lineage-structured societies. The ancestors are made the repositories of authority over the affairs of the living, but evidence of the supernatural power of ancestors can only be had after the fact, generally through divination. In divination, though the diviner himself may command a certain amount of respect, he must generally produce a divination which is in accord with the general body of public opinion and fitting to the normal pattern of divination for his report to be accepted. Failing this, he or other diviners may be asked to repeat the entreaty to the spiritual world until the signs offered are in accord with present social constraints and standards. In other words, the ancestors have all formal authority, but no intentional power. They 'act' to express the will of the community, and thus act with a great deal of moral and social strength.[41] But the range of possible actions which the ancestors may sanction is limited; ancestral authority cannot readily be used to support a new concerted collective action, but may order the activity of the members of a community over extended periods of time and sanction the defence of this social order.

We may understand the notion of 'moral economy' in a similar sense. E. P. Thompson has recently brought it into currency to refer to the slowly evolved but carefully maintained community consensus on many fundamental issues which ordered and legitimated responses to the upset of the community's way of life. Thus, food riots in pre-industrial England were not blind or instinctive responses of base and hungry creatures. They were indeed responses to crises, but:

The men and women in the crowd were informed by the belief that they were defending traditional rights or customs: and, in general, that they were

---

[41] This is not to suggest that the ancestors are necessarily very democratic – elders may have a greater ability to shape publice opinion. They are, after all, apt to be at the centre of networks of social relations, and it is relations out of which community is made and therefore through which the authority of the community is exercised. See C. J. Calhoun 'The Authority of Ancestors among the Tallensi of Northern Ghana' (unpublished thesis, Manchester, 1975), esp. chs. 1, 6 and 9.

supported by the wider consensus of the community. On occasion this popular consensus was endorsed by some measure of licence afforded by the authorities. More commonly, the consensus was so strong that it overrode motives of fear or deference.[42]

Two particular interesting questions are raised by this passage. One concerns the relationship of community, consensus and the taking of collective action; the other involves the relationship of authority and power to community. Taking the latter first, we are immediately confronted with a problem of terminology. Authority is not the same as power; furthermore, those who speak with authority may speak also with a varying proportion of private or sectional motives and a varying amount of power. As we shall see, it is communal consensus as to what is right which confirms the voice of authority. 'Right', in this context, may refer interrelatedly to the right which may invest a particular social actor with authority, and the rightness of is actions. Who were 'the authorities' of pre- and early industrial England? Thompson seems to have in mind 'men of substance', landowners and particularly magistrates. The extent to which these men spoke with authority as opposed to exercising material power is open to question. If the former, they must have been spokesmen for the principles which ordered the whole web of social relationships, and their words enforced less by the active exercise of power than by the sanctions implicit in the multiplex relations of community members. To fail to follow authority is to fail to maintain one's place in the web of social relations of which it is a part. But clearly, in the early years of English industrialization, it was necessary on occasion to back up the word of authority with economic sanctions and public bloodshed – in other words with power. The local 'authorities' were not always voicing the consensus of the community, and the implicit sanctions were not

---

[42] E. P. Thompson 'The Moral Economy of the English Crowd in the Eighteenth Century', *Past and Present*, L (1971), p. 78. The reader should be aware that Thompson is unclear to the point of contradiction when he considers this moral economy in temporal perspective. On the one hand, he wants to show it developing; on the other hand, he feels it being stolen from traditional workers' communities by the onset of capitalist relations of production and consumption. The passage quoted in the text is a description of the eighteenth century crowd given in protest against those who would call it a 'mob'. Among this latter number we mst count an earlier Edward Thompson: 'It is indeed, this collective self-conscious loss, with its corresponding theory institution, discipline and community values which distinguishes the nineteenth century working class from the eighteenth century mob.' (E. P. Thompson, *The Making of the English Working Class*, Revised edn. (Harmondsworth, 1968), p. 463. Generally I think one is safer to follow Thompson's developmental assertions – though not to the end – than his romantic belief in the virtues of the past. See also R. Williams, *The City and the Country* (St Albans, 1973), p. 131, on the active community of workers' protest movements as opposed to the mutuality of the oppressed.

always working.[43] Community itself was changing, but perhaps more important its place in the overall structure of social relationships was changing. The ties of the landed élite to the rest of the population underwent shifts, generally a weakening, even in the small rural parishes.[44] At the same time, the extent to which there was an inclusive hierarchy of social groups, ordered by common principles, was called into question.[45]

There are, of course, always exceptions to the rule of authority; man is not completely socialized. No society is so completely free of contradictions, either, that the breaking of customary rules is not normal, and does not require the active exercise of power if it is to be kept in check. Authority is, however, weakest at the joints of corporte and/or communal organization. It is, crudely, when those who are most socially important to an individual support his violation of authority that power is most likely to be necessary. Feuds thus occur in ancestor-worshipping societies, despite the existence of overarching common authority. Similarly, crises of authority occur where counter-balancing and cross-cutting ties are absent or weak, and a social split develops in what had hitherto been a more unified community. Such a crisis of authority is what made for the extension of the death penalty and then the campaign for reform of the criminal justice system in late-eighteenth- and early-nineteenth-century England.[46] Resistance to the rule of law was not new, but it was intensified, and the traditional bridges across the 'ranks' of society became increasingly hard to maintain. As Hay has described the eighteenth century:

The fabric of authority was torn and reknit constantly. The important fact remains, however, that it was reknit readily. The closer mesh of economic and social ties in rural society, the public nature of those relationships compared to the complexity and obscurity of much metropolitan life,

---

[43] We parallel again inexactly S. F. Moore's distinction of legal from moral obligations cited above. In fact, this is a return under yet another guise of the contrast between social orders based on status and contract.

[44] The accelerated building of great houses, the increasing proportion of absentee landlords, the growing importance of clerical (and thus non-native) magistrates and the centralization of land holdings all are aspects of this growing apart. Perhaps none was more important than the simple increase in the scale of local populations, especially those which turned to outwork and/or factories, industrial discipline was also increasingly impersonal and a multitude of other factors could also be adduced.

[45] This question is reflected in the contrast between 'interests' and 'classes' often drawn to distinguish the units of social organization at a large scale before and after industrialization. H. Perkin, for example, has made much of this contrast in *The Origins of Modern English Society* (London, 1969).

[46] L. Radzinowicz, *A History of English Criminal Law*, Vol. I, *The Movement For Reform* (London, 1948).

allowed the creation of an ideology that was much more persuasive than in London.[47]

In the nineteenth century, many of the landowners on whom the traditional system of authority depended worked to maintain their political positions at the expense of close ties to their communities.[48] Perhaps more important, the proportion of the total population which lived in the more traditional communities shrank rapidly, if unevenly. In the new industrial districts new ties had to be formed; traditional communal bonds did not support an established system of authority, and before a new paternalism was forged (to the extent it ever was) power was especially important.

The regulation which some magistrates attempted to provide was not the self-regulation of an integrated community, but an order imposed by external agency. Other magistrates who opposed the encroachments of market relations frequently tolerated or encouraged the actions of crowds against grain dealers and other middlemen. This sort of authority, however, allowed magistrates to give licence rather more than to take action. As defenders of a way of life and a set of values, they might implicitly or explicitly approve of actions against middlemen, but they had little or no power to move against these engrossers and forestallers themselves. To the extent that the role of the middlemen and other shifts in the relations of production were new, the magistrates were made ineffective by the very conservatism of their own authority. They were slow to realize the threat to their way of life, and slower still to adopt 'popular' solutions, but this can only partly be attributed to personal failings. The intrinsic limitations of authority were also involved:

As a regulatory capacity, authority is legitimated and identified by the rules, traditions, and precedents which embody it and which govern its exercise and objects. Power is also regulatory, but is neither fully prescribed nor governed by norms and rules. Whereas authority presumes and expresses normative consensus, power is most evident in conflict and contraposition where dissensus obtains.[49]

Such power as the magistrate had came from the central government, and this put them in an ambivalent position. On the one hand, their authority depended on their status in the local community, and the

[47] D. Hay 'Property, Authority and the Criminal Law', in D. Hay, P. Linebaugh and E. P. Thompson (eds.), *Albion's Fatal Tree* (London, 1975), p. 55.
[48] F. M. L. Thompson, *English Landed Society in the Nineteenth Century* (London, 1963), p. 183.
[49] M. G. Smith, '*A Structural Approach to Comparative Politics*', p. 104.

congruence of their activities with public opinion. On the other hand, their power obliged them to represent interests sometimes contrary to those of their local communities.[50]

On the local level, the authority of magistrates enabled them to carry out proceedings which were backed by the apparent opinion of the community. In general, this meant proceedings against particular individuals who transgressed against the laws. The community might either support the specific laws or at least the general right of King and Parliament to establish such laws and magistrates to enforce them. This did not necessarily mean that the community members individually felt compelled to follow these laws.[51] Unpopular laws (or interpretations of the law), moreover, might engender opposition as well as disobedience. Herein entered the difficulty. To put down popular opposition always meant to act against the community, not simply against members of the community. It made it obvious that, far from being representatives of the community, and of public opinion, the magistrates were acting on behalf of external interests, and were using external powers. Magistrates were increasingly called upon to enforce certain abstract rights (such as that of selling commodities at the price one chooses) against the weight of custom. Not infrequently a large domestic army was needed to back up the magistrates as these attempted to enforce laws which lacked authority in local communities.[52]

The crucial issue here is the breakdown of the structure of hierarchical incorporation which knit local communities into the society as a whole. The authority of the law in the eighteenth century was maintained in part by the collaboration if the interlinked levels. Thus suspects might be apprehended locally, tried by visiting justices (representing national authority) and convicted. After conviction, local authorities might petition regional or national ones in order to

---

[50] This ambivalence also characterized African village headmen under British colonial rule. Generally headmen were less likely to have inherited a wealth which set them and their families apart as a social class than British landowners were. None the less, it is interesting to speculate as to the extent to which the British Government followed a less explicit policy of indirect rule over its domestic population well before it formulated its approach to colonial governance. See on headmen, J. A. Barnes, J. C. Mitchell and M. Gluckman 'The Village Headman in British Central Africa', *Africa*, XIX (2) (1959), pp. 82–106

[51] Indeed, people did *not* feel compelled to obey the law for authority's sake in all circumstances. But they were surprisingly willing to grant the authorities the right to punish them if they were caught. Thus, popular literature's frequent contrasts between 'French Tyranny' and 'British Liberties' suggested that a fault of the former system was its attempt at preventative action. The Englishman had the liberty of stealing game and getting hanged if he were caught.

[52] Simultaneously, magistrates found that they had little if any ability to take recourse against employers who refused to obey the injunction of the Bench: they had no power to bring to bear. See Elie Halévy, *England in 1815* (London, 1961), p. 336.

obtain a commutation of the sentence by royal mercy.[53] In this way, local notables upheld the law and alleviated the sufferings of the members of the community (upon the satisfaction of certain criteria of worthiness, not the least of which was being well integrated into the web of social relations). In the course of thus managing the ambiguity of their position, they were able to demonstrate to the locals that they had the ear of the people at court (either directly or indirectly). Such a process still obtains at a local level and within many institutions. Nationally, it is attenuated beyond all recognition. If one writes to one's MP to get a wrong redressed, one generally writes as just 'a constituent', not as someone 'personally very well known to . . .' – a standard eighteenth and nineteenth-century locution. Other 'rationalized' mechanisms have take the place of personal connection in seeing that most transactions between local and national levels are accomplished (though of course one's standing in the social hierarchy may influence the performance of bureaucrats). During the period of the Industrial Revolution, however, the older hierarchical organization of authority underwent its crisis without an effective substitute being provided. This is one of the factors which caused community to be reorganized along class lines in Britain.[54]

As the fissure of class distinction began more and more to be recognized, and as demographic and other factors made self-regulating working-class communities possible, the identification of the bonds of community shifted. The corporate system into which people were most strongly linked did not cross the major lines of class. Friendly societies, trade unions and political unions linked workers primarily to each other. At the same time, the growth of working-class collective action depended on the social integration of working-class communities.[55] Hierarchical splits existed within the ranks of the workers as well as between them and other sections of society; in addition, social and geographical mobility, long hours of work, and active oppression of corporate groups all worked against the sociation of workers. A

---

[53] See D. Hay's illuminating article on 'Property, Authority and the Criminal Law . . .'. L. Radzinowicz's *A History of English Criminal Law*, remains the most important general work; see vol. I, ch. 4 on commutation of the death penalty.

[54] Workers certainly tried to make the old system work at least as often as they pushed for anything new. Petition after petition flowed into parliament expressing their grievances. Parliament seldom considered these petitions, let alone took positive action. On a few occasions, workers had statute law on their side (such as the Statute of Artificers, 42 Eliz. cap. 63); parliament then suspended or repeated the laws.

[55] As J. Foster notes, 'The effective practice of illegal unionism demanded more than just the elaboration of a mass of insitutional supports. It compelled the formation of a labour *community*' (*Class Struggle in the Industrial Revolution* (London, 1974), p. 48 original emphasis)). It is one of the merits of Foster's book to give serious attention to this issue.

traditional localism gave way to a somewhat greater consciousness of commonality within a class, at least for a time. In the end, of course, workers did not achieve either a fully autonomous social organization or dominance in English society. It is also clear that this was the aim of only a minority of workers, even of those workers actively engaged in collective social and economic struggles.

Societies which have had revolutions have shown much more complete and autonomous community among the 'masses' and much less hierarchical inter-linkage between classes than existed in England. This is an important reason why 'wars of national liberation' are more common than wars against wholly indigenous rulers (let alone exploiters). In part, this is a matter of the clearer identification of 'them' and 'us' afforded by alien rule. In this way, the more alien and separate a ruling class becomes, the more vulnerable it becomes. But there is another important factor. Wars of national liberation generally pit a hierarchically inclusive corporate society, a highly systemic society with strong community foundations, against an external power.[56] War within a class society is a very different matter. A class very seldom has the social strength and community basis of a traditional society, nor does it have the economic and intellectual self-sufficiency a more 'complete' society may have. This is particularly true in highly mobile societies of advanced industrial capitalism. The social foundations for a revolution, and for a social and political organization to follow it, are not inherited from earlier stages of class society, as they are from pre-colonial society. Would-be revolutionaries must struggle to build such social foundations, and against extraordinary odds.

Widespread agreement that some particular political (or social) change ought to be effected is not enough to mobilize people in favour of that change. Concerted collective action depends on more than consensus, for individuals are interested in many goods; and collective goods, like others, have costs. If people are to co-operate in some costly undertaking, they require some assurance that everyone will contribute his share.[57] A collective good (one which can only be enjoyed in common with some aggregate of people) will generally only be provided under one of two conditions: either one actor's anticipated benefits from the collective good must outweigh his costs, therefore making it worthwhile for him to provide the good by himself, or there must be coercion or selective inducements to ensure the contributions of the entire collectivity.[58] Coercion is generally

[56] This is obviously a matter of degree, as many would-be nations are rent by deep schisms.

[57] Less assurance is required, of course, as there are fewer good alternatives available to the individual. This is better described perhaps, as a reduction in the (opportunity) costs.

[58] See M. Olson, *The Theory of Collective Action.*

treated as an application of external force. It is apparent, however, that community, in the way in which we have defined it, may also provide the coercion or inducements necessary to ensure collective action. Community, indeed, may even mobilize people for collective action over long periods of time, in pursuit of highly uncertain goals and at high personal costs. The amount of external force required to achieve the same ends would be vast, if even then the intentional application of force could achieve the same combination of strength and flexibility as community.

Community is a matter of long-term co-operation. Many of the results of this co-operation are not conscious goals in the minds of participants. More exactly, many actions may fit these 'goals' without being explicitly instrumental. At particular junctures people may decide to pursue one or another task of societal development; practices they consider as instrumental may later be taken for granted. At the simplest level, we all need to limit the range of possibilities which we take into consideration when choosing an action. Habit is by no means the least important way in which this is done; cultural rules are another; social constraints on the availability of information add to the limitation.[59] The efficiency of habit and culture clearly depends on the familiarity of situations and events. Community both depends on this familiarity and helps to produce it. Being able to predict the behaviour of those with whom one must deal is one of the social advantages of community membership. This ability comes not only from long observation of particular persons, but from the systematicity of the communal organization, and the multiplicity of communal relationships. The former provides for collective definitions of relationships and the obligations they entail and expectations they justify. The latter increases people's investment in particular relationships, and causes them to be much more influenced by the wishes of others. For these reasons, it is inaccurate to see people in communities taking action solely as individuals (as much microeconomic theory and both psychologistic and economistic exchange theory do). Moreover, members of communities often desire that benefits should accrue to large social units with which they identify – kinship and descent groups, for example. If we fail to look at community, and instead look only at individuals, including individuals collectively described as action sets or social networks, a very significant part of social life must elude our analyses.

[59] Thus, H. A. Simon has stressed the limited nature of rationality in his important discussions of the necessity for 'satisficing' rather than maximizing in decision-making. See H. A. Simon, *Administrative Behaviour* (New York, 1957).

Part II
INTERPRETATION

Introduction

How to arrange in sequence the six contributions to this section? Alphabetically?

According to the historical period with which each is mostly concerned – eighteenth to nineteenth centuries? Thus: Laslett, Thompson, Neale, Foster, Himmelfarb, Perkin?

According to the emphasis each places upon theory, the least explicitly theoretically first? Thus: Himmelfarb, Thompson, Laslett, Perkin, Foster, Neale?

According to the concept of class central to the model of class used? Thus: Laslett (one-class), Thompson and Foster (two-class), Perkin (four-class), Neale (five-class), Himmelfarb (anti-class models)?

According to the degree to which each model of class used approximates to a conventional Marxist schema of class, the least Marxist first? Thus: Himmelfarb, Laslett, Perkin, Thompson, Neale, Foster?

Each of these arrangements would do injustice to the complexity of argument in one or more or all of the contributions, and would impose a false lineage on this fragment of recent historiography. It would be simpler to arrange the contributions chronologically according to the date of publication and add the rider, that such a chronological sequence has no implication of a chronological sequence of ideas. Indeed, while each contributor addresses him/herself to the question of class consciousness and to the question of the use of theory in history, only Himmelfarb directly confronts one of the other authors (Neale) with a counter argument. On the surface each of the authors seems an island unto himself. Yet the debate betwen them is no less real for being implicit – their silences are eloquent. And, while a chronological ordering of the contributions might be thought to imply a simplistic acceptance of the importance of linear time, it does best convey the variety and fertility of English/American historiography in the period 1963–77. (Such an ordering also shows the problems that would be involved in writing a linear history of historical writing in that period.) Only considerations of space prevent this section of the collection including contributions published as recently as 1981. I attempt to remedy that deficiency in my Afterword.

The contributions should be read here for the argument about theory and about class which is in each of them, for the context they provide for each other, and for the intellectual puzzles they collectively pose to the reader (ideally, of course, reading these extracts should send students to the originals – only Himmelfarb is reprinted in full). I keep my solutions to some of these puzzles for the Afterword.

7

Class Consciousness

E. P. THOMPSON

PREFACE

This book has a clumsy title, but it is one which meets its purpose. *Making*, because it is a study in an active process, which owes as much to agency as to conditioning. The working class did not rise like the sun at an appointed time. It was present at its own making.

Class, rather than classes, for reasons which it is one purpose of this book to examine. There is, of course, a difference. 'Working classes' is a descriptive term, which evades as much as it defines. It ties loosely together a bundle of discrete phenomena. There were tailors here and weavers there, and together they make up the working classes.

By class I understand an historical phenomenon, unifying a number of disparate and seemingly unconnected events, both in the raw material of experience and in consciousness. I emphasize that it is an *historical* phenomenon. I do not see class as a 'structure', or even as a 'category', but as something which in fact happens (and can be shown to have happened) in human relationships.

More than this, the notion of class entails the notion of historical relationship. Like any other relationship, it is a fluency which evades analysis if we attempt to stop it dead at any given moment and anatomize its structure. The finest-meshed sociological net cannot give us a pure specimen of class, any more than it can give us one of deference or of love. The relationship must always be embodied in real people and in a real context. Moreover, we cannot have two distinct classes, each with an independent being, and then bring them *into* relationship with each other. We cannot have love without lovers, nor

The Preface (pp. 9–13) and a section on class consciousness (pp. 807–32) from E. P. Thompson, *The Making of the English Working Class* (Victor Gollancz, London, 1963).

deference without squires and labourers. And class happens when some men, as a result of common experiences (inherited or shared), feel and articulate the identity of their interests as between themselves, and as against other men whose interests are different from (and usually opposed to) theirs. The class experience is largely determined by the productive relations into which men are born – or enter involuntarily. Class-consciousness is the way in which these experiences are handled in cultural terms: embodied in traditions, value-systems, ideas, and institutional forms. If the experience appears as determined, class-consciousness does not. We can see a *logic* in the responses of similar occupational groups undergoing similar experiences, but we cannot predicate any *law*. Consciousness of class arises in the same way in different times and places, but never in *just* the same way.

There is today an ever-present temptation to suppose that class is a thing. This was not Marx's meaning, in his own historical writing, yet the error vitiates much latter-day 'Marxist' writing. 'It', the working class, is assumed to have a real existence, which can be defined almost mathematically – so many men who stand in a certain relation to the means of production. Once this is assumed it becomes possible to deduce the class-consciousness which 'it' ought to have (but seldom does have) if 'it' was properly aware of its own position and real interests. There is a cultural superstructure, through which this recognition dawns in inefficient ways. These cultural 'lags' and distortions are a nuisance, so that it is easy to pass from this to some theory of substitution: the party, sect, or theorist, who disclose class-consciousness, not as it is, but as it ought to be.

But a similar error is committed daily on the other side of the ideological divide. In one form, this is a plain negative. Since the crude notion of class attributed to Marx can be faulted without difficulty, it is assumed that any notion of class is a pejorative theoretical construct, imposed upon the evidence. It is denied that class has happened at all. In another form, and by a curious inversion, it is possible to pass from a dynamic to a static view of class. 'It' – the working class – exists, and can be defined with some accuracy as a component of the social structure. Class-consciousness, however, is a bad thing, invented by displaced intellectuals, since everything which disturbs the harmonious co existence of groups performing different 'social rôles' (and which thereby retards economic growth) is to be deplored as an 'unjustified disturbance-symptom'.[1] The problem is to determine how best 'it' can

---

[1] An example of this approach, covering the period of this book, is to be found in the work of a colleague of Professor Talcott Parsons: N. J. Smelser, *Social Change in the Industrial Revolution* (1959).

be conditioned to accept its social rôle, and how its grievances may best be 'handled and channelled'.

If we remember that class is a relationship, and not a thing, we can not think in this way. 'It' does not exist, either to have an ideal interest or consciousness, or to lie as a patient on the Adjustor's table. Nor can we turn matters upon their heads, as has been done by one authority who (in a study of class obsessively concerned with methodology, to the exclusion of the examination of a single real class situation in a real historical context) has informed us:

Classes are based on the differences in legitimate power associated with certain positions, i.e. on the structure of social rôles with respect to their authority expectations. . . . An individual becomes a member of a class by playing a social rôle relevant from the point of view of authority. . . . He belongs to a class because he occupies a position in a social organization; ie. class membership is derived from the incumbency of a social rôle.[2]

The question, of course, is how the individual got to be in this 'social rôle', and how the particular social organization (with its property-rights and structure of authority) got to be there. And these are historical questions. If we stop history at a given point, then there are no classes but simply a multitude of individuals with a multitude of experiences. But if we watch these men over an adequate period of social change, we observe patterns in their relationships, their ideas, and their institutions. Class is defined by men as they live their own history, and, in the end, this is its only definition.

If I have shown insufficient understanding of the methodological preoccupations of certain sociologists, nevertheless I hope this book will be seen as a contribution to the understanding of class. For I am convinced that we cannot understand class unless we see it as a social and cultural formation, arising from processes which can only be studied as they work themselves out over a considerable historical period. This book can be seen as a biography of the English working class from its adolescence until its early manhood. In the years between 1780 and 1832 most English working people came to feel an identity of interests as between themselves, and as against their rulers and em-ployers. This ruling class was itself much divided, and in fact only gained in cohesion over the same years because certain antagonisms were resolved (or faded into relative insignificance) in the face of an insurgent working class. Thus the working-class presence was, in 1832, the most significant factor in British political life.

[2] R. Dahrendorf, *Class and Class Conflict in Industrial Society* (1959), pp. 148–9.

The book is written in this way. In Part One I consider the continuing popular traditions in the 18th century which influenced the crucial Jacobin agitation of the 1790s. In Part Two I move from subjective to objective influences – the experiences of groups of workers during the Industrial Revolution which seem to me to be of especial significance. I also attempt an estimate of the character of the new industrial work-discipline, and the bearing upon this of the Methodist Church. In Part Three I pick up the story of plebeian Radicalism, and carry it through Luddism to the heroic age at the close of the Napoleonic Wars. Finally, I discuss some aspects of political theory and of the consciousness of class in the 1820 and 1830s.

This is a group of studies, on related themes, rather than a consecutive narrative. In selecting these themes I have been conscious, at times, of writing against the weight of prevailing orthodoxies. There is the Fabian orthodoxy, in which the great majority of working people are seen as passive victims of *laissez faire*, with the exception of a handful of far-sighted organizers (notably, Francis Place). There is the orthodoxy of the empirical economic historians, in which working people are seen as a labour force, as migrants, or as the data for statistical series. There is the 'Pilgrim's Progress' orthodoxy, in which the period is ransacked for forerunners – pioneers of the Welfare State, progenitors of a Socialist Commonwealth, or (more recently) early exemplars of rational industrial relations. Each of these orthodoxies has a certain validity. All have added to our knowledge. My quarrel with the first and second is that they tend to obscure the agency of working people, the degree to which the contributed, by conscious efforts, to the making of history. My quarrel with the third is that it reads history in the light of subsequent preoccupations, and not as in fact it occurred. Only the successful (in the sense of those whose aspirations anticipated subsequent evolution) are remembered. The blind alleys, the lost causes, and the losers themselves are forgotten.

I am seeking to rescue the poor stockinger, the Luddite cropper, the 'obsolete' hand-loom weaver, the 'utopian' artisan, and even the deluded follower of Joanna Southcott, from the enormous condescension of posterity. Their crafts and traditions may have been dying. Their hostility to the new industrialism may have been backward-looking. Their communitarian ideals may have been fantasies. Their insurrectionary conspiracies may have been foolhardy. But they lived through these times of acute social disturbance, and we did not. Their aspirations were valid in terms of their own experience; and, if they were casualties of history, they remain, condemned in their own lives, as casualties.

Our only criterion of judgement should not be whether or not a man's actions are justified in the light of subequent evolution. After all, we are not at the end of social evolution ourselves. In some of the lost causes of the people of the Industial Revolution we may discover insights into social evils which we have yet to cure. Moreover, this period now compels attention for two particular reasons. First, it was a time in which the plebeian movement placed an exceptionally high valuation upon egalitarian and democratic values. Although we often boast our democratic way of life, the events of these critical years are far too often forgotten or slurred over. Second, the greater part of the world today is still undergoing problems of industrialization, and of the formation of democratic institutions, analogous in may ways to our own experience during the Industrial Revolution. Causes which were lost in England might, in Asia or Africa, yet be won.

Finally, a note of apology to Scottish and Welsh readers. I have neglected these histories, not out of chauvinism, but out of respect. It is because class is a cultural as much as an economic formation that I have been cautious as to generalising beyond English experience. (I have considered the Irish, not in Ireland, but as immigrants to England). The Scottish record, in particular, is quite as dramatic, and as tormented, as our own. The Scottish Jacobin agitation was more intense and more heroic. But the Scottish story is significantly different. Calvinism was not the same thing a Methodism, although it is difficult to say which, in the early 19th century, was worse. We had no peasantry in England comparable to the Highland migrants. And the popular culture was very different. It is possible, at least until the 1820s, to regard the English and Scottish experiences as distinct, since trade union and political links were impermanent and immature.

★ ★ ★ ★ ★

CLASS CONSCIOUSNESS

'A Sort of Machine'
'The present mischief these two men [Owen and Hodgskin] have in some respects done is incalculable,' noted Francis Place.[3] The 'mischief' is written across the years 1831–5. And at this point the limits of this study have been reached; for there is a sense in which the working class is no longer in the making, but has been made. To step over the threshold, from 1832 to 1833, is to step into a world in which the working-class presence can be felt in ever county in England, and in most fields of life.

[3] Add. MSS. 27,791 f. 270.

The new class consciousness or working people may be viewed from two aspects. On the one hand, there was a consciousness of the identity of interests between working men of the most diverse occupations and levels of attainment, which was embodied in many institutional forms, and which was expressed on an unprecedented scale in the general unionism of 1830–4. This consciousness and these institutions were only to be found in fragmentary form in the England of 1780.

On the other hand, there was a consciousness of the identity of the interests of the working class, or 'productive classes', *as against* those of other classes; and within this there was maturing the claim for an alternative *sytem*. But the final definition of this class consciousness was, in large part, the consequence of the response to working-class strength of the middle class. The line was drawn, with extreme care, in the franchise qualifications of 1832. It had been the peculiar feature of English development that, where we would expect to find a growing middle-class reform movement, with a working-class tail, only later succeeded by an independent agitation of the working class, in fact this process was reversed. The example of the French Revolution had initiated three simultaneous processes: a panic-stuck counter-revolutionary response on the part of the landed and commercial aristocracy; a withdrawal on the part of the industrial bourgeoisie and an accommodation (on favourable terms) with the *status quo*; and a rapid radicalization of the popular reform movement until the Jacobin cadres who were tough enough to survive through the Wars were in the main little masters, artisans, stockingers and croppers, and other working men. The twenty-five years after 1795 may be seen as the years of the 'long counter-revolution', and in consequence the Radical movement remained largely working-class in character, with an advanced democratic 'populism' as its theory. But the triumph of such a movement was scarcely to be welcomed by the mill-owners, iron-masters and manufacturers. Hence the peculiarly repressive and anti-egalitarian ideology of the English middle classes (Godwin giving way to Bentham, Bentham giving way to Malthus, M'Culloch, and Dr Ure, and these giving rise to Baines, Macaulay and Edwin Chadwick). Hence also the fact that the mildest measure of reform, to meet the evident irrationalities of Old Corruption, was actually *delayed*, by the resistance of the old order on the one hand, and the timidity of the manufacturers on the other.

The Reform Bill crisis of 1832 – or, to be more accurate, the successive crises from early in 1831 until the 'days of May' in 1832 – illustrates these theses at almost every point. The agitation arose from 'the people' and rapidly displayed the most astonishing consensus of opinion as to the imperative necessity for 'reform'. Viewed from one aspect, England was without any doubt passing through a crisis in these twelve months in which revolution was possible. The rapidity with which the agitation extended indicates the degree to which experience in every type of constitutional and quasi-legal agitation was present among the people:

The systematic way in which the people proceeded, their steady persever-ance, their activity and skill astounded the enemies of reform. Meetings of almost every description of persons were held in cities, towns, and parishes; by journeymen tradesmen in their clubs, and by common workmen who had no trade clubs or associations of any kind. . . .

So Place wrote of the autumn of 1830, adding (of February 1831):

. . . yet there was not even the smallest communication between places in the same neighbourhood; each portion of the people appeared to understand what ought to be done. . . .[4]

'The great majority' of those who attended the swelling demonstra-tions, the King's private Secretary complained in March 1831 to Grey, 'are of the very lowest class.' The enormous demonstrations, rising to above 100,000 in Birmingham and London in the autumn of 1831 and May 1832, were overwhelmingly composed of artisans and working men.[5]

   'We did not cause the excitement about reform,' Grey wrote a little peevishly to the King, in March 1831: 'We found it in full vigour when we came into office.' And, viewed from another aspect, we can see why throughout these crisis months a revolution was in fact impro-bable. The reason is to be found in the very strength of the working-class Radical movement; the skill with which the middle-class leaders, Brougham, *The Times*, the *Leeds Mercury* both used this threat of working-class force, and negotiated a line of retreat acceptable to all but the most die-hard defenders of the *ancien régime*; and the awareness on the part of the Whigs and the least intransigent Tories that, while Brougham and Baines were only blackmailing them, nevertheless if a compromise was not come to, the middle-class reformers might no longer be able to hold in check the agitation at their backs.

   The industrial bourgeoisie desired, with heart and soul, that a

⁴ Add. MSS. 27,789.
⁵ See Jephson, *The Platform* (1892), II, Ch. XV.

revolution should not take place, since they knew that on the very day of its commencement there would be a dramatic process of radicalization, in which Huntite, trade unionist, and Owenite leaders would command growing support in nearly all the manufacturing centres. 'Threats of a "revolution" are employed by the middle classes and petty masters,' wrote the *Poor Man's Guardian*. But –

a violent revolution is not only beyond the means of those who threaten it, but is to them their greatest object of alarm; for they know that such a revolution can only be effected by the poor and despised millions, who, if excited to the step, might use it for their own advantage, as well as for that of themselves, who would thus . . . have their dear rights of property endangered: be assured that a violent revolution is their greatest dread. . . .[6]

The middle-class reformers fought skilfully on both fronts. On the one hand *The Times* came forward as the actual organizer of mass agitation: 'We trust there is not a county, town, or village in the United Kingdom which will not meet and petition for a reform . . .' It even urged upon the people 'the solemn duty of forming themselves into political societies throughout the whole realm.' It supported – as did Edward Baines, before cheering throngs, at Leeds – measures of enforcement which led directly on towards revolution: the run on the Banks, refusal to pay taxes, and the arming of members of Political Unions. On the other hand, the riots at Nottingham, Derby and Bristol in October 1831 underline the dual function of the Political Unions on the Birmingham model:

These Unions were to be for the promotion of the cause of reform, for the protection of life and property against the detailed but irregular outrages of the mob, as well as for the maintenance of *other* great interests against the systematic violences of an oligarchy. . . .[7]

These middle-class incendiaries carried in their knapsacks a special constable's baton. There were occasions when the Tories themselves hoped to outwit them, by encouraging the independent working-class reform movement to display itself in a form so alarming that Brougham and Baines would run to Old Corruption for protection. When the National Union of the Working Classes proposed to call a demonstration in London for manhood suffrage, and in resistance to the Whig Reform Bill, the King himself wrote (4 November 1831):

[6] 1 October 1831.
[7] *The Times*, 1 December 1830, 27 October 1831; see Jephson, *op. cit.*, II, pp. 69, 107. During the Bristol riots, the authorities were forced to call in the leaders of the Bristol Political Union to restore order. See *Bristol Mercury*, 1 November 1831.

His Majesty is by no means displeased that the measures contemplated by the meeting in question are so violent, and . . . objectionable, as he trusts that the manifestation of such intentions and such purposes may afford the opportunity . . . of checking the progress of the Political Unions. . . .[8]

Throughout the country middle-class and working-class reformers manoeuvred for control of the movement. In the earliest stages, until the summer of 1831, the middle-class Radicals held the advantage. Seven years before Wooler had closed the *Black Dwarf* with a sadly disillusioned final Address. There was (in 1824) no 'public devotedly attached to the cause of parliamentary reform'. Where hundreds and thousands had once clamoured for reform, it now seemed to him that they had only 'clamoured for bread'; the orators and journalists of 1816–20 had only been 'bubbles thrown up in the fermentation of society'.[9] Many of the working-class leaders of the late 1820s shared his disillusion, and accepted the anti-political stance of their master, Owen. It was not until the summer of 1830, with the rural labourers' 'revolt' and the July Revolution in France, that the tide of popular interest began to turn back to political agitation. And thenceforward the insanely stubborn last-ditch resistance of the die-hards (the Duke of Wellington, the Lords, the Bishops) to *any* measure of reform dictated a strategy (which was exploited to the full by the middle-class Radicals) by which popular agitation was brought to bear behind Grey and Russell, and in support of a Bill from which the majority had nothing to gain.

Thus the configuration of forces of 1816–20 (and, indeed, of 1791–4), in which the popular demand for reform was identified with major Cartwright's platform of manhood suffrage, was broken up. 'If any persons suppose that this Reform will lead to ulterior measures,' Grey declared in the House in November 1831:

they are mistaken; for there is no one more decided against annual parliaments, universal suffrage, and the ballot, than I am. My object is not to favour, but to put an end to such hopes and projects.

This was clearly enough seen by the older Radicals, the majority of whose articulate spokesmen poured scorn on the Whig Bill until the final 'days of May'. 'It mattered not to him', declared a Macclesfield Radical, 'whether he was governed by a boroughmonger, or a whoremonger, or a cheesemonger, if the system of monopoly and corrup-

[8] Cited in Jephson, *op. cit.*, II, p. 111. The demonstration of the National Union was, in fact, pronounced seditious and prohibited. It was a risk too great to take.
[9] Final Address, prefacing *Black Dwarf*, XII (1824).

tion was still to be upheld.'[10] Hunt, from his place as Member for Preston (1830–2), maintained the same prepositions, in only slightly more decorous language. George Edmonds, the witty and courageous Radical schoolmaster, who had chaired Birmingham's first great post-war demonstration on Newhall Hill (January 1817), declared:

I am not a house-holder. – I can, on a push, be a musket-holder. The nothing-but-the-Bill does not recognize George Edmonds as a citizen! – George Edmonds scorns the nothing-but-the-Bill, except as cut the first at the national robber.[11]

This was the position also of the élite of London's Radical artisans, enrolled in the National Union of Working Classes and Others, whose weekly debates in the Rotunda in 1831 and 1832 were reported in Hetherington's *Poor Man's Guardian* – undoubtedly the finest working-class weekly which had (until that time) been published in Britain. The debates were attended by Hetherington himself (when not in prison), William Lovett, James Watson, John Gast, the brilliant and ill-fated Julian Hibbert, and old William Benbow (the former colleague of Bamford and of Mitchell), now pressing his proposal for a 'Grand National Holiday', or month's general strike, in the course of which the productive classes would assume control of the nation's government and resources.[12] The debates increasingly turned upon the definition of class. William Carpenter, who shared with Hetherington the honour of initiating the struggle for the 'unstamped' press, offered a dissentient opinion. The Whig Bill ought to be supported, as a 'wedge'. He complained that the *Poor Man's Guardian* used the words 'middle men' and 'middle class' as 'convertible terms', whereas the middle classes 'are not only *not* a class of persons having interests different from your own. They are the *same* class; they are, generally speaking, *working* or *labouring* man.'[13] Throughout the entire crises the controversy continued. After the Bill had passed, the *Poor Man's Guardian* recorded its conclusion:

The promoters of the Reform Bill projected it, not with a view to subvert, or even remodel our aristocratic institutions, but to consolidate them by a reinforcement of sub-aristocracy from the middle-classes. . . . The only

[10] *Poor Man's Guardian*, 10 December 1831.

[11] G. Edmonds, *The English Revolution* (1831), p. 5. Edmonds went on to play an active part in the Chartist movement.

[12] See A. J. C. Rüter, 'Benbow's Grand National Holiday', *International Review of Social History* (Leiden), I (1936), pp. 217 et seq.

[13] W. Carpenter, *An Address to the Working Classes on the Reform Bill* (October 1831). See also the ensuing controversy in the *Poor Man's Guardian*.

difference between the Whigs and the Tories is this – the Whigs would give the shadow to preserve the substance; the Tories would not give the shadow, because stupid as they are, the millions will not stop at shadows but proceed onwards to realities.[14]

It is problematical how far the militant Owenities of the Rotunda represented any massive body of working-class opinion. They commenced by representing only the intelligentsia of the artisans. But they gathered influence most rapidly; by October 1831 they were able to organize a massive demonstration, perhaps 70,000 strong, many wearing the white scarves emblematic of manhood suffrage; perhaps 100,000 joined their demonstrations against the National Fast in March 1832. Place regarded the Rotundists (many of whom he wrote off as 'atrocious') as constituting the greatest of threats to the middle-class strategy, and much of his manuscript history of the Reform Bill crises (upon which historians have placed too much reliance) is devoted to the unscrupulous manœuvres by which he sought to limit their influence, and displace it by that of his rival National Political Union. The Duke of Wellington himself saw the contest as one between the Establishment and the Rotunda, which he compared to two armies '*en présence*'. It confused his military mind very much to reflect that he could place no river between the armies, with adequate sentinels and posts on the bridges. The enemy was installed at sensitive points within his own camp.[15]

The procession of October 1831, however, was mainly composed (it seems) of 'shopkeepers and superior artisans'. And while the numbers called out were impressive, they compare poorly with the even greater demonstrations at Birmingham, drawn from a smaller population. It would seem that, while the London artisans had at last succeeded in building a cohesive and highly articulate leadership, there remained a wide gulf between them and the mass of London labourers, and workers in the dishonourable trades. (This problem was to recur time and again in the history of London Chartism.) The position was caricatured in the pages of a scurrilous and alarmist pamphlet by Edward Gibbon Wakefield. He saw the Rotundists as 'Desperadoes' and idealists, whose danger lay in the fact that they might unleash the destructive energies of the criminal classes, 'the helots of society', who were crammed in the lanes and alleys off Orchard Street, Westminster, or Whitechapel. Here were the thousands of unpolitical (but danger-

[14] *Poor Man's Guardian*, 25 October 1832; see A. Briggs, *The Age of Improvement* (1959), p. 258.
[15] See J. R. M. Butler, *The Passing of the Great Reform Bill* (1914), pp. 292–3, 350; Add. MSS., 27,791 f. 51; Memorandum on 'Measures to be taken to put an End to the Seditious Meeting at the Rotunda', *Wellington Despatches*, second series (1878), VII, p. 353.

ous) 'costermongers, drovers, slaughterers of cattle, knackers, dealers in dead bodies and dogs' meat, cads, brickmakers, chimney-sweeps, nightmen, scavengers, etc.' His attitude to the Owenite Socialists of the Rotunda was ambiguous. On the one hand, they were mostly 'sober men, who maintain themselves by industry – men plainly marked off by superior talents from the dangerous classes. On the other hand, many were 'loose single men living here and there in lodgings, who might set fire to London without anxiety for helpless beings at home':

In manner they are rather gentle than rough; but touch one of them on his tender point; – only say that you think the stimulus of competition indispensable to the production of wealth; – and he will either turn from you in scorn, or . . . tell you, with flashing eyes, that you are paid by the Government to talk nonsense. Any thing like a compromise is what annoys them even more than decided opposition.

Many, he said (with some truth), 'are provided with arms':

If an insurrection of the London populace should take place, they will be found at the most dangerous posts, leading the thieves and rabble, pointing out the most effectual measures, and dying, if the lot fall on them, with cries of defiance.

'These will be the fighting men of our revolution, if we must have one.'[16]

The picture is overdrawn; but it is not wholly without truth.[17] The danger, from the point of view of authority (whether Whig or Tory), lay in a possible conjunction between the artisan Socialists and the 'criminal classes'. But the unskilled masses in London inhabited another world from that of the artisans – a world of extreme hardship, illiteracy, very widespread demoralization, and disease, which was dramatized by the cholera outbreak of the winter of 1831–2. Here we have all the classic problems, the hand-to-mouth insecurity, of a metropolitan city swollen with immigrants in a period of rapid population-growth.[18]

[16] E. G. Wakefield, *Householders in Danger from the Populace* (n.d. October 1831?).

[17] While Lovett and his circle believed in the maximum of pressure short of physical force (and maintained some relations with Place), others, including Benbow and Hibbert, were preparing for an armed struggle.

[18] It is interesting to speculate upon how far Place's frequent assertions as to the improvement in the manners and morals of the London populace expressed the truth, or merely the widening gulf between the artisans and unskilled, the narrowing of Place's own circle of experience, and the pushing of poverty out of the City's centre towards the east and the south. On the whole problem of metropolitan growth and demoralisation (and its 'biological' foundation), see L. Chevalier, *Classes laborieuses et classes dangereuses à Paris pendant la première moitié du XIX Siècle* (Paris, 1958), which suggests many new lines of research into London conditions.

The unskilled had no spokesmen and no organizations (apart from friendly societies). They were as likely to have followed the lead of a gentleman as of an artisan. And yet the severity of the political crisis which commenced in October 1831 was sufficient to crack the crust of fatalism, deference, and need, within which their lives were enclosed. The riots of that month in Derby, the sacking of Nottingham Castle, the extensive riots at Bristol – all were indicative of a deep disturbance at the foundations of society, which observers anxiously expected to be followed by the uprising of London's East End.

The Birmingham Political Union was an acceptable model, which *The Times* itself could commend, because the local industrial context favoured a reform movement of the masses which still remained firmly under middle-class control. The history of Birmingham Radicalism is significantly different from that of the north Midlands and the north. There was no basis in its small-scale industries for Luddism, and the 'father' of the Political Unions, Thomas Attwood, first gained public-prominence when he led, in 1812, a united agitation of the masters and artisans against the Orders in Council. There were undoubtedly groups of 'physical force' Radicals in the Black Country in 1817–20, but – whether by good fortune or good judgement – they were never exposed by any abortive movement like the Pentridge and Grange Moor affairs.[19] As Professor Briggs has shown, Thomas Attwood was able in 1830 to 'harmonize and unite' the diverse 'materials of discontent' because the Industrial Revolution in Birmingham had 'multiplied the number of producing units rather than added to the scale of existing enterprises'. There had been little displacement of skilled labour by machinery; the numberless small workshops meant that the social gradients shelved more gently, and the artisan might still rise to the status of a small master; in times of economic recession masters and journeymen were afflicted alike.[20] Hence, class antagonism was more muted than in Manchester, Newcastle, and Leeds. Throughout the Reform Bill crisis, Attwood controlled the Birmingham Union with 'such a show of good-nature' (O'Brien later recalled) 'that the Brummagem operatives seemed really to believe that they would be *virtually*, though not actually, represented in the "reformed" parliament'. And, in a tribute impressive from so stern a critic, O'Brien added:

[19] It is difficult to discount Oliver's circumstantial account of Birmingham contacts (Narrative in H.O. 40.9). See also evidence in H.O. 40.3 and 6.

[20] See Cobbett's angry comment: 'Do you imagine that the great manufacturers, and merchants, and bankers are crying for REFORM, because they have been converted to a love of *popular rights*! Bah! . . . [Financial causes] have made them raise their wages; these they cannot pay and *pay tithes and taxes* also. . . . Therefore, are they *reformers*; therefore, they throw their lusty arms around the waist of the Goddess'; *Political Register*, 17 October 1831.

To this body, more than to any other, is confessedly due the triumph (such as it was) of the Reform Bill. Its well-ordered proceedings, extended organization, and immense assemblages of people, at critical periods of its progress, rendered the measure irresistible.[21]

In such centres as Leeds, Manchester, and Nottingham the position of the middle-class reformers was very much more uneasy. At Manchester (as in London) rival political Unions co-existed, and from October 1831 onwards the manhood suffrage Union made the running. At Bolton in the same month the rejection of the Bill by the House of Lords resulted in a split in the Political Union, the largest (manhood suffrage) section organizing a demonstration 6,000 strong, behind the banners: 'Down with the Bishops!', 'No Peers!'[22] In the Midlands and the north such incidents were repeated dozens of times. 'Walk into any lane or public-house, and where a number of operatives are congregated together,' wrote Doherty in January 1832:

and listen, for ten minutes, to the conversation . . . In at least seven out of every ten cases, the subjects of debate will be found to bear upon the appalling question of *whether it would be more advantageous to attack the lives or the property of the rich?*[23]

Indeed in the winter of 1831–2 the ridicule poured upon the Bill and upon its attendant proceedings in the *Poor Man's Guardian* takes on a somewhat academic air. No doubt the Rotundists were right to designate the Bill as a trap (and as a betrayal of the Radical movement). But the well-nigh neolithic obstinacy with which Old Corruption resisted *any* reform led on to a situation in which the nation stepped, swiftly and without premeditation, on to the threshold of revolution. Belatedly, the *Poor Man's Guardian* adjusted its tactics, publishing as a special supplement extracts from Colonel Macerone's *Defensive Instructions for the People* (a manual in street-fighting).[24] Throughout the 'eleven days of England's apprehension and turmoil' which preceded the final passage of the Bill through the Lords in may, Francis Place held his breath. On the evening of the day when it passed, he returned home and noted:

We were within a moment of general rebellion, and had it been possible for the Duke of Wellington to have formed an administration the Thing and the people would have been at issue.

---

[21] *Destructive*, 2 February and 9 March 1833; A. Briggs 'The Background of the Parliamentary Reform Movement in Three English Cities', *Cambridge History Journal*, 1952, p. 293, and *The Age of Improvement*, p. 247.

[22] W. Brimelow, *Political History of Bolton* (1882), I. p. 111.

[23] *Poor Man's Advocate*, 21 January 1832.   [24] *Poor Man's Guardian*, 11 April 1832.

There would have been 'Barricadoes of the principal towns – stopping circulation of paper money'; if a revolution had commenced, it 'would have been the act of the whole people to a greater extent than any which had ever before been accomplished.'[25]

In the autumn of 1831 and in the 'days of May' Britain was within an ace of a revolution which, once commenced, might well (if we consider the simultaneous advance in co-operative and trade union theory) have prefigured, in its rapid radicalization, the revolutions of 1848 and the Paris Commune. J. R. M. Butler's *The Passing of the Great Reform Bill* gives us some sense of the magnitude of the crisis; but his study is weakened by an insufficient awareness of the potential openness of the whole situation, evinced in such comments as this (upon the National Union of the Working Classes):

. . . it disgusted sensible people . . . by its arrogant silliness, as when the Bethnal Green branch petitioned the King to abolish the House of Lords, or the Finsbury section urged the Commons to confiscate the estates of the 199 peers. . . .[26]

Some assessment less complacent than this is required. The fact that revolution did not occur was due, in part, to the deep constitutionalism of that part of the Radical tradition[27] of which Cobbett (urging the acceptance of half a loaf) was the spokesman; and in part to the skill of the middle-class Radicals in offering exactly that compromise which might, not weaken, but strengthen both the State and property-rights against the working-class threat.

The Whig leaders saw their rôle as being that of finding the means to 'attach numbers to property and good order'. 'It is of the utmost importance,' Grey said, 'to associate the middle with the higher orders of society in the love and support of the institutions and government of the country.'[28] The extreme care with which this line was drawn is evinced by a survey undertaken by Baines in 1831, to discover 'the numbers and respectability of the £10 householders in Leeds'. The results were communicated to Lord John Russell in a letter which should be taken as one of the classic documents of the Reform Bill crisis. Baines' pioneering psephological canvassers –

[25] Add. MSS., 27,795 ff. 26–7.

[26] Butler, *op. cit.* p. 303.

[27] See Gladstone's comment: 'I held forth to a working man . . . on the established text, reform was revolution . . . I said, 'Why, look at the revolutions in foreign countries, meaning of course France and Belgium. The man looked hard at me and said . . . "Damn all foreign countries, what has old England to do with foreign countries"; This is not the only time that I have received an important lesson from a humble source.' J. Morley, *Life of Gladstone* (1908), I, p. 54.

[28] See A. Briggs, 'The Language of "Class" in Early 19th-century England', *op. cit.*, p. 56.

stated *unanimously*, that the £10 qualification did not admit to the exercise of the elective franchise a single person who might not safely and wisely be enfranchised: that they were surprised to find how comparatively few would be allowed to vote.

In answer to Russell's enquiry as to the proportion which £10 house-holders bore to the rest of the population, the canvassers reported:

. . . in the parts occupied chiefly by the working classes, not one householder in fifty would have a vote. In the streets principally occupied by shops, almost every householder had a vote. . . . In the township of Holbeck, containing 11,000 inhabitants, chiefly of the working classes, but containing several mills, dye-houses, public-houses, and respectable dwellings, there are only 150 voters. . . . Out of 140 householders, heads of families, working in the mill of Messrs. Marshall and Co, there are *only two* who will have votes. . . . Out of 160 or 170 householders in the mill of Messrs. O. Willan and Sons, Holbeck, there is *not one* vote. Out of about 100 householders in the employment of Messrs. Taylor and Wordsworth, machine-makers, – the highest class of mechanics, – *only one* has a vote. It appeared that of the working classes not more than one in fifty would be enfranchised by the Bill.

Even this estimate would appear to have been excessive. Returns made to the Government in May 1832 showed that in Leeds (population 124,000) 355 'workmen' would be admitted to the franchise, of whom 143 'are clerks, warehousemen, overlookers, etc.' The remaining 212 were in a privileged status, earning between 30s. and 40s. a week.[29]

Such surveys no doubt reassured the Cabinet, which had meditated raising the franchise qualification to £15. 'The great body of the people,' Place wrote, 'were self-assured that either the Reform Bills would be passed by Parliament, or that they should, by their own physical force, obtain much more than they contained, if they were rejected . . .'[30] It is the threat of this 'much more' which hung over both Tories and Whigs in 1832, and which enabled that accomodation to be made, between landed and industrial wealth, between privilege and money, which has been an enduring configuraion of English society. Upon the banners of Baines and Cobden were not *égalité* and *liberté* (still less *fraternité*) but 'Free Trade' and 'Retrenchment'. The rhetoric of Brougham was that of property, security, interest. 'If there is a mob,' Brougham said in his speech on the second reading of the Reform Bill,

there is the people also. I speak now of the middle classes – of those hundreds of thousands of respectable persons – the most numerous and by far the most

[29] Baines, *Life of Edward Baines* (1859), pp. 157–9.
[30] Add. MSS., 27790.

wealthy order in the community, for if all your Lordships' castles, manors, rights of warren and rights of chase, with all your broad acres, were brought to the hammer, and sold at fifty years' purchase, the price would fly up and kick the beam when counterpoised by the vast and solid riches of those middle classes, who are also the genuine depositaries of sober, rational, intelligent, and honest English feeling . . . Rouse not, I beseech you, a peace-loving, but a resolute people . . . As your friend, as the friend of my order, as the friend of my country, as the faithful servant of my sovereign, I counsel you to assist with the uttermost efforts in preserving the peace, and upholding and perpetuating the Constitution. . . .[31]

Divested of its rhetoric, the demands of the middle-class Radicals were voiced by Baines, when the Bill had been passed:

The fruits of Reform are to be gathered. Vast commercial and agricultural monopolies are to be abolished. The Church is to be reformed. . . . Close corporations are to be thrown open. Retrenchment and economy are to be enforced. The shackles of the Slave are to be broken.[32]

The demands of working-class Radicalism were less clearly formulated. A minimum political programme may be cited from the *Poor Man's Guardian*, the organ of the National Union of Working Classes:

Extirpation of the Fiend Aristocracy; Establishment of a Republic, viz. Democracy by Representatives elected by Universal Suffrage; Extinction of hereditary offices, title and distinctions; Abolition of the . . . law of primogeniture; . . . Cheap and rapid administration of justice; Abolition of the Game Laws; Repeal of the diabolical imposts on Newspapers . . .; emancipation of our fellow-citizens the Jews; Introduction of Poor Laws into Ireland; Abolition of the Punishment of Death for offences against property; Appropriation of the Revenues of the 'Fathers in God', the Bishops, towards maintenance of the Poor; Abolition of Tithes; Payment of every Priest or Minister by his Sect; the 'National Debt' not the debt of the Nation; Discharge of the Machinery of Despotism, the Soldiers; Establishment of a National Guard.[33]

This is the old programme of Jacobinism, with little development from the 1790s. (The first principle of a declaration of the National Union, drawn up by Lovett and James Watson, in November 1831, was: 'All property (honestly acquired) to be sacred and inviolable.')[34] But around this 'much more' other demands accrued, according to the grievances foremost in different districts and industries. In Lancashire,

[31] See J. R. M. Butler, *op. cit.*, pp. 284–5.

[32] Baines, *op. cit.*, p. 167.

[33] Cited in A. L. Morton and G. Tate, *The British Labour Movement* (1956), p. 59 and attributed (erroneously) to *Poor Man's Guardian*, 3 March 1831.

[34] See Lovett, *op. cit.*, I. p. 74.

Doherty and his supporters argued that 'universal suffrage means nothing more than a power given to every man to protect his own labour from being devoured by others'.[35] The Owenites, the factory reformers, and 'physical force' revolutionaries like the irrepressible William Benbow were pressing still further demands. But, in the event, the terms of the contest were successfully confined within the limits desired by Brougham and Baines. It was (as Shelley had foreseen in 1822) a contest between 'blood and gold'; and in its outcome, blood compromised with gold to keep out the claims of *égalité*. For the years between the French Revolution and the Reform Bill had seen the formation of a middle-class 'class consciousness', more conservative, more wary of the large idealist causes (except, perhaps, those of other nations), more narrowly self-interested than in any other industrialized nation. Henceforward, in Victorian England, the middle-class Radical and the idealist intellectual were forced to take sides between the 'two nations'. It is a matter of honour that there were many individuals who preferred to be known as Chartists or Republicans rather than as special constables. But such men – Wakley, Frost of Newport, Duncombe, Oastler, Ernest Jones, John Fielden, W. P. Roberts, and on to Ruskin and William Morris – were always disaffected individuals or intellectual 'voices'. They represent in no sense the ideology of the middle class.

What Edward Baines had done, in his correspondence with Russell, was to offer a definition of class of almost arithmetical exactitude. In 1832 the line was drawn in social consciousness by the franchise qualifications, with the crudity of an indelible pencil. Moreover, these years found also a theorist of stature to define the working-class predicament. It appears almost inevitable that he should have been an Irish intellectual, uniting in himself a hatred of the English Whigs with the experience of English ultra-Radicalism and Owenite Socialism. James 'Bronterre' O'Brien (1805–64), the son of an Irish wine merchant, and a distinguished graduate of Trinity College, Dublin, arrived in London in 1829 'to study Law and Radical Reform'.

My friends sent me to study law; I took to radical reform on my own account . . . While I have made no progress at all in law, I have made immense progress in radical reform. So much so, that were a professorship of radical reform to be instituted tomorrow in King's College (no very probable event by the way), I think I would stand candidate . . . I felt as though every drop of blood in my veins was radical blood. . . .[36]

[35] A. Briggs, *op. cit.*, p. 66.
[36] *Bronterre's National Reformer*, 7 January 1837. O'Brien in fact was qualified in law at the Bar in Dublin.

After editing the *Midlands Representative* during the Reform Bill crisis, he moved to London and assumed the editorship of the *Poor Man's Guardian*.

'We foresaw,' he wrote of the Reform Bill, 'that its effect would be to detach from the working classes a large portion of the middle ranks who were *then* more inclined to act with the people than with the aristocracy that excluded them'.[37] And in his Introduction to Buonarotti's history of the Conspiracy of Equals, he drew a parallel: 'The Girondists would extend the franchise to the small middlemen (just as our English Whigs did by the Reform Bill) in order the more effectively to keep down the working classes.' 'Of all governments, a government of the middle classes is the most grinding and remorseless.'[38]

It was a theme to which he often returned. His anger was refreshed by each new action of the Whig administration – the Irish Coercion Bill, the rejection of the 10 Hour Bill, the attack on the trades unions, the Poor Law Amendment Act. 'Previously to the passing of the Reform Bill,' he wrote in 1836:

the middle orders were supposed to have some community of feeling with the labourers. That delusion has passed away. It barely survived the Irish Coercion Bill, it vanished completely with the enactment of the Starvation Law. No working man will evey again expect justice, morals or mercy at the hands of a profit-mongering legislature.[39]

A refugee from a middle-class culture himself, he took especial pleasure in writing of his own class in terms which imitated its own drawing-room small-talk about the servant classes: 'The pursuits and habits [of the middle classes] are essentially debasing. Their life is necessarily a life of low cunning and speculation . . .':

These two classes never had, and never will have, any community of interest. It is the workman's interest to do as little work, and to get as much for it as possible. It is the middleman's interest to get as much work as he can out of the man, and to give as little for it. Here then are their respective interests as directly opposed to each other as two fighting bulls.

And he sought, with considerably genius, to twist together the tradition of ultra-Radicalism with that of Owenism, into a revolutionary

---

[37] *Destructive*, 9 March 1833.

[38] O'Brien, *op. cit.*, pp. xv, xx. For O'Brien, see G. D. H. Cole, *Chartist Portraits* (1941), Ch. IX; T. Rothstein, *From Chartism to Labourism* (1929), pp. 93–123; Beer, *op. cit.*, II, pp. 17–22.

[39] *Twopenny Despatch*, 10 September 1836.

Socialism, whose goals were political revolution, the expropriation of the propertied classes, and a network of Owenite communities:

We must have what Southey calls 'a revolution of revolutions'; such an one as Robespierre and St. Just projected in France in the beginning of 1794; that is to say, a complete subversion of the institutions by which wealth is distributed . . . Property – property – this is the thing we must be at. Without a change in the institution of property, no improvement can take place.

Such a revolution (he hoped) would come, without violence, in the immediate aftermath of the attainment of manhood suffrage: 'From the *laws of the few* have the existing inequalities sprung; by the laws of the many shall they be destroyed.'[40]

Historian today would certainly not accept O'Brien's over-crude assimilation of the post-Reform Whig administration to the interests of the 'middle-class'.[41] (Old Corruption had more vitality than that, as the protracted struggle for the repeal of the Corn Laws was to show.) Nor is it proper to select this one theorist (middle-class in his own origins) as expressive of the new consciousness of the working class. But at the same time, O'Brien was very far from being eccentric at the edges of the movement. As editor of the *Poor Man's Guardian* and other journals he commanded a large, and growing, working-class audience: he was later to earn the title of the 'Schoolmaster' of Chartism. His writings are a central thread through the abundant agitations of the early 1830s, providing a nexus for the old democratic claims, the social agitations (against the New Poor Law and for Factory Reform), the Owenite communitarian experiments, and the syndicalist struggles of the trade unions. O'Brien was, as much as Cobbett and Wooler in the post-war years, an authentic voice of his times.

For most working men, of course, disillusion in the Reform Bill came in less theoretical forms. The proof of the pudding was in the eating. We may see the eating in microcosm in a few of the incidents at one of the contests in the ensuing General Election – at Leeds. Here Baines, who had already used his influence to instate Brougham as the Yorkshire member, brought forward in the Whig interest Marshall, one of the largest employers in Leeds, and Macaulay (or 'Mr Mackholy' as one of the tail of Whig shopkeepers noted in his diary) Macaulay was one of the most complacent of the ideologists of the Reform Bill

---

[40] *Destructive*, 9 March, 24 August 1833; *People's Conservative*; and *Trade's Union Gazette*, 14 December 1833.

[41] O'Brien himself came to regret the vehemence of his dismissal of the entire 'middle class', when an opportunity for alliance between the Chartists and elements from the middle class occurred in the 1840s: see Beer, II, p. 126.

settlement, translating into new terms the Tory doctrine of 'virtual representation':

The higher and middling orders are the natural representative of the human race. Their interest may be opposed, in some things, to that of their poorer contemporaries, but it is identical with that of the innumerable generations which are to follow.

'The inequality with which wealth is distributed forces itself on every body's notice,' he lamented, while 'the reasons which irrefragably proved this inequality to be necessary to the well-being of all classes are not equally obvious.' Mr Marshall was not equal to him as a theorist; but, if a Radical election sheet is to be believed, he was of the view that 12s. a week was a good wage for a man with a family, he considered that the working classes might better their conditions by emigration, and:

In Mr Marshall's mill, a boy of 9 years of age was stripped to the skin, bound to an iron pillar, and mercilessly beaten with straps, until he fainted.[42]

The Tory candidate, on the other hand, was Sadler, leading parliamentary spokesman of the 10 Hour Movement. Oastler had launched, with the Short-Time Committees, his passionate campaign against child labour two years before. The amazing 'Pilgrimage to York' had taken place in the previous April; and the 10 Hour agitation (like the Owenite agitation) continued without pause during the Reform Bill crisis months. In such a contest, therefore, Oastler could be counted upon to side with Sadler against Baines, who had conducted a mealy-mouthed defence of the mill-owners in the *Leeds Mercury*. Cobbett could be counted upon to do the same. Indeed, he gave a reference for Baines which reminds us of the latitude of the libel laws of the time:

This great LYING PUFFER of Brougham . . . who has always taken care to have one member, at least, to do more mischief to public liberty than any other fifty members in the House of Commons; this swelled-up, greedy, and unprincipled puffer, who has been the deluder of Yorkshire for twenty years past. . . .[43]

A Tory-Radical alliance was therefore inevitable behind Sadler. It was also inevitable that the greater part of the Non-conformist 'shopocrat'

[42] J. R. M. Butler, *op. cit.*, pp. 262–5; *Cracker*, 8 December 1832.

[43] *Political Register*, 24 November 1832. Cobbett was recalling the former Yorkshire country member, Wilberforce.

vote would go to 'Mr Marshall Our Townsman and Mr Mackholy the Scotchman' (as our diarist put it):

. . . as to Sadler he never has done any good nor he never will do . . . for he has always been inventing something that has tended to injure the inhabitants of the Town of Leeds . . . he was the first promoter of the Improvement Act and that has cost the Inhabitants a manny thousands and the Burthen has cheefly fallen upon Shopkeepers and what I call the Middling Class of People . . . its true he is one of our Magestrate Party but he is not better for that. . . .[44]

The working-class Radicals in Leeds, maintained the independent press and organization. The men of Leeds (they declared) who 'have assembled in evil report and good report; . . . been instant in season and out of season', had now been betrayed by the men who, in the days of May, had addressed their great assemblies and promised Reform or barricades:

Messrs Marshall and Macaulay may . . . be very friendly to Reforms of all sorts and sizes, both in church and state; they may also be in favour of the abolition of all monopolies except their own, those of mill-men and place-men; but let the operativee of Leeds remember that if they support them, they do what they can to put legislative power into the hands of their enemies.

Moreover, the Radicals declared that the old forms of electoral bribery and influence employed by the aristocratic interest were now finding insidious new forms in the service of the manufacturing interest. Although the workers did not have votes, great efforts were made to offset the effects of 10 Hour demonstrations in favour of Sadler by compelling factory-hands to declare for Marshall and Macaulay at the hustings:

We could name more than a dozen mills, all the hands of which have received positive orders to be in the Yard on Monday, and to hold up their hands for the Orange candidates . . . on pain of instant privation of employment. . . . They have each their stations assigned in the yard, where they are to be penned like flocks of sheep, surrounded on all sides by overlookers, clerks and other understrappers, for the purpose of enforcing the high mandate of the counting-house.

In the event, the scene on the hustings turned into riot, where Oastler and the 10 Hour men 'rang matins on the thick skulls of the flying oranges'. When Sadler was defeated at the poll, Marshall and Macaulay

[44] MS. Letterbook of Ayrey (Leeds Reference Library).

were burned in effigy in the same city centre where Paine had been burnt by the loyalists in 1792.[45]

This Leeds election of 1832 was of more than local significance. It had focussed the attention of factory reformers throughout the country, drawing addresses in Sadler's favour from thousands of signatories in northern towns. There is no mistaking the new tone after 1832. In every manufacturing district a hundred experiences confirmed the new consciousness of class which the Bill had, by its own provisions, so carefully defined. It was the 'reformed' House of Commons which sanctioned the transportation of the Dorchester labourers in 1834 ('a blow directed at the whole body of united operatives'),[46] and who launched, with 'the document' and the lockout, the struggle to break the trade unions, whose intensity and whose significance (in both political and economic terms) is still too little understood. Against the manifesto of the masters, the Yorkshire Trades Union issued its own:

The war cry of the masters has not only been sounded, but the havoc of war; war against freedom; war against opinion; war against justice; and war without justifying cause. . . .

'The very men,' declared one Leeds trade unionist, 'who had pampered Political Unions, when they could be made subservient to their own purposes, were now endeavouring to crush the Trades Unions':

It was but the other day that the operatives were led in great numbers to the West Riding meeting at Wakefield, for the purpose of carrying the Reform Bill. At that time, the very individuals who were now attempting to put down trades' unions, were arraying them to carry by the force of numbers, a political reform which he was sure would not otherwise have been obtained from the aristocracy of this country. That reform which had thus been obtained appeared to him to have been the ultimate means of strengthening the hands of corruption and oppression.[47]

The line from 1832 to Chartism is not a haphazard pendulum alternation of 'political' and 'economic' agitations but a direct progression, in which simultaneous and related movements converge towards a single point. This point was the vote. There is a sense in which the Chartist movement commenced, not in 1836 with the pro-

[45] *Cracker*, 8, 10, 21 December 1832. See also A. Briggs, 'The Background of the Parliamentary Reform Movement in Three English Cities', *op. cit.*, pp. 311–14; E. Baines, *Life*, pp. 164–7; C. Driver, *Tory Radical*, pp. 197–202.

[46] Speech of William Rider, Leeds stuff-weaver and later to be a prominent Chartist Leader, *Leeds Times*, 12 April 1834.

[47] *Leeds Times*, 12, 17, 24 May 1834.

mulgation of the 'Six Points', but at the moment when the Reform Bill received Royal Assent. Many of the provincial Political Unions never disbanded, but commenced at once to agitate against the 'shopocrat' franchise. In January 1833 the *Working Man's Friend* was able to announce that the fortress of middle-class Radicalism had been stormed: '. . . in spite of all the opposition and chicanery of a RAG MERCHANT MONARCHY, the Midland Union of the Working Classes was formed by the brave, but, till then, misled people of that country.'[48] The characteristic ideology of Birmingham Radicalism, which united employers and journeymen in opposition to the aristocracy, the Banks, the National Debt, and the 'paper-money system', was beginning to fall apart. For a time Attwood himself was carried with the new current, partly through loyalty to the regiments to which he had made large promises before. Once again, a monster demonstration gathered on Newhall Hill (May 1833), at which an attendance of 180,000 was claimed, and at which there was expressed –

. . . a sentiment of common hatred to the parties whom, having been mainly instrumental in forcing into power, they now assembled to express their disgust of the . . . treachery which they had manifested.

The attendance was swelled by colliers from Walsall, iron-workers from Wolverhampton, outworkers from Dudley. The process of Radicalization which was to make Birmingham a Chartist metropolis had begun.[49]

But the content of this renewed agitation was such that the vote itself implied 'much more', and that is why it had to be denied. (The Birmingham of 1833 was not the Birmingham of 1831: it was now the home of an Equitable Labour Exchange, it was the headquarters of the socialist Builders' Union, it housed the editorial office of the *Pioneer*.) The vote, for the workers of this and the next decade, was a symbol whose importance it is difficult for us to appreciate, our eyes dimmed by more than a century of the smog of 'two-party parliamentary politics'. It implied, first, *égalité*: equality of citizenship, personal dignity, worth. 'Instead of bricks, mortar, and dirt, MAN ought to be represented,' wrote one pamphleteer lamenting the lot of 'the miserable, so-called "free-born" Englishman, excluded from the most valuable right that man can enjoy in political society.'[50] 'Be we, of the working millions,' wrote George Edmonds –

---

[48] *Working Man's Friend and Political Magazine*, 5 January 1833.
[49] *Report of the Proceedings of the Great Public Meeting &c., 20 May 1833*.
[50] 'I.H.B.L.', *Ought Every Man to Vote?* (1832).

never more seen at baby-shows, Lord Mayor penny-peeps, and gingerbread
Coronations – be not present as accomplices in such national fooleries. Let
the tawdry actors have all the fun to themselves.

'Like the wild Irish of old, the British millions have been too long
insolently placed without the pale of social governments':

I now speak the thoughts of my unrepresented fellow millions, the Wild
English, the free-born slaves of the nineteenth century.[51]

But in the context of the Owenite and Chartist years, the claim for
the vote implied also further claims: a new way of reaching out by the
working people for *social control* over their conditions of life and
labour. At first, and inevitably, the exclusion of the working class
provoked a contrary rejection, by the working class, of all forms of
political action. Owen had long prepared the ground for this, with his
indifference to political Radicalism. But in the post-1832 swing to
general unionism, this anti-policital bias was not quietist but em-
battled, militant, and even revolutionary. To examine the richness of
the political thought of these years would take us further into the
history of general unionism – and, indeed, into the early years of
Chartism – than we intend to go. They are years in which Benbow
canvassed his notion of the 'Grand National Holiday' in the industrial
districts; in which the printing-worker, John Francis Bray, carried
forward Hodgskin's ideas, in lectures to Leeds artisans, later published
as *Labour's Wrongs and Labour's Remedies*; in which the Builders' Union
and the Grand National Consolidated Trades Union rose and fell; and
in which Doherty and Fielden founded the 'Society for National
Regeneration' with its remedy of the General Strike for the Eight-
Hour Day. The Owenite communitarians were fertile with notions
and experiments prefiguring advances in the care of children, the
relations between the sexes, education, housing, and social policy.
Nor were these ideas canvassed among a limited intelligentsia only;
building workers, potters, weavers, and artisans were willing, for a
while, to risk their livelihood to put experiments to the test. The
swarming variety of journals, many of which made exacting demands
upon the readers, were addressed to an authentic working-class
audience. In the silk mills of the Colden Valley, isolated on the
Pennines between Yorkshire and Lancashire, the Owenite journals
were read.

Two themes only may be mentioned of those which arose again and

---

[51] G. Edmonds, *The English Revolution* (1831), pp. 5, 8.

again in these years. The first is that of internationalism. This was, to be sure, part of the old Jacobin heritage; and one which the Radicals had never forgotten. When Oliver tramped with the Leeds cropper, James Mann, and another revolutionary, to the rendezvous at Thornhill Lees (in 1817) he found, from their discourse, that 'the recent news from the Brazils seemed to cheer them with greater hopes than ever.'[52] Cobbett could always find time to add a stop-press to his journals:

I have just room to tell you, that the people of BELGIUM, the *common people*, have *beaten the Dutch armies*, who were marched against them to compel them to *pay enormous taxes*. This is excellent news.[53]

The French Revolution of 1830 had a profound impact upon the people, electrifying not only the London Radicals but working-class reformers in distant industrial villages. The struggle for Polish independence was followed anxiously in the working-class press; while Julian Hibbert, in the Rotunda, carried a vote of sympathy with the Lyons weavers, in their ill-fated insurrection, likening them to the weavers of Spitalfields. In the Owenite movement this political tradition was extended to embrace social and class solidarities. In 1833 a 'Manifesto of the Productive Classes of Great Britain and Ireland' was addressed to 'the Governments and People of the Continents of Europe and of North and South America', commencing: 'Men of the Great Family of Mankind . . .' By the end of the same year, the question of some common alliance between the trade unionists of England, France, and Germany had already come under discussion.[54]

The other theme was that of industrial syndicalism. When Marx was still in his teens, the battle for the minds of English trade unionists, between a capitalist and a socialist political economy, had been (at least temporarily) won. The winners were Hodgskin, Thompson, James Morrison and O'Brien; the losers were James Mill and Place. 'What is capital?' asked a writer in the *Pioneer*. 'It is reserved labour!' cries M'Culloch. . . . From whom and what was it reserved? From the clothing and food of the wretched.'[55] Hence the workers who had been 'insolently placed without the pale of social government' developed, stage by stage, a theory of syndicalism, or of 'Inverted Masonry'.[56] 'The Trades Unions will not only strike for less work, and more wages,' wrote 'A Member of the Builder's Union',

[52] Narrative of Oliver, H.O. 40.9.
[53] *Two-Penny Trash*, 1 October 1803.
[54] See, e.g. *Destructive*, 7 December 1833.
[55] *Pioneer*, 13 October 1833.
[56] *Man*, 13 October 1833.

but they will ultimately ABOLISH WAGES, become their own masters, and work for each other; labour and capital will no longer be separate but they will be indissolubly joined together in the hands of the workmen and work-women.

The unions themselves could solve the problem of political power; a 'Parliament' of the industrious classes could be formed, delegated directly from workshops and mills: 'the Lodges send Delegates from local to district, and from district to National Assemblies. Here are Universal Suffrage, Annual Election, and No Property Qualification, instanter.'[57] The idea was developed (in the *Pioneer*) of such a House of Trades:

which must supply the place of the present House of Commons, and direct the commercial affairs of the country, according to the will of the trades which compose associations of the industry. This is the ascendancy scale by which we arrive to universal suffrage. It will begin in our lodges, extend to our general union, embrace the management of trade, and finally swallow up the whole political power.[58]

This vision was lost, almost as soon as it had been found, in the terrible defeats of 1834 and 1835. And, when they had recovered their wind, the workers returned to the vote, as the more practical key to political power. Something was lost: but Chartism never entirely forgot this preoccupation with social control, to the attainment of which the vote was seen as a means. These years reveal a passing beyond the characteristic outlook of the artisan, with his desire for an independent livelihood 'by the sweat of his brow', to a newer outlook, more reconciled to the new means of production, but seeking to exert the collective power of the class to humanise the environment: – by this community or that co-operative society, by this check on the blind operation of the market-economy, this legal enactment, that measure of relief for the poor. And implicit, if not always explicit, in their outlook was the dangerous tenet: production must be, not for profit, but for *use*.

This collective self-consciousness was indeed the great spiritual gain of the Industrial Revolution, against which the disruption of an older and in many ways more humanly-comprehensible way of life must be set. It was perhaps a unique formation, this British working class of 1832. The slow, piece-meal accretions of capital accumulation had

[57] *Man*, 22 December 1833.
[58] *Pioneer*, 31 May 1834.

meant that the preliminaries to the Industrial Revolution stretched backwards for hundreds of years. From Tudor times onwards this artisan culture had grown more complex with each phase of technical and social change. Delaney, Dekker and Nashe: Winstanley and Lilburne: Bunyan and Defoe – all had at times addressed themselves to it. Enriched by the experiences of the 17th century, carrying through the 18th century the intellectual and libertarian traditions which we have described, forming their own traditions of mutuality in the friendly society and trades club, these men did not pass, in one generation, from the peasantry to the new industrial town. They suffered the experience of the Industrial Revolution as articulate, free-born Englishmen. Those who were sent to gaol might know the Bible better than those on the Bench, and those who were transported to Van Diemen's Land might ask their relatives to send Cobbett's *Register* after them.

This was, perhaps, the most distinguished popular culture England has known. It contained the massive diversity of skills, of the workers in metal, wood, textiles and ceramics, without whose inherited 'mysteries' and superb ingenuity with primitive tools the inventions of the Industrial Revolution could scarcely have got further than the drawing-board. From this culture of the craftsman and the self-taught there came scores of inventers, organisers, journalists and political theorists of impressive quality. It is easy enough to say that this culture was backward-looking or conservative. True enough, one direction of the great agitations of the artisans and outworkers, continued over fifty years, was to *resist* being turned into a proletariat. When they knew this cause was lost, yet they reached out again, in the Thirties and Forties, and sought to achieve new and only imagined forms of social control. During all this time they were, as a class, repressed and segregated in their own communities. But what the counter-revolution sought to suppress grew only more determined in the quasi-legal institutions of the underground. Whenever the pressure of the rulers relaxed, men came from the petty workshops or the weavers' hamlets and asserted new claims. They were told that they had no rights, but they knew that they were born free. The Yeomanry rode down their meeting, and the right of public meeting was gained. The pamphleteers were gaoled, and from the gaols they edited pamphlets. The trade unionists were imprisoned, and they were attended to prison by processions with bands and union banners.

Segregated in this way, their institutions acquired a peculiar toughness and resilience. Class also acquired a peculiar resonance in English life: everything, from their schools to their shops, their chapels to their

amusements, was turned into a battle-ground of class. The marks of
this remain, but by the outsider they are not always understood. If we
have in our social life little of the tradition of *égalité*, yet the class-
consciouness of the working man has little in it of deference. 'Orphans
we are, and bastards of society,' wrote James Morrison in 1834.[59] The
tone is not one of resignation but of pride.

Again and again in these years working men expressed it thus: 'they
wish to make us tools', or 'implements', or 'machines'. A witness
before the parliamentary committee enquiring into the hand-loom
weavers (1835) was asked to state the view of his fellows on the
Reform Bill:

Q. Are the working class better satisfied with the institutions of the country
since the change has taken place?
A. I do not think they are. They viewed the Reform Bill as a measure
calculated to join the middle and upper classes to Government, and leave
them in the hands of the Government as a sort of machine to work according
to the pleasure of the Government.

Such men met Utilitarianism in their daily lives, and they sought to
throw it back, not blindly, but with intelligence and moral passion.
They fought, not the machine, but the exploitive and oppressive
relationships intrinsic to industrial capitalism. In these same years, the
great Romantic criticism of Utilitarianism was running its parallel but
altogether separate course. After William Blake, no mind was at home
in both cultures, nor had the genius to interpret the two traditions to
each other. It was a muddled Mr Owen who offered to disclose the
'new moral world', while Wordsworth and Coleridge had withdrawn
behind their own ramparts of disenchantment. Hence these years
appear at times to display, not a revolutionary challenge, but a resistance movement, in which both the Romantics and the Radical craftsmen opposed the annunciation of Acquisitive Man. In the failure of the
two traditions to come to a point of junction, something was lost.
How much we cannot be sure, for we are among the losers.

Yet the working people should not be seen only as the lost myriads
of eternity. They had also nourished, for fifty years, and with in-
comparable fortitude, the Liberty Tree. We may thank them for these
years of heroic culture.

---

[59] *Pioneer*, 22 March 1834; see A. Briggs, 'The Language of "Class" in Early Nineteenth
Century England, *op. cit.*, p. 68.

8

Class and Class Consciousness in Early Nineteenth Century England: Three Classes or Five?

R. S. NEALE

The three-class model of social structure in the early nineteenth century is that in which, for the sake of convenience, individuals are placed into one of three categories: Aristocracy, Middle Class, Working Class. The boundaries of the classes, particularly of the two lower ones, are rarely clearly or explicitly explained, and there is little general agreement among writers about the bases of classification. Nevertheless this model and these categories are regularly used in analysing the interplay of economic, social, political, and cultural forces.

It is my contention that both model and categories have outlived their usefulness for any rigorous analysis of the relationship between class, class-consciousness, and political ideology in the early nineteenth century.

Of course it may be that historians and others only use the three-class model of Victorian society as a convenient shorthand form of expression for something which, implicitly, they recognize to be more complex. If this is so, then in order to communicate with each other, we need to be sure of two things. Firstly, we need to be sure that each of us uses the same shorthand symbol for the same idea, that is, we need a key to the shorthand. Secondly, we need to be sure that our system of shorthand has as many symbols as we have ideas worth expressing. It is in connection with this second observation that I wish to press my point.

From *Victorian Studies*, XII(1) (September 1968), pp. 5–25. Section V of the article is omitted.

Generations of students brought up on the conventional shorthand are too frequently hamstrung by it. Either they find difficulty in comprehending that the social structure is indeed more complex than the conventional shorthand indicates, and cling desperately to the signs they know, however unhelpful they are in pointing the way, or, when they find that the shorthand does not describe the real world, they reject altogether the possibility of handling history through the medium of aggregative concepts like class.

Some students grow up to be historians. If they do, unless they clearly and explicitly add new symbols to the shorthand and continuously refine their concepts they will find difficulty in advancing the frontiers of their discipline. They will become Schoolmen.

Take as an example the continuing debate on the standard of living between 1780–1850. By the early 1960s it had reached a stalemate because both optimists and pessimists seemed increasingly happy to regard labour as an homogeneous class experiencing and participating in the process of industrialization as a whole, and both sides were content to use one or more global indicators like mortality rates, consumption indices, and figures of national income per capita. Such an approach has its uses. For the purpose of amassing evidence about broad shifts in the rate of economic development, the growth rates of income per capita have a place. But the same approach immediately becomes useless if the problem is to say something about the welfare of specific groups of short-lived workers and to relate changes in the welfare of these groups to other phenomena. This was the reason for suggesting that historians should and could move away from the position of stalemate simply by employing a more fruitful disaggregative, regional, and multi-class approach to the problem.[1]

Recent discussion on the relationship between various social classes, class-consciousness, and ideology during the early nineteenth century seems to point to a similar stalemate. It is my purpose in this article, therefore, to take a close look at the usefulness of the conventional three-class apparatus. My schema is: (I) Show something of the limitations of the three-class model by commenting on two recent contributions to the problem of class and ideology in the early nineteenth century. These initial comments should also show that in taking to task those historians who use the three-class model as an analytical tool I choose real historians and not straw men; (II) Suggest the need for a clarification of the terminology of class; (III) Using this improved terminology and empirical data, discuss the relationship of Philosophic

---

[1] R. S. Neale, 'The Standard of Living, 1780–1844: A Regional and Class Study', *Economic History Review*, XIX (Dec. 1966), pp. 590–606.

Radicalism to English society with the purpose of showing that this relationship can be fully comprehended only if the three-class model is explicitly rejected; (IV) Suggest that we would do well to try to increase the number of concepts we can handle by abandoning the three-class model. The five-class model to replace is it described. Its purpose is to focus attention on the crucial role of a dynamic, achievement-motivated, Middling Class which, as a political class throughtout the 1820s and 1830s, was neither Middle nor Working Class; (V) Finally, use the concept of the Middling Class to throw some light upon the problem of the Charter and its relationship to class-consciousness.

I

The first contribution which shows the limitation of the three-class model is that by D. J. Rowe on the 'People's Charter'.[2] Rowe begins by positing the existence of *a* middle-class consciousness vis à vis the aristocracy and the labouring classes. He contrasts this with the absence of *a* working-class consciousness. That is, he adopts the conventional three-class descriptive model into which he incorporates the new orthodoxy about middle-class and working-class conscious-ness. Rowe then attempts to show that the Charter was not a political manifestation of working-class consciousness because the Charter, and the forerunner of the London Working Men's Association, the Association of Working Men to Procure a Cheap and Honest Press, were themselves the product of a *radical middle-class initiative*.

In arguing thus the author introduces another concept, 'a radical middle class', and makes the next analytical step, using what is in fact a four-class model. This is a useful advance. But it is so only if its main implication is made explicit. It is that the author sees the possibility of two images of social class-consciousness developing in one social class, i.e., that the one middle class in the descriptive model can generate a *radical* middle-class consciousness as well as one which is, presumably, purely *a* middle-class consciousness. The recognition of the possibility of such a phenomenon is itself a denial of the intial assumption about the existence of *a* middle-class consciousness. It could be that a more rigorous attempt to delineate the various social strata and social classes in the omnibus term 'Middle Class' might help to account for the dualism in middle class social class-consciousness which changes Rowe's model from a three-class to a four-class one.

[2] D. J. Rowe, 'The People's Charter', *Past and Present*, XXXVI (Apr. 1967), pp. 73–86.

In this same article, there is an implicit identification of *a* working-class consciousness with a 'proletarian' social consciousness. But, to approach the problem of the connection between class-consciousness and the Charter with the preconception that what one is looking for is a 'proletarian' social class-consciousness means that the historian is constrained within a mental straitjacket as soon as he attempts to show of which social class-consciousness the London Working Men's Association and the Charter were organizational and political manifestations. Again it could be that discussion of the existence of working-class consciousness would be improved given a more rigorous attempt to differentiate workers according to social stratum and social class.

Another historian, Joseph Hamburger, in attempting to identify the Philosophic Radicals, correctly concluded that their political philosophy was not an expression of middle-class aspirations.[3] But, because he began his analysis within the framework of the three-class model and because, as it were, he never went into a constituency, he also concluded that it was a political philosophy devoid of all class interest or connection. The essence of his position seems to be something like this. The Philosophic Radicals were hostile to the aristocracy. Yet they were not representative of the middle class and clearly not associated with the working class. If this was the case, where did they come from and how did they develop as a political faction? The answer given is that Philosophic Radicalism was a mental construct in the minds of its adherents owing nothing to the existence of social classes or class-consciousness, except, perhaps, that it did have a distant connection with the Philosophic Radicals' own concept of 'the People'.

In this manner, the answer narrows the range of concepts available to us. It offers the two-class model employed by the Philosophic Radicals themselves and requires us to admit their claims that they represented no class except the People in their struggle against the Aristocracy. We are asked to comprehend these historical figures according to their own self-evaluation though we know, on general grounds, that it is not uncommon for leaders of political parties to set out programmes and contribute to ideologies which they claim to be above class and other factional interests, but which, nevertheless, attract class or factional support.

An answer to the question, 'Was there any class content in the doctrines and policies of the Philosophic Radicals?' cannot be resolved simply by asking the Philosophic Radicals what the thought about the matter, or by using a three- or two-class model to find it. It can only be

[3] Joseph Hamburger, *Intellectuals in Politics: John Stuart Mill and The Philosophic Radicals* (New Haven, 1965).

found by approaching the problem of class and class-consciousness in the manner already suggested and through detailed local studies of constituency politics. Furthermore, a clarification of the class content in Philosophic Radicalism might throw additional light on the problem of class-consciousness and the Charter.

II

Historians who may be concerned with identifying the derivation and nature of class-consciousness and of political class in the early nineteenth century face problems similar to those faced by the sociologists concerned with the same question in the mid-twentieth century. These problems fall into two categories: conceptual and methodological, and empirical. Most probably the empirical problems in each period will have to be resolved in different ways. But with regard to the shared conceptual and methodological problems the concerns and methods of attack of historians and sociologists should be the same.

Four principal concepts will need to be distinguished.[4] They are social stratification, social class, class-consciousness, and political class.

Social stratification will probably be determined by some objective, measureable, and largely economic criteria such as source and size of income, occupation, years of education, or size of assets. Some aspects of stratification, however, are more likely to be identified by other less easily quantifiable criteria, i.e., by things like values, social custom, and language. Many of these criteria will be particularly difficult to identify since, in addition to the problem of measurement, they may exist in the minds of members of a social stratum only as norms which are not always matched by behaviour.

Social classes, however, are really conflict groups arising out of the authority structure of imperatively coordinated associations.[5] Social class defined in this way can be objectively identified, at least in part, by setting out the authority structure of associations. But this in itself is not enough for the identification of social class as a conflict group. At best it will produce a sorting-out of people with similar authority or subjection positions into what Ginsberg and Dahrendorf have called

[4] Since the first draft of this article was written, Irving Kraus in the *Sociological Review* has made similar observations for the benefit of sociologists (See 'Some Perspectives on Social Stratification and Social Class', XV (July 1967), pp. 129–140).

[5] An imperatively coordinated association will be any group of people in which authority is unequally distributed and in which those in dominant positions exercise legitimate authority. The State and industrial enterprises are examples of such associations.

quasi-groups. Quasi-groups, however, function as recruiting fields for classes.[6]

Whether a quasi-group produces or becomes a social class will depend upon the technical, political, and social conditions of organization and the generation of class-consciousness within it. These, in turn, will depend on the specific historical conditions. Nevertheless, the formation of a social class as a conflict group will always have much to do with the growth of sensations of collective identity of interest amongst individuals in a quasi-group vis à vis other groups or social classes, and much to do with relationships of authority and subjection as felt and experienced in a quasi-group. The crucial notion to grasp is that there is a distinction between social stratification and social class, and that social classes are conflict groups based on relationships of authority and subjection.

The existence of social class as a political class will be most easily inferred from the existence of continuously organized political and/or industrial action.

It is at the point of determination of the existence of class-consciousness that the investigator should be especially careful to make explicit his preconceptions about class-consciousness. It is all too easy, as the example of Rowe shows, to slip into assuming that a working-class consciousness must be a 'proletarian' one. Historians who do assume this will, of course, look for what they assume. Consequently it will be what they find or do not find. The same will be true of the search for a middle-class consciousness. In connection with this problem Lockwood has recently reminded us that in the twentieth century there is at least a trinity of working-class social consciousness: 'proletarian', 'deferential', and 'privatized'.[7] The first two terms are readily understood, but the 'privatized' worker is one whose work situation is socially isolating and whose social consciousness will approximate most nearly to a pecuniary model of society in which the cash nexus is the dominant relationship between individuals. It is important that, with some modification, we carry this reminder with us into the study of the early nineteenth century.

---

[6] Morris Ginsberg, *Sociology* (London, 1953), p. 40; Ralf Dahrendorff, *Class and Class Conflict in an Industrial Society* (Stanford, Cal., 1959), p. 180. Much of the general theoretical underpinning for this article is derived from a simplified version of Dahrendorf's brilliant exposition, particularly pp. 157–205.

[7] David Lockwood, 'Sources of Variation in Working Class Images of Society', *Sociological Review*, XIV (Nov. 1966), 249–67; John H. Goldthorpe and David Lockwood, Affluence and British Class Structure', *Sociological Review*, XI (July 1963), pp. 133–63; see also E. A. Nordlinger, *The Working Class Tories* (London, 1967).

III

Any attempt to describe social stratification and social class for the early nineteenth century must incorporate at least two broad groups of factors if it is to bear any relation to the world as contemporaries saw it. These are: for social stratification, things like occupation, income, wealth, and manners; and, for social class, authority positions derived from ascribed status as conferred according to the consensus of opinion and convention about rank, pedigree, and authority. In contemporary opinion authority positions derived from ascribed status generally outweighed income, wealth, and occupation whilst the latter, by themselves, rarely granted status and authority. Because of the difficulty in weighing these opposing elements in some rational balance, much of early nineteenth-century literature centred on the problem of social identity. This problem of social identity was further complicated as the traditional status of high-ranking social classes was eroded through the increase in geographic and social mobility associated with rapid economic growth. Nevertheless, for a large part of the nineteenth century an important determinant of social class, and a very important element in relationships of authority and subjection, was derived from ascribed status and authority.[8]

[8] One of the most perceptive comments on the subtleties of barriers at the end of the nineteenth century between the Upper Middle classes, the county families, and the aristocracy on the one hand and an aspiring member of the professional classes on the other is given in Leonard Woolf's autobiography. It places him in my Middling Class and is worth quoting at length: 'I was glad when the tour of introductions ended. The children of Sir Leslie Stephen had, at the turn of the century, when their father died, broken away from the society into which they were born. That society consisted of the upper levels of the professional middle class and county families, interpenetrated to a certain extent by the aristocracy. But, although Vanessa, Virginia, and Adrian had broken away from it and from Kensington and Mayfair to live in Bloomsbury what seemed to their relations and old family friends a Bohemian life, there was no complete rupture; they still from time to time saw socially their Stephen and Duckworth relations and the old family friends. It was a social class and way of life into which hitherto I had only dipped from time to time as an outsider, when, for instance, I stayed as a young man with the Stracheys. I was an outsider to this class, because, although I and my father before me belonged to the professional middle class, we had only recently struggled up into it from the stratum of Jewish shopkeepers. We had no roots in it. The psychology of the different strata of English society is extremely important in its effects upon the individual (or was 50 years ago). The Stephens and the Stracheys, the Ritchies, Thackerays, and Duckworths had an intricate tangle of ancient roots and tendrils stretching far and wide through the upper middle classes, the county families, and the aristocracy. Socially they assumed things unconsciously which I could never assume either unconsciously or consciously. They lived in a peculiar atmosphere of influence, manners, respectability, and it was so natural to them that they were unaware of it as mammals are unaware of the air and fish of the water in which they live. Now that I was going to marry Virginia and went round to see her relations I began to see this stratum of society from the inside. I said in *Sowing* that I know that I am ambivalent to aristocratic societies, disliking and despising them and at the same time envying them their insolent urbanity. In a milder form there was the

In these circumstances it is unlikely that any social class–consciousness, other that a deferential one, will be found at the lower end of the social stratification and social class spectrums. Likewise, where the barriers to higher status for the most economically successful of the aspirants for higher status are surmountable at some level of achievement, the social class-consciousness of new members of the highest social strata is likely to be deferential vis à vis those with high ascribed status, and they are likely to be more willing than unwilling to conform to the mores of those already strong in an authority derived from it. In practice they are likely to be desperate for approval. Therefore, one should look elsewhere for situations more likely to be productive of conflict between those with and without authority, hence more likely to be productive of a social class-consciousness resulting in the formation of a political class.

Such a situation is one in which there appears to be an unresolvable incongruity between the positions men have according to social stratification and ascribed status. Where men possessed of a high need for achievement[9] move from lower to higher social strata whilst retaining low ascribed status and are geographically concentrated in regions in which insistence on the observance of traditional relationships remains strong, a quasi-group generating a social class-consciousness which is highly privatized or individuated and non–deferential is likely to emerge. Furthermore, because of the geographic concentration and strength of traditional relationships, this social class-consciousness is likely to lead to attempts by individuals in the quasi-group to overcome their isolation and produce a political class hostile to traditional authority.[10] The point is that men come to recognize a personal conflict and begin to identify their own dilemma with those conflict situations in society at large which may be formulated in

---

same ambivalence in my attitude to the society which I found in Dalingridge Place and St. George's Square. I disliked its respectability and assumptions while envying and fearing its assurance and manners. I should, perhaps, add that the class stratum or strata which I have been writing about in this paragraph are now practically extinct; they were almost destroyed by the 1914 war and were finally wiped away in the 1939 war' (Leonard Woolf, *Beginning Again: An Autobiography of the Years 1911–1918* (London, 1964), pp. 74–5). Gissing was the writer who best expressed the predicament of the less successful members of the Middling Class after their brief moment of glory during the early nineteenth century.

[9] I consider this concept self-explanatory. However, any reader interested in it and in the possibility of its connection with economic growth should start with David C. McClelland, *The Achieving Society* (Princeton, N.J., 1961). In my view McClelland has made out a *prima facie* case for a close causal relationship between high achievement motivation and high rates of economic growth.

[10] Evidence for this generalization is in R. S. Neale 'Class and Ideology in a Provincial City: Bath 1800–1050', *Our History*, Pamphlet 42 (Summer 1966). Also see below.

general or philosophic terms. In these circumstances class conflict is likely to be intense. This, in short, was the basis of class conflict and of the emergence of a Middling Class with a social class-consciousness making them receptive to the ideas of the Philosophic Radicals through the 1820s and 1830s. It came about as follows.

In the course of the eighteenth century there was an acceleration in the rate of industrial growth and change. Consequently there were more opportunities for advancement. At the same time population grew and there were many more applicants for both old and new opportunities. This increase of applicants was the result of the increase in family size and the uncertainties of economic life which repeatedly reduced erstwhile economically successful families to indigence. Probably the number of respectable places for the increasing number of sons grew less than the number of applicants.[11] On the other hand many of the places that were created were still allocated through nepotism, influence, and graft.[12] Even where opportunities for economic advancement existed traditional restraints associated with

[11] Very little work has been done on the standard of living or the employment opportunities of the Middling Class during the early nineteenth century; nevertheless, a number of studies suggest that economic growth faltered and the real income of many social strata declined during the 1830s:

	Growth rate of total national product per capita	
1801/11 – 1831/41	1.5% p.a.	
1811/21 – 1841/51	1.4% p.a.	
1821/31 – 1851/61	0.9% p.a.	

(Phyllis Deane and W. A. Cole, *British Economic Growth, 1688–1959: Trends and Structure* [Cambridge, 1962], p. 172.)

	Income per capita	Prices (1800 = 100)
1831	£25.90	69
1841	£23.99	76

(Phyllis Deane 'Contemporary Estimates of National Income in the First Half of the Nineteenth Century', *Economic History Review* VIII (Apr. 1956), 353.)

	Real wages in Bath (1838 = 100)
1833	114
1837	93
1839	102

(Neal, 'The Standard of Living' 1780–1844', Appendix B, p. 604.)
In giving evidence before Edwin Chadwick in 1834 the Assistant Overseer of the Parish of St. George in Southwark said, 'Indeed the malady of Pauperism has not only got amongst respectable mechanics, but we find even persons who may be considered of the middle class, such as petty masters, small master bricklayers and other such persons, who have never before been seen making application to parish officers, now applying' *(Report From His Majesty's Committee for Inquiring into the Administration and Practical Operation of the Poor Laws, Parliamentary Papers, 1834* [44], xxvii, p. 26).

[12] *The Extraordinary Black Book* ..., ed. John Wade (London, 1832), particularly pp. 452–590; *Luke Graves Hansard, His Diary, 1814–1841: A Case Study in the Reform of Patronage*, ed. Percy and Grace Ford (Oxford, 1962). At the level of local and parish politics see *The Resolutions and Petition of the Freeholders, Householders and Inhabitants of the City of Bath 1817*, and *The Report of the Committee appointed to examine into and control the Receipts and Expenditure of the Parish of Walcot 1817*, both in the Bath Public Library.

status continued to bear heavily. Furthermore the growth of urban communities created large pockets of these aspiring and marginally disaffected men.

In more concrete terms, the early stages of industrialization in Britain brought about a proliferation of petty producers, retailers, and tradesmen – collectively the petit bourgeois – and a class of professional men, as well as bringing into existence the big industrial, commercial, and professional capitalist – the big bourgeois. The children of the petit bourgeois and of the professionals flooded the grammar and private school systems only to be turned out half-educated, half-gentlemen unfitted for industrial employment.[13] Accustomed to living standards something above subsistence, they feared a decline to some lower social strata. Many of them also lacked the capital and connections as well as the education which might have brought them the rewards they had come to feel were properly theirs. As this group of what I call 'literates' came to maturity they added to the competition for the limited number of respectable places.

In this manner the middle classes came to include at least two sub-groups or social strata whose economic experience and status relationships with other groups created conditions favourable to the development of a social class-consciousness which was especially highly individuated and non-deferential. These were the petit bourgeois and the professionals, and the literates. Many of the latter might well be described as underemployed intellectuals. Such was James Mill. Such, too, were the ninety-seven barristers contending for eighty-nine briefs at the York Assizes in 1840.[14] Members of the literate and professional social strata possessed of few liquid assets and having no property or connections were particularly inclined to assert the rights of man as against the rights of property, status, and traditional authority. Prominent among them were doctors as well as lawyers.

By the 1820s, individuals in these social strata were also members of a social class in the sense that enough of them were sufficiently class-conscious to cooperate with each other in organized political

[13] See the *Reports of the Charity Commissioners* printed between 1815 and 1839. There is an instructive account of the changing class origin of university students in W. M. Mathew, 'The Origins and Occupations of Glasgow Students, 1740–1839', *Past and Present*, XXXIII (Apr. 1966), pp. 74–94, particularly p. 80. For a case study of the son of a government official see the author's 'H. S. Chapman and the Victorian Ballot', *Historical Studies: Australia and New Zealand*, XII (Apr. 1967), pp. 506–21. For an account of the fortunes of the son of a merchant in the Atlantic trade ruined by the revolt of the colonies, see 'The Letters of William Neate Chapman', with a preface by Sir F. R. Chapman, holograph collection in the Mitchell Library, Sydney, Location A1974.

[14] See *Westminster Review*, XXXIV (1840), p. 134.

activity, particularly at local level. They were becoming a political class to be reckoned with. Sometimes, as in their opposition to aristocratic privilege, they appear to be submerged in the omnibus 'Middle Class'. Indeed in the 'Middle Class' agitation for reform the men who did the work in the constituencies and the political unions were often men from these two social strata.[15] Nevertheless a distinctive element in their social class-consciousness was a sense of difference from other sections of the 'Middle Class'.[16] Their social class-consciousness was not always at one with that of the more cautious, propertied, and outstandingly successful members of the commercial and industrial bourgeoisie, the older gentry, senior military and naval men, successful professional men, or those on fixed incomes.

Edward Gibbon Wakefield, who had squandered a small fortune and slipped a few rungs on the social ladder as a result, had a collective name for both the petit bourgeois and the underemployed literates. It was the 'Uneasy Class'. 'Distress,' he wrote,

is not confined to those small capitalists who employ a material capital. The learning, skill and reputation, united, of a professional man may be called his capital. Great professional capitalists, those who possess all at once great skill, great learning and a high reputation still make large incomes: but none of those, whose learning or skill or reputation is small, make enough to live upon. . . . Two thirds, therefore, at the very least, of professional men may be reckoned amongst the uneasy class. . . . The general rule with daughters of men of small income, whether fixed or not is a choice between celibacy and marriage with one of the uneasy class. Now, a great proportion of young men in the uneasy class dread marriage, unless there be a fortune in the case, as the surest means of increasing their embarrassment. This is one of the most important features in the social state of England.[17]

The point to be noted is the belief that the 'Uneasy Class' existed as a class which included lesser professional men who had interests dif-

[15] In London, Francis Place. In Birmingham, George Edwards and even Joseph Parkes – see G. J. Holyoake, *Life of Holyoake: Sixty Years of an Agitator's Life* (London, 1906), pp. 26–32, Asa Briggs, 'Thomas Attwood and the Economic Background of the Birmingham Political Union', *Cambridge Historical Journal*, IX (1948), p. 196; Mrs Grote, *The Personal Life of George Grote* (London, 1873), p. 79; also the discussion on Parkes in Hamburger. In Leicester, John and William Biggs – See A. Temple Patterson, *Radical Leicester* (Leicester, 1954), pp 181–9 In Bath, Thomas Falconer, George Cox, and a score of others – see R. S. Neale, 'Economic Conditions and Working Class Movements in the City of Bath, 1800–1850', unpublished M. A. thesis, Bristol University (1963) and *Bath 1680–1850: A Social History* (London, 1981).

[16] See n. 8, and the bitter correspondence between George Cox, a successful master hatter and the superintendent of a Baptist Sunday School, and H. E. Carrington, editor of the *Bath Chronicle*, in the *Bath Journal*, 10 June 1833, *Bath Chronicle*, 13 June 1833, and the *Bath and Cheltenham Gazette*, 18 June 1833.

[17] *England and America* (London, 1833), pp. 94–5.

ferent from those of the successful professional men just as the
interests of the petit bourgeois were different from those of the big
bourgeois. Distressed they may have been, aspiring they certainly
were. In this they were like the petit bourgeois. Whatever the real
reasons for the frustration of the ambition of these people they came to
believe that a very important one was the weight of ancient restriction
and aristocratic and oligarchic privilege. What was additionally galling
were the attitudes of superiority adopted by people who were regarded
by the petit bourgeois and the literates as inferior to themselves, at
least in terms of usefulness and intellect.

The most successful and systematic political ideology to which the
class-conscious in the two social strata most readily subscribed was
Philosophic Radicalism. But even the Philosophic Radicals were not
always unanimous or united.[18] Like other political groupings they
spread over a spectrum, which in their case is best expressed in terms
not of left and right, but of ultra and whiggish. By the mid-1830s the
ultra wing circulated loosely around the waspish and doctrinaire J. A.
Roebuck who, according to J. S. Mill, was that unique figure in
English politics, a Napoleon-Ideologue.[19] Perhaps, since Mill was
himself atypical, his comment about the politcal uniqueness of Roebuck
should act as a warning against any easy acceptance of the proposition
that the political ideology of Roebuck and his associates was a manifestation of something called a middle-class consciousness.[20] There is also
reason to doubt whether the phrase 'radical middle class' is an adequate
shorthand term for them. It is vague and can easily be used in a way
which makes it only a little less inclusive than the parent term, 'Middle

[18] The political question distinguishing the Philosophic Radicals most clearly from other
radicals was the Ballot, and that distinguishing 'ultra' Philosophic Radicals from the rest was
their support for the French Canadians even when the latter became rebels.

[19] See Mill to Carlyle, 22 Oct. 1832, to John Nicol, 10 July 1833, to Gustav D'Eichthal,
29 Nov. 1834, to Aristide Guilbert, 19 Mar. 1835, in *The Ealier Letters, 1812–1848*, ed. F. E.
Mineka, Vol. XII of *The Collected Works of John Stuart Mill*, ed. J. M. Robson (London, 1963).
For the ineffectiveness of Grote as leader right from the start see Mill to D'Eichthal, 29 Nov.
1834, and to Carlyle, 22 Dec. 1833 – 'Grote has gradually sunk into a state always too congenial
to him of thinking that no good is to be done and who therefore will certainly never do any'. See
also Mrs M. G. Fawcett, *Life of Sir William Molesworth* (London, 1901), p. 122. Nevertheless, see
H. S. Chapman to H. Chapman, 4 Mar. 1847: 'Roebuck set up to lead a party – he might have led
a small party of Radicals, but – I doubt if any of the radical party of 1835, when the party was
strong would have acted with him. The Roebuck Pamphlets show his arrogant assumption of
superiority, and it was by the early numbers of it that he lost some personal friends; Grote,
Molesworth, the Romillies' (Chapman Holograph Letters MSS, Papers 53 Chapman IIb,
Alexander Turnbull Library, Wellington).

[20] Morse Peckham has recently suggested that most outstanding literary Victorians were in
fact anti-Victorian; see 'Can "Victorian" have a Useful Meaning?', *Victorian Studies*, X (Mar.
1967), pp. 273–7. In many ways the Philosophic Radicals were also politically anti-Victorian
although their ideas did much to shape Victorian England.

Class'. Leading Philosophic Radicals were themselves aware of this danger. Consequently they attempted to dissociate themselves from other forms of radicalism and to identify themselves with the dynamic elements in society by referring to themselves either as Philosophic Radicals or as exponents of 'movement' radicalism.[21] Like Marxist socialists they turned their backs on utopian forms of their basic ideology and claimed to be rigorously scientific. A further qualitative difference between the Philosophic Radicals and those often described as 'the radical middle class' is best comprehended by those who have grasped something of the qualitative difference between the Bolsheviks and the Mensheviks.

It is, indeed, difficult to place the leaders of the Philosophic Radicals into any one social spectrum or social class. As an income group they were spread wide, from Sir William Molesworth, who paid £4,000 out of income to support the *London Review*, through J. S. Mill on £1,200 a year to H. S. Chapman struggling in the best years on a mere £260.[22] They ranged in social status from Charles Buller, Esquire, who was a darling man and of Cornwall's best, to Mr Francis Plate, a successful breeches maker, or to Roebuck himself, the barrister stepson of a Canadian farmer. On occasion they touched shoulders with deviant aristocrats who were among the leading men in the country, like Lords Durham and Brougham. In terms of education, although not of intellect, the range was equally great.

Nevertheless, neither the diversity of origin of the intellectual and parliamentary leaders, nor the doctrinal nature of their political beliefs, nor yet their claim to represent the whole of 'the People' should divert attention away from the fact that Philosophic Radicalism was an ideology with appeal to a clearly differentiated class in the constituencies. Philosophic Radicals who were also members of parliament, like Roebuck, Hume, Grote, and Charles Buller, rested solidly on the electoral support of tradesmen, artisans, petty producers, and a few military and professional men. Roebuck, for example, had the active support of both Napiers, and of a great many shopkeepers and producers; and his right-hand man in many a national issue was H. S. Chapman, an ex-bank clerk and unsuccessful commission agent turned political journalist and agitator. That contemporaries recognized the class nature of this movement is suggested by the fact that, in the Tory

[21] Mill To Albany Fonblanque, 30 Jam. 1838, in *The Earlier Letters*; J. S. Mill, *Autobiography*, Signet Edn. (New York, 1964), pp. 89–93; H. S. Chapman, letters in *The Western Vindicator* dated 7 Feb. to 2 Mar. 1835, in Chapman Papers, Scrap Book M. G. 24 B31, Public Archives of Canada. See also *Pamphlets for the People*, various authors, June 1835 through Feb. 1836; and Hamburger.

[22] At one stage they also included Charles Austin, a barrister earning £40,000 a year.

and Whig press, these supporters of the Philosophic Radicals were execrated by, and on behalf of, the gentry and the middle class. In Bath, for example, the opponents of Roebuck frightened the respectable middle classes, as well as the aristocracy, with images of blood, the French Revolution, republicanism, and American democracy.[23]

Roebuck and the ultras constituted the group which, above all others, attempted to translate intellectual Philosophic Radicalism into a political programme at constituency level. After the demise of the *Poor Man's Guardian* in 1835 they were also the main agents disseminating radical propaganda to lower social strata. It is true that they included members of the 'Middle Class' among their converts and adherents. Indeed some Philosophic Radicals believed that they ought to confine their educational activities to the 'Middle Class'. J. S. Mill for example, advised the Saint Simonian Missionaries to this effect.[24] Roebuck on the other hand believed in trying to get through to those social strata whose members did not normally read the literary reviews and political quarterlies. To achieve this object Roebuck, assisted by Chapman and others, produced a series of *Pamphlets for the People* which retailed at 1½d. and reached a circulation of 10,000 in 1835 and the early part of 1836. These pamphlets represented a sustained attempt to present a systematic political doctrine based on Philosophic Radicalism to be a section of the reading public much wider than anything one could call 'Middle Class' or even 'Radical Middle Class'. They were also part of the campaign against the Newspaper Stamp at the head of which was a committee on which Dr J. R. Black and Francis Place (allegedly representative of middle-class consciousness) worked with Chapman, Thomas Falconer (another ultra), and others, to promote 300 petitions to Parliament on the subject.[25]

At the heart of these pamphlets and of Roebuck's programme was a seven-point Radical Charter. This Charter, written by H. S. Chapman and published in 1835, demanded an occupier suffrage, abolition of the property qualification, the Ballot, abolition of the existing method of registration, equal electoral districts, shorter parliaments, and abolition of the Newspaper Stamp.[26] Elsewhere the ultras emphasized the importance of the Ballot, the case for single-chamber government, a wholesale reform of the law, national education, the abolition of all

[23] See Mrs Grote, *Life of Grote;* Neale, 'The Standard of Living, 1780–1844'; 'The Diary of Fanny Chapman', in the Rosenberg Collection, Christchurch. In 1832 Charles Buller was returned unopposed for his old constituency of Liskeard.

[24] Mill to D'Eichthal, 7 Nov. 1829, and 9 Feb. 1830, in *The Ealier Letters*, especially p. 49.

[25] C. D. Collet, *History of the Taxes on Knowledge: Their Origin and Repeal* (London, 1933), p. 25.

[26] J. A. Roebuck, *Pamphlets for the People*, No. 22.

monopolies and privilege, municipal reform, and, through a reduction in government expenditure, a reduction in taxation. They also gave their support to the Canadian Radicals through two rebellions, and opposed Durham's ordinance and the Durham Report.

The social class to which these views appealed was made up of those who were low in the traditional scale of status and privilege, i.e., towards the bottom in relationships of authority and subjection, and those in this position who aspired to rise and could only do so through their own unaided efforts, whether efforts of mind and skill in trade and manufacture, or in the professions. It was, therefore, and whatever its theoretical or philosophic origin, a political philosophy well suited to a society of petty producers and petit bourgeois. It mirrored that individuated, privatised, and non–deferential social class–consciousness which grew amongst a middling set of people in a rapidly expanding and changing society, but which in no modern or late-nineteenth-century sense was 'Middle Class'. This set of people or quasi-group included compositors as well as doctors, artisans as well as small producers, self-employed shopkeepers as well as bigger and more successful retailers. In Bath, where these groups were physically concentrated, despised by their customers, untouched by large-scale industry and technological innovation, and unacquainted with the phenomenon of an urban proletariat as distinct from the traditional urban poor and unskilled, their consciousness of themselves as a cooperating political class became particularly strong. There was less distinction in social stratification, status and social class-consciousness between employers and employed, between skilled and professional workers, than there was between producers (of all kinds) and aristocratic consumers, and between regularly employed artisans and the mass of the poor. There was also little point of contact between the 'factoryized' proletariat of the northern regions and the local artisans.[27]

[27] See Neale 'Class and Ideology'; Conrad Gill, *Manor and Borough to 1865*, Vol, I in *The History of Birmingham* (London, 1952), pp. 200–13; and Asa Briggs, 'Thomas Attwood and the Economic Background of the Birmingham Political Union', pp. 199–200, for a similar view of Birmingham. The following letter shows something of the privatized and non-deferential characteristics of highly skilled and scarce artisans:

Thomas Rodda to Guest Lewis and Co.   William & Mary Mine,
                                                       Tavistock, Devon, April 23rd,
                                                       1837

In answer to your letter that I received from you on the 21st instant, I cannot think of agreeing with you for that wages which you have offered me 28/- per week, and as you have added the Blast pumps to the pit work, which I have no doubt but what the Blast pumps will require a great deal more tendance than the water lifts in the mine. You say you are not in the habit of allowing house rent and coals which i understand that House rent is very high. I should be very happy to engage in your service if the money you have offered would be sufficient to maintain my

This class of petit bourgeois and literates to which we have added the artisans, was the vanguaged of 'the People' so much admired by leading Philosophic Radicals. And 'the People' was really a Middling Class which was still neither Middle Class nor Working Class. Indeed because of the insistence of Philosophic Radicals on the need for education and enlightenment it seems very likely that their image of 'the People' was dominated by their own self-image and by their image of the industrious and literate workman and shopkeeper: by their image of a Middling Class. Certainly 'the People' addressed by Roebuck and others in the *Pamphlets for the People* were deemed to be rational, literate, and respectable, even though they ranked low in the order of social stratification and social class. And, although the concept of 'the People' was meant to include everyone outside the ranks of the aristocracy, it was never intended to be used as a concept including the mob or the masses. Indeed James Mill expressly excluded half the population from his image of 'the People' since for him women were not people. The idea the concept was meant to convey was that of the mob or the masses after having been provided with the means of economic independence and after their transformation into respectable and responsible members of the middling set of people through a universal education based on associationist psychology.[28] Roebuck made no bones about it: 'My object has been through life to make the working man as exalted and civilized a creature as I could make him. I wanted to place before his mind a picture of civilized life such as I see in my own life . . . my household has been a civilized household. It has been a household in which thought, high and elevated ideas of literature, and grace and beauty, have always found everything that could recommend them . . . I wanted to make the working man like me.'[29]

---

famely. i see it will not answer to remove them before i see the work. If you will alow me half of my expenses of coming to Dowlais Iron Works, which will be about £3, I will come and see you before I make any agreement, which I have no boubt but what I should agree with you for the work and give you every satisfaction that you require from me.
(*Iron in the Making: Dowlais Iron Company Letters, 1782–1860* (Cardiff, 1960), p. 26.)
For an indication of the extent of mobility between the upper and lower social strata in the hosiery industry, see Charlotte Erickson, *British Industrialists: Steel and Hosiery, 1850–1950* (Cambridge, 1959), pp. 94–9.

[28] The importance of education in this connection is nowhere more clearly emphasized than in the *Report of the Royal Commission on Hand Loom Weavers (Parliamentary Papers*, 1841 [296], 273) and the *Reports of Assistant Commissioners (Parliamentary Papers*, 1839 [159], 511 and 1840 [217], xxiv, 1; [220], xxiv 373). See particularly the report on the West Riding of Yorkshire; also Roebuck's election address for 1832. A twentieth-century version of what the Philosophic Radicals had to say about the social function of eduction is in H. G. Johnson, 'An Economic Approach to Social Questions', *Economica* XXXV (Feb. 1968), particularly pp. 17–21.

[29] R. Eadon Leader, *Autobiography of Rt. Hon. J. A. Roebuck* (London, 1897), p. 325. Compare Lovett's very similar view in *Life and Struggles of William Lovett* (London, 1967), p. 78.

The print by Henry Harris of 'The Gathering of the Unions in Birmingham in 1832'[30] is a pictorial representation of this image. Harris created the impression of numbers through dots signifying countless thousands of bodyless heads, and he emphasized the significance of individuals through the detail of the figures in the foreground. The women, a minority amongst them, are properly shawled and bonneted. The men are toppered and best-suited. Everywhere there is earnest conversation and attentions. There is only one beer or mineral water drinker with his back to the procession, but he is dressed in a smock. The slogan most clearly readable is 'An honest man is the noblest work of God.'

As for the general question of the apparent separation of Philosophic Radicalism from social class, it was Marx who, in another context, suggested an answer. Writing of the coalition between the petit bourgeois and the workers in 1848, and of the content of French social democracy, he said,

This content is the transformation of society in democratic way, but a transformation within the bounds of the petty bourgeoisie. Only one must not form the narrow-minded notion that the petty bourgeoisie, on principle, wishes to enforce an egoistic class interest. Rather, it believes that the *special* conditions of its emancipation are the general conditions within the frame of which alone modern society can be saved and the class struggle avoided. Just as little must one imagine that the democratic representatives are indeed all shopkeepers or enthusiastic champions of shopkeepers. According to their education and their individual position they may be as far apart as heaven from earth. What makes them representative of the petty bourgeoisie is the fact that in their minds they do not go beyond the limits which the latter do not go beyond in life, that they are consequently driven, theoretically, to the same problems and solutions to which material interest and social position drive the latter practically. This is, in general, the relationship between the *political* and *literary* representatives of a class and the class they represent.[31]

It certainly seems to have been part of the relationship between the ultra wing of the Philosophic Radicals and their constituency workers and supporters.

The general point which I would like to make in connection with this brief survey is that we should not engage in an endless round of argument, based on limited alternatives, as to whether this or that political phenomenon was or was not the manifestation of a Middle- or Working-Class consciousness. A more fruitful approach would be

---

[30] This print is reproduced in Gill, p. 210.
[31] Karl Mark and Friedrich Engels, *Selected Works in Two Volumes* (London, 1950); see Vol. I, The Eighteenth Brumaire of Louis Bonaparte, pp. 249–50.

to discard the three-class model altogether and open up a greater range of possibilities by using a basic model containing a minimum of five classes and employing the category of a Middling Class.

IV

Before the five-class model is introduced it is worth observing that although early Victorians often talked collectively of the 'middle class', and the 'labouring classes', 'the people', and even the 'working class', they behaved as if there was a multiplicity of classes the nuances of which were comprehensible to the population at large. Anyone accustomed to reading early nineteenth-century directories and local newspapers will be well acquainted with the usage, whereby a man with the name John Smith would be placed in any one of a number of categories: John Smith Esq.; Mr John Smith; John Smith carpenter or butcher; John Smith labourer; or just John Smith. At the bottom, of couse, was John Smith's wife. Formal lists, like the lists of arrivals in the City of Bath,[32] would begin higher up with Lord John Smith, and work down through Sir John Smith, Col. John Smith, Rev. or Dr John Smith, to John Smith Esq. The result, a division into ten degrees or orders. Yet other works like Webster's *Encyclopaedia of Domestic Economy*[33] divided the five orders, ranging from Lord John Smith to John Smith Esq, into nine divisions according to income and number of servants. They ranged from 'An estalishment of the first rate fit for a nobleman with an income of over £5,000 p.a. employing twenty to twenty-four domestics', to one of the ninth rate with an income of £150 to £200 per annum employing a maid of all work. In addition, servants were carefully ranked in twenty-two categories.

A society as status conscious as this will appear to be cramped even within a five-class model. If, however, it is borne in mind that this approach to the ranking of people is concerned not with social classes as defined above but simply with social stratification, and if it is realised that each of the five social classes can embrace more than one social stratum however delineated, and if women are recognized as a sub-group in each social class, then the model could be made complex enough even for those historians who deny the usefulness of the

---

[32] Published weekly in the *Bath Chronicle*.

[33] T. A. Webster, *Encyclopaedia of Domestic Economy* (London, 1844), pp. 330–1. An enlightening discussion on relationships between these orders is in Brougham's review of Isaac Tomkins, *Thoughts upon the Aristocracy of England* in the *Edinburgh Review*, CXXIII (Apr. 1835), 64–70.

concept of class.[34] Nevertheless, for the purpose of understanding the nature and existence of social and political class, five classes make better sense that many even if many could be shown to exist.

The basic five-class model is made up as follows:

(1) *Upper Class*, aristocratic, landholding, authoritarian, exclusive.

(2) *Middle Class*, industrial and commercial property owners, senior military and professional men, aspiring to acceptance by the Upper Class. Deferential towards the Upper Class because of this and because of concern for property and achieved position, but individuated or privatized.

(3) *Middling Class*,[35] petit bourgeois, aspiring professional men, other literates, and artisans. Individuated or privatized like the Middle Class but collectively less deferential and more concerned to remove the privileges and authority of the Upper Class in which, without radical changes, they cannot realistically hope to share.

(4) *Working Class A*, industrial proletariat in factory areas, workers in domestic industries, collectivist and non-deferential, and wanting government intervention to protect rather than liberate them.

(5) *Working Class B*, agricultural labourers, other low-paid non-factory urban labourers, domestic servants, urban poor, most working-class women whether from Working Class A or B households, deferential and dependent.

This model is a static one. Yet one thing certain about early Victorian England is that it was changing. How then to incorporate a dynamic element?

The first thing to do is to cease visualizing or conceptualizing social strata or social classes as separate boxes, whether arranged vertically as in the traditional and United Nations models, or horizontally as in the

---

[34] Some historians consider that model-building has no value: see W. A. Speck, 'Social Status in Late Stuart England', *Past and Present*, XXXIV (July 1966), pp. 127–9. Yet the fact remains, unless our minds are blanks, that each of us *does* have a set of preconceptions which is carried around with, and mixed up in, whatever happens to be our favourite stereotype. For example, those who believe that history can best be treated by having regard to the uniqueness of each person either as an individual capable of a rational free choice or as the psychological product of a unique set of circumstances, are also model-building. In their models every individual is in a stratum or class of his own and relationships between strata and classes are unique to each group of strata or classes concerned. The corollary of such a model is that history is biography and that there can be no history until all the biographies are written. One supreme value in model-building is that it serves to make explicit the essence of the conceptual apparatus used, and of the assumptions which are always made.

[35] For examples of contemporary uses of this term see Asa Briggs 'The Language of "Class" in Early Nineteenth Century England', in *Essays in Labour History*, ed. Asa Briggs and John Saville (London, 1960), pp. 40–73.

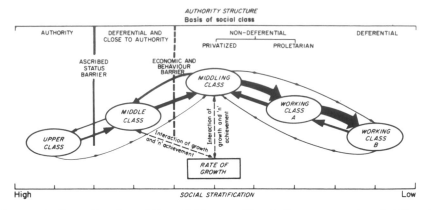

Arrows indicate direction of flow. Thickness of line indicates guessed probability of moving from one class to another circa 1800 (probabilities will vary with rate of growth, 'n' achievement, time, population growth, and the strength of barriers). Given sustained growth the probabilities of moving from low to high increase, the probabilities of moving from high to low decrease.

Figure 1 *Diagram of the five-class model*

San Gimignano model.[36] Instead, think of the five classes, each embracing a number of social strata, as separate pools of water linked together by streams of water and located on a convex but asymmetrical hill with the Middling Class on the summit exposed to all the elements. The Upper and Middle Class pools lie on the sheltered sunny side of the hill and both Working Class pools lie on the higher and more exposed northern slope. The stream linking the summit or Middling Class pool to the Middle and Upper Class pools is controlled by traditional sluices between each pool. The two Working Class pools are linked to each other and the Middling Class pool by more sluggish streams but there are not obstacles to the downward flow of water although eddies will result in water moving backwards and forwards between any two pools.

Visualized in this way the Middling Class will begin to appear as the central and most unstable class. It undergoes continuous replacement from a variety of sources; from successful occupants of upper social strata in Working Class A, although very rarely from Working Class B, from less successful occupants, and their children, of the Upper and Middle Classes, as well as from its own natural increase. It also loses population to all other classes. Consequently the Middling Class itself

[36] For a discussion of the United Nations and San Gimignano models of social stratification and structure see Lawrence Stone 'Social Mobility in England, 1500–1700', *Past and Present*, XXXIII (Apr. 1966), pp. 16–55.

displays divergent political and social tendencies. In times of rapid economic growth and when traditional ascriptive relationships of authority and subjection are weak or absent there is likely to be a shift of many people to higher social strata and social classes. Where, however, traditional relationships of authority and subjection remain strong men may move from low to higher social strata without any effect on their authority positions. In this circumstance there will develop a strong Middling Class consciousness the essence of which is that it is individuated and non-deferential. The political class engendered by this class-consciousness will contend for power against established authority. At other times the political way in which the disparate, because individuated or privatized, elements of the Middling Class will jump, will depend on specific historical conditions.[37]

By the 1820s enough people in the social strata covered by the Middling Class had generated sufficient similar social class-consciousness to develop as a political class at least in some regions. The Upper and Middle Classes were also class-conscious and productive of political classes. Working Class A was beginning to develop a distinctive proletarian social class-consciousness, again in some regions, and was beginning to emerge as a political class. Working Class B, however, was a long way from developing a social class-consciousness that was anything other than deferential, and a long way from appearing as a distinctive political class.

The essential purpose of the model, in contrast with the three-class one, is that it represents an attempt to formulate a conceptual apparatus which focuses attention on a number of crucial aspects of early nineteenth-century England. These are: the existence of a Middling Class, the dynamic political and economic role of this class, the difference between social stratification and social class, movement between social strata, and the rise and fall of political classes associated with economic growth.

As a theory of social change which seeks to link conflict-induced social and political change to economic change, the model is only set out in outline. Of course it might be helpful to write it down in precisely formulated mathematical functions. Nevertheless what it would gain in mathematical precision could be offset by too great an abstraction from reality. My guess is that the most fruitful method would be to use a probability model based on a Markov-chain

---

[37] The role of the colonies in drawing off some of the pressure from the petit bourgeois, the professionals, and impecunious younger sons is suggested by the five hundred entries in the *Australian Dictionary of Biography*, Vol. I, 1788–1850. See the review of the volume by A. W. Martin in *Historical Studies: Australia and New Zealand*, XII (Apr. 1967), pp. 584–6.

analysis. In such a model the probability of moving from one stratum to any other could be expressed as a function of (a) the rate of economic growth, (b) the level of achievement motivation, (c) population growth, (d) time. But even these would not express all the determinants of such probabilities. However, it should be possible to calculate something close to the real probabilities from existing data and to see how they are influenced, if at all, by the four factors, a, b, c, d, above. Even so, this exercise would tell us nothing mathematically about the probability of the emergence of social class-consciousness or the formation of political class.

The point is that in all historical studies we should distinguish between the usefulness of a model as a cognitive and explanatory apparatus, and as a predictive one. I do not with to claim any kind of predictive power for the Five-Class Model other than that, just like any other aid to understanding in history, it might be an aid to thinking about the present.

9

The Birth of Class

HAROLD PERKIN

The most profound and far-reaching consequence of the Industrial Revolution was the birth of a new class society. A class society is characterized by class feeling, that is, by the existence of vertical antagonism between a small number of horizontal groups, each based on a common source of income.[1] Such vertical antagonism and the horizontal solidarity of each class transcend the common source of income which supports them. 'The essence of social class,' T. H. Marshall has pointed out, 'is the way a man is treated by his fellows (and, reciprocally, the way he treats them), not the qualities or the possessions which cause that treatement.'[2] This is precisely because the qualities and the possessions which cause the treatment may equally support, as in the old society which was to give birth to class, a totally different social structure, characterized by horizontal antagonism between vertical interest pyramids, each embracing practically the whole range of status levels from top to bottom of society. In the old society, as we saw in Chapter II, class feeling was often latent, but when it emerged in the form of industrial or political 'insubordination' it was ruthlessly suppressed. The birth of class was the process by which the old society itself generated new vertical economic conflicts powerful enough not only to burst through the old bonds of patronage and dependency but to replace the old structure of relationships with a new.

Such a process of social reproduction was necessarily lengthy, pre-

Extracts from *The Origins of Modern English Society, 1780–1880* (Routledge & Kegan Paul, London, 1969), pp. 176–7; 218–27, 231–44; 251–60; 266–7. Cross-references to chapter and section refer to the original.

[1] Cf. K. Marx, *Capital* (Chicago, 1909), III, chap. lii, p. 1031–2, where he considers the idea that class is based on 'the identity of their revenues and their sources of revenue', but then rejects it, presumably as undermining his theory of class struggle – see below, chap. vii, §4.
[2] T. H. Marshall, *Citizenship and Social Class* (1950), p. 92.

ceded by a long gestation with faint but unmistakable symptoms even in the earliest stages of industrialism, and followed by a long infancy in which the child only gradually escaped from the domination of its mother. If, therefore, we found anticipations of class conflict in the old society, we shall equally find relics of 'connection' and 'interest' in the new. The Anti-Corn Law League itself, 'that uniquely powerful instrument in the forging of middle-class consciousness, as Asa Briggs has called it,[3] we shall find at times behaving very like an eighteenth-century interest group.

In was also a complex, syncopated process, operating at different speeds in different areas. Not only did the old society survive much longer in the countryside, but the new came to birth much more slowly in some towns than in others. 'In 1830,' its modern historian has written, 'Coventry still epitomized the old order, in which there were many ranks and conditions of men within a single, homogeneous society. But Coventry could not stand still while England moved, and in the end Coventry succumbed to the standards of the nineteenth century all the more painfully for her long resistance to them.'[4] Nevertheless, one of the distinguishing features of the new society, by contrast with the localism of old, was the nationwide character of the classes, in appeal if not always in strength. At some point between the French Revolution and the Great Reform Act, the vertical antagonism and horizontal solidarities of class emerged on a national scale from and overlay the vertical bonds and horizontal rivalries of connection and interest. That moment, which it is one purpose of this chapter to isolate, saw the birth of class.

★ ★ ★ ★ ★

THE STRUGGLE BETWEEN THE IDEALS

The new class society did not, like Pallas Athene, spring into existence full-grown and fully armed. It had a great deal of growing up to do before it became the viable class society of mid-Victorian England. In 1820 the classes were still very immature and scarcely knew their own strength and limits. Contemporaries often talked of the higher, middle and lower or working *classes*, each in the plural, and this was more than a hangover from the pluralistic ranks and orders of the old society. It reflected the vagueness of the social facts, the existence of numerous layers and sections within the three major classes which only time and

[3] Asa Briggs, 'The Language of "Class" in Early 19th-century England', in A. Briggs and J. Saville (eds.), *Essays in Labour History* (1960), p. 59.
[4] John Prest, *The Industrial Revolution in Coventry* (Oxford, 1960), pp. x-xi.

the experience of class conflict would hammer into something like compact entities.

Nevertheless, it was from the beginning one of the functions of class consciousness to draw a sharp line between each class and the next by means of the conflict taking place across it. The hotter the firing, the better the troops knew where the front line was, and the less they cared about internal divisions – though there would always be those who neither knew nor cared which side they were on, and others whose hearts were on the other side. What kept the armies together was the competition for income between rent, profits and wages, and in the secular deflation which lasted from the post-war slump of 1815–1820 down to the late 1840s the competition for income was extremely sharp. Whatever happened to them in real terms – and this, as we have seen, is still the subject of much dispute amongst historians – rents, profits and wages between 1815 and 1848 were all under severe pressure, and the general trend of all three in terms of current values was downward.[5] The great conflicts of the age were all at bottom struggles for income: the struggle over the corn laws classically so, and even Parliamentary Reform was, in large part, a struggle for the control of government spending and taxation, which weighed far more heavily on some incomes than on others. Certainly, the industrial conflicts of this seminal period of trade unionism were obviously so, while Chartism was basically, in the words of J. R. Stephens, 'a knife and fork question'.[6]

Yet income alone, though a necessary, was never a sufficient motivation for class antagonism, or class would be as old as rent, profits and wages. What was also required was a conscious image of the class in its relation to rival classes, and of the ideal society in which it would find its rightful place. The troops, or at least a considerable portion of them, had to have some notion of the army as a whole and its position relative to the enemy, and of the objective at which they were aiming. Moreover, since morale was half the battle, the image has to be flattering to one's own side and demoralizing to one's opponents: it had to be an ideal image of the representative member of one's class as the lynchpin of society, the only role-bearer who fully justified his place, the ideal citizen whom the rest should emulate, and of the ideal society as one in which this ideal citizen would be suitably honoured and rewarded.

[5] Cf. W. W. Rostow, *British Economy*, p. 8; P. Deane and W. A. Cole, *British Economic Growth, 1688–1959* (Cambridge, 1962), p. 23; F. M. Thompson, *English Landed Soceity in the 19th Century* (London, 1963), pp. 231–5.
[6] G. D. H. Cole, *Chartist Portraits* (London, 1965), p. 74.

The class ideal thus sublimated the crude material self-interest of the competition for income, sanctified the role of class members by the contribution they made to society and its well-being, and so justified the class and its claim to a special place and special treatment within the social framework. It had a twofold function: first, to act as a catalyst in the formation and growth of class, a 'seed' around which the class could crystallize and coagulate, a magnetic pole radiating lines of force throughout the beneficiaries of the common source of income and orienting them towards itself; second, to operate as an instrument of propaganda or psychological warfare *vis-à-vis* the other classes, to undermine their confidence in their own ideal, and try to win them over one's own. In other words, it was a means of educating both the class itself to class-consciousness, and the rest of society to accept it at its own valuation.

The class which was most successful in this educational and moral struggle, in uniting its own members and imposing its ideal upon others, would win the day and have most influence in determining the actual society in which all had to live and in approximating it more or less closely to its own ideal. The primary conflict in the newly born class society of the early nineteenth century was a struggle for the minds and hearts of men. It was a struggle between the ideals.

Perhaps the most significant effect of the sublimation of the competition for income into a struggle between ideals was that it allowed men to embrace ideals other than that which sprang from their own source of income. If this had not been so the old society in which the aristocratic ideals of the leisured gentlemen and of the open aristocracy based on property and patronage were universally accepted, could never have existed, while in the new society victory would automatically have gone to the biggest battalion, the working class, which it manifestly did not. Further, it helps to explain one of the most puzzling phenomena of class conflict, the large proportion of leaders and spokesmen who led or spoke for classes other than their own. These 'social cranks', as they may be called – men like Professor Malthus, the premier apologist of the landed class, Ricardo their landed opponent, James Mill the civil-servant spokesman of the capitalist class, and Robert Owen, William Thompson and Feargus O'Connor, the respectively capitalist, landowning and gentleman-journalist champions of the working class – played a part out of all proportion to their rarity in the class conflict of their day. Indeed, it might almost be said that only the social crank could be sufficiently disinterested to possess the fervour and evoke the passionate response of charismatic leadership. Certainly, no landowner, capitalist or workman could have made the outrageous claims for their class which Malthus, James Mill and Feargus O'Connor did for those which they adopted. Finally, since as we shall see there was in the professional middle class a whole ready-made class of potential social cranks, it helps to explain the very special role of professional men in the class conflicts of the new society.

Not that the leaders and spokesmen invented the ideals and imposed them on their followers. For one thing, they were at least as much chosen by the class as the class by them: they 'spoke to their condition', and when they did not were rejected. For another, the ideals of all the major classes had their origins deep in the old society, and welled up to the surface when the old ground was broken up. There was in each enough nostalgia for certain aspects of the old social structure to ease the transition to the new. In other words, the new class ideals were a transmutation of the older elements in the heat generated by class conflict. As such they were not the novel creation of any one man or small band of leaders, but the spontaneous response of large social groups to the release of deep and long suppressed yearnings which had been latent in the old society.

1 *The entrepreneurial ideal*

The ideal citizen for the bulk of the middle class was, naturally, the capitalist, and the ideal society a class society based on capital and competition. Yet these terms were used in a more specific sense than today, and they were much more disruptive of the old society than at first sight appears. The capitalist of the ideal was the active owner-manager of the Industrial Revolution, not the passive or remotely controlling financier of later corporate capitalism. So much was he the typical business man of the age that neither Adam Smith nor the Ricardians thought it necessary to distinguish him from any other kind of capitalist, and it was left to the Continentals like J. B. Say to differentiate between the *entrepreneur* and the *rentier*. Capital likewise was active property, as remote – as least until the capitalists's retire-ment – from the passive investment of the fundholder or (in theory) of the landowner as a work-horse from a hunter. Competition was not the bloodless competition between material products and between abstract corporations of the modern 'free enterprise' economy: it was *individual* competition, the competition of flesh-and-blood men for wealth, power and social status. For these reasons it may, with judicious anachronism, be called not just the capitalist by the entre-preneurial ideal.

The entrepreneur, according to the ideal, was the lynchpin of society. Although labour was the source of all wealth, it was capital which called it forth and set it in operation. The entrepreneur was the impressario, the creative force, the initiator of the economic cycle. He it was who conceived the end, found the means, bore the burden of risk, and paid out the other factors of production. All this he did for the meagre return of a profit fixed by competition, unable ever to rise more than momentarily above the common rate, and subject to a long-term natural tendency to fall as, with the increasing cost and difficulty of producing food, wages and rent trenched in upon it.[7] The worker, although indispensable and deserving of the highest wages which society could afford, took no thought for the morrow and had nothing to do but to perform at the entrepreneur's bidding a full day's work for a wage fixed by competition at the level of customary subsistence.[8] The landlord, on the other hand, was a mere parasite, a member of the 'unproductive class', whose rent was an unearned income equivalent to the whole surplus produce after the subsistence wages and the common rate of profit had been paid.[9] If the worker was the horse and the landlord the non-paying passenger, the entrepreneur was driver, conductor, pathfinder, caterer and provider of provender all rolled into one.

Capital, it followed, was the mainspring of the economic machine: 'that fund by whose extent the extent of the productive industry of the country must always be regulated'. The national capital – the total fund for the employment of labour in the hands of the entrepreneurs – was the real wealth and strength of the country. It could never be too large: 'there is no amount of capital which may not be employed in a country, because demand is only limited by production.'[10] Derived entirely from the capitalist's self-denying abstention from consumption, savings were automatically invested in further production, raising wages and, via the demand for food, the landlord's rent. Capital could easily be diminished, by the selfishness or fecklessness of the other two classes: by the landed rulers who imposed heavy taxes on profits or transferred a portion to themselves by means of corn laws, or by the working class who might underbreed, and so raise wages at the expense of profits, or overbreed beyond the capaicty of capital to employ them, and so hasten the 'stationary state' of mass poverty.[11] Capital was the chief benefactor of society, the parent of all

[7] Ricardo, 'Principles of Political Economy and Taxation', in *Works and Correspondence* (ed. Sraffa), I, pp. 110–27; cf. J. S. Mill, *Principles of Political Economy* (1904 ed.), p. 416.

[8] Ricardo, *Works and Correspondence*, I, p. 162; and cf. I, pp. 94, 100–1.

[9] *Ibid.*, I, pp. 270, 335.

[10] *Ibid.*, I, pp. 151–2, 290.

[11] *Ibid.*, I, pp. 108–9.

progress, the only bulwark between prosperity and the poverty of countries such as Ireland, with 'labourers unfed for want of employment, and land unproductive for want of labour. . . . The connecting link is capital, and that link is wanting.'[12]

It was also, or ought to be in an ideal society, undistorted by aristocratic corruption and jobbery, the chief determinant of social status. In this it was the exact equivalent of property in the old society, except that the emphasis was, naturally, on active acquisition rather than passive endowment. In the words of a typical early Victorian capitalist, 'society will ever remain composed of classes. Some are born with fortune; more are born without any, and the struggle for it is very serious. It is the best educated of these, the most talented and industrious, who take the prize; but *all* may possess industry which is, after all, the starting point and by far the most valuable power.[13]

The change of emphasis is significant, for it introduces the second principle of the entrepreneurial ideal society, competition. Competition did for capital what patronage did for property in the old society: buttressed its selection to positions of power, wealth and prestige, and filled those positions which the first principle along could not fill. Indeed, it played a larger part in their ideal than patronage had done in the old society: for whereas passive property, in land or the funds, required active exertion to get rid of, active capital by its nature required constant attention to keep it in being. While patronage, therefore, was never more than an adjunct to property, competition was inherent in the very idea of capital and inseparable from it.

Patronage, as we have seen, contained an element of selection by merit, measured by the judgment and importance of the patron. Competition, on the other hand, appealed to a far more impartial judge, 'fortune', 'market forces', or material success. Adam Smith's 'invisible hand' of competition was doubly benevolent. It led the self-interest of the individual to promote the good of the whole community, and, conversely, it guaranteed success to the most meritorious: those who best served the interest of the whole best promoted their own interest. The elegant moral symmetry of 'the competitive system', which ran through classical economics down to the first edition of J. S. Mill's *Principles*, appealed most powerfully to both the moral self-righteousness and the material self-interest of the middle class.[14] Competition, in contrast to the 'monopoly, 'privilege' and

---

[12] [John Wilson], 'The Real State of Ireland in 1827', *Blackwood's*, XXII, (1827), p. 25.

[13] Edmund Potter, *A Picture of a Manufacturing District* (Manchester, 1856) pp. 54–5.

[14] Smith, *Wealth of Nations*, I, 456, Mill, *Principles* (1848), I, p. 239; cf. L. Robbins, *The Theory of Economic Policy in English Classical Political Economy* (1952), pp. 11–19, 150.

'restriction' of the old economic system, was universally beneficial. It kept up supply and kept down prices in the market' it maintained profits at a remunerative level, neither so high as to exploit the consumer nor so low as to discourage saving and future production; and it fixed wages at exactly the level which was best for the worker and society, low enough to provide full employment for all workers and to make it necessary for them to work full-time in order to earn their customary standard of living, high enough to guarantee them subsistence and to produce the next generation of workers. The only member of society to escape its beneficent discipline was the landlord who, since he provided no service save that of permitting access to nature's gifts, merely enjoyed the fruits of others' competition.

It was, above all, socially beneficial. 'The theory of self-dependence', as J. S. Mill (or Harriet Taylor) was to call it in contrast to 'the theory of dependence and protection' of 'the patriarchial or paternal system',[15] evoked not only manly self-respect and responsibility but also the ambition to rise in social status which was the chief source of the energy and drive behind the progress of society. Cobden challenged the maternal charity of the squire's wife and daughters with that of his own class:

Mine is the masculine species of charity which would lead me to inculcate in the minds of the labouring classes the love of independence, the privilege of self-respect, the disdain of being patronized or petted, the desire to accumulate and the ambition to rise.[16]

By individual competition anyone with energy and ability, however humble his birth, could climb the ladder of entrepreneurial society. From this belief logically stemmed one of the most powerful instruments of propaganda every developed by any class to justify itself and seduce others to its own ideal: they myth of the self-made man. As Samuel Smiles was to put it in *Self-Help*, 'What some men are, all without difficulty might be. Employ the same means, and the same results will follow'. The self-made man was the ideal entrepreneur, the man without any initial property or patronage, any education other than self-education, or any advantage other than native talent, who by self-help and force of character made his way to wealth and status. It was a real myth, in that it had a sufficient basis in fact – as Samuel Smiles' *Lives of Engineers* from James Brindley to George Stephenson

[15] Mill, *Principles* (1904), pp. 455–6; for Harriet Taylor's influence cf. Mill's *Autobiography* (World's Classics, 1958), p. 208.
[16] J. Morley, *Life of Cobden* (1903), p. 137.

bears witness – to make it eminently plausible, while remaining utterly ficticious as a sociological explanation of the entrepreneurs as a class. The number of industrialists even in the Industrial Revolution who began without capital or connections of any kind was a minute fraction of the whole, yet 'what some men are all without difficulty might be' was an argument which overwhelmed statistics and made the self-made man to the nineteenth century what the football pool winner is to the twentieth. The myth was the apotheosis of the entrepreneurial ideal. In it, as we shall see, the notions of active capital and beneficent competition were fused with that of the entrepreneur as the autogenous benefactor of society into the decisive weapon of the class struggle.

The entrepreneurial ideal, like the other class ideals, had its roots in the old society. Capital, admittedly, was from a neutral standpoint but old society property in its active phase, and implicit in Locke's labour theory of property. 'Who sees not,' Hume, the link between Locke and the Utilitarians, asks on the active swing of the pendulum, '. . . that whatever is produced or improved by man's art or industry ought, for ever, to be secured to him, in order to give encouragement to such *useful* habits and accomplishments?' and, immediately returning of the passive swing, 'That the property ought also to descend to children and relations, for the same *useful* purpose?'[17] No family-founding capitalist, least of all Ricardo, could disagree with that.

Competition, similarly, was rooted in the dynamism of the old society, and its justification of inequality. As Malthus, the rearguard of the old system, put it, in the passage already quoted, 'If no man could hope to rise or fear to fall in society; if industry did not bring its own reward, and indolence its punishment; we could not hope to see that animated activity in bettering our own condition which now forms the master-spring of public prosperity.[18] The condemnation of idleness and the commendation of self-help and independence were old themes amongst the puritans and mercantilists of the old society's middle ranks, as, for example, Thomas Starkey in the 1530s on 'idle and unprofitable persons' or Sir Josiah Child in 1698 on high interest rates which suffer 'Idleness to suck the Breasts of Industry'.[19]

And the ideal of the self-made man was potential, at least, in the pride of the middle ranks in the endless stream of 'new men' who rose

---

[17] D. Hume, *Essays, Moral, Political, and Literary* (ed. T. H. Green and T. H. Grose, 1875), II, p. 189.

[18] T. R. Malthus, *Essays on Population* (Everyman, 1951), II, p. 254.

[19] T. Starkey, *A Dialogue between Cardinal Pole and Thomas Lupset* (ed. J. M. Cowper, 1871), p. 89; J. Child, *A New Discourse on Trade* (1698), p. 21.

to landed property in the old society.[20] It became quite explicit in Tory opponents of the entrepreneurial ideal who nevertheless defended Lord Chancellor Eldon as 'a man who began the world with no fortune but his education and his talents – with no connexions whatever – with no pretence to any sort of external aids . . . Self-raised and self-sustained . . . a splendid example of the power of merit – a living witness that there is at least one country in the world where merit can do everything.'[21]

The close connections with the older ideal, however, only carried the thrusts of the new one nearer the heart. Active capital, open competition and the productive entrepreneur were a standing indictment of passive property, closed patronage and the leisured gentleman. By the light of capital, property meant idleness. Adam Smith bequeathed to the classical economists the distinction between the productive and the unproductive members of society, and singled out the landlords as men who 'love to reap where they never sowed'; but he said worse things about business men, who were in a continuous conspiracy against consumers, against their workers and against the public at large, while the interest of the landlords, like that of the labourers, was 'strictly and inseparably connected with the general interest of society.'[22] It was left to Ricardo and his followers to kick out this prop, and leave the landlords not merely unproductive but parasitic, compared with the least active capitalist. As Nassau Senior put it,

Wages and profits are the creation of man. They are the recompense for the sacrifice made, in the one case, of ease; in the other, of immediate enjoyment. But a considerable part of the produce of every country is the recompense of no sacrifice whatever; is received by those who neither labour nor put by, but merely hold out their hands to accept the offerings of the rest of the community.[23]

And J. S. Mill: 'They grow richer as it were in their sleep, without working, risking or economizing. What claim have they, on the general principle of social justice, to this accession of riches?'[24] Business men were even more outspoken that the economists. A Glasgow merchant and Tory critic of aristocratic 'abdication' condemned 'the

---

[20] Cf. chap. ii, §3, above.

[21] The Late Whig Attacks on the Lord Chancellor, *Blackwood's,* XIV 1823, p. 202; Eldon did not in fact begin without fortune: his father was a prosperous Tyneside coal-fitter and 'new man' – cf. E. Hughes, *North Country Life,* I, pp. 165–6.

[22] Cf. Smith, *Wealth of Nations,* I, pp. 67, 101, 134, 148, 263, 265, 432, 459.

[23] N. W. Senior, *Political Economy* (1872 ed.), p. 89.

[24] J. S. Mill *Principles,* p. 492.

enormous free incomes of the modern landlords' who had shed their responsibilities as 'custodians of the soil, for the behoof of the nation at large' and 'have been reduced to the condition of DRONES', thus anticipating a whole literature of anti-landlord metaphor down to Joseph Chamberlain's 'they toil not, neither do they spin.'[25]

* * * * *

2 The working-class ideal

The working class was never so united or self-confident as the capitalist middle class, partly because it was by its nature more fragmented, still more because its ideal was ambiguous in itself and led to diverse and conflicting means of pursuing it. The divisions of the working class, between urban and rural, skilled and unskilled, 'aristocracy of labour' and common or garden workers, were proverbial right down the nineteenth century. A defender of the old society with its infinity of ranks wrote in 1825:

The case is the same with the lower orders. The ploughmen hold the mechanics in contempt as an inferior race of beings, although the latter can earn the best wages: the journeymen cabinet-makers cannot degrade themselves by associating with the journeymen tailors: the journeymen shoe-makers cannot so far forget their dignity as to make companions of the labourers: the gentleman's lacquey cannot, on any account, lower himself to the level of the carman.[26]

The working-class ideal had to be stretched to bridge such gulfs, and its ambiguity owed much to the attempt. Its ideal citizen was the productive, independent worker, and its ideal society an equalitarian one based on labour and co-operation. Every one of these terms was ambiguous. The productive, independent worker normally meant the manual wage-earner on whom the capitalist system rested and for whom freedom from dependence on the arbitrary will of the capitalist was demanded; but for the nostalgic like Cobbett and the domestic workers who formed so large a part of his following the ideal was narrowed to the (in theory) self-employed 'little masters' of the old domestic system, while for some of its more forward-looking protagonists like Thomas Hodgskin it was widened to include the master manufacturer: 'The labour and skill of the contriver, or of the man who arranges and adapts a whole, are as necessary as the labour and

[25] 'Bandana' [John Galt], 'Hints to Country Gentlemen' *Blackwood's*, XII (1822), pp. 483–4; J. L. Garvin, *Life of Chamberlain* (1931–51), I, p. 392; cf. The Tenure of Land, *Westminster Review*, XXVI (1864), p. 122; 'The position of our landlords, "who toil not, neither do they spin", . . . is fast becoming unique'; and same phrase in W. Lovett, *Life and Struggles*, p. 131.

[26] [Robinson], 'The Nobility', *Blackwood's*, XVIII (1825), p. 337.

skill of him who executes only a part, and they must be paid accordingly.'[27] One view might lead to an attempt to return to an idealized past which never existed; another to acceptance of the capitalist present with mere political safeguards for the worker's rights and welfare; a third to the pursuit of a millennial future in which capitalist and landlord were no more, and only the productive, independent worker remained.

An equalitarian society, likewise, could mean a merely political democracy or a socialist utopia, the latter either replacing the class society comprehensively and immediately or growing alongside it in the form of co-operative communities. As for labour, both aristocratic society and entrepreneurial society were admittedly based on it, in the sense that both passive property and active capital justified themselves by Locke's labour theory.[28] The rights of labour might mean anything from a fair day's pay for a fair day's work, which was all the craft unions for example demanded, to the complete abolition of landed property and/or industrial capital demanded by the Spenceans and extreme socialists. Working-class co-operation, too, could mean anything from friendly societies and trade clubs for mitigating the worst effects of competition to the primitive communism of Owen's parallelograms or the socialist commonwealth achieved by the general strike.

The ideal, nevertheless, was the only principle which could hope to unite the working class, and its ambiguity was to some extent a virtue. It united the divergent elements more by what it opposed than by the monolithic nature of what it stood for. The ideal of the productive, independent worker was a more logical criticism of the unproductive landowner and rentier than the ideal of the entrepreneur, who had to keep open the door to retirement and passive investment. The ideal of labour as the sole justification of remuneration, recruitment and promotion in society was a standing criticism of all forms of unearned income and of recruitment by anything but merit defined as hard work, and above all of the unequal advantages and bargaining power of capital. The ideal of co-operation was a moral condemnation of the selfish, mutually destructive principle of competition.

[27] [T. Hodgskin], *Labour Defended against the Claims of Capital*, by 'A Labourer' (1825, ed. G. D. H. Cole, 1922), pp. 88–9.

[28] Cf. Arthur Young, *Tour in Ireland* (1780) Appendix, p. 18: the poor 'form the basis of public prosperity; they feed, clothe, enrich, and fight the battle of all the other ranks of the community'; and *P.P.*, 1817 (462), VI. 1, *S. C. on the Poor Laws*, p. 4 '. . . those exertions on the part of the labouring classes on which, according to the nature of things, the happiness and welfare of mankind has [sic] been made to rest.' For the basis of capital in labour, cf. Hume, *loc. cit.*, and §1, above.

Like the entrepreneurial ideal, the working-class ideal was rooted in the old society. Justification by labour was implicit in the Lockeian labour theory of property, and became explicit in Adam Smith, who asserted that 'the produce of labour constitutes the natural recompense or wages of labour,' and contrasted the early and rude state of society, 'in which the whole produce of labour belongs to the labourer,' with the capitalist system in which the labourer 'must share it with the owner of the stock which employs him.'[29] From the publication of *The Wealth of Nations* (if not before) it was open to critics of property and capital to assert the workers' 'right to the whole produce of labour'. It was so asserted by William Ogilvie in 1782, but with the same confusion as Locke and Hume about the inheritance of the right: 'Whoever enjoys any revenue, not proportioned to industry or exertion of his own, *or of his ancestors*, is a freebooter, who has found means to cheat and rob the public'; and more unequivocally by Charles Hall in 1805: 'Wealth consists not in things but in *power* over the labour of others.'[30] Robert Owen, who was then more a paternalist critic of the new manufacturing system than a socialist, spoke in 1815 of the 'industry of the lower orders, from whose labour this wealth is now drawn.'[31]

Yet it was only with the emergence of a separate working-class consciousness after the Wars that the right to the whole produce of labour became a dynamic instrument of class conflict. This it did most notably, of course, with the so-called Ricardian socialists of the 1820s.[32] They were not specifically Ricardian, except in the sense that Ricardo was then the chief representative, though not the most vulnerable, of the economists whose ideas they were standing on their head. If Ricardo perpetuated the labour theory of value, at least he was free from the confusion between productive and unproductive workers, between the producers of goods and the suppliers of services, which was the orthodox niche into which the heretical doctrine of the right to the whole produce of labour grafted itself. If any one man influenced them all, it was Patrick Colquhoun, the Benthamite popularizer of Adam Smith, whose statistical tables of civil society with

[29] *Wealth of Nations*, I, pp. 48, 50, 65.

[30] W. Ogilvie, *Essay on the Right of Property in Land* (1781) p. 46 (my italics); C. Hall, *The Effects of Civilisation on the People in European States* (1805, 1849 ed.), p. 39.

[31] R. Owen, *Observations on the Effect of the Manufacturing System* (1815) in *A New View of Society, etc.* (Everyman, 1927), p. 121; Owen derived his labour theory of value, along with his idea of villages of co-operation, from the Quaker philanthropist, John Bellers, *Proposals for Raising a Colledge of Industry of all Useful Trades and Husbandry* (1695) – cf. M. Beer, *A History of British Socialism* (1953 ed.) I, pp. 174–5.

[32] First so called by H. S. Foxwell, Introduction to Adolf Menger, *The Right to the Whole Produce of Labour* (1899) p. lxxxiii.

their invidious distinction between the productive and the unproductive classes were a gift which no critic of contemporary society
could ignore.[33]

Still less were they all socialists. On the contrary, they were fairly
evenly divided between those who, like the anonymous author of *A
Letter to Lord John Russell* (1821), the Tory democrat 'Piercy Raven-
stone', and the Radical ex-naval officer, Thomas Hodgskin, would
retain the present structure of society, with political safeguards for the
labourer, and avoided socialist remedies, and those who, like the clerk
turned professional lecturer John Gray and the Irish landowner William
Thompson, advocated forms of socialism.[34] Both groups, however,
equally used the ideal of labour to denounce capital and competition.
Thomas Hodgskin defined capital as labour, past or present:

If . . ., as I say, circulating capital is only co-existing labour, and fixed capital
only skilled labour, it must be plain that all those numerous advantages, those
benefits to civilization, those vast improvements in the condition of the
human race, which have been in general attributed to capital, are caused
in fact by labour, and by knowledge and skill informing and directing
labour.[35]

Profit and the capitalist – though not, apparently, the manager – were
unnecessary. William Thompson denounced 'competition with its
unequal remuneration – prizes for the few, blanks, want, and misery
for the many; prizes for the idle, blanks for the industrous – mutual
antipathy for all,' and opposed to it his system of 'Association, or of
labour by Mutual Co-operation.'[36]

This group of anti-capitalists, individualist and socialist, are of the
first importance in the intellectual history of socialism and their influence, especially through John Francis Bray and Bronterre O'Brien,
on Marx and all later socialists is beyond question.[37] Yet this is not to
say that this motley collection of 'social cranks' invented the ideal and
foisted it on the working class. At best they formulated it in striking

[33] Colquhon, *Treatise on . . . British Empire*, pp. 29–47; his tables were used by Robery Owen
and John Gray, and repeated by John Wade in *The Extraordinary Black Book* (1831), p. 216; cf.
Foxwell, in Menger, *The Right to the Whole Produce of Labour*, pp. xlii–xliii, and Briggs 'The
Language of "Class" . . .', pp. 49–50, 51n.

[34] Cf. Beer, *A History of British Socialism*, I, pp. 183–4; for a bibliography of their works see
Menger, *The Right to the Whole Produce of Labour*, Appendix.

[35] Hodgskin, *Labour Defended against the Claims of Capital*, pp. 108–9.

[36] W. Thompson, *Labor Rewarded*, by 'One of the Idle Classes' (1827), p. 30; and 'Appeal on
One Half of the Human Race', p. 199.

[37] Cf. Foxwell, in Menger, *The Right to the Whole Produce of Labour*, pp. lxv–lxxi; A. Plummer,
'The Place of Bronterre O'Brien in the Working-Class Movement', *Economic History Review* II,
(1929), 61f.

form and 'spoke to their condition'. But the working class were not only ready to accept the message: some at least were already in possession of it. The first 'Co-operative and Economic Society' and the first propaganda organ of the co-operative movement, *The Economist* – both names are significant – were started as early as 1821, and the London Co-operative Society was set up in 1824, contemporary with Thompson's first book, and before the publication of all the rest of the group, 'to restore the whole produce of labour to the labourer.'[38] It is true that they were influenced by Owen, but if ever there was a case of a leader being chosen by his followers, this was it. Practically the whole working-class co-operative movement began either without his knowledge or against his opposition, and it was only in 1829 after the failure of his American experiment and the manifest success of theirs that he was reluctantly persuaded to lead them.[39]

By then the working-class ideal was well established. It was used to justify universal manhood suffrage: a speaker in Manchester in 1826 declared that 'the purpose of parliamentary reform was to secure to the labourer the fruits of his own labour,' and the argument became a standard one with working-class Radicals.[40] Francis Place, commenting in 1831 on the National Union of the Working Classes (an offshoot of the original Owenite British Association for Promoting Co-operative Knowledge of 1829), remarked:

The 'Union' had great influence over a considerable portion of the working class, more especially in the great manufacturing counties. During the time the Reform Bills were before the Parliament this was particularly the case. The attention of the whole people was then drawn to the subject, and the working people were quite as much excited as any class whatever. The consequence of this excitement was a general persuasion that the whole produce of the labourers' and workmen's hands should remain with them.[41]

The ideal captured the working-class press, joining forces with the Painites – The Carliles, Hetheringtons and Cleaves – who had kept alive the old Jacobin tradition of political democracy, and transformed the merely political Rights of Man into the social revolutionary Rights of Labour. Joshua Hobson announced in the first number of his unstamped *Voice of the West Riding* in 1833:

[38] Beer, *A History of British Socialism*, I, p. 185.
[39] Cf. G. Wallas, *Place*, pp. 269–72.
[40] *Wheeler's Manchester Chronicle*, 28 October 1826; Briggs, 'The Language of "Class" . . .', p. 66.
[41] Wallas, *Place*, p. 266n.

It is intended to publish a Weekly Penny Paper, to be called the 'Voice of the
West Riding', advocating the Rights of Man against the 'exclusives', and the
Rights of Labour against the 'Competitives' and the 'Political Economists',
and especially to vindicate the Working Classes from the calumnies and
misrepresentations of our parasitical scribes who figure in the Provincial
Newspapers.[42]

Wherever it succeeded, it transformed the working-class movement
from an ameliorative one which accepted the basic structure of the
new class society into a revolutionary one which rejected it altogether.
As a disillusioned bricklayer put it at a trade union conference in 1839,

Trade unions are for botching up the old system; Chartists are for a new one.
Trade unions are for making the best of a bad bargain; Chartists are for a fresh
one; and everyone must admit that trade unions partake of the tampering
spirit of monopoly.[43]

There were many ways in which outright rejection of the system
could show itself – too many for the unity of the working class. There
was the frontal attack, via political agitation for Reform, aimed at
proletarian control of government, or, if that failed, violent revolution
as advocated by the physical-force Chartists. There was the undermining operation of syndicalist trade unionism, culminating in a
revolutionary general strike – William Benbow's 'national holiday' or
'sacred month' – as in Owen's Grand National Consolidated Trade
Union of 1834. And there was the attractively non-violent method of
simply opting out of the competitive system, by setting up proletarian
cells or islands within it based on the ideal of labour instead of that of
capital. Even these, however, could take various forms, the basic
choice lying between millennial co-operative communities on the
Owenite model and nostalgic individualist colonies of independent
peasants on the lines of O'Connor's Chartist Land Plan.

The fragmentation of the ideal, in practice as well as theory, was its
fundamental weakness. Moreover, an apparently unequivocal decision for outright rejection had a habit not merely of failing – which
rejectionist experiments did with dismaying regularity – but of evol-
ving by imperceptible degrees into acceptance of the system. This
happened in different ways, as we shall see later, to syndicalist trade
unionism, the co-operative movement, and even to phsycial-force
Chartism. Meanwhile, the working-class ideal, for all its greater
plausibility, was extremely vulnerable to seduction by the other two

[42] *Voice of the West Riding,* 8 June 1833.
[43] E. R. Wickham, *Church and People in an Industrial City* (1957), p. 102.

ideals, the more surprisingly by the remarkable revival of the aristocratic ideal which took place in the 1820s.

3 *The revival of the aristocratic ideal*

The aristocratic ideal never quite died. At its weakest, in the agitation
for the abolition of the poor laws between Waterloo and the Queen's
Trial, an etiolated sense of reponsibility of the lower orders managed
to survive amongst the aristocracy. The Lords' Committee on the
Poor Laws of 1817 was 'decidedly of the opinion, that the general
system of these laws, interwoven as it is with the habits of the people,
ought . . . to be essentially maintained'.[44] Even at this low ebb,
schemes for the state-aided welfare of the poor, like John Christian
Curwen's National Benefit Society' or Robert Owen's Plan for
Villages of Co-operation, could still get a serious hearing in Parliament, though they were seen chiefly as cheap alternatives to poor relief,
and even so had little chance of breaking through the prevailing belief
of the Government in *laissez-faire*.[45]

Paternal discipline, on the other hand, survived in despotic strength
in its home territories, the English countryside and London 'Society'.
A Tory paternalist in 1824 advocated English landlordism as a cure for
Ireland's woes:

None but those who have been familiarized with English farmers and
cottagers can conceive the degree of awe which actuates them in regard to
their landlords . . . The English landlord's influence does not slumber. We
have ourselves seen farmers deprived of their farms for frequent drunkenness
– for leading immoral lives – for being bad cultivators; – and we have seen a
farmer compelled to marry a girl whom he had seduced . . . This operates in
the most powerful manner, in preventing vice and crime; and in giving the
best tone to what may be called the rustic world.[46]

Francis Place complained in 1831 of the difficulty of working with
'gentlemen' Reformers who feared 'being looked upon as ungenteel'
or of 'being discountenanced by Holland House people and Brooks'
Club people' and would sacrifice the public cause so as 'not to lose
caste with their fashionable friends and acquaintances.'[47]

The countryside and the West End were not the whole of England,

[44] *P. P.*, 1818, V, 100, *S. C. of H. of L. on the Poor Laws, 1817*, p 7

[45] J. C. Curwen, *Sketch of a Plan for Bettering the Condition of the Labouring Population* (1817) and
Parliamentary Debates, XXXIV. 871; R. Owen, *Report to the County of Lanark of a Plan for Relieving
Public Distress* (1820) and *P. P.*, 1823, VI, *S. C. on Mr. Owen's Plan*.

[46] 'Y.Y.Y.' [Robinson], 'The Instruction of the Irish Peasantry', *Blackwood's*, XV 1824,
p. 502.

[47] Wallas, *Place*, pp. 260–2.

however, and in other spheres the ruling class were not merely yielding ground to the new entrepreneurial ideal, but actually making the pace in accepting its principles. During the 1820s Tory Governments brought in increasing doses of free trade (Huskisson and Peel's reduction of the customs duties, 1823 onwards, and especially the sliding – and lower – scale of corn duties, 1828), free trade in labour (repeal of the Combination Acts and of the laws forbidding the emigration of artisans, 1824–5), and free trade in religion (repeal of the laws against Dissenters and Roman Catholics, 1828–9). The protectionist High Tories were alarmed. As early as 1826 *Blackwood's* was complaining that 'Our policy has been greatly changed – some of our most important laws and systems have been changed – some of the leading relations and regulations of society have been changed,' and that the defenders of the old system had had 'to oppose both the Ministry and the Opposition, a united Parliament, a united Press, and to a very great extent, public opinion.' 'What is the great object of the new system?' it asked in 1827, 'To carry competition to the highest point. . . .' And it hounded Canning, Huskisson, Peel, and even Wellington, for selling out to 'the Faction' of Whigs and Political Economists, in terms of which the following is a fair sample: 'Saying nothing of the others, Mr Peel's pubilic life has been one continuing course of despicable, grovelling, mercenary faithlessness to principles and party. . . .'[48] The very shrillness of the tone betrays the nostalgic protectionists as defenders of a lost cause.

Yet there was at the same time and in the same group a remarkable revival of the paternal aristocratic ideal. Malthus has usually been considered the main champion of the leisured, unproductive landed class, and this amongst the classical economist he certainly was. He was himself aware of it: 'It is somewhat singular that Mr Ricardo, a considerable receiver of rents, should have so much underrated their importance; while I, who never received, nor expect to reveive any, shall probably be accused of overrating their importance.'[49] For Malthus, the unproductive landlord was not only a useful but the most necessary member of society. Not only was rent 'an exact measure of the *relief* from labour in the production of food granted to [man] by a most kind Providence,' which 'will always afford a fund for the

[48] 'Christopher North' [John Wilson *et al.*,], Preface to *Blackwood's*, XIX (1826), pp. xviii–xix; [Robinson], 'The Surplus Population of the United Kingdom', 'The Faction, and Political Economy, No. IV', *ibid.*, XXI (1827), XXII, 379, pp. 403–31, and XXVII (1830), p. 41.

[49] Malthus, *Principles* (1820), p. 238n.; Ricardo bought estates worth £275,000 in Gloucestershire, Herefordshire, Worcestershire, Warwickshire and Kent – Ricardo, *Works* (ed. Sraffa), X. pp. 95–9.

enjoyments and leisure of society, sufficient to leaven and animate the whole mass,' and 'the reward of present valour and wisdom, as well as of past strength and cunning', 'a boon most important to the happiness of mankind'. It also supplied the demand which made the landlord the lynchpin of society, the initiator of the economic cycle, the unproductive consumer without whom the productive classes could not continue to produce more than they consumed: 'In the ordinary state of society, the master producers and capitalists, though they may have the power, have not the will, to consume to the necessary extent. And with regard to their workmen, it must be allowed that, if they possessed the will, they have not the power'. It followed, therefore, that 'it is absolutely necessary that a country with great powers of production should possess a body of unproductive consumers.'[50]

On this Ricardo drily remarked: 'A body of unproductive labourers are just as necessary and as useful with a view to future production, as a fire, which should consume in the manufacturers warehouse the goods which those unproductive labourers would otherwise consume.'[51] Malthus's *Principles* and Ricardo's *Notes* on it constitute a dialogue between the aristocratic and entrepreneurial ideals unique in candour and sincerity, which nevertheless breaks off time after time in mutual incomprehension – symbolically, it may be said, since this was the normal relationship betwen the two ideals.

Yet it was not Malthus who fathered the revival of the aristocratic ideal. On the contrary, he was one of the chief objects of the revivalists' wrath. For Malthus was the champion of the ideal at its most irresponsible, the apologist of power without responsibility, who armed it – and the entrepreneurial ideal – with what his opponents considered the most diabolical instrument ever invented for disciplining the lower orders and grinding the faces of the poor. The 'principle of population' – 'the constant tendency in all animated life to increase beyond the nourishment prepared for it'[52] – was used to mock every attempt to improve the condition of the working class, from the poor laws to Owen's 'parallelograms'. The fact that the principle formed, along with Ricardo's theory of rent which was based on it through the law of diminishing returns, one of the twin pillars of the classical school of economics has masked the extent to which it was a product of 'the abdication on the part of the governors.' In its original form it was intended to counteract entrepreneurial criticism of 'idleness'.

[50] Malthus, *Principles*, pp. 229, 237–9, 463, 471.
[51] Ricardo, *Works*, II. 421n.
[52] Malthus, *Essay on Population* (Everyman, 1951), I. p. 5.

Francis Place, the first neo-Malthusian, pointed out, 'Mr Malthus denies to the unemployed poor man the right to eat, but he allows the right to the unemployed rich man.'[53] Nassau Senior, who found the principle 'made the stalking horse of negligence and injustice, the favourite objection to every project for rendering the resources of the country more productive,' later wrote in the report of a Royal Commission:

the general proposition that such is the influence of the principle of population, that no increase in the supply of provisions can permanently benefit the labouring class, we believe to be absolutely false. That proposition owed its origin to some expressions of Mr Malthus, not sufficiently qualified by him, and repeated in a still more unqualified form by many of his followers. It owed its currency to the relief which it afforded to the indolence and selfishness of the superior classes. But it is contradicted by the evidence of all experience.[54]

The revivalists of the aristocratic ideal were reacting as much against the betrayers of paternalism as against the new entrepreneurial ideal. They not only bracketed for common enmity Malthus and the other economists, but singled him out for special attack. Michael Thomas Sadler, the acknowledged leader of the High Tory paternalists, made his name by his attack on Malthus. A Leeds linen merchant, and thus a notable 'social crank', he had the leadership of the revivalists thrust upon him the moment he entered Parliament in 1829.[55] To the principle of population he opposed his own 'law of population', that 'the prolificness of human being . . . varies inversely as their number' [i.e. density], and to Malthus's purely hypothetical ratios he opposed massive empirical statistics drawn from all over the world to show that human fertility fell as population density, urbanization and comfort increased.[56] It was 'disproved' by Macaulay in the *Edinburgh Review* by the dishonest manipulation of his statistics,[57] and laughed at or ignored by the economists. Nevertheless, in spite of being couched in theological terms of God's providence and 'the ample provision Nature has made for all creatures,' Sadler's 'law' was essentially the belief accepted

[53] Wallas, *Place*, p. 165.

[54] N. W. Senior, *Two Lectures on Population* (1829), Appendix (Correspondence with Malthus), p. 89; *Extracts from the Reports of the Commissioners on . . . Handloom Weavers* ed. R. Currie, 1841), p. 12.

[55] [Samuel O'Sullivan], 'Review of the last Session of Parliament', *Blackwood's*, XXVI 1829, pp. 234–7.

[56] M. T. Sadler, *The Law of Population* (1830); for Malthus's ratios, see *Essay on Population* (*ed. cit.*), I. 10–11.

[57] [R. B. Seeley], *Memoirs of M. T. Sadler* (1842), pp. 630–4.

by modern economists that economic growth and higher living standards are the main prerequisite of population control.[58] Mr Sadler alleged that the only efficient checks to population were, ease and comfort, increasing to luxury'. It led to a conclusion diametrically opposed to Malthus's: 'If you really apprehend an overflow of this kind, the best way to check it, is to improve the condition of the people.'[59]

To be fair to the economists, it must be admitted that Malthus favoured high wages – though he clearly doubted the working class's capacity for 'moral restraint' by which alone they could keep their numbers small enough to obtain them – while Ricardo believed that 'the natural price of labour . . . essentially depends on the habits and customs of the people,' and that 'a taste for comforts and enjoyments' should be encouraged as the best 'security against a superabundant population.'[60] But that their position was poles apart from Sadler's can be seen from their attitude to the poor laws: their pernicious tendency, says Ricardo, 'has been fully developed by the able hand of Mr Malthus; and every friend to the poor must ardently wish for their abolition.'[61] Sadler, by contrast, argued 'the absolute necessity of such a provision, as regards the labouring classes of England,' and of their extension to Ireland: 'The institution of the Poor Law of England encourages the demand for, and increases the value of labour, as well as abates distress; In Ireland, in consequence of the want of such a law, labour is discouraged, and distress increased.'[62]

To Malthus's 'Selfish System', therefore, Sadler opposed his 'Paternal System'. It was not merely that the rich ought to be charitable towards the poor out of prudence and benevolence. Protection and maintenance were the right of the poor and a duty of the rich implicit in the privilege of property: 'a real and indisputable right, that, after the institutions of the country have sanctioned the monopoly of property, the poor shall have some reserved claims to the necessaries of life.'[63] This was the revival of the aristocratic ideal in all its pristine purity. *Blackwood's* commented on his first session in Parliament:

The Economists for the first time heard their fallibility called in question, and felt their ascendancy in danger. . . . These sages of the Satanic school in politics

[58] Cf. W. A. Lewis, *Theory of Economic Growth* (1955), pp. 313–15, 434–5; and cf. recent studies by animal behaviourists, who have found a psychological reluctance to breed in overcrowded conditions amongst laboratory mice and amongst species of kangaroo on islands off Western Australia.
[59] Seeley, *Memoirs of M. T. Sadler*, p. 182; contrast Malthus, *Principles*, p. 472.
[60] Ricardo, *Works*, I, pp. 96–7, 100.   [61] *Ibid.*, I. 106.
[62] Sadler in H. of C., 3 June 1830; Seeley, *Memoirs of M. T. Sadler*, p. 203.
[63] *Ibid.*, pp. 167, 208.

encountered an adversary by whom their favourite measures were opposed, and their most familiar axioms disputed; . . . Sadler had done this. Be he right or wrong, he is the man whose warning voice called the attention of the honourable House . . . to the first principles of the Economists; who bid them turn their eye from the capitalist to the labourer; and who had the spirit and the feeling to ask them . . . whether that could be a good system . . . under the influence of which capital must increase at the expense of humanity; where what is called wealth only serves to oppress and to paralyse industry; and national prosperity is made to . . . proceed upon its course amidst the sweat, and the blood, and the groans of its victims.[64]

Sadler was the key figure in the revival of the aristocratic ideal. His part in its most successful manifestation, the campaign for factory reform, and his post-mortem influence through his disciples, Richard Oastler and John Wood, on the attack on the New Poor Law of 1834, make him the chief link between the ideal of the old society and all later attempts to unite the upper and the working classes in common opposition to the capitalist middle class. As the youngest son of a large yeoman or small country gentleman, apprenticed to a linen merchant in one of the largest of the northern industrial towns, and as an Anglican brought up under the influence of the Tory Wesleyans, he was specially fitted for the role. But he was the channel rather than the originating spring of the revival. He belonged to a widespread current of social thought which was flowing strongly in the 1820s before it carried him to the top, provided him through the patronage of the Duke of Newcastle with a pocket borough seat in Parliament, and chose him as its leader. That current of thought, signally defeated by the Reform Act (which overthrew Sadler himself), by the New Poor Law, and by the triumph of free trade, and then dissipated in the romantic feudalism of Disraeli, Lord John Manners and 'Young England', has suffered the neglect and misunderstanding of most lost causes. Yet in the 1820s it produced, quite apart from Sadler's contribution, a counter-attack on aristocratic 'abdication' and the entrepreneurial ideal which not only rejected outright the whole canon of classical economics but anticipated in great measure both Keynesian economics and the social outlook of the Welfare State. . . .

★ ★ ★ ★ ★

Why did the attempt to revive the aristocratic ideal, so deeply rooted in the traditional interests of the ruling class and so brilliantly argued in the most widely read journal of the day, fail? For fail it did, despite the partial success of Sadler and his followers in the factory

[64] [O. Sullivan], Review of the last Session of Parliament, *Blackwood's*, XXVI 1829, p. 235.

reform agitation. It failed because the revivalists were fighting for a cause already lost. Paternal discipline without paternal responsibility was too attractive a principle for most of the landed class to resist. The fact that it made them more vulnerable to the criticisms of the entrepreneurial ideal merely weakened its hold on them still more: the attack on paternalism as a whole had already gone too far for the revival of its better side to save it.

Indeed, the revivalists themselves helped to undermine its defences. In their disgust with the Parliament which had betrayed paternalism and embraced free trade in commerce, labour, and religion, they denounced it more fiercely even than the Radicals, and so, since there were more of them in the old Parliament than there were Radicals, more effectively ensured the success of Reform. Because of 'the notorious incompetency of the present House of Commons,' because the close borough members had become mere tools and mercenaries of a tacit coalition of renegade Tories and treacherous Whigs who had betrayed paternalism and the Church, the High Tory opponents of Reform came to 'feel that no change could well give them a worse House of Commons than the present system gives them, and that the elective franchise could not be in more dangerous hands than those which now hold it.'[65] In the event it was the decision of the High Tories, led by Sadler, to oppose Wellington's Government and let in the Whigs which decisively opened the doors to Reform, and to the new Parliament which was to bury the aristocratic ideal.[66] The ideal did live to see a transfigured resurrection, in Victorian Oxford and Cambridge and, surprisingly, in the East End of London.[67] But that is another story, which involves another class ideal.

4 *The forgotten middle class*

The aristocratic, entrepreneurial and working-class ideals, then, were the three major class ideals contending for supremacy in early nineteenth-century England. Yet there was another class and another ideal, without analysing which it is still not possible to understand the struggle between them. An extraordinary proportion of the spokesmen of the first three ideals were members of none of the three classes: James Mill, Henry Brougham, and Nassau Senior, for example, of the entrepreneurial ideal; Charles Hall, Thomas Hodgskin, John Gray, and Bronterre O'Brien, of the working-class ideal; T. R. Malthus,

---

[65] [Robinson], A Dissolution of Parliament, *ibid.*, XXVI 1829, pp. 251–9; cf. [O'Sullivan], Review of the last Session of Parliament, XXVI, pp. 224–37, and [Robinson], The Reform of the House of Commons, XXVII 1830, pp. 640–58.

[66] Seeley, *Memoirs of M. T. Sadler*, pp. 221–2.

[67] Cf. chap. x, §3, below.

John Wilson (editor of *Blackwood's*), Coleridge and Southey, of the aristocratic ideal.[68] To what class did this collection of lawyers, doctors, public officials, journalists, professors and lecturers belong? To the middle class, certainly, but not to the capitalist middle class. They belonged to the non-capitalist or professional middle class, a class curiously neglected in the social theories of the age, but one which played a part out of all proportion to its numbers in both the theory and the practice of class conflict.

To treat them as a separate class seems at first sight to be perverse. Most theorists have treated them as middle class, *tout court*. Marx, who was aware of them to his own embarrassment, treated them in his ciriticism of their unregenerative role in existing societies as a mere adjunct of the ruling class: 'within this class one part appears as the thinkers of the class (its active conceptualizing ideologist, who make it their chief livelihood to develop and perfect the illusions of the class about itself)'; but in his hopes for their aid in establishing the socialist society of the future, as 'workers by brain', or super-proletarians.[69] All three views express an element of the truth about this Protean class, which could assume the guise of any other class at will. Yet underlying each disguise was Proteus himself, a class, sub-class, or socio-economic group whose members had enough in common to support a separate social ideal which had a profound effect upon the rest of society.

Curiously enough, their existence as a separate class follows logically from Marx's own definition of class as determined principally by source of income. Indeed, when Marx came to wrestle systematically with his definition, in the abortive last chapter of *Capital*, he uncovered Proteus, and shied away:

what constitutes a class? . . . What constitutes wage-labourers, capitalists and landlords as the three great social classes? At first glance it might seem that the identity of revenues and of sources of revenue is responsible. . . . However, from this point of view, doctors and officials would also form two distinct classes, for they belong to two different social groups, and the revenues of the members of each group come from the same source.

And he tailed off in an infinite regression of different sub-classes of workers, capitalists and landowners.[70]

Doctors and officials do indeed belong to a distinct class. They

[68] Mill was an India Office official, Brougham a K.C., Senior a Master in Chancery, Hall an M.D., Hodgskin a half-pay naval officer turned lecturer, Gray a commercial clerk turned lecturer, O'Brien a lawyer turned journalist, Malthus and Wilson professors, Coleridge and Southey professional authors.

[69] Marx, *German Ideology* (1845–6), in Bottomore and Rubel, *Karl Marx: Selected Writings in Sociology and Social Philosophy* (Penguin, 1963), p. 79.

[70] Marx, *Capital* (Chicago, 1909), III, chap. xlii, pp. 1038–40.

receive incomes which differ less from each other than they do from rent, profits and wages. Though not altogether immune from market forces, their incomes are not the direct result of bargaining in the market, but are in a sense set aside by society according to the value set by it on their services, under their persuasion. The first profession was that of the clergy, whose income, significantly, was called a 'living': an income set aside by the laity, not as a reward for their service – which, once incumbent in the living, they were free except in conscience to supply or omit – but a guaranteed income to enable them to perform their office. The second and third were those of law and medicine, in which fees might seem to bear some relation in detail to piece-rates and in aggregate to profits. Yet fees, too, were not (in theory) fixed by competition, but by the value set by the profession, and accepted by society, on services which the client could not judge and had therefore to take on trust. All 'true' professions stem from these three, and are characterized by expert, esoteric service demanding integrity in the purveyor and trust in the client and the community, and by non-competitive reward in the form of a fixed salary or standard and unquestioned fee.

This is not, of course, to say that either the professional man or the community always lived up to these high standards. In the old society there were always plenty of 'hedge priests', 'pettifogging attornies', 'dishonest apothecaries', 'fee-snatching office-holders', and 'writers prostituted to Ministers'; and both clients and society were apt to treat all but the very highest levels of the professions with scant respect and scantier reward, viz. the underpaid curate, the apothecary at the tradesman's entrance, and the threadbare government clerk. The professional man could then be anything from rich, respected *savant* through dependent retainer or licensed jester to despised charlatan. Being by nature hierarchical interests dependent on patronage, stretching from the aristocracy of office on the bishops' and judges' benches down to the level of the petty tradesman, the professions fitted snuggly into the old dependency society.

The Industrial Revolution, however, which emancipated the entrepreneur and the wage-earner, also emancipated the professional man. With urbanization and the rise of living standards, doctors, lawyers, writers, and even the clergy (including dissenting ministers) found an enlarged demand for their services, which reduced their dependence on the few rich and increased that on the many comfortable clients of their own social standing. The transition enabled them to acquire a greater measure of self-respect, and to demand corresponding respect from society. 'Respectability' was the conscious aim of the 'gentlemen practisers' who set out to substitute for the eighteenth-century one of the 'pettifogging attorney' the nineteenth-century one of the 'respectable solicitor', through the local societies which culminated in the Law Society of 1825.[71] The surgeons and apothecaries, the general practitioners of the eighteenth century, achieved enhanced status through the Royal College of Surgeons of 1800 and the Apothecaries' Act of 1815.[72] Even the Anglican clergy, the most dependent of professions and the most consistent defenders of the aristocratic system, were not immune. In raising the standards, self-respect and independence of the profession the Evangelical and Oxford movements were for once on the same side, the first by demanding a more sober standard of conduct, morality, speech and dress than the average gentlemanly cleric of the eighteenth century, the second by emphasizing the sacerdotal character of the clerical office which segregated them from the laity and freed them from lay control.[73]

At the same time new professions proliferated, and organized themselves to demand the same kind of status and independence as the old: the civil engineers in 1818, the architects in 1837, the pharmacists in 1841, the mechanical engineers in 1847, and so on – though many of these took some time to differentiate themselves from the adjacent entrepreneurial occupations of building and contract, shop-keeping, machine-making, and the like.[74]

More significant than any of these particular developments, however, was the general rise in the status of the professional intellectual in society. This can best be seen in the most intellectual of professions, the profession of letters, at both the mundane and sublime levels. At the mundane level, authorship at last became a profession in the material sense. It was no longer mainly a pastime for gentlemen like Dryden, Addison and Pope and a low-paid occupation for Grubb Street hacks like Defoe or Johnson, but a regular profession at which a Walter Scott, a Southey or a Cobbett could make a comfortable, sometimes handsome living.[75] Aristocratic clients like Thomas Moore might condemn the 'lowering of standards that must necessarily arise from extending the circle of judges; from letting the mob in to vote, particularly at a time when the market is such an object to authors', but

[71] R. Robson, *The Attorney in 18th-Century England* (Cambridge, 1959), esp. chap. x, 'The Road to Respectability'.

[72] C. Newman, *The Evolution of Medical Education in the 19th Century* (1957), pp. 2, 73.

[73] Cf., *inter alia*, M. M. Hennel, *John Venn and the Clapham Sect* (1958) and Geoffrey Faber, *Oxford Apostles* (Penguin, 1954).

[74] G. Millerson, *The Qualifying Professions* (1964), pp. 121, 126.

[75] Cf. J. W. Saunders, *The Profession of English Letters* (1964), esp. chaps. viii and ix.

they could not resist the rewards of the mass market for best-sellers.[76]

At the sublime level — whatever one thinks of the rise or fall of literary standards — there is no doubt that inordinately higher claims were made in the early nineteenth century for the importance and influence of authors. They were no longer Adam Smith's 'unprosperous race of men, commonly called men of letters', but Shelley's 'unacknowledged legislators of the world'; Coleridge's 'men of genius' whose imagination was 'an echo in the finite mind of the eternal act of creation in the infinite I am'; Carlyle's 'Man-of-Letters Hero . . . our most important modern person . . . the light of the world; the world's Priest: — guiding it like a sacred Pillar of Fire in its dark pilgrimage through the waste of Time.'[77] The evolution of the romantic conception of genius deserves an unromantic monograph, but meanwhile it can be said that the romantic movement represents a social emancipation of the intellectual and the artist exactly parallel to the birth of class.

What characterized the emancipated professional men as a class was their comparative aloofness from the struggle for income. It was of course only comparative. Individuals found the struggle only too real, while each profession collectively knew that its value in the market could be increased by restricing entry and 'closing the shop' like any skilled trade union. Nevertheless, there was a sense in which professional incomes were only indirectly influenced by the market, or rather, that it was implicit in the professional outlook to pretend that the rewards demanded for their services were not be to questioned. At any rate, once established, the professional man could generally rely on a steady income not subject to the same mutual competition as rent, profits and wages. To a certain extent, then, he was above the economic battle, with the same freedom to take sides, to turn his thumbs up or down, as a spectator in the Roman Colosseum. More often than not, no doubt, he went with the crowd, or the most influential part of it, the middle tiers or the patrician boxes. But, not being involved, he had the more freedom to choose on the merits of the contest. He was, in short, a ready-made 'social crank', who could be relied upon to come to the aid of any class but his own.

In any other class, to be a 'social crank' required great strength or at least perversity of character. 'No high-sounding maxims can influence

<hr/>

[76] T. Moore, *Memoirs, Journal and Correspondence* (ed. Lord John Russell, 1853–1856), VII. 46; Murray, the publisher, was said to have paid Moore £3,000 for *Lallah Rookh* – J. W. Saunders, *The Profession of English Letters*, p. 177.

[77] Smith, *Wealth of Nations*, I, 38; P. B. Shelley 'A Defence of Poetry', in *Essays and Letters* (ed. E. Rhys, 1886) p. 7; S. T. Coleridge, *Table Talk* (1835), II, 87; T. Carlyle, *Heroes and Hero-Worship* (1893 ed.), pp. 144–6.

the rich as a body,' that remarkable 'social crank', the Owenite land-owner William Thompson, pointed out. However, 'a few individuals may rise above the impulses of their class'; these few should be 'numbered among the heroes and philosophers of society.'[78] Professional men, once emancipated, did not need to be heroes. They were the philosophers of society by inclination and training. It was they who supplied the major part of the social analysis and terminology used by the three major classes. It was Adam Smith and the Scottish historical school of philosophy, academics all, who first systematized the language of class.[79] It was the classical economists, all professional men except Ricardo, who, according to their opponents, set the classes at loggerheads. Their professional opponents thought in exactly the same terms of the tripartite class system: Carlyle of 'Workers, Master Workers, and Master Unworkers', Mathew Arnold of 'Barbarians, Philistines, and Populace', F. D. Maurice of 'the aristocracy, the trading classes, and the working classes'.[80] Indeed, what J. S. Mill said of the political economists could be applied to them all:

They revolve in their eternal circle of landlords, capitalists and labourers, until they seem to think of the distinction of society into those three classes, as if it were one of God's ordinances, not man's and as little under human control as the division of day and night.[81]

They were the forgotten middle class, in short, because they forgot themselves. Except when postulating a place for their idealized selves in other classes' ideal societies, they generally left themselves out of their social analysis. Nevertheless, professional men had a separate, if sometimes subconscious, social ideal which underlay their versions of the other class ideals. Their ideal society was a functional one based on expertise and selection by merit. For them trained and qualified expertise rather than property, capital or labour, should be the chief determinant and justification of status and power in society. For James Mill, for example, it was 'intellectual powers', not birth or wealth, which alone fitted men to rule. For Carlyle the natural rulers were 'the unclassed Aristocracy by nature . . . "who derive their patent of nobility direct from Almighty God".'[81]

[78] R. K. P. Pankhurst, *William Thompson . . . 1775–1833* (1954), pp. 21–2.
[79] Cf. chap. ii, §1, above.
[80] Carlyle, *Past and Present* (1893 ed.), pp. 5–6; M. Arnold, *Culture and Anarchy* (1869), chap. iii; F. D. Maurice, *On the Reformation of Society* (Southampton, 1851), pp. 10–13.
[81] 'A' [J. S. Mill], 'On Miss Martineau's Summary of Political Economy', *Monthly Repository*, VIII (1834), p. 320; Briggs, 'Language of "Class",' VIII (1834), p. 44.
[82] J. Mill, *Government*, p. 7; Carlyle, 'Shooting Niagara, and After?', *Macmillian's Magazine* XVI (1867), 319.

Similarly, selection by merit, rather than patronage, market competition (as distinct from competitive examination), or co-operative endeavour, ought to be the supporting principle of recruitment. Merit of course entered into all systems of recruitment: merit adjudged by the partron, by the impersonal market, or the acceptance of one's fellow workers. But in the professional ideal merit meant ability and diligence in one's chosen field of expertise, and could be judged only by other professional experts in the same field. The principal technique for such selection was the examination. The cult of the examination amongst the Benthamites is proverbial. Bentham himself regarded it as the perfect device for 'maximizing aptitude' and 'minimizing expense', and it was the cornerstone of his followers' educational endeavours from the Lancastrian schools of 1808 to the Society of Arts Examination Board of 1854.[83] It was no less a cult amongst their rivals: Thomas Arnold laid a new emphasis on examinations at Rugby, where in addition he replaced free entry for local boys by scholarship examinations, while his son Matthew devoted his professional career to examining elementary schoolchildren.[84] Examinations inevitably preoccupied the new professional institutes of the nineteenth century, and were absorbed into the framework of the State by Macaulay's and Trevelyan and Northcote's reforms of the Indian and home civil services.[85]

Examinations were a method of ensuring that the candidate was capable of performing the function for which he was selected. For the ideal society was a functional one in which trained and qualified experts provided efficiently and disinterestedly the services necessary to keep it functioning. The professions were bound to justify the privileges – incorporation, self-government, control of entry, and ultimately a legal monopoly of the occupation – which they increasingly claimed from the State, by the service which they provided for the community. They naturally extended the demand for justification by service to the rest of society. The Ricardians, for example, justified the capitalist by his service of managing industry and initiating the cycle of economic activity, and condemned the landlord for giving nothing in return for his unearned rent. Malthus, on the other hand,

[83] Cf. Brian Simon, *Studies in the History of Education, 1780–1870* (1960), pp. 79–84, 149–50; F. F. Foden, 'A History of Technical Examinations in England to 1918', PhD dissertation, Leicester University, 1961, pp. 3–4, 10–14, 19–20.

[84] T. W. Bamford, *Thomas Arnold* (1960), chap. xii; M. Arnold, *Reports on Elementary Schools* (1910).

[85] Millerson *The Qualifying Professions*, pp. 120–9; Wyn Griffith, *The British Civil Service, 1854–1954* (1954), pp. 12–16; E. W. Cohen, *The Growth of the British Civil Service, 1780–1939* (1941), pp. 118–23.

justified the landowner by his service of unproductive consumption which initiated the activities of the other classes. John Gray, the professional lecturer, hoped that all men would justify themselves in the society of the future by their labour, manual or mental:

In the old world, men are respected in proportion as they are enabled by the profession of wealth to command the labour of others. . . . In the new, we hope to secure to all men the value of their services to society in whatever way they may be given; to respect man in proportion of their *utility* in promoting in any shape or way, the happiness of our species; and to attach value, not to pieces of metal, but to *every thing* which tends to improve the condition of the human race, physically, morally, or intellectually.[86]

Gray's definition of service in terms of human happiness and improvement was characteristic of the professional idea. It followed naturally from the concern with function, which could be defined as the increasingly efficient satisfaction of human needs. The Benthamite 'principle of utility', of 'the greatest happiness of the greatest number', obviously fits the same model:

the only rational foundation of government . . . is, expediency – the general benefit of the communtiy. It is the duty of a government to do whatever is conducive to the welfare of the governed.[87]

More remarkably, the anti-Benthamite professional thinkers used identical language. For Coleridge the 'outward object of virtue' was 'the greatest producible sum of happiness of all men', and his 'positive ends of the State' were:

1 To make the means of subsistence more easy to each individual:
2 To secure to each of its members the hope of bettering his own condition or that of his children:
3 The development of those faculties which are essential to his humanity, that is, to his rational and moral being.[88]

The concern of professional men with happiness, progress and efficiency was not entirely altruistic. It was the function of the nineteenth century, Sir George Young has said, 'to disengage the disinterested intelligence, to release it from the entanglements of party and sect, . . . and to set it operating over the whole range of human life

[86] J. Gray, *A Lecture on Human Happiness* (1825), p. 3.
[87] N. W. Senior, Oxford Lectures, 1847–48, in *Industrial Efficiency and Social Economy* (ed. S. L. Levy, 1929), II, p. 302.
[88] Coleridge, *Aids to Reflection* (1825), p. 39; *Second Lay Sermon* (1839), p. 414.

and circumstance.'[89] In so far as it did this institutionally, it was the disintersted intelligence of professional men – doctors, lawyers, civil servants, engineers, scientists, social workers, teachers and professional thinkers – which it brought to bear upon its problems. These men were not necessarily superior, morally and intellectually, to their fellows in other classes, but they had a professional interest in disinterestedness and intelligence. It was their interest to 'deliver the goods' which they purveyed: expert service and the objective solution of society's problems, whether disease, legislation, administration, material construction, the nature of matter, social misery, education, or social, economic and political theory.

★ ★ ★ ★ ★

It was not to be expected that the other classes should share their self-admiration. There was in all three major classes a built-in suspicion of intellectuals, of men who were too disinterested to be reliable, who had no hard economic interest to bind them to their adopted class. This was in fact an extension of the suspicion of all 'social cranks', whose whimsicality had led them into the quixotic championship of a different class, and might at any moment lead them out again. Suspicion of intellectuals led the TUC to exclude Frederic Harrison and all other middle-class sympathizers from membership in 1883, and suspicion of the 'advanced Liberals', the middle-class 'cranks', both professional and capitalist, who were leading the Liberal Party into both land and social reform was to help to alienate the Whig landowners and Liberal business men who drifted to the Tories in the last quarter of the century.[90] In the long run the attempt by professional thinkers to moralize the other class ideals failed, as moralizing without a material *quid pro quo* is apt to do.

[89] G. M. Young, *Victorian England, Portait of an Age* (1960).
[90] S. and B. Webb, *Trade Unionism*, p. 347n.; R. C. K. Ensor, 'Some Political and Economic Interactions in Later Victorian England', *Trans. R.H.S.*, 1949.

10

A One-Class Society

PETER LASLETT

A one-class society may appear at first sight to mean one where there is no inequality, because everyone belonged to the same class.[1] But it has already been laid down that this cannot have been so in the pre-industrial world, at least in Europe. The *ancien régime*, as the historians call it, was marked by a very sharply delineated system of status, which drew firm distinctions between persons and made some superior, most inferior. There were various gradations, all authoritatively established and generally recognized. If class were simply a matter of social status, of the various degrees of respect in which men are held by their fellows, then it could not be said that the world we have lost was a

Extracts from the section 'Social divisions and power relations amongst nobility and gentry, townsmen and peasants' in *The World we have Lost*, (Methuen, London, 1971), pp. 23–41, 44–9, 52–4.

[1] Weber's concepts of class, status and power in relation to pre-industrial European society have been much written about, especially with relation to England, but there is no work specifically addressed to the theory of the subject. The position taken up in this chapter about class and status generally is roughly that of W. G. Runciman: see his contribution, 'Class, Status, Power?', in J. A. Jackson (ed.), *Social Stratification* (Cambridge, 1968), and his *Social Science and Political Theory* (1963), ch. VII: compare also the reader compiled by R. Bendix and S. M. Lipset, *Class, Status and Power* (1967). J. H. Hexter expresses contemporary scepticism about multi-class division in early modern England: see his *Reappraisals* (1965) expecially on The Myth of the Middle-class in Tudor England, and Storm over the Gentry. This latter essay is a contribution to the vast literature on the rise of the gentry, and contains a list of works, which can be filled in from Lawrence Stone, *Social Change and Revolution, 1540–1640*, (1967). Social structural description, especially of the gentry themselves, has gone forward as an incidental to this controversy, but there have been some studies specifically directed to it. The yeomen are dealt with by Mildred Campbell, *The English Yeoman* (1942), and the labourers are well described by Alan Everitt in J. Thirsk (ed.), *Agrarian History*, vol. IV, 1500–1640 (1967): see also G. Batho on the landlords. A recent critical description of the early Stuart social structure is found in Zagorin, *Court and Country* (1969).

Original sources for this chapter, apart from Cambridge Group File 3, are the works published and in manuscript, of Gregory King and such descriptions of English society as Edward Chamberlayne, *Angliae Notitia*, 1669, 1670, 1671 . . . 20th Edition (1702).

one-class society. On the contrary, it would have to be described as a society with a considerable number of classes, as many as there were distinct steps in the graduated system of status.

But when the word class is used, in conversation and by historians, it does not merely refer to status or to respect. The distribution of wealth and power is also at issue. This is obvious when the phrase class-conflict appears. For it nearly always seems to imply the clash of groups of persons defending and enhancing not simply a common status but also interest and power. The emphasis is on the solidarity of classes as groups of persons which act in championship of their con-flicting aims. Such classes have a further characteristic in ordinary usage: they are nation-wide.

It is in this sense that we shall claim that there was, in England at least, only one class in pre-industrial society. A distinction will be drawn between a status group, which is the number of people enjoying or enduring the same social status, and a class, which is a number of people banded together in the exercise of collective power, political and economic. The argument will be that there were a large number of status groups but only one body of persons capable of concerted action over the whole area of society, only one class in fact.

It is unfortunate that an introductory study of this character should have to be concerned with anything as difficult, contentious and tehnical as the question of class. It is unfortunate also that the only vocabulary which is open to us to discuss it should be that designed for nineteenth- and twentieth-century society. 'Status groups' and 'class' do not fit at all well as description of sets of people belonging to Stuart England, and most of the rest of the terminology used by sociologists is inappropriate too. These expressions have implications belonging to rather different social structures. But literary critics, even novelists have talked about traditional England in these terms, as well as historians and sociologists. We cannot direct our attention to the everyday life of our ancestors and the scale on which they lived it out without any notion of the overall shape of their society, its macro-structure as it might be called, in contrast to its micro-structure where, as we have seen, the family was the key. The macro-structure of Stuart society moreover has become a subject of world-wide discussion because a good part of the contemporary world has to believe in a particular version of what is called The English Revolution for political reasons. Class conflict in the age of Charles I and Cromwell is not simply a matter of social antiquarianism.

There is a sense, of course, in which the phrase 'class-conflict' might be appropriate to pre-industrial society, even if it did contain only one class. For the conflict could be between those who were included within it and everyone else. Perhaps if the expression were always used in this very restricted sense, it would be acceptable as a rough description of what went on. It is certainly not part of our purpose to deny that conflict existed at this time. But historians have not in fact used the phrase in such a restricted way, or in any very closely defined fashion at all. When they have discussed rising and falling classes they have obviously had in mind interaction of a very different kind. Sometimes, perhaps not very often because their language has been so vague, they have made the precise error of confusing a status group with a class and have proceeded as if status groups could rise, fall, conflict, be self-conscious, have a policy. Let us leave these generalities for a moment and look more closely at status symbols and systems in our industrial society as well as in that of our ancestors.

We now inhabit a world of immeasurable wealth and many of us are possessed of a power and a consequence never before known on such a scale. Our society is therefore marked by an intense search after status and after symbols to express it. The most important of those symbols is a personal title, an addition to a man's name, proclaiming who he is, how much success he has had and how much he ought to be respected. There is a whole study of the part which titles and other less satis-factory and specific symbols of status have to play in our contem-porary world and on its social, economic, even its political stage. The difficult problem for us in our day is to find out how status and its symbols are to do their necessary psychological work unless they belong to a recognizably coherent system. This used to exist in pre-industrial times but change since then has been so rapid and profound that it survives today only in a form so attenuated that it can hardly fulfil its functions any longer.

The reasons for this are complex, but the most obvious is that we want contradictory things – a system of status and universal social equality. It is easy to illustrate the difficulties. Some issues of relative social importance can still be settled fairly simply; we can put a managing director, for example, on a level with a lieutenant-colonel, though it begins to be a little puzzling when we consider whether the executive secretary of a professional society, say of electrical engineers, is in the same category of status. When it comes to extremes, our status system breaks down altogether. We have no intelligible methods for relating a world-ranking pop musician and a cardinal-archbishop. We know that they are both influential people, and must be treated with due deference, but we cannot relate them satisfactorily one to another.

We cannot weigh them up against each other, but even if we could we have no set of symbols universally recognized which could give even a rough expression of their relative importance. The pop-star can, and will, collects as many signs of superiority as possible, of an enormously variegated sort, but none of them help very much when we compare them to the traditional titles of the senior and successful cleric. For the symbolic superiority of a cardinal-archbishop belongs to an ordering which the master of the media of our day can never hope to share. This ordering is an inheritance from the world we have lost.

'Lost' may not be quite the proper word here, and for two reasons. One is that in some contemporary societies and for certain purposes, the status system of the traditional, pre-industrial world is still in use with all its necessary symbols: near imaginary use perhaps we ought to say, since the effectiveness both of the traditional status and its trappings are so much reduced. Just as the English still seem to want to live in the structures of the pre-industrial world, prizing the thatched cottage and the half-timbered house as the proper place for the proper Englishman to dwell in, so also do the English go on awarding the symbolic titles which belong to the status system of the world we have lost. We go on creating knights and barons, setting up industrial peerages, and calling cricketers and jockeys 'Sir', though we no longer understand the system which informed these honorifics and are uneasily aware that their distribution may not correspond to the true distribution of consequence in our society. This is typical of the way in which the world we have lost is in some sense still present with us, or at least of the difficulty we have in becoming conscious of its ghostly persistence, and so addressing ourselves to the problem of putting something else in its place.

But the second reason why the word 'lost' is somewhat paradoxical when we talk of the system of status and its symbols in the pre-industrial world is that elsewhere it was not a case of losing but of rejecting. Titles of honour were deliberately obliterated, first in the United States, then in France and so successively in other European countries, at their 'revolutions'. Great Britain is one of a handful of countries which has not yet found it proper to abolish them by law. The subject of status and its symbols is, therefore, of particular interest to English historians. Here is something in our present which we know to affect the lives of everybody, since the hierarchy of status we preserve so meticulously is by no means confined to titles of nobility and marks of gentility, yet which can only be explained by reference to a past we have nearly forgotten. This is one of the ways in which our country, which was the first to be industrialized and to lose most of the economic institutions of the traditional Europe, has nevertheless clung for the longest and with most affection to little, unrelated fragments of the world we have lost.

We live, in England, among the material remains of a patriarchal society of peasants and craftsmen: those stately churches, spacious manor houses, farmsteads, cottages, millhouses, bridges, all built for itself by the familial social order which is the subject of this essay. We find them interesting, often quaint and picturesque, and always, if we are honest, a little puzzling too. We are puzzled in exactly the same way when we try to decide whether to put 'Esq.' or 'Mr' on a letter. If we ask ourselves why we use these abbreviations at all, we find that we do not quite know. Yet these are the most common of all status symbols and we use them every day.

We call each other *gentlemen* as well, although we have some difficulty in deciding what the word means. Defining *gentleman* indeed, and disputing about the qualities which go to make one, is a favourite pastime of those who write impressionists' accounts of social history. The rest of us, if ever it occurs to us to decide, dismiss the expression as having by now no meaning at all. It can no longer be defined by contrast since everybody expects to be called a gentleman, and to be addressed in writing as *esquire*. So it is not difficult to guess that the descriptions 'Mister' and 'Esquire' must one have implied that the person addressed was in fact a gentleman. But further than that we usually cannot go.

There could be no more vivid illustration of our dim and partial understanding of the pre-industrial world. In that society of peasants, craftsmen, labourers, husbandmen, and a very few gentry and nobility, the word *gentleman* meant something tangible, substantial enough, if uncertain in precise definition. It was a grade amongst other grades in a carefully graduated system of social status and had a critically important use.

The term gentleman marked the exact point at which the traditional social system divided up the population into two extremely unequal sections. About a twenty-fifth, at most a twentieth, of all the people alive in the England of the Tudors and the Stuarts, the last generations before the coming of industry, belonged to the gentry and to those above them in the social hierarchy. This tiny minority owned most of the wealth, wielded the power and made all the decisions, political, economic and social for the national whole. It you were not a gentleman, if you were not ordinarily called '*Master*' by the commoner folk, or '*Your Worship*'; if you, like nearly all the rest, had a Christian and a surname and nothing more; then you counted for little in the world outside you own household, and for almost nothing outside your small village community and its neighbourhood.

'Nothing' is too strong a word perhaps, and in every society, however constituted, even the smallest unit, the weakest influence, is of some account, has to be allowed for in the general social process. The plain Richard Hodgsons, Robert Boswells, Humphrey Eltons and John Burtons of the English villages, the labourers and husbandmen, the tailors, millers, drovers, watermen, masons, could become constables, parish clerks, churchwardens, ale-conners, even overseers of the poor. They had something of a public life, within the tiny boundaries of the village, and this might give them a minor consequence in the surrounding villages. If they happened to be technically qualified, they might even cast a vote at an election. But in none of these capacities did their opinion matter very much, even in the last. They brought no personal weight to the modest offices which they could hold. As individuals they had no instituted, recognized power over other individuals, always excepting once again those subsumed within their families. Directly they acquired such power, whether by the making or the inheriting of wealth, or by the painful acquisition of a little learning, then they became *worshipful* by that very fact. Then and then only could they know anything substantial of the world, which meant everything which went on outside their own localities, everything rather which was inter-local, affecting more communities and localities than one.

To exercise power, then, to be free of the society of England, to count at all as an active agent in the record we call historical, you had to be a gentleman. When you came to die you had to hold one of those exceptional names in a parish register which bore a prefix or a suffix, about one name in fifteen or twenty seems to have been the average. The commonest addition to a name to be read in a register is *Mr*, for the word 'Master', and *Mrs*, for the word 'Mistress', applied to the maidens as well as the wives and widows. *Gent.* and *Esq.* are rare amongst the additions, as is the word *Dame*, the designation of their wives, and *Knight* and *Baronet* are, of course, much rarer still. The reader with the whole population in his mind, as distinct from the reader with an eye only for the interesting and attractive, will, or course, occasionally come across the titles *Lord* or *Lady*, and the ceremonious phrase 'The Right Honourable the . . .' which was often used to introduce them. But the higher titles of nobility are absent for all practical purposes when the whole population is under review. They are rather like the four-leaved clover to the collector of flowers, or perhaps the winning ticket numbers in a national lottery; one knows they must exist because the system demands it, but one never sees them. Nevertheless, page after page, year after year, decade after decade in the books recording, conscientiously, the burials in an ordinary English parish church will show some title or other for 3 per cent, 5 per cent or at most 10 per cent of the names, never very much more unless the parish had extraordinarily aristocratic or even Royal connections. All the rest of the entries are for simple names and surnames.[2]

Yet the history books we read are studded with much grander titles, and no one seems to appear in them who was without any title at all, except perhaps in the cursory chapter heading 'social'. Which is one way to show again that *England* in the pre-industrial era meant a small minority of the English, small, select and special. Not everyone who belonged to the majority of those who were nobodies felt this exclusion; contemporaries comment often enough on the rich yeoman, for a yeoman was the rank or status immediately below the critical divide, who refused to 'bear the port or mien of a gentleman'. But if the yeoman himself did not wish it, his son or grandson would find it difficult to resist the temptation and the pressure to assume the title and responsibility of gentry. Most of those on the way up in the world needed little persuasion, for when a man was successful the reward was tangible and important, and the higher a family went the more remarkable the difference was from the situation in which its rise began. The great nobles of the traditional world lived a life of superiority which we can no longer imagine, because we no longer possess so clear and overt a system of status.

However lofty the traditional social structure was, the point of transformation was the change which came with the transition from the commonalty to the gentry. Here was a society which has no devices for the saving of labour, none that is when we compare it with our own. The simplest operation in everyday life needed effort; drawing water from the well, striking steel on flint to catch the tinder

---

[2] Some parsons and parish clerks, naturally, were more generous, and others less generous, in distributing titles to their entries and it would be foolish to expect any rigorous consistency. We have used the burial entries as the most revealing for the purpose, and results of such analysis (along with those for marriages, see below) will be published in due course. Here are three arbitrary examples: Manchester, 1653–5, 3.9 per cent of 2,380 death entries contained some title like 'gentleman' or higher, and the addition of those marked *Mr* or *Mrs* brought the total up to 11.3 per cent. Of those buried at Ludlow in Shropshire, between 1632 and 1641 5.2 per cent bore some such title, and between 1599 and 1633 the proportion was 6.6 per cent as Wem in the same county. Studies have been sent to the Cambridge Group of the registers of a group of Yorkshire parishes, showing that persons actually named as gentry in birth or death entries there in the eighteenth century varied from less than 1 per cent (Addingham, 1767–1812) to over 3 per cent (Otley, 1721–40, Ilkley, 1718–1810) – work of Mrs Mary Pickles.

alight, cutting goose-feather quills to make a pen, they all took time, trouble and energy. The working of the land, the labour in the craftsmen's shop, were infinitely taxing. The surviving peasantry in Western Europe still shock us with their worn hands and faces, their immeasurable fatigue. Yet the primary characteristic of the gentleman was that he never worked with his hands on necessary, as opposed to leisurely, activities.

The simple fact of leisure dividing off this little society of the privileged – it had to be little at a time when the general resources were so small – is the first step in comprehending the attitude of our forefathers to rank and status. The law of the land laid it down how long common men should work and how little they should rest:

And be it further enacted by the authority aforesaid, That all artificers and labourers being hired for wages by the day or week shall, betwixt the midst of the months of March and September, be and continue at their work, at or before five of the clock in the morning, and continue at work, and not depart, until between seven and eight of the clock at night (except it be in the time of breakfast, dinner or drinking, the which times as most shall not exceed two and a half hours in a day, that is to say, at every drinking one half-hour, for his dinner, one hour, and for his sleep, when he is allowed to sleep, the which is from the midst of May, to the midst of August, half an hour at the most, and at every breakfast one half-hour). And all the said artificers and labourers, between the midst of September, and the midst of March, shall be and continue at their work from the spring of the day in the morning, until the night of the same day, except it be in time afore appointed to breakfast and dinner.

This was laid down in 1563 in the famous Elizabethan Statute of Artificers,[3] as it is usually called, which made compulsory by law the common practice of the time. At the County Assizes, the judges had to inquire whether there were workers who 'do not continue from Five of the Clock in the Morning till Seven at Night in the Summer and from Seven till five in the Winter'.[4] No mention of sleeping-time here, even in the heat of harvest. Still Breughel's sleeping harvester was an ordinary working man acting on his rights; he was no visionary, no drowsy peasant drunkard.

Although those in work for wages lived a life of rough, incessant toil – no Saturday afternoons, none even of the safeguards of the early

---

[3] The Statute of Artificers, (5 Eliz. c 4), para. IV, quoted from R. H. Tawney and E. Power, *Tudor Economic Documents*, 1924 (1951) vol. I, p. 342, modernized.

[4] Serjeant Thorpe, Judge of Assize for the Northern Circuit, his charge to the Grand Jury at York Assizes March 20th, 1648, printed in *Harleian Miscellany*, vol. II, (1744), p. 12.

Factory Acts – not all the common people were caught up in productive work. This is outstandingly evident from Gregory King's famous table of the structure of English society, reproduced as Table 1. It was drawn up in the 1690s and applied to the year 1688. It divides up the population of the country in such a way as to show that more than half the people then alive were dependent – 'Decreasing the Wealth of the Kingdom' is the expression appearing in King's *General Account*.[5]

King's calculation was made on extensive and probably fairly reliable evidence, and was the only one ever worked out by a contemporary for a European society in wholly pre-industrial times. It is now supposed that the reason why so large a proportion of the population could not wholly support itself was because there was not enough productive work to do.[6] The more impressionistic writers in Gregory King's time and before it did not hesitate to call everyone below a certain level by insulting names: the *rascals*, or *rascality*, the *proletarii*. In the 1560s Sir Thomas Smith, a respected lawyer, spoke his mind in this way, and his is an instructive comment on the common people of England in their relations with their social superiors.

For this observer, English society had a fourfold division:

1 'The first part of the Gentlemen of England called *Nobilitas Major*'. This is the nobility, or aristocracy proper.
2 'The second sort of Gentlemen called *Nobilitas Minor*'. This is the gentry and Smith further divides it into Knights, Esquires and gentlemen.
3 'Citizens, Burgesses and Yeomen'.
4 'The fourth sort of men which do not rule.'

We shall concern ourselves in due course with the relationship between these four divisions. Our present interest is in Smith's detailed description of the lowest of them. These are his words:

[5] King's table was printed by Charles Davenant in his *Essay upon the Probable Methods of Making a People Gainers in the Ballance of Trade*, in the year 1699. This version is reproduced here on pages 36–7. It differs in detail from that which forms part of a manuscript treatise entitled *Natural and Politicall Conclusions Upon the State and Conditions of England*, by Gregory King, Esqr, Lancaster Herald at Armes, AD 1696, along with other tables of importance for the study of pre-industrial society. In this work, which was never published in King's lifetime, no explanation is advanced as to why the general distinction was made, and very little evidence to justify any of the statistical work is offered. We have found, however, that King's figures are surprisingly accurate wherever we have been able to provide independent checks on them. King's manuscript treatise was printed from an original in the British Museum (Harleian MSS 1898: there are other manuscripts) in 1802 by George Chalmers as an appendix to an edition of his *Estimate of the Comparative Strength of Great Britain*, and again from the same source in Baltimore, USA in 1936 by George E. Barnett under King's title.

[6] See the very important article of D. C. Coleman, 'Labour in the English Economy of the 17th Century', *Economic History Review*, new series, VIII, 3 (1956).

The fourth set or class amongst us is of those which the old Romans called *capite sensu proletarii* or *operarii*, day labourers, poor husbandmen, yea merchants or retailers which have no free land, copyholders, and all artificers, as tailors, shoemakers, carpenters, brick-makers, brick-layers, etc. These have no voice nor authority in our commonwealth and no account is made of them, but only to be ruled and not to rule other, and yet they be not altogether neglected. For in cities and corporate towns, for default of yeomen, inquests and juries are impanelled of such manner of people. And in villages they are commonly made churchwardens, aleconners, and many times constables, which office toucheth more the commonwealth.[7]

Even though Smith was prepared to use the word *proletarii* of these people, the old Roman expression meaning those able to produce nothing but offspring, *proles*, as their contribution to society, it does not appear that this description includes the humblest of all. These 'low and base persons' as Smith goes on to call them may not have made up the complete whole of the majority of the population which was 'decreasing the wealth of the kingdom' and some of them may have been increasers. The really large groups of lowly persons are not mentioned by Smith. Though King's 'labouring people' appear, his 'cottagers and paupers' are not mentioned at all. The truly poor, the begging poor, had no craft and could never have become constable or ale-conners, as could the proletariat of Sir Thomas Smith.

Begging was universal, as it is today in some of the countries of Asia; beggars at the door, outside the churches, in the market-places and wandering along the roads. Men sometimes took fright at their numbers, especially in Tudor times, and the savage laws against sturdy vagabonds have become notorious in the textbooks. Everyone knows that Elizabeth made each parish responsible for its own poor, and that when a pauper could be identified as from another community, he or she was sent along the highway from place to place until the place of settlement was reached. These outcasts have left their sad traces in the registers of deaths in our churches: 'a poor walking woman buried', 'a wandering beggar lad', 'a poor woman name unknown who had crept into Mr Miller's barn'.

Yet crowds of destitute people were not typical of poverty in the old world in quite the way that queues of unemployed are typical of industrial poverty. The trouble then, as we have hinted, was not so much unemployment, as under-employment, as it is now called, and

---

[7] Sir Thomas Smith, *The Commonwealth of England* (1560s) (published 1583, edition of 1635) p. 66. The parish records of the seventeenth century make it clear that labourers did hold office as churchwardens and constables, and often attempted administrative tasks beyond their capacities as readers and writers.

Table 1 *Gregory King's Scheme of the income & expence of the several*

Number of Families	Ranks, Degrees, Titles and Qualifications	Heads per Family	Number of Persons
160	Temporal Lords	40	6,400
26	Spiritual Lords	20	520
800	Baronets	16	12,800
600	Knights	13	7,800
3,000	Esquires	10	30,000
12,000	Gentlemen	8	96,000
5,000	Persons in greater Offices and Places	8	40,000
5,000	Persons in lesser Offices and Places	6	30,000
2,000	Eminent Merchants and Traders by Sea	8	16,000
8,000	Lesser Metchants and Traders by Sea	6	48,000
10,000	Persons in the Law	7	70,000
2,000	Eminent Clergy-men	6	12,000
8,000	Lesser Clergy-men	5	40,000
40,000	Freeholders of the better sort	7	280,000
120,000	Freeholders of the lesser sort	5½	660,000
150,000	Farmers	5	750,000
15,000	Persons in Liberal Arts and Sciences	5	75,000
50,000	Shopkeepers and Tradesmen	4½	225,000
60,000	Artizans and Handicrafts	4	240,000
5,000	Naval Officers	4	20,000
4,000	Military Officers	4	16,000
500,586		5⅓	2,675,520
50,000	Common Seamen	3	150,000
364,000	Labouring People and Out Servants	3½	1,275,000
400,000	Cottagers and Paupers	3¼	1,300,000
35,000	Common Soldiers	2	70,000
849,000		3¼	2,795,000
	Vagrants; as Gipsies, Thieves, Beggars, &c.		30,000
	So the general Account is		
500,586	Increasing the Wealth of the Kingdom	5⅓	2,675,520
849,000	Decreasing the Wealth of the Kingdom	3¼	2,825,000
1,349,586	Neat Totals	4¹/₁₃	5,500,520

families of England calculated for the year 1688*

Yearly income per Family		Yearly income in general	Yearly income per Head			Yearly expense per Head			Yearly increase per Head			Yearly increase in general
£	s.	£	£	s.	d.	£	s.	d.	£	s.	d.	£
3,200		512,000	80	0	0	70	0	0	10	0	0	64,000
1,300		33,800	65	0	0	45	0	0	20	0	0	10,400
800		704,000	55	0	0	49	0	0	6	0	0	76,800
650		390,000	50	0	0	45	0	0	5	0	0	39,000
450		1,200,000	45	0	0	41	0	0	4	0	0	120,000
280		2,880,000	35	0	0	32	0	0	3	0	0	288,000
240		1,200,000	30	0	0	26	0	0	4	0	0	160,000
120		600,000	20	0	0	17	0	0	3	0	0	90,000
400		800,000	50	0	0	37	0	0	13	0	0	208,000
198		1,600,000	33	0	0	27	0	0	6	0	0	288,000
154		1,540,000	22	0	0	18	0	0	4	0	0	280,000
72		144,000	12	0	0	10	0	0	2	0	0	24,000
50		400,000	10	0	0	9	4	0	0	16	0	32,000
91		3,640,000	13	0	0	11	15	0	1	5	0	350,000
55		6,600,000	10	0	0	9	10	0	0	10	0	330,000
42	10	6,375,000	8	10	0	8	5	0	0	5	0	187,500
60		900,000	12	0	0	11	0	0	1	0	0	75,000
45		2,250,000	10	0	0	9	0	0	1	0	0	225,000
38		2,280,000	9	10	0	9	0	0	0	10	0	120,000
80		400,000	20	0	0	18	0	0	2	0	0	40,000
60		240,000	15	0	0	14	0	0	1	0	0	16,000
68	18	34,488,800	12	18	0	11	15	4	1	2	8	3,023,700
									Decrease			*Decrease*
20		1,000,000	7	0	0	7	10	0	0	10	0	75,000
15		5,460,000	4	10	0	4	12	0	0	2	0	127,500
6	10	2,000,000	2	0	0	2	5	0	0	5	0	325,000
14		490,000	7	0	0	7	10	0	0	10	0	35,000
10	10	8,950,000	3	5	0	3	9	0	0	4	0	562,500
		60,000	2	0	0	4	0	0	2	0	0	60,000
68	18	34,488,800	12	18	0	11	15	4	1	2	8	3,023,700
10	10	9,010,000	3	3	0	3	7	6	0	4	6	622,500
32	5	43,491,800	7	18	0	7	9	3	0	8	9	2,401,200

* See note 5.

once more the comparison is with the countries of Asia in our own century. Too many members of a family were half-busied about an inadequate plot of infertile land; not enough work could be found for the women and children to do round the cottage fire, in some districts none at all, for there was no rural industry in them. Everywhere work of all kinds varied alarmingly with the state of the weather and of trade, so that hunger was not very far away, as we shall see. Starvation, we perhaps ought to add at once, cannot yet be shown to have been a present menace to the poor Stuart times.

No one could call a life of this sort a life of leisure, even if it was not a life of ceaseless toil for everybody, and leisure as had been said was a mark of the gentleman. The most celebrated Elizabethan definition of a gentleman comes from Harrison's *Description of Britain*, published in 1577. Besides the sons of gentlemen already recognized, he says:

Whosoever studieth the laws of this realm, who so abideth in the university giving his mind to his books, or professeth physic [that is medicine of course] and the liberal sciences, or beside his service in the room of captain in the wars, or good counsell given at home, whereby his common-wealth is benefitted, can live without manual labour, and thereto is able and will bear the port, charge and countenance of a gentleman, he shall for money have a coat and arms [coat of arms, etc.] bestowed upon him by the heralds (who in the charter of the same do of custom pretend antiquity, service and many gay things) and thereunto being made so good cheap, be called master, which is the title that men give to esquires and gentlemen, and reputed for a gentleman ever after.[8]

Any professional man, any university graduate, any officer in the royal forces, therefore, was a gentleman in England by that very fact, and the business of coats of arms, ancestry and public service could all be assumed; the heralds who were responsible would make it all up if required. Harrison is a little obscure when it comes to the matter of money necessary to attain gentility, but popular opinion was much more straightforward: 'In England gentry is but ancient riches'. The historian is always coming across families which obey this simple rule. If a family had the money for long enough, just over one succession was generally sufficient, it graduated to the gentry. By money here is meant means sufficient to enable a family to live without doing manual work.

Gentility and its ranks were objective realities as well as honorifics: they counted for example when taxation systems were devised. The Poll Tax, imposed in 1660 for the first time was graduated according

[8] William Harrison, *Description of England* (1577, 1587) (1968), pp. 113–14.

to rank: a really ordinary person paid only 6*d*. a year, but a gentleman paid £5, an esquire paid £10, a knight £20, a baronet £30, a baron paid £40 and his heir £30, a viscount £50 (£35), an earl £60 (£40) and a duke £100 (£60).[9] The time when you could be legally compelled to dress according to your rank was passing, though private correspondence is full of resentment at common people wearing the clothes reserved to the socially superior. But the distinction between those who were and those who were not within the gentry was still of overriding importance. It could be said without much distortion of the very elusive facts that this distinction in the eyes of our ancestors was only less significant than the sharpest of all distinctions, that between the Christian and a heathen. Indeed the very phrase 'A Christian and a gentleman', a typical survival of the values of that vanished world, suggests such a comparison. It also leaves open the possibility that a man could in some sense be a gentleman without being a Christian.

The system of status does not seem to have prevented social mobility. Movement into the select minority was straightforward enough in Harrison's view; a man simply had to have the necessary qualifications and be acceptable to those already there. But this is not the end of the matter. A great deal more will have to be found out about the family background and economic resources of men who were able to get entrance to a university, or to a profitable profession, or to commissioned rank in the army and so on, before it will be clear exactly how often gentlemen were recruited in this fashion. All that can be said with much confidence is that it did happen and that it was noticed and accepted by contemporaries.

When we come to consider social mobility rather more closely, we shall find ourselves having to assume that it must have been going on all the while in pre-industrial England, if only because of vital statistics. The scale of this movement may have been small and it undoubtedly varied from time to time, but it went on in both directions, downwards as well as upwards. In fact rather more people must have descended than ascended in society. Social mobility is always most pronounced as the frontiers, so to speak, and in traditional society this meant at the crucial divide between the minority which ruled and the mass which did not rule. The fact that this movement was constantly happening was one of the circumstances which made it possible for the single ruling group to maintain its supremacy and to adapt its membership to changing conditions.

In such a situation it seems hardly likely that simple upward motion in society can have been the final effective cause of political strife and

[9] Act of 12 Car. II, Cap. IX.

civil commotion. There were other reasons for social mobility than vital statistics; obviously an imcompetent family above the line of division which mis-managed its affairs and dissipated its fortune was likely to go down, and a family of capable people below the line which was making money was likely to go up. In spite of the elaborate arrangements to maintain the community of the privileged in their position, which was far easier to ensure in that agrarian society than it is in our own industrial society, interchange due to such influences could not be entirely prevented, and presumably happened most often at time of pronounced economic change. It is possible therefore that periods of particularly intense economic change might have been marked by unusually pronounced social mobility, and this might conceivably have led to unrest and conflict, particularly if there was any blockage, so to speak, any threat of resistance from those unwilling to be replaced. But if what is called the English Revolution was like this, then it was very different from a conflict of classes as that term has ordinarily been used. It leaves little room for the rise of a class, the capitalist or middle class as a group of persons. Even some of those who wish to retain a modified version of the rise-of-a-capitalist-class view of social development in pre-industrial times have begun to recognize that the capitalists as a group of persons capable of coming into conflict with other groups of persons are unlikely ever to be identified in England under pre-industrial conditions.[10] Rather it is now supposed that the whole of the English gentry, in our own terminology the whole of the ruling segment, was imbued with bourgeois values by the middle years of the seventeenth century. According to this view the world of gentleman, parson, peasant, craftsman and pauper was already a 'fully possessive market society', where conflict must presumably have been due to the internal contradictions of capitalism rather than to the clash of bourgeoisie and aristocrats. If this was so, the rivalries and clashes between Englishmen in Stuart and even Tudor times, intellectual, political and military, can hardly have been of an inter-class character. They must have gone on within the one class.

[10] See for example the books of Christopher Hill. The position taken up in his very stimulating and influential general history of England in Stuart times, *The Century of Revolution* (Edinburgh, 1961), is rather different from that which he took up in 1949, when he made the following statement about events in England from 1640 to 1660: 'Very briefly summarised, our subject here is the story of how one social class was driven from power by another.' (*The Good Old Cause* edited by C. Hill and E. Dell (1949), p. 19.) Professor Brough Macpherson is responsible for the general reformalation of the position about capitalism (or the 'market society') and seventeenth-century England. See his important book *The Political Theory of Possessive Individualism, Hobbes to Locke* (Oxford, 1962).

Social change and development in the pre-industrial world need not, therefore, be thought of in terms of classes which rise, conflict and fall. It perhaps ought to be emphasized once again that this does not mean that opposition of economic interest was absent from that society. No sharper clash of interest, material, economic or even biological, can be easily imagined than that between those with and those without access to the land. In an agrarian economy not far removed from the subsistence level in some areas and in some periods, this might have meant that when harvests were bad some men could count on surviving, whilst others, the landless, could not be so sure. But this confrontation of class interest in the sense that whole un-organized masses of persons were on the one side and a few, concerted persons were on the other, is very different from an overt or covert collision between the rising bourgeoisie on the one hand and the falling feudality on the other. Rather it was an opposition between all those within and all those without the possessing minority which we have already referred to.[11]

The graduated ladder from top to bottom of the social scale has already been referred to as the status system. Status depended for the most part on the position a man occupied on that ladder, though there was some admixture of status which arose from his actual function in society and his personal achievement. Status, that is to say, did not come exclusively from the title a man had inherited or had conferred on him. Nearly all the height of the social ladder was to be found within the ruling minority, within that part of the whole society which contained the nobility and the gentry, though the men below that line did share to some extent in the status system. I have tried to represent the facts in the chart given as Table 2, drawing the dividing line below Gentleman.

At the very top of the society came the monarchy, but it was related to the whole in many other ways than that of status and its very special position is not our present concern. Under the Throne came the nobility, two hundred families, a thousand people or so, in a popula-

[11] No more general claim is made for the definitions of class and status in the text than that they seem to correspond to the uses made of the concepts in the loose discussions of historians, particularly Marxian and post-Marxian historians. Only action groups are by definition of importance for them because only action groups can enter into historical events, such as rebellion, revolution or governmental action. Obviously if the common work-situation of individuals be taken as the critical characteristic of class, as for example by David Lockwood (see *The Blackcoated Worker* (1958)), or if 'the way a man is treated by his fellows' is taken to be its essence, as it is by T. H. Marshall, *Citizenship and Social Class* (Cambridge, 1950), it would be possible to identify many social classes in Stuart England, but none of them, it is claimed, was likely to ever come into relation with another, or other, of them, in such a way that collective group conflict, such as the Civil Ware of 1642–8 could possibly have been created.

Table 2 *Chart of Rank and Status, Stuart England*

Grade	Title	Form of Address	Status Name	Occupational Name
GENTRY — NOBILITAS MAJOR (Greater Nobility) — LORDS AND LADIES				
1 Duke, Archbishop	Lord, Lady	Honourable Right Honourable	Noblemen	None
2 Marquess		The Lord		
3 Earl		My Lord My Lady		
4 Viscount		Your Grace (for Grade 1)		
5 Baron, Bishop		Your Lordship Your Ladyship, etc.		
NOBILITAS MINOR (Lesser Nobility) — GENTLEMEN				
6 Baronet	Sir	The Worshipful Your Worship, etc.	Gentlemen	[*Professions*] Army Officer Medical Doctor Merchant etc.
7 Knight	Dame*†			
8 Esquire	Mr			
9 Gentleman	‡Mrs			
Clergyman	[† Sir]			[Your Reverence]
10 Yeoman	†Goodman	†Worthy	Yeoman	
11 Husbandman	†Goodwife (Goody)			Husbandman
Craftsman	None	Name and Surname only	None	Name of Craft (Carpenter, etc.)
12 Tradesman				
Artificer				
13 Labourer				Labourer
14 Cottager Pauper				None

*　Often called *Lady* by courtesy.
†　Occasional, absolescent usage.
‡　For unmarried as well as married women.

General note to scheme of Ranks

The common tendency for a person to be called by a rather higher title than the one to which he was strictly entitled was already present. For example the wives of Knights and Baronets were called *Lady* rather than *Dame*. Usage was stricter amongst the nobility and also somewhat complicated. Any nobleman might be called *Lord* (Lord Norfolk, Lord Shaftesbury), but in the higher ranks the actual grade was almost always specified on each occasion (the Duke of Norfolk, the Earl of Shaftesbury). Most noblemen had titles of honour different from their family names (Anthony Ashley Cooper, Earl of Shaftesbury). Occasionally however the family and the title were identical (Ralph Montagu, Duke of Montagu). Some courtesy titles were in use for their heirs: more usually, the heirs to noble titles would be called *Lord* followed by the family name, but the brothers and sisters of heirs of noble titles were often called plain *Mr* or *Mrs*. They were all entitled of course to the general designation *Honourable* as an additional forms of address. The grandsons of holders of titles were quite usually called *Mr* without the *Honourable* and so came to be recognized as plain gentry. Usage below the line of gentry, as is emphasized in the text, was very much more uncertain because what status there was was associated with occupation.

The clerical equivalents given above represent usage, but status was uncertain and some clerics (especially those without benefices) were often regarded as below the line of gentry. The status name applied to all members of a family, that is to say the wife and children of a nobleman, were all noble, and of a knight, all gentle. In the case of the clergy, wives and children were always in an equivocal position. There was a tendency for the occupational name of a professional man to be associated with his status name, so that the son of a merchant would be described as a merchant. Below the gentry line this tendency seems to have taken the form of associating the children with the status below that of the head of the family, so that a yeoman's sons would call themselves husbandmen and husbandmen's sons labourers.

tion of some five and a half million – by 1690 in Gregory King's reckoning (see Table 1).[12] Yet most of the gradations in the system of honour were contained within this little gilded network; his Grace the Duke (or the Archbishop), the Marquess, the Earl, the Viscount, and lowest of all, His Lordship the Baron (or the Bishop). These were the *nobilitas major* of Sir Thomas Smith, but described by him as belonging to the gentlemen of England all the same. Every step in the honorific grading was meticulously marked and every noble family strove to mount the next one upwards of the glittering steps. Differences in wealth sometimes made the distinctions unrealistic, for even in Stuart times a viscount on the coal measures might outweigh a marquess on the Northern moors, but it could not obliterate them.

It cannot be said that the whole society of the nobility ever acted as a group; their identification with the gentry as a whole was reality, not a piece of legal fancy. We now know for certain that a majority of all marriages made by the English nobility from the sixteenth century until the twentieth were made with commoners, mainly with the gentry.[13] This may mark off our English titled families from their continental counterparts, and hierarchy was notoriously less rigid in England than elsewhere in Western Europe. But they had a remark-able privilege of their own nevertheless which gave them a defined, active institution and consolidated political power; they had the House of Lords. It may seem extraordinary to assert that in spite of this the peerage in England was for all purposes except the details of their status at one with the rest of the ruling segment, the gentry as a whole, yet this was undoubtedly the case. To look on the peerage as a class apart, to see it simply as an element surviving from the feudal age, resenting, and in rivalry with, the humbler members of the privileged order, is only a partial understanding of the system of status.

★ ★ ★ ★ ★

Baronet, knight, esquire, gentleman – these were the grades below the peerage in Tudor and Stuart time, Smith's *Nobilitas Minor*. All these titles, like the title of nobility, were honorifics only, not descrip-

---

[12] About 200 seems to be the number of such families referable to England and Wales in successive editions of Chamberlayne. King allots 6,400 *persons* to his 160 noble families, but all except 4 or 5 in each family must have been servants.

[13] See Hillingsworth, *Demography of the Peerage* (1964). Nearly 40 per cent of peers' sons born between 1550 and 1674 married daughters of peers; this proportion fell to 25 per cent for peers born 1700–1749. Mr D. N. Thomas, in his M.Phil. thesis for the University of London (*Marriage Patterns in the British Peerage in the 18th and 19th Centuries* (1969)) shows that peers marrying outside their order chose mostly partners from the gentry, but married extensively into the bourgeoisie and the professional classes, sometimes even into the lower levels of society.

tions of function. But we have seen that Harrison does talk of a man's function as qualifying him for gentle status, since a physician, a don, a military officer were gentlemen, he thought, by virtue of doing what they did. Another fiscal measure of the Stuart parliaments, an Act passed in 1694,[14] which goes into status to a degree of minuteness which has to be read to be believed, is even more straightforward about who and who was not a gentleman. It imposed a tax to be collected 'upon burial of every Gentleman or reputed Gentleman, or owning or writing himself such'. Phrases of this sort are quite common in legal discussion of the crucial difference between those who belonged to the privileged and ruling minority. In fact a man's reputation as a gentleman depended to a considerable degree on what he did, when it was not obvious to all who knew him that he had been born to that status. The Poll Tax quoted earlier lists a whole range of holders of legal, ecclesiastical and even commercial offices as being liable to taxation at levels corresponding to grades of the nobility and gentry. The equivalent grades were usually rather modest ones, except for certain lucrative legal offices.[15]

Such provisions as these amount to an overt, legal recognition of movement into the gentry, even deliberate provision for ensuring that anyone making money or attaining any form of social consequence should succeed to gentle status. Let us pursue the hierarchy of status below the critical divide, and into the largely undifferentiated mass of ordinary people. Before we do so we may notice that the lowest grades of gentry enormously outnumbered the titled grades. With less than two hundred noble families in his table (Table 1), it was reckoned by Gregory King that there were in 1688 eight hundred families of baronets and six hundred of knights, but three thousand families of esquires and twelve thousand of gentlemen. This only makes up a third or more of the full number of those who must be reckoned to have composed the ruling segment at that time, a third of the one in twenty we referred to earlier. The other two-thirds must have been

[14] 6 and 7 William and Mary, c.6. This act, and the returns to which it gave rise up to the time of its repeal in 1705, are of great importance to English history both demographic and sociological. The listings of inhabitants in Cambridge Group, File 3 on which so much has to be based, are commoner for the period 1695–1705 than for any other in pre-census times, and there is a danger that our view of pre-industrial social structure as a whole may for this reason (and because of the connected work over the same years of Gregory King, see note 5) be true of the 1690s only. The act, its origin, its importance, its research possibilities, its workings, are authoritatively discussed by Professor Glass: see Glass, 1965, 1966, 1968, 1969.

[15] See note 9. In the twelve first companies (Goldsmiths, Drapers, etc.) the assesment went like this: Master £10 (equivalent to that for an Esquire), Liveryman £5 (equivalent to that for a gentleman); the liverymen were ex-masters or potential masters and of the same social standing), yeoman £3 (above a clergyman £2, but below a gentleman).

those with the title 'master' (*Mr* on our letters), self-reputed or locally recognized gentlemen rather than those living on estates in land. This was what might be called the penumbra of the privileged group and again will concern us when we come to social mobility.

Status amongst the common people, the vast majority, went with occupation in so far as it was marked at all; it was a matter of function, not description. The only status name as such which men recognized below the line, so to speak, was the name 'yeoman' (see Table 2). Even this was to some extent a functional term, since a yeoman had to be a fairly substantial owner (not renter) of land which he had to work himself, for he emphatically did not come under the idleness rule which defined gentlemanliness. Alternatively, and here the much greater vagueness of terms for these lower statuses is already to be seen, such a man might be called a freeholder, a greater freeholder (much more likely to have the alternative title yeoman) or a lesser freeholder (probably a freeholder without the vote, that is with less than 40s. a year from his own land). Sometimes, during the final generations of the old order, he might be called a farmer, and this is a functional name altogether. It has survived as the only term we now use for those occupied in agriculture.

Yeoman then, was the status name of the most successful of those who worked the land. This was a name which became sentimentalized very early, whilst the men who had held it under the old order became farmers under the new. It is interesting that there was a *yeoman* status even in the companies of craftsmen in the cities and that it should have come below the status of *master* in those associations. The word yeoman has survived in our vocabulary, whilst the functional name based upon what we call farming, working the land, the word *husbandman* has disappeared. All yeomen were husbandmen, because they worked the land, but not all husbandmen were yeomen by any means, because most of them had neither the qualifications nor the status. Since a yeoman's sons worked the land without owning it, they were often called husbandmen too, and most husbandmen were workers of land they did not own but rented. There was a very special sense in which even a gentleman might sometimes describe himself, in his letters, shall we say, as a *husbandman*. For a gentleman had to direct work on his land, even if he was not supposed to engage in the labour itself.

Husbandman, then, was an extremely common description of men in the old world, because it was the description of what so many of them were engaged in, tending the animals and tilling the soil. Alongside of husbandmen came all the other callings, the craftsmen.

Husbandmen and craftsmen are given no titles in our table and were addressed always by simple name and surname, followed where necessary by their occupational name. The word *worthy* would sometimes be used as a sort of prefix to their names, though never in quite the way in which *worshipful* was associated with gentry. Yeomen would be called *worthy* more readily, and the occasional use of this word emphasizes the very considerable variation which men called husbandmen or crafsmen might show in their prosperity and importance. There was an enormous difference between a draper in the City of London engaged in large-scale cloth dealings and a tailor or a blacksmith in a village, even if the draper was not substantial enough to be regarded as worshipful and gentle.

'Mechanick' was the title often given to the meaner handicrafts: John Bunyan, the tinker, was thought of as a 'mechanick preacher'. The craftsmen in the towns must nearly always have worked on a larger scale than those in the countryside, but in town and in country the overriding impression of the grade of craftsman was of its multifarious variety. Miller, tailor, ploughwright, weaver, plumber, dyer, bricklayer, carpenter, mason, tanner, innkeeper, all these are still familiar words and many of them common surnames. Some of the occupations of craftsmen which the historian finds have disappeared so completely from our memory that the ordinary reader does not usually recognize them: there were the fletchers (arrow-makers), badgers (corn-dealers), cordwainers (leather-workers), whittawers (sadlers). How many readers would know that hedge-cutting or hedge-laying, was probably what the *plasher* did, who is listed as living at Clayworth in Nottinghamshire in 1688?

All these men, and the yeomen too, were described simply by their Christian and surnames whenever they were mentioned: plain John Hart, husbandman, or James Buckland, carpenter. It had been some centuries since ordinary Englishmen had lacked surnames, but it can easily be seen how natural it was when surnames came in to call Peter the Smith, Peter Smith. On the Continent of Europe the older naming custom survived longer; in Holland for example the common folk did not acquire second names until the time of Napoleon.

There were three further names of common people: *labourer, cottager* and *pauper*. Only *labourer* in any sense described status or function. A *labourer* could be either of the other two, and a man who called himself that could not call himself a husbandman, because he did not work land on his own account. He could have no other calling-name, because he had no specific calling; he just worked for other people. *Cottager* was a description, not of a calling but of a means of livelihood which was not specific. Getting a living where you, you and your whole family, could make one, and wringing all that was possible out of the land which might be attached to the hovel you lived in. This is an unwieldy description, but it is as short a way as I have found of placing a cottager in the old order. The final term, *pauper*, speaks for itself.

According to Gregory King (see Table 1), the largest group of families in England was in fact made up of 'Cottagers and Paupers', 400,000 out of 1,350,000. If we regard these as the lowest in the social scale, in spite of the recognition that 'scale' does not strictly apply below the line, the enormous inequality of life in the world we have lost immediately becomes apparent. Not all of these wretched families must be counted as permanently below the level of subsistence, as the early sociologists used to say, or in what was once called primary poverty. But they were for varying periods in poverty of some sort, in need of relief. In fact that whole half and more of the population which Gregory King described as decreasing the wealth of the kingdom may well be supposed to have been living in intermittent poverty in the England of 1688. Indeed it is probably safe to assume that at all times before the beginnings of industrialization a good half of all those living were judged by their contemporaries to be poor, and their standards must have been extremely harsh, even in comparison with those laid down by Victorian poor law authorities.[16]

There is another important characteristic of King's figures which we must not overlook, because it demonstrates a general principle which

[16] *The poverty line in seventeenth-century England.* The families which Gregory King names as making up that half of the population which was 'decreasing the wealth of the kingdom' seems a rather miscellaneous assemblage: seamen, 'labouring people and outservants', cottagers and paupers, common soldiers and vagrants (see above). Evidently King was not anxious to be specific about the poor, and the major interest in these descriptions is what they did not include. Obviously King did not think that 'shopkeepers and tradesmen', 'artisans and handicrafts' were in permanent poverty since he places them above the 'decreasing' line, but this does not mean that the carpenters, bricklayers, masons, thatchers, weavers, coopers and so on were always out of poverty. It seems much more likely that they were in poverty at certain times of their lives, or in bad seasons, or for some weeks even in good seasons, but not perpetually dependent in the way that labourers, cottagers, paupers and the common soldiery were. This was the pattern of the industrial proletariat in the late nineteenth century and the early twentieth century when they were studied by Rowntree and Booth.

The statement in the text is true if King's estimates are reliable. In an economy of the type he was describing any person in receipt of a transfer income from the wealthier people must surely be in need of such an income in order to subsist, and this is the sense in which it seems best to understand King's concept of 'increasing or decreasing' the national wealth. It is very difficult to believe that such transfers were taking place in order to equalize wealth, or to add to the incomes of those who already had enough to keep them out of poverty. No doubt such transfers did go on in favour of the craftsmen who were sometimes liable to poverty, but on balance craftsmen appear to have been self-sufficient, which was perhaps why King did not think of them as permanently among the decreasers.

was a striking feature of social arrangements as they were in his day. The total number of people he gives as five and a half million, of which we have seen a little over half (2, 825,000) were 'decreasing the wealth of the kingdom' and a little under half (2, 675,520) were increasing it. But the difference in the number of 'families' (we should now, of course, use the word 'household') between these two halves was very much greater; only 501,000 'families' were in the richer section as against 849,000 'families' in the poorer section. Poor people, therefore, lived in small households, and rich people in big ones, though some members of rich households, the servants, came from poor homes and might themselves die in poverty. The general principle, then, runs as follows: the higher the status of the household or family, the larger it was, and the humbler people were, the smaller were the houscholds they lived in. The majority of households were the small, poorer ones, and the minority the large, richer ones, even though more people in total lived in them than in the smaller ones. Humble families in fact lost some of thcir members, as servants to richer families. We shall return to the size of the family and household in due course; all we are registering here is its connection with the hierarchy of status.

If the phrase middle class seems to have so many misleading associations when it is used of any part of Stuart society, there was of course a middle range of income and status in the plain numerical sense as thcrc always must be. Indeed the 'middling sort of people' began to enter into social descriptions in Stuart times and it is interesting to find that the term was mostly used of the towns. We must look a little closer at the townsfolk and the bourgeoisie in order to decide the extent to which they can be said to havc lived apart from the rest of the population, even though like cverybody else they found themselves under the domination of the ruling minority. Can it be said that the two thousand familics of 'Mcrchants and Traders by Sea' which Gregory King estimated as existing in 1688, or ten thousand of them in all if the lesser ones are included, really formed the bourgeoisie in pre-industrial England? Or would it be realistic and useful to call Sir Thomas Smith's third sort of men, 'Citizens, Burgesses and Yeomen' by the title middle class?

Though yeomen and merchants must have come from the same stock, and though there might seem to be some rough sort of equivalencc in the position of the more modest burgesses with that of the substantial peasantry, Smith is exceptional in linking them together in this way. In the provincial towns – how insignificant they were will become obvious later – the local grazier who was also a butcher had already appeared in the sixteenth century and his is a figure which persisted until the twentieth century. Nevertheless the towns had a life of their own, small as they were, and any acquaintance with municipal records will show how intense such a community feeling could be. It was at the top that the linkage with society as a whole is to be seen, and it was the link between the gentry and the merchants which preoccupied the men of the time.

* * * * *

Perhaps the phrase a 'one-class society' would fit no other European country as well as it seems to fit pre-industrial England, even with all the complicated exceptions and reservations which have had to be made in the course of this chapter. This title gives rise to no expectation that the workers of the pre-industrial world can be thought of as a community apart from the rest, which is a further advantage over the usual phraseology. Detailed analysis of the working force, or the labour force as the economists say, cannot be undertaken here and it is one more of the subjects which will have to be pursued elsewhere for itself alone. There was a considerable number of wage-earners even before large-scale industry made the wage packet the almost universal form of payment and support. Indeed there is evidence that even in Tudor times well over a half or even two-thirds of all households received some part at least of their income from wages. Nevertheless the paupers, when they were fortunate enough to receive wages, the labourers, the artificers, even the husbandmen and the yeomen who pocketed such payments from their employers were in a very different position from the worker in the factory, the shop or the office. They did not all share a common work situation by any means, as do the members of the working class in the contemporary industrial world.

A considerable part of the labour force, moreover, cannot have been householders at all. These were the servants living in the households of their masters and the grown and growing children still at home and at work at the bench or in the fields. Most of them were young, but some of them were as old as the heads of their households, and a very few even older, unmarried and now largely unmarriable. They were separated into the myriad familial cells which went to make up the society. Here we return once agan to the minute scale of life, the small size of human groups, before the coming of industry. Working persons were held apart from each other by the social system. Many or most of them were subsumed, as we have said, within the personalities of their fathers and masters. If it had not been for the terminology which was invented for a society like our own, it would never have occurred to us even to wonder whether they could be thought of as a community, a class of their own.

The working families were poor, and we have seen men of the time openly talking of them as the proletariat. 'Miserable men,' Westcote calls them, 'in regard of their labour and poverty.'[17] Everyone was quite well aware throughout the life of that social order that the poorer peasantry might at any time break out into violence. Talking about the 'pulling and contest' after money at a time of deflation, John Locke said in 1692 that this struggle usually went on between 'the landed men and the merchant'.

For the labourer's share, being seldom more than a bare subsistence, never allows that body of man time or opportunity to raise their thoughts above that, or struggle with the richer for theirs (as one common interest), unless when some common or great distress, unting them in one universal ferment, makes them forget respect, and emboldens them to carve to their wants with armed force, and then sometimes they break in upon the rich and sweep all like a deluge. But this rarely happens but in the mal-administration of a neglected or mismanaged government.[18]

Journeymen out of their time, but unable to set up for themselves; small masters miserably dependent on the capital of rich masters; husbandmen pinched for their rent by avaricious landlords; these were likewise looked upon as dangerous men who might sometimes become desperate.

But the head of the poorest family was at least the head of something. The workers did not form a million *outs* facing a handful of *ins*. They were not in what we should call a mass situation. They could not be what we should call a class. For this, it has been claimed, if the expressed can be used at all, was a one-class society. It must be clear that the question of how the *élite*, the ruling segment, was related to the rest is not an easy one to answer. A great deal of patient, intricate work of discovery and analysis will have to be undertaken by the historians before they can begin to decide such issues as these. They will have to show an imaginative sensitivity to all those subtle influences which enable a minority to live for all the rest. When they come to do this, it is the symbolic life of our ancestors which will be the most difficult to handle, and especially their symbols of status.

[17] T. Westcote, *A View of Devonshire*, (1845), p. 52.
[18] *Some Considerations of the Consequences of Lowering of Interest* (1692) *Works* (1801), vol. 5, p. 71.

11

Class Struggle and
Social Structure

JOHN FOSTER

The question is not what this or that proletarian, or even the whole of the proletariat, at the moment considers its aim. The question is what the proletariat is, and what, consequent upon that being, it will be compelled to do.[1]

SOLIDARITY AND FRAGMENTATION: SOME MEASUREMENTS

The previous chapter ought to have made it clear that some sort of move from trade union to class consciousness did take place in Oldham during the 1830s and early 1840s. It should also have indicated the importance of industrial factors in this process – a finding that would support the argument that the main *previous* social trend (during the period of coercive trade union solidarity) had been the formation – or at least strengthening – of industrially based occupational cultures. If this was so, and if a radical erosion and replacement of these cultures then took place, at least something of it ought to show up in terms of social structure. Compared with Shields (still in the stage of trade union consciousness) and the even less advanced Northampton, one would expect Oldham to reveal a markedly greater degree of social closeness between working people of different occupational backgrounds. Indeed, the mere growth of mass class consciousness ought to have brought with it a corresponding repudiation of any system of occupational hierarchy based on bourgeois values. What follows is an attempt to see whether this was in fact so.

From *Class Struggle and the Industrial Revolution: Early Industrial Capitalism in Three English Towns* (Weidenfeld & Nicolson, London, 1977) pp. 125–49.
[1] K. Marx, and F. Engels, *Holy Family* (written in 1844) (Moscow, 1956) p. 53.

Figures 1 and 2 show the principal measures that have been used: tests of how far working families with different occupational backgrounds (and particularly craftsmen and labourers) intermarried and lived next door to each other.[2] Obviously, marriage is a much more reliable test than housing because where people live also depends on what they can afford and its distance from where they work. Obviously, too, in making comparisons between towns, it is necessary to take into account the income differentials in each. If, for instance, the average incomes of skilled and labourer families are much closer in Oldham than Shields, they would – as a result of this alone – be more likely to live next door to each other, possess similar ways of life and consequently intermarry. So, to allow for this Figure 1(a) gives the degree of income overlap between craft and labourer families in relation to the poverty line (calculated in the same way as we have done before). Taking this into account, the results are quite surprising. They show that it was Shields – the town that comes out as having the greatest income overlap – that also had least intermarriage or neighbouring, and conversely Oldham with the least overlap that had the most intermarriage. To this extent, the evidence supplies fairly striking confirmation for the overall argument.

Plainly, the figures are not completely foolproof. Because of the deficiency of early marriage registration, they refer to a period considerably later than one would like: 1846–56 instead of the late 1830s and early 1840s. They are also mostly calculated from far too small a base (unfortunately even using the entire mass of several thousand marriages taking place in this period, the statistical likelihood of any two particular occupations intermarrying, turns out to be quite small). Worst of all, the figures do not reveal trend. They show the position at the end of the 1840s, but not how it developed. As a result they cannot rule out the possibility (admittedly a small one) that the exceptional social cohesion of Oldham's working population was a cause – not a consequence – of radical political consciousness.

Nonetheless, whatever the qualifications (and there are a number of others), there can be no doubt that the figures as a whole are mutually consistent and fit in with the purely descriptive evidence. Shields, for instance, did have quite pronounced occupational cultures. The secretary of its improvement commission found it possible to list occupations by precise neighbourhoods when replying to the health of towns commission in 1842:

---

[2] A full description of these sources and the methods used is given in appendix 2 [of *Class Struggle and the Industrial Revolution*, not reprinted here].

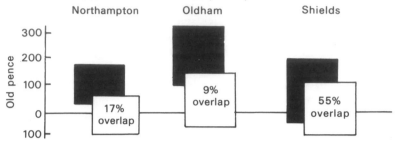

(a) POVERTY (1849)[3]
overlap of experience–distance (in pence) of the central cluster of craft and labour families from the poverty line

Northampton   Oldham   Shields

Old pence

300
200
100
0
100

17% overlap
9% overlap
55% overlap

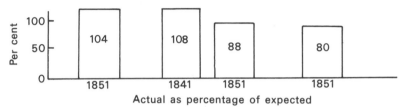

(b) HOUSING[4]
likelihood of a labourer family living next door to a craft family. 100 per cent–number of expected housing relations, given relative sizes of the groups in the population

Per cent

100
50
0

104   108   88   80

1851   1841   1851   1851

Actual as percentage of expected

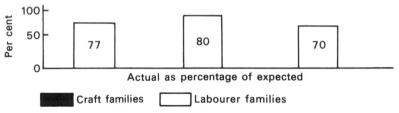

(c) MARRIAGE (1846–56)[5]
likelihood of a labourer family intermarrying with a craft family. 100 per cent–number of expected marriages, given relative sizes of the groups in the population

Per cent

100
50
0

77   80   70

Actual as percentage of expected

■ Craft families   □ Labourer families

Figure 1 *Social distance between craftsmen and labourers*

[3] The 'central cluster' represents (statistically) those families within one standard deviation of the mean income for the group. Craft occupations are defined as metal crafts, building crafts, printers, furniture and coachmakers and (in Shields) shipbuilders. Labourer families include paupers and washerwomen. The samples are the same as those used in the poverty survey described in appendix 1. The reults turn out to be quite contrary to the preliminary assumption made in Foster, 'Class Dimension', *Studies in Urban History*, ed. H. Dyos (1968) that – as today – the existence of work for women and children would tend to reduce the effect of male differentials. In fact, it was the skilled workers (presumably with more influence in the factories) who secured the lion's share of this work for their own families. This itself is eloquent testimony to the pressures which even the 'better-off' families were then exposed to.

[4] Using the significance test described in appendix 2, the figures for Oldham in 1841 are significant at 20 per cent ($X^2 = 1.87$) against those for Oldham in 1851 and at 5 per cent ($X^2 = 3.82$) against those for Shields in 1851. In Northampton (1851) the sample of 5,110 households

Marriages between the children of labourers and those of other workers how many
times more (or less) than chance expectation (1864–56)

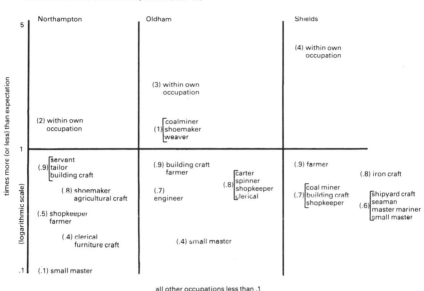

Figure 2 *Social distance within the labour force: three towns*[6]

The inhabitants may be classed and distributed as follows. First, the pilots
living in parts of districts six and fourteen (The Lawe). Second, the sailors
chiefly confined to the streets bordering the river. Third, the glassmakers.
Fourth, the labourers in the alkali works. Fifth, the pitmen (Templetown).
Sixth, the tradesmen and shopkeepers in the principle streets.[7]

And looking at the 'nationality' aspect of labour fragmentation (Figure
4) one finds Shields' Irish families (mainly alkali workers) considerably
more segregated in 1851 than Oldham's comparable sized Irish population in 1841 – when men of Irish origin (like John Doherty) occupied
leading positions in the south Lancashire labour movement.

---

included 1,097 neighbouring relations involving craft workers and 1,066 involving labourer
families. Of these 119 were *between* the two categories as against a 'random expectation' of 114.
Oldham (1841): total 2,748; craft 553; labourers 490; cross 54 against 50 expectation. Oldham
(1851): total 5,889; craft 1,474; labourer 1,546; cross 171 against 194 expectation. Shields (1851):
total 2,069; 701 craft; 707 labourer; cross 96 against 119 expectation.

[5] In Northampton there were 159 craft/labourer marriages against 206 expectation (3,146 total
marriages), Oldam 81 against 101 (5,550 total) and in Shields 53 against 76 (3,180 total).

[6] The same hierarchies are repeated (with one or two minor variations) if one follows through
the mutual interrelations of the component occupations.

[7] RC state of towns, second report part 2, appendix p. 185 (PP 1845 XVIII).

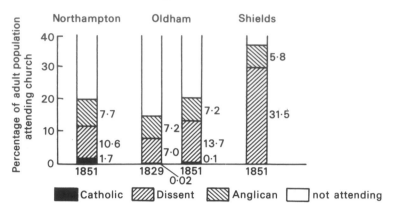

Figure 3 *Religious attendance, 1851: three towns*[8]

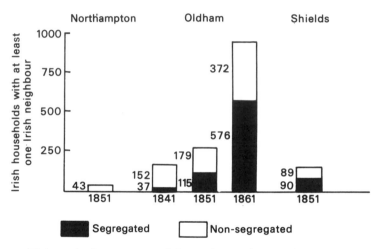

Figure 4 *Segregation of the Irish population: three towns*[9]

[8] The 1851 figures are taken from the religious census returns PRO HO 129/168 (Northampton) 475 (Oldham) and 550 (South Shields). For Oldham the returns relating to churches outside the parliamentary borough (in Tonge and Middleton) have been taken out. The figures are for congregations on 30 March 1851 and do not include Sunday school children. Following E. Hennock ('Birmingham Dissent'. Cambridge PhD, (1956), p. 265) 'real' attendance has been abstracted from the usual two or three Sunday services by taking the total attendance at the largest and half that at the next largest. The Oldham figures for 1829 come from the return made to the clerk of the peace by constables of 'the total number of places of worship not of the Church of England . . . and the total number of each sect' within each township (LRO QDV 9//267, 301 and 309) and for the Church of England the 1821 visitation report (Chester RO EDV 7/6) of 'usual attendance'.

[9] Census schedules. The figures are for households, not *families* or *houses*. One could find more than one family in a household and more than one household in a house.

Moreover, if Shields' social structure was a reflection of trade union consciouness, the results for Northampton fit in with what one would expect from a population still under direct bourgeois influence. Simple occupation was clearly less important as a basis for culture. Indeed in 1851 (though not 1841) one finds more craft–labourer neighbouring than in Oldham. Far more decisive were divisions which transcended occupation and expressed themselves in terms of social behaviour and consumption: how far a family was (or was not) 'respectable and hard working' in the eyes of its immediate local task masters. It was such divisions that largely dominated the villages from which Northampton's population mostly came, and in the town itself one can definitely find such differences cutting across occupation. This was particularly so among the shoemakers. A good proportion were definitely not 'respectable'. According to a *Morning Chronicle* journalist in 1851 their 'principle source of amusement . . . appears to be the "Free and Easy",'[10] and some years later another writing in *Good Words* noted a prevalence of drink and demoralization:

In the lowest parts of London I have never heard such *general* superfluity of obscene naughtiness issuing from youthful lips as I heard during my stay in Northampton. After nightfall on week days the . . . Market Square is disgraced by scenes of juvenile depravity quite as shameless as those which may be witnessed . . . on Sunday evenings in Upper Street, Islington.[11]

Yet, against this, one finds among Northampton shoemakers a bigger segment of 'respectable' chapel families than among any group of workers in the other two towns. Table 1 gives places of marriage by occupation.

The figures for church marriages are not strictly comparable. In Shields and Oldham it was the administrative custom for all but Non-conformist marriages to take place in church while in Northampton Registry Office marriages were already common. But looking at Nonconformist marriages alone (and in Northampton itself at the spread between all three types) it seems clear that there were radically different social allegiances *within* individual occupations. And, as the last chapter showed, it was in Northampton also that a significant portion of the labour force still remained under the fairly direct cultural control of their employers.

---

[10] *Morning Chronicle*, 23 January 1851.
[11] *Good Words*, 1 November 1869, p. 758.

Table 1 *Place of marriage by occupation of parents, 1846–56*[12]

Northampton % marrying in	Anglican church per cent	Nonconformist chapel per cent	Registry Office per cent
professional	95	5	0
tradesman	71	29	0
small employer	59	35	6
shopkeeper	69	16	15
farmer	79	13	8
metal craft	84	4	12
furniture craft	80	10	10
building craft	71	12	17
shoemaker	57	11	32
servant	72	6	22
labourer	65	12	23

Oldham	church per cent	chapel per cent	Shields	church per cent	chapel per cent
large employer	80	20	large employer	89	11
tradesman	91	9	tradesman	86	14
small employer	95	5	small employer	89	11
shop	94	6	shop	90	10
farm	97	3	farm	94	6
supervisory	92	8	master mariner	83	17
metal craft	98	2	shipyard craft	94	6
building craft	98	2	building craft	96	4
spinner	96	4	seaman	96	4
weaver	98	2	coalminer	97	3
hatter	98	2	labourer	96	4
labourer	98	2			

[12] Taken from the same survey of marriage certificates used in appendix 2. Up to 1838 all marriages (apart from special dispensations for Quakers) had *by law* to be performed in Anglican churches. Afterwards they could be conducted in Registry Office or any other duly licensed place of worship (Anglican or not). But it was still far easier to be married the traditional way and in Oldham the district registrar's office was anyway associated with the introduction of the new poor law (of whose machinery it was an integral part).

WORKING-CLASS LEADERSHIP

By and large, therefore, the social structure of the three towns does seem to reflect their differing levels of political consciousness. What remains to be examined – at least for Oldham – is the process of interaction itself. If in the course of the 1830s a labour consciousness was heightened into class consciousness, if occupational consciousness was indeed transcended, the actual people who achieved all this still remain unidentified. To really prove our point, what still has to be established is the existence of some sort of real-life struggle between old and new types of labour leaders.

This poses a good number of problems. Some simply concern evidence. In themselves the sources are rich. Home Office and legal records, diaries and newspapers make it possible to name not just dozens but hundreds of people active in Oldham working-class politics between 1830 and 1850 – certainly quite enough to destroy any notion that the town's working-class activity was just spontaneous mob violence. What we lack is *complete* information. Only a small part of any individual's total activity is recorded and probably up to half of those active slip through the net altogether. Of the twenty-one people arrested on conspiracy and sedition charges in 1842 (and who unlike those held for riot might be expected to have been active previously), only ten are recorded as having been so. This means that any attempt to build up coherent groupings of working-class leaders by matching particular campaigns and slogans can really only be used as a rough backing for more impressionistic findings.

The other main problem is that posed by the facts themselves. At any rate at first glance, the existing material (Table 2) does not indicate any decisive change in leadership during the early 1830s. Indeed, almost the reverse. Comparing the lists of leaders for these years with those before 1830 (mainly from 1815–20) two things are immediately apparent. The key men remained roughly the same throughout: Knight, Fitton, Haigh, Mills, Swire. And at least in occupational terms the composition of the leadership becomes less (not more) proletarian as one moves on in time. It is only after 1830 that one gets the appearance of significant numbers of shopkeepers, publicans and small employers.

Partly, the explanation is simply a matter of definition. The figures we have refer solely to those who were *politically* active – not to industrial militants as such. So if there is continuity, it is that of the Jacobin hard core (the only group likely to have been politically involved in the semi-legal conditions of the early decades). But, even granting this, there still remains the problem of non-proletarian elements – shopkeepers and publicans especially – joining after 1830. One can see why they did not do so before. As men occupying a relatively public and exposed position (and until recently playing a key role in the old system of social control), they had every reason to lie low during periods of popular disturbance. Certainly, their absence is conspicuous in 1816 and 1819. But why did they come forward after 1830?

Table 2 *Occupations of main working-class leaders*[13]

	1795–1830	1830–50
magnate	1	1
small employer	0	5
small master	2	2
shopkeeper, publican	0	9
beerhouse, cookshop	1	3
schoolmaster	1	2
'doctor'	3	2
building craft	1	2
metal craft	1	1
other craft	0	3
factory skilled	0	2
spinner	1	9
factory semi-skilled	0	1
weaver	10	0
hatter	3	1
tailor, shoemaker	0	4
labourer	1	3
not known	8	10
	33	60

It is, in fact, this apparent contradiction that supplies the best clue to the precise nature of the changes then taking place. The situation was not so much that of radicals taking over any existing movement, but rather of drawing under their control a whole number of previously

[13] 'Main working-class leaders' are defined as those whose names are *recorded* as being active three or more times in different years or who were arrested for sedition. 'Other craft' includes cloggers and basket makers (both occupations highly organized)'. Factory skilled are dressers, carders and twisters, and semi-skilled weavers.

fragmented parts of the working population. This is why the changed position of the shopkeepers is so significant. Previously, their ability to keep out of politics at least partly reflected the survival of a narrow 'non-political' labour consciousness which as publicans and shop-keepers they had good reason (and opportunity) to sustain. Now, in the new situation, the sheer momentum of radical politics (particularly exclusive dealing and the control of local government) forced them to become part of the larger movement, and to do so, what is more, on terms largely dictated by the working-class radicals. If, therefore, one wants evidence for a decisive change in labour's leadership (and by inference for the erosion of the social bases which previously sustained 'non-political' leaderships), it will best be found by examining the nature of this new political unity.

Insofar as the evidence allows, three distinct social groupings can be distinguished within it: the continuing group of working-class radi-cals, the shopkeepers and publicans, and a number of small employers. On the committee of the 1831 Political Union their members were represented in the ration of five, three and two, and this seems a fair weighting of their respective influence.[14]

The shopkeepers make their appearance during the later phases of the 1830–2 reform campaign (they played no part in the original attempt to establish a political union in June 1830 nor in the French revolution celebrations of August that year).[15] At times they attempted to maintain an independent course. They framed their demands in terms of the reform of a corrupt establishment (rather than class representation) and at the biggest of the mass meetings in October 1831 their acknowledged leader, Alexander Taylor, successfully intervened on the side of the employers, blocking a motion from Knight and Fitton in favour of annual Parliaments and the ballot.[16] Only during the election campaign which followed did they finally become inte-grated into the radical alliance. It was during these crucial months (July to December 1832) the working class radicals at last found themselves in a position to focus, on this small but socially key group of two to three hundred people, the full force of popular opinion. It was, they argued, not just Oldham's representation that depended on shopkeepers' votes but the whole larger fate of what was then the central concern of all working people in Oldham: the new Factory Act.

[14] Butterworth diary, 8 November and 30 December 1831. The radicals were Mills, Swire, Augustus Taylor, Wilde and Knight – who was secretary; the tradesmen Holladay and Halliwell.
[15] *Ibid.*, 14 June and 16 August 1830.
[16] *Ibid.*, 13 October 1831.

It is indisputable that the shopkeepers hold the power to separate their interests from the people, for if they vote for the return of Bright and Burge, who will not promise to reform one single abuse in the state, they identify themselves with that system by which you are injured, destroying at once that reciprocity of interest which should exist between you . . . and it is evident that your interest in their welfare is absolutely annihilated. . . .[17]

Under such pressures Oldham's shopkeepers finally capitulated. How far such enforced solidarity also developed a genuine commitment of its own remains unclear. Certainly, the shopkeepers were (in marriage terms) socially very close to the working population, as well as being uniquely well placed to understand the *generality* of economic distress. During the 1836–7 lock-out they demanded that the spinners be relieved out of the rates (and not by private subscription): 'The more they considered the causes of the affair the more evident would appear the obduracy of the employers. What advantage could there be in a subscription when every retail dealer and shopkeeper had been sub-scribing week after week to assist the sufferers, while the masters passed resolutions weekly to bring the men to compliance by starva-tion.'[18]

Yet against this has to be set the fact that the men who emerged as spokesmen (and mediators for a perhaps still less radical shopkeeper body) were not, in the last resort, reliable. Though Alexander Taylor, Knott, Stump and Stepney all spoke in favour of universal suffrage and the Charter, the campaigns with which they were particularly associated tended to be more aligned to the redevelopment of a limited labour consciousness: organizing aid to strikers and opposition to the new poor law and police (Table 3). Moreover, whenever things came to the crunch – as in August 1842 – it was Taylor and his colleagues who appeared with the compromise solution and eventually in the later 1840s (when the force of working-class mobilization started to disintegrate) played a key role in forming a new alliance with the employers.[19]

The characteristic ambiguity of the group can best be summed up by a brief description of Taylor himself. Taylor (1800–53) began his life as a powerloom weaver and then sometime in the later 1820s set up as a retail flour dealer. Between 1830 and 1850 there was almost no public meeting at which he did not speak and by the mid-1840s he had

[17] William Spier, *A List of Voters in the Borough of Oldham* (Manchester n.d.).

[18] Butterworth diary, 20 December 1836.

[19] This 'compromise' move (a committee to 'confer with the employers') must be distinguished from the local Chartist attempt to keep their members in line till the national executive had met (Butterworth diary, 12 August 1842).

Table 6 *Oldham working-class leaders: shopkeepers and publicans*[20]

Activity		Campaigns and slogans	
active before 1830	0	1832 – reform	2
reform campaign	5	1832 – class	0
short time 1831–3	6	1842 strike	0
Regeneration Society	0	1842 compromise	2
Charter 1838–41	4	Owenite Socialism	0
active 1842	0	1840s factory campaign	2
arrest 1842	1	Anti-poor law	5
Holladay support 1847	2	Anti-police	4
Cobbett support 1847	2	Strike support	6
active 1848	0	Ireland protest	0

Total number for which *any* information: 16

established a personal dominance over the popularly controlled parts of local government. At his death he was assessed on £5,000 personalty, giving some weight to the charges that he made a good thing out of exclusive dealing and the workhouse (which he ran till 1847).[21] His great strength lay in his ability to manipulate local government: he could intimidate the vestry and stage-manage crowds. He also understood the essentials of extra-legal unionism. From 1840 till 1847 Taylor led the fight against the new government-controlled rural police.[11] He moved the 1843 police commission motion against the use of the Town Hall as barracks; opposed the swearing of constables during the 1847 election.[23] In the poor law campaign his job was to produce crowd effects for Fielden's parliamentary campaign. This was how Fielden wrote to Taylor in November 1845: 'I have drawn up a few reasons in the shape of resolutions which you may either adopt or reject at your meeting tomorrow evening. You may in your speeches say much more severe things . . . but so far as resolutions go I think an appeal to reason is more likely to stay their proceedings.'[24] Fielden to Taylor, February 1846: 'If the overseers are [firm], why not re-elect

[20] These figures include all shopkeepers and publicans (though not beerhousekeepers, coffee shops or cookshops) for whom there is *any* reference of radical political activity.

[21] 1841 census schedule and will (LRO proved June 1853). B. Grime, *Memory Sketches 1832–52* (Oldham, 1887), pp. 59, 212 and 269.

[22] Butterworth diary, 2 January 1840, for some particularly outspoken statements by Taylor.

[23] Police commission minute book 1843–9 (Oldham Town Clerk's Office), 4 January 1843. *Manchester Guardian*, 8 July 1847.

[24] Fielden to Taylor, 23 November 1845 (OPL).

them? If not, get others who will be firm to succeed them.'[25] Taylor could see to this without much difficulty. And to give an idea of his mob appeal (as well as his anti-establishment – rather than anti-capitalist – rhetoric), here he is haranguing a mass meeting held to protest against the coronation in 1838:

It was a most gratifying and delightful spectacle to behold such an immense mass of human being met together, not like the lords and the squires and the gentry and the rest of the small fry that followed close upon their heels for the purpose of filling their bellies with luxuries they could not, would not and did not earn; and of exhibiting their embroidered coats and lace hats which had to be paid for by the labouring millions; they were not met for the purpose of exhibiting a loyalty they did not feel like hundred of the nobility and gentry were doing at that moment; and expressing an attachment to the queen which was only inspired by their love of pensions and places which had to be paid for out of the sweat and toil of an industrious, insulted and plundered people. . . .[26]

But Taylor was also the man who gave Oldham radicalism its formal death blow by concluding an electoral alliance with the Tories in 1852.

Like the shopkeepers, the other main subordinate social grouping, the small employers, were only drawn into the alliance during the final phases of the 1832 election campaign. Though somewhat less vulnerable than the shopkeepers, they occupied as economically marginal position in the town's economy and had certain common interests with organized labour, particularly the statutory enforcement of short-time. A considerable number were also engaged in wholesale trading and so potentially exposed to popular pressure.[27] The men responsible for handling their political affairs (it would probably be putting it too strongly to call them leaders of the small employers as a *body*) were largely dissenters – Holladay, William Halliwell, Quarmby – and their politics markedly anti-clerical and anti-establishment. (Indeed, the one occasion when they broke ranks was when they put up O'Connor as a counter-candidate to Morgan Cobbett in 1835 in a protest against his record on disestablishment.)[28] However, their most interesting characteristic was their fairly sudden espousal of Owenite Socialism. This – at least in a gutted 'union of industry' form – seems to have provided an ideological let-out for the somewhat forced alliance in which they found themselves. In the mid-1830s the group's

[25] Fielden to Taylor, 23 February 1846 (OPL).
[26] *Northern Star*, 7 July 1838.
[27] See below for details of this.
[28] Butterworth diary, 31 April and 20 December 1834. E. Butterworth, *Oldham* p. 207. *Manchester Advertiser*, 27 June 1835, 4 and 18 July and 29 August 1835.

principal spokesman, James Holladay, supplied much of the energy for setting up Oldham' Socialist Society, and in 1838 acted as host to Owen during his visit to Oldham.[29] Later on (after the collapse of mass working-class pressure) it was also under the pseudo-Owenite slogan of a 'union of the industrious classes' that Holladay finally broke with the working-class radicals and attempted to stand as parliamentary candidate against Morgan Corbett.

Looking at both these groupings, therefore, it does seem to have been the early 1830s that saw them largely abandoning any independent line of their own and being forced (for a time) into a one-sided alliance with the working-class radicals. To this extent one can legitimately claim the period as one of acute struggle between old and new forms of leadership: between an old structure that (in various

Table 4 *Oldham working-class leaders active in 1832, 1842 and 1848*[30]

Occupations		Activity		Campaigns and slogans	
large employer	1	pre-1830	11	Owenite Socialism	4
small employer	0	industrial	11	factory movement 1840s	3
small master	2	short-time 1831	7	anti-poor law	4
shop-pub	3	Regeneration	7	anti-police	6
beerhouse	4	Charter 1838–41	17	strike support	5
schoolmaster	4	active 1842	22	Ireland protest	10
'doctor'	1	arrest 1842	11		
building craft	3	Holladay 1847	4		
metal craft	1	Cobbett 1847	2		
other craft	5	active 1848	16		
factory skilled	3				
spinner	9				
factory semi	3	Total number on which any information: 57			
handweaver	1				
hatter	1				
shoe/tailor	4				
labourer	3				
not known	9				

[29] *Northern Star*, 7 July 1838, Butterworth diary, 10 September 1838. John Holladay (1798–1852) was originally a millwright who set up a small cotton factory in 1835 in partnership with a Rochdale tea dealer. By 1846 he employed 136 persons. In 1828 he became a trustee of Queen Street Congregational Church.

[30] Includes all those active in the political campaigns of 1832, 1842 and 1848 which involved confrontation with the authorities. 'Schoolmaster' includes one 'Socialist lecturer' (Richard Cooper) and a 'dissenting minister'. 'Shop-pub' includes John Haigh who only became a shopkeeper after being victimized as a cotton spinner.

ways) fragmented the working population and a new one whose strength derived from uniting it. All that now remains is to have a closer look at the working-class radicals themselves.

Table 4 gives the occupations and campaign associations of those involved – from a radical standpoint – in three of the main struggles between 1830 and 1850. This time there can be no question about their proletarian composition. The great bulk were manual workers and even those listed a shopkeepers and beer-housekeepers were often (like John Haigh, Len Haslop and James Greaves) victimized industrial militants. The biggest single group are the spinners, the occupation which had now replaced weaving as the focus of industrial struggle. Moreover, it is also noteworthy that in contrast to the shopkeepers the most common campaign associations tend to be on larger national issues: not so much poor law, police or strike support (although quite a number were also active industrially) as the question of state power itself and – also significantly – Ireland.

However, the group's essential feature – its cohesion – does not show up in the figures at all. Though there were always tactical disagreements and a constant stream of new recruits, what strikes one most from the descriptive evidence is the degree to which members saw themselves as part of a continuing tradition. Radical allegiances tended to be inherited within families and associated with particular neighbourhoods. The Swires, Earnshaws and Warwicks were all families that produced at least two generations of radicals. And of neighbourhoods the best example is perhaps the 'Jacobin village' of Royton. In 1807 Chippendale noted that it was Royton which supplied almost all the audience and speakers at a peace meeting: 'Partington . . . a determined Jacobin . . . read the resolutions . . . he was attended by several of that family of Taylors whom I have often mentioned to you under the name of O'Calebs and others of the same kidney . . . particularly the schoolmaster Winterbottom.'[31] Again in 1812 he described Royton as 'a place in which every inhabitant (with the exception of five or six) are the most determined revolutionary Jacobins'.[32] And in 1818 Colonel Fletcher wrote to the home secretary: 'During the course of my correspondence I have more than once had occasion to notice the hostility of this village towards his majesty's government. Fitton . . . is an atheist, and so also is Kay, and probably most of the others . . . The reformers decry religion under the name of bigotry and superstition and vow its utter destruction. . . .'[33] An effective

---

[31] Chippendale to Fletcher, 25 December 1807 (HO 42/91).
[32] Chippendale to Ryder, 22 May 1812 (HO 42/123).
[33] Fletcher to Sidmouth, 29 March 1818 (HO 42/175).

summing up can be found in a speech by Fielden (himself an old Jacobin) at the celebration dinner following the 1832 election:

I know many persons in this borough who have been persecuted – persecuted, hunted down like wild beasts. . . . When I look at the company by which I am now surrounded, when I take a retrospective view of what they have done and suffered; when I consider the violence with which they have been abused, calumnated and persecuted; and when I consider the occasion we are now celebrating, it gives me a full conviction, if anything were wanted to give me that conviction, that the cause for which you have suffered is the cause of truth. . . .[34]

But if this community of experience and tradition was important, just as critical was the not unrelated ability to change and develop. It is this that provides Oldham's radicals with their strongest claim to be a genuine vanguard group. Because the main component of the tradition *was* radical opposition to the system itself, so one finds the members of the group stepping in to express each successive mass issue in terms of the overall political struggle. This is what brought the radicals into the leadership of the industrial struggles of 1794–1801. It was this which placed them in the forefront of the factory movement in the 1820s. And consequently one also finds their political analysis moving in step with (and expressing) the system's own emerging contradictions, as reflected in the changing nature of mass struggle. This is perhaps strikingly demonstrated by the career of John Knight.

Knight, born in 1763, was originally a small manufacturer in the hills behind Saddleworth.[35] Politically, he first appears as a 'determined Jacobin', imprisoned for two years following the 1794 clash at Royton. In 1801 he was on the county executive of the United Englishmen and in 1812 again arrested as one of the suspected organizers of the guerilla campaign.[36] After the war he was editor in turn of the *Manchester Political Register* (1816) and the *Manchester Spectator* (1818).[37] On both occasions the government suspended *habeas corpus* (1817 and 1819). Knight was one of the people they took care to put

[34] *Cobbett's Register*, 29 December 1832.

[35] In 1801 'John and William Knight' of Stonebreaks, Saddleworth still had £1,500 of stock insured (Royal Exchange fire register 7253/42). The collapse of the firm seems to have come some time after 1812 (probably as a result of Knight's repeated imprisonment). Obituary by William Fitton in *Norther Star*, 22 September 1838. Some biographical information is also included in Cole's edition of Cobbett, *Rural Rides* (1930), vol. III, p. 998.

[36] *The Trial of the Thirty-Eight Men from Manchester or Lancaster on 27 August 1812* (Manchester, 1812, MPL 942.730731 P70). Already in 1812 Knight was writing 'labour (the poor man's only property) ought to be held as sacred as any other'.

[37] The *Register* ran from 4 January to 1 March 1817. It was printed by Wardle. For Knight as editor of the *Spectator*, Norris to Home Office, 18 November 1818 (HO 42/182).

inside (on the Home Office index of suspected persons he is marked as 'violent' and 'one of the thirty-eight tried in 1812').[38] After some years away from Oldham in the early 1820s (in Burnley it seems) he re-appears in 1827 and in 1831 he became secretary of the Political Union.[39] At the same time he also played an important part in the Spinners Union (and was accused in 1834 of being its secretary).[40] In 1836 he saw to it that the Oldham Political Union adopted the principles of O'Connor's London and Marylebone Radical Associa-tion. Five months before his death in 1838 he was appointed salaried treasurer of the town poor relief fund.[41]

Knight's greatest contribution, however, was his ability to keep thinking. For fifty years he went on trying to make political sense of what was happening. He started as a Tom Paine Jacobin. By the 1810s he had merged the struggle for political freedom with the larger struggle of labour against property.[42] When he saw the effect of machine production in the late 1820s and early 1830s – how wages fell as output rose – he worked out (or at least propagated) a primitive labour theory of value. And in the years immediately before his death, after watching the failure of one working-class movement after another, he was arguing that political activity would only be suc-cessful if it was by labour 'as a whole' – and if it was action for complete power. For the moment it will be enough to quote part of a speech he made, beside Alexander Taylor at the anti-coronation meeting, two months before his death. It is quite different from Taylor's and shows, if anything does, the way he thought and the close responsiveness of his leadership:

the ministers had settled upon the Queen an income of more than £1,000 a day while hundreds on thousands of her subjects were starving on 2½d, 1¾d and 1d per day. Something had been said about six shillings per day; he would like to see how many people there were before him who were earning six shillings per day. What, no one? . . . Well, how many of you get four shillings then? What, only five or six hands up yet? How many of you get three shillings and six pence? Oh, you can show a few now. [About twenty or thirty were held up for three shillings.] How many of you can obtain only two shillings per day? Ah, you put them up by hundreds now. But how many of you cannot obtain more than one shilling per day by reason of want

[38] 1817 index (HO 40/5 (7)).

[39] W. Bennett, *History of Burnley* (Burnley, 1948) for Knight in Burnley.

[40] In 1834 he was put on trial for forging a workman's reference and was described by the *Manchester Guardian* as the union's secretary (*Manchester Guardian*, 11 October 1834). Knight denied this in the *Manchester Advertiser*, 10 December 1834.

[41] Fitton's obituary in *Northern Star*, 22 September, 1838.

[42] Knight's introduction to the 1812 *Trial*.

of work and low wages put together? Ah, you hold them up in larger numbers than I expected you to.[43]

MASS ACTION

We now reach the more or less final question. How far did this *ideological* development also express itself in mass activity? So far we have looked at the way the radicals won support in industry, at changes in social structure and labour leadership. What we have not yet tackled is the far more difficult problem of pinpointing the difference between revolutionary mass action in the 1830s and 1840s and the apparently just as revolutionary action of the 1810s. If we can answer this, we should be well on the way to getting some estimate of its overall social significance.

Certainly, it is impossible to deny the very real degree of continuity. This shows up in both the popular response to crisis and in the tactics and strategy of the leadership.

On popular reactions in the later period we have already quoted descriptions from 1834 to 1842. But it would be just as difficult to make much immediate distinction between 'the near prospect was that of the monarch dethroned and all her followers . . . in headlong flight to escape the vengeance of an oppressed and vindictive people. This is no fancy sketch; it is a fair picture of the wandering day-dreams of the whole body of what were called the working classes forty years ago' (which is an ex-cotton worker remembering 1848) and Chippendale's contemporary description of Oldham during the earlier crises.[44] *April 1818*: 'A strange ferment was excited in the speeches and its effect spread through the country like wildfire . . . the strongest conviction exists that the grand struggle is approaching . . . an evident change in their habits in consequence . . . their minds are quite in an unsettled state and they are evidently engrossed in the contemplation of the great day. . . .'[45] *January 1819*: 'The delusion that prevails in this part of the country is lamentable. It is impossible to form any conception of it but by supposing an immense majority of both sexes throughout the working class to be the complete dupes of the indendiaries. . . .'[46] *July 1819*: 'The minds of the lower orders in these parts are exclusively occupied with political discussions and the expectation of an approaching explosion which is to produce a complete change in the present

[43] *Northern Star*, 7 July 1838.
[44] B. Grime, *Memory Sketches*, p. 81.
[45] Chippendale to Fletcher, 20 April 1818 (HO 42/176).
[46] 'XY' to Fletcher, 10 January 1819 (HO 42/183).

order of things.'⁴⁷ And if one wants evidence for the disintegration of 'value systems' and deference, here is Chippendale describing a mass meeting of two thousand Oldham workers in 1817. A journeyman mechanic had got hold of a loyalty declaration by the 'principle inhabitants'. He read the names over 'one by one with a considerable pause betwixt each of them. . . . This pause was filled up with some sort of indecent remark accompanied by a characteristic gesticulation . . . all the most respectable people for character and property in the town were made the subject of popular derision.'⁴⁸

So, if (after Lenin) one describes these brief moments of revolutionary release as 'festivals of the oppressed', the earlier periods qualify just as fully as those that came later. And, turning to leadership, one again finds a continuity that goes beyond a mere overlap of personnel. By and large, the problems (and solutions) also stayed the same. It is important to remember that even in the 1810s one is dealing with men who *already* had great experience in handling proletarian mass movements. Another quotation from Chippendale makes this point very well. It relates to the very beginning of the postwar crises in September 1816:

The work of disaffection is going on very rapidly in this neighbourhood, and the activity and industry of the malcontents is beyond conception. By their exertions meetings are established in every part of the country. There is not a village or hamlet or fold of houses anywhere but has its periodical meeting and committee. There is invariably one or more of the Royton agitators at these meetings. The activity of these people is to me most astonishing. . . . [Chippendale then goes on to give an account he had from an agent of one of these meetings at Miles Platting. The chairman introduced the meeting and then] inquired if there were any Royton people present. He was answered in the affirmative by three or four persons who stood together in the crowd. He requested some one of them to address the meeting and called upon Kay in particular. But Kay and the others declined saying it was more proper for some immediate neighbour to speak first. [There were then other speakers till one man made a 'violent' speech.] 'It is idle', said he, 'to expect anything from so vile and corrupt a source as the British House of Commons – let them proceed by force at once . . . we have only to unite and be firm. . . .' At this period he was interrupted by the Roytonians. . . . The Roytonians succeeded in silencing him . . . and he appeared to acquiesce. One of the Royton men, Fitton, then made a speech marked by great moderation. He said if they proceeded in the way recommended by the speaker who preceded him they would get stopped by the authorities as once. He concluded by recommending the formation of a committee. . . . [A committee was then ap-

---

⁴⁷ Chippendale to Sidmouth, 6 July 1819 (HO 42/189).
⁴⁸ Chippendale to Sidmouth, 10 February 1817 (HO 40/10).

pointed, future meetings fixed and the meeting ended.] The Royton people
then returned towards home, and my informant mixed with them upon the
road . . . in course of conversation upon the way they freely commented upon
the speech of the violent man . . . they perfectly coincided with him in
sentiment but the present was not the time for such opinions to be broached.
They must wait a little longer.[49]

And this, of course, remained the dilemma throughout. However
long they waited, whatever the period of mass mobilization, the
confrontation ultimately had to come. As the radicals knew only too
well, state power would not be conceded until the disenfranchised
possessed (and were ready to use) an effective preponderance of outright force. So, although there were certainly changes in strategy, they
tended to be variations on the same, basically insurrectionist, theme.
Naturally, such strategy was evolved at a regional and national level,
and this is not the place to go into it in detail. But because it was at the
heart of so much radical activity, it is important to note its basic
continuity.

1812, for instance, came immediately after the successful use of
guerilla tactics in Spain and looked back to the failure of the London-
based coups of 1802–3. It seems to have envisaged the use of industrial
violence for mass mobilization in much the same way as peasant
violence had been used in Ireland in 1798 (when, of course, many of
the Lancashire leaders had been active in the United Englishmen).
1816–17 combined local insurrections with an attempt to overcome
the weakness in London by marching south a mass of northern
industrial workers. After the failure of this, 1818 saw a return to
industrially based activity culminating in a general strike (during
which one local spy reported that 'the main actors of 1812 have been
heard to say that their projects have again been botched – and they fear
that the different trades cannot be *roused* to the assertion of the people's
rights . . .').[50] 1819 moved from a fairly sophisticated (and nationally
concerted) plan of mass mobilization – in which the government was
successfully cast as the initiator of violence – to an old-style insurrection in April 1820. 1830–2 saw a return to the 1819 mobilization
plans (with Hunt again leading the action) while 1834 attempted to
harness the rising momentum of extra-legal unionism to a more
syndicalist challenge to state power. The various fiascos of 1839 are
well known (and the north-west was probably wise to keep clear of
them). But 1842 was largely a north-west affair and incorporated the

[49] Chippendale to Fletcher, 4 September 1816 (HO 42/153).
[50] Fletcher to Home Secretary, 20 October 1818 (HO 42/181), reporting AB.

experience of three decades in an attempt that came nearer to success than any other. After a month of confused hostilities the home secretary was still worried: 'We have had a very dangerous struggle, a sort of servile war, which is checked, but by no means overcome.'[51] The strategy involved the use of masses of armed, highly organized but ambivalently peaceful strikers to engulf and isolate troops – whose loyalty was uncertain. This was tried again in May–June 1848. After its failure, August 1848 saw an almost straight repeat of the insurrectionist plans of 1817 and 1820: surprise midnight attacks in the big cities (with the Oldham contingent once more marching off to join others in Manchester).

Nor should it be forgotten that these radical strategies were put into effect and that some time or other during most crises badly armed men clashed with regular troops. It does less than justice to those involved not to take this as seriously as it was at the time. With the treason laws being what they were, detailed evidence is inevitably sparse. But enough survives to indicate that most mass actions were carefully and responsibly led. The drilling of 1819 was professionally organized by recently demobbed soldiers:

This morning the number assembled on Tandle Hill was not less than two thousand. The order and regularity that prevailed among them astonished my informant as much as the progress they have made in discipline. The rifle company was very conspicuous as usual. The pivot men were discharged riflemen in uniform. While they stood in close column one of the buglers sounded the call. About twenty-eight drill instructors turned out and five adjutants were chosen out of them.

(General Byng's comment: 'It is an evil if not put down soon will grow to such an extent as to be eminently dangerous'; the Peterloo massacre came six days later.)[52] The mobs of 1842 at first seemed harmless, until it was discovered that they controlled Manchester.

Applications have been received [wrote Colonel Warre requesting immediate reinforcements from London] from Oldham, Ashton, Staleybridge and Stockport soliciting the aid and protection of troops, which I am utterly unable to afford them, as I have but a very inadequate force in this town [Manchester] under the altered state of things from the organisation among the working classes . . . I did not expect that a general turnout would take

---

[51] Graham to Lyndhurst, 21 August 1842 (Graham papers, microfilm spool, 32 Cambridge University Library).

[52] Chippendale to Byng, 8 August 1819 (HO 42/191). Byng to Sidmouth, 10 August 1819 (HO 42/191).

place . . . and that they should venture to march in bodies into Manchester notwithstanding the police and the garrison.[53]

General Arbuthnot later conducted an enquiry into the composition of these mobs and reported them highly organized and directed from meetings which his agents found 'impenetrable'.[54] Even a wild Oldham plugging riot of May 1848 turns out to be more than it seems. Mark Benson, an Irish labourer, was captured. From the evidence against him it appears at first that he was no more than a chance victim. One policeman: 'I went along with them [the crowd]. . . . I saw the prisoner . . . he had with him a long willow stick the upper part painted green with a small green ribbon at the top.' Another policeman saw Benson with his stick in the crowd that plugged Clegg's mill 'nearly in the front and there might be a thousand persons'. The manager of Greaves' saw 'Benson with his stick' in the mob which forced the mill gates. Another witness saw Benson in the crowd as it poured through Waterhead plugging one mill after another. But, then, as the crowd started back towards Oldham, the report makes clear that this was something more than random violence and Benson something more than a victim. 'They were off, and Benson had got five or six yards down the street when a man ran after him and said, "Come back, the other boiler is not off yet." Benson said, "We must have it off." He returned and said, "Come on, lads. We must have this other boiler plugged".' Another man then reported the arrival of police. Benson: 'We must stone the buggers off as we did the two at Tommeyfield. We must have it off.' That afternoon was fixed for a march on Manchester (along 1842 lines); every man had to be on the streets and every mill stopped. Four years before Benson had been imprisoned for taking part in an attack on the new (government-controlled) county police.[55]

After all this, therefore, the case for continuity would seem un-challengeable. Whether in the tactics and strategy of the leadership or in the experience of crisis itself, the basic form of each successive bid remained much the same. It is against this background that we now have to pick out the differences.

Probably the best place to start is not so much the crises themselves as the periods between them. One would, in fact, expect the crises to be roughly the same. These were the moments when the whole objective basis of the social system seemed to be visibly breaking up

[53] Warre to Home Office, 10 August 1842 (HO 45/268).
[54] Arbuthnot to Home Office, 17 September 1842 (HO 45/268).
[55] Depositions *Regina* v. *Benson* QJD 1/215, *R.* v. *McCabe* QJD 1/214 (LRO). Magistrates of Oldham to Home Office, 31 May 1848 (HO 45/2410A).

and all that the radicals had to do was to point to current events themselves. John Haigh, April 1818: 'National bankruptcy was certainly at hand. He enjoined the people to persevere a short time longer and their deliverance would be obtained. Indeed, he said, it is already accomplished for nothing can prevent the arrival of the crisis. . . . By the natural course of events the great change must necessarily be brought about. . . .'[56] Such circumstances would be bound to produce sudden shifts of allegiance away from any leaders intellectually implicated in the existing system (and this certainly included the 'non-political' labour leaders of the 1810s). Clearly, too, the resulting breakdown of sectional discipline would tend to produce just those burst of social liberation already described. But equally clearly the great weakness of these earlier periods of radical consciousness was their lack of staying-power. Only a few months after the great upsurge of 1816–17 the *Manchester Chronicle* could congratulate itself on the state of domestic peace:

In every direction, in the metropolis, in cities, in towns, in villages the call to insurrection was heard. The apostles of revolution swarmed over the land. . . . The partly unemployed . . . grew reckless of partial relief in anticipation of general amelioration. . . . It is impossible to contrast the present situation of the country with what it was twelve months ago, and not seem gratified for our deliverance. . . .[57]

As soon as the objective conditions of each crisis subsided (and a few military counter-measures had been taken), people seemed to slip back into their old attitudes remarkably quickly. Conversely, each time a new crisis developed, the radicals had to fight a new battle for supremacy in the movement with the 'non-politicals'.[58] Indeed, by 1818 this interior struggle was seen as so much part of crisis development that the government was deliberately intervening to strengthen the hands of the 'moderates' by getting employers to grant wage increases.[59]

It seems to have been this that marked the really key difference with the later period. In 1839 and 1842 the big struggles were not between 'politicals' and 'non-politicals' but between two lines of *political* action

[56] Fletcher to Hobhouse, 25 April 1818 (HO 42/176).

[57] *Manchester Chronicle*, 23 September 1817.

[58] 'XY' to Byng, 3 August 1818, Chippendale to Fletcher, 4 August 1818, Fletcher to Sidmouth, 5 August 1818 and Norris to Sidmouth, 13 August 1818 (all HO 42/179) gives a running commentary on the struggles between 'moderates' and 'extremists' among the weavers and colliers.

[59] Chippendale to Fletcher, 25 July 1818 (HO 42/178). Hobhouse to Fletcher, 30 July 1818 (HO 79/3). Fletcher to Hobhouse, 5 August 1818 (HO 42/179).

and (as was shown earlier) the whole nature of the change in working-class leadership during the early 1830s derived from the *permanent* subordination of all sections of the working population to radical control. It is here that ideological developments (linked, of course, to the development of capitalism itself) played such a key role.

It was not just that developments in the early 1830s made it possible to give long-standing industrial demands a radical content. Far more important was the fundamental *intellectual* reorientation they demanded. In cotton and coal the form of struggle itself provided a constant re-education in anti-capitalist assumptions. It was now *economic* reconstruction that was seen as the ultimate goal, and political change only the precondition for it. Previously, things had been the other way round. 'National bankruptcy' was just one more step on the road to some ill-defined Jacobin republic. And reading the speeches of the earlier period, what strikes one most – despite the reference to changing 'the present order of things' and the undoubted spirit of radical egalitarianism – is the failure to make any long-term organic linkage between economic and political campaigns. 'Non-political' labour leaders could still present economic action as a credible *alternative* to political.

This difference also shows up in the cultural field. Although the evidence is somewhat scanty, there does not seem to have been any *sustained* rejection of bourgeois forms till well into the second period. When it came, however, it seems to have been sufficiently deep (and wide) to sustain something otherwise extremely rare: a distinctly new tradition of collective *class* expression. Putting on one side for the moment Oldham's own satirists of bourgeois manners there is the biggest and most undeniable development of all a mass readership of the radical press. While this cannot be precisely measured, the descriptive evidence indicates that the London and Lancashire working-class newspapers achieved something near a monopoly in Oldham. The 1830s also saw church attendance falling to what was probably its lowest level of the century (Figure 3), and atheist lecturers like Carlile and Hetherington collecting paying audiences running into hundreds.[60] And though one would certainly like much more evidence on the directly cultural side, the following assessment by W. J. Fox, Oldham's MP from 1847 and a leading proponent of liberalization, seems fairly realistic:

There was one peculiar fact which could not but strike every reflecting person at the present day, and that was the number of writers springing up among

[60] Butterworth diary, May 1832, 9 September 1833, October 1833.

the working classes – writers who did not like the authors of former days rest on patrons and patronage – writers who wanted no class above them, but who retained strong within them the feelings of the working class in which they were born and bred. Nothing like this was known in former times. . . . Their works were animated by a peculiar spirit – a spirit the result of the political circumstances of the class to which they belonged. They had in them the rich racy spirit of our old English writers . . . when the whole of this literature was considered it would be found pervaded by a spirit of indignation which would arise among men who felt themselves reduced to a slave class, threatening the disruption of that national unity which had hitherto constituted the glory of this country. The stream of mind was separated into two distinct courses; if they did not recognise its claims . . . the genius of the country would become suicidal by the antagonism of its elements.[61]

If, therefore, one wants to distinguish between the two periods, it does seem to have been this permanence of intellectual commitment which was the really decisive factor. And while it is easy to criticize the movement's theory – its somewhat unsystematized economic analysis and its lack of Leninist rigour about state power – the key point is that it worked. As far as the northern factory population is concerned it passed the test of practice. It succeeded in the most difficult task of relating the struggle for a non-capitalist society to the immediate experience of working people. It took the system's apparently most insoluble failings – its inability to function without periodic bursts of overproduction and wage-cutting – and turned them into political issues: political issues whose solution was barred by the existing state-power set-up. It was this which was the great achievement of the campaign on poor law, police and above all factory reform, and it was precisely this connection that John Knight made it his special task to underline in the years immediately before his death:

The making and administering of the laws is exclusively enjoyed by men of property, and, therefore, in the promotion of their own interests they are continually diminishing the rights of all the labouring classes. No plan hitherto laid for the benefit of the labourers has been successful; and so far as the legislative power remains exclusively in the hands of the men of property, no such plan will ever be effectual. In all disputes between employers and workmen . . . the magistrates almost invariable protect the employers. . . . Such is the phalanx of power opposed to the working class that until their influence does actively preponderate in the House of Commons, there is no possibility of their circumstances being bettered. . . . No change favourable to the working class will be obtained unless for some object beneficial to the

[61] Hansard, XCIX c 933–944 (20 June 1848).

whole of them and for which they will unitedly, strenuously and perseveringly continue even to death itself.[62]

Which finally brings us to the most crucial question of all and the one that will occupy the rest of the study: why, if the movement was so effective in mobilizing mass support, it ultimately collapsed so completely. A good many explanations have been suggested, and most blame the movement itself: the primitive level of its theory, the splits in its leadership, the failure to expand mass support beyond a few limited areas. All stress that it was the movement's own weakness that was the basic cause.

Here a somewhat different line is taken. The movement's eventual collapse was, it will be argued, in part the result of its earlier effectiveness: of its ability to force capitalist society to the point of crisis and then hold it there for a decade and a half. It is important not to be taken in by the professional pessimism of the academic historians. Compared with later proletarian movements this primitive English working class is remarkable for the long-sustained level its mobilization (it should be remembered that even Lenin's revolutions required the external stimulus of war). As a movement it was perhaps unlucky not to find any such external stimulus itself. But even in its absence it was sufficiently powerful to bring about a profound modification in the structure of English capitalism. What destroyed it was, it will be argued, more its inability to maintain its offensive under the impact of these changes . . .

[62] *Manchester Advertiser*, 25 September 1834.

12

Social History and the Moral Imagination

GERTRUDE HIMMELFARB

There was a dramatic moment in a symposium a few years ago on 'New Trends in History'. Frank Manuel was contrasting his own mode of writing history to that of Charles Tilly: where Tilly would do an exhaustive quantitative study of strikes and strikers in nineteenth-century France, Manuel would analyse the personalities of the strikers and the values prevalent at the time. There was no meeting ground between them, he concluded, only the tolerant understanding that each be allowed to do his own thing in his own way. Lawrence Stone was moved to protest: 'If this is true, I think it is tragic. It is appalling if two men studying a single phenomenon just walk past each other and have nothing to say to each other.'[1]

Stone was describing an experience that is becoming all too familiar – among historians most dramatically, with the development of quantitative and psychoanalytic history, but in other disciplines as well. For all of the brave talk about interdisciplinary studies, scholarship has never been as factionalized and polarized as it is today. Two scholars working on the French Revolution are apt to produce books so disparate one can hardly recognize in them the same subject; they might be dealing with events centuries and continents apart. This has come about not, as was once feared, because of a fragmentation of learning, a division of labour with each scholar intensively cultivating his own small piece of turf. Nor is it because the 'two cultures' have created disciplines so specialized and recondite that their practitioners can no longer understand each other. In spite of the technical apparatus of the 'new' methods, the quantifiers and psychoanalysers of history can still

From *Art, Politics and Will – Essays in Honor of Lionel Trilling*, edited by Quentin Anderson (Basic Books, New York, 1977), pp. 28–58.
[1] New Trends in History, *Daedalus* (Fall, 1969), p. 894.

understand each other, and the traditional historian can understand them both. In one respect they understand one another all too well. This, indeed, is the difficulty. For what they understand is that each school is staking out for itself not a part but the whole of the subject, each is laying claim to the deepest level of understanding, each thinks it has exclusive access to the truth. If they agree to tolerate each other, as Manuel suggests, it is out of sheer civility. But they do not really communicate with each other because they insist upon speaking different languages, with different vocabularies, different rules of syntax, different intonations and gestures – all reflecting profoundly different interpretations of reality.

The situation would be harmless if it applied only to such relatively limited topics as strikes in nineteenth-century France. What makes it serious, and what Stone was properly exercised about, is the fact that the largest, most comprehensive, and most crucial themes are treated in the same disparate manner. Take, for example, a subject that has been said to be at the heart of all history, that to some degree impinges upon most human activities – the subject of class. There are periods and events in history which are unintelligible without reference to the phenomenon of class, centuries of literature and entire genres (the novel, most notably) which have drawn sustenance from it, philosophies and ideologies of the greatest practical as well as theoretical import which make of it the central fact of life. When this subject is treated as diversely as it has been in recent years, to the point where serious scholars 'walk past each other and have nothing to say to each other', we may well be disturbed.

The problem has only recently become acute. Twenty-five years ago, when *The Liberal Imagination* was published, the historian, no less than the literary critic, could read that book as a testament of his own faith. When Lionel Trilling spoke of the social reality that was the substance of the novel, when he deplored the misguided liberalism that thought it enlightened to ignore the fact of class, as if that fact were demeaning to the critic and belittling to the individual, the historian took heart, recognizing that social reality as the stuff of history. But if the historian was emboldened by this message, he was also forewarned by Trilling's admonition to avoid the opposite extreme, the philistine pretense that facts had nothing to do with ideas, that social reality stood apart from and independent of the exercise of mind. In Trilling's concept of 'the moral imagination', the historian, as much as the literary critic, could find his own mission: to examine the assumptions and preconceptions, the attitudes, beliefs, and ideas which are as much the facts of history as of culture. And the facts of history in both senses of 'history'; if the moral imagination shaped the past, it must to the same degree shape our thinking and writing about the past.[2]

But that was 25 years ago. Today a generation of historians is being trained to write a kind of history that is as nearly devoid of moral imagination as the computer can make it. It was one of Trilling's heroes, Matthew Arnold, who characterized as 'barbarians' and 'philistines' those in his own day who were 'inaccessible to ideas' and therefore obsessively concerned with the 'machinery' of life. But neither Arnold nor Trilling could have anticipated the mechanization of ideas that is even more insidious than the mere use of computers.

In place of the moral imagination, we are more and more confronted with something that might be called the sociological imagination. The sociologist *cum* historian assimilates history to the social or behavioural sciences. He prides himself on using only 'hard' data, precise and unambiguous, the kind that can be counted, sorted, added, weighed, and arranged in tables, charts, graphs. In a more sophisticated variant of this method, he goes beyond the empirical, quantitative method and constructs models intended to represent the abstract essence of the data.

Model-building has recently emerged as the *ne plus ultra* of the sociological imagination. The model seems to have all the advantages of the quantitative method and more. It is abstract as well as precise; it lends itself readily to comparative analysis; it is scientific, objective, and 'value-free'; it makes explicit what might otherwise remain implicit; it evokes the largest statements, generalizations, and theories. Most important, as one disciple of the method has said, it liberates history from the conventional, undisciplined, 'impressionistic' historian who, instead of defining and theorizing, take refuge in 'literary grace', in 'paradox, antithesis, innuendo, and gratuitous irony'.[3]

Although any aspect of history is amenable to quantification and model-building (it has become a measure of the ingenuity of the sociological historian to apply his methods to political, diplomatic,

---

[2] In a memorable passage of the *Reflections on the Revolution in France*, Edmund Burke attacked those rationalists who should strip the 'moral imagination' of its authority, leaving the individual and the polity exposed to the brute facts of power: 'All the pleasing illusions, which made power gentle, and obedience liberal, which harmonized the different shades of life, and which, by a bland assimilation, incorporated into politics the sentiments which beautify and soften private society, are to be dissolved by this new conquering empire of light and reason. All the decent drapery of life is to be rudely torn off. All the superadded ideas, furnished from the wardrobe of a moral imagination, which the heart owns, and the understanding ratifies, as necessary to cover the defects of our naked shivering nature, and to rise it to dignity in our own estimation, are to be exploded as a ridiculous, absurd, and antiquated fashion.' (World's Classics ed. p. 84.)

[3] S. G. Checkland, 'The Historian as Model Builder', *Philosophical Journal*, 7 (Jan. 1969), p. 37.

military, even religious history), social history is the special province of the sociological historian. And within social history, the subject he has staked out for himself is that of class. In reading the recent literature on this subject one can easily get the impression that the sociological historian invented, or at the very least discovered, the phenomenon of class. One is tempted to forget that the consciousness of class was as old as class itself, and that in some periods, in nineteenth-century England most notably, contemporaries spoke of class with a candour and clarity that may come as a shock to some latter-day historians.

The most ambitious attempt to build a class model for early nineteenth-century England may be found in an article by R. S. Neale originally published in 1968 and recently reprinted.[4] Dissatisfied with the conventional three classes, Neale proposes a five-part division: upper class, middle class, middling class, working class A, and working class B. To the unsophisticated eye, this may look like the familiar distinctions of upper, upper-middle, lower-middle, upper-lower, and lower-lower. But Neale intends to signify by his divisions not more or less of the same thing but different things; thus he distinguishes his classes in terms of the distinctive sources of their income, their professions or occupations, their attitudes toward themselves, and their relations with each other.

So far, Neale concedes, his five-class model is essentially static and therefore inappropriate for an England where the only certainty was the fact of change. To convey the dynamic nature of the model, the classes are visualized not as separate boxes in the usual manner, but as pools of water:

... Think of the five classes, each embracing a number of social strata, as separate pools of water linked together by streams of water and located on a convex but asymmetrical hill with the Middling Class on the summit exposed to all the elements. The Upper and Middle Class pools lie on the sheltered sunny side of the hill and both Working Class pools lie on the higher and more exposed northern slope. The stream linking the summit or Middling Class pool to the Middle and Upper Class pools is controlled by traditional sluices between each pool. The two Working Class pools are linked to each other and the Middling Class pool by more sluggish streams but there are no obstacles to the downward flow of water although eddies will result in water moving backwards and forwards between any two pools.[5]

---

[4] R. S. Neale, 'Class-Consciousness in Early Nineteenth-Century England: Three Classes or Five?', *Victorian Studies*, 12 (Sept. 1968), pp. 5–32; reprinted in *Class and Ideology in the Nineteenth Century* (London, 1972).

[5] *Ibid.*, pp. 23–24.

But even this verbal account cannot describe the model in all its precision, abstraction, and complexity. Only the diagram (see Figure 1) can do justice to it.

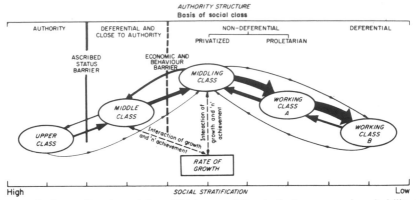

Arrows indicate direction of flow. Thickness of line indicates guessed probability of moving from one class to another circa 1800 (probabilities will vary with rate of growth, 'n' achievement, time, population growth, and the strength of barriers). Given sustained growth the probabilities of moving from low to high increase, the probabilities of moving from high to low decrease.

Figure 1 *Diagram of the five-class model*

Neale has taken us far from an old–fashioned 'impressionism' (the quantifier's invidious term for conventional history), or even an old–fashioned mode of quantification. The language of the model suggests a high order of sociological sophistication: 'authority' and 'deferential' levels, 'social stratification', 'status' and 'behaviour' barriers, 'ascribed' and 'privatized'. And these concepts are presented in such a manner as to connote a correspondingly high degree of precision: lines are solid or broken, of varying thicknesses, graduated in equal parts, pointing in one or another direction. The model even contains something resembling a formula: 'Interaction of growth and "n" achievement'. And a note appears to give directions for calculating the 'probability' or movement from one class to another: 'Probabilities will vary with rate of growth, "n" achievement, time, population growth, and the strength of barriers.'

It may seem churlish, after all this, to complain that one does not know what it all means or what it all adds up to. What good is a formula in which some of the variables cannot be quantified because the historian lacks the necessary data (the 'rate of growth' at any particular time), and in which other of the variables are by their nature unquantifiable ('the strength of barriers')? If the formula is only intended to point to the presence of these factors, does one need either a formula or a diagram to do that? Is a 'guessed probability' indicated by the 'thickness of a line' a better guess, more exactly 'indicated', than that which might be conveyed verbally by such notoriously inexact words as 'more' and 'less'? Does the whole of this elaborate diagram really tell us anything more than the admittedly imprecise accounts of the conventional historian?

The diagram does have one important virtue: it offers an alternative to the traditional three-class model. But that alternative emerges earlier in the article without benefit of diagrams, charts, or even statistics. It is on the basis of the usual kinds of literary, 'impressionistic' evidence – excerpts from commission reports, articles, memoirs, letters, buttressed by an occasional reference to a secondary source – that the author was moved to challenge the traditional three-class model. But if he finds three classes insufficient to account for the complexities of the social reality, why stop at five? Would it not be more precise to separate some of the disparate groups lumped together in the 'Middling Class' – 'petit bourgeois, aspiring professional men, other literates, and artisans' – or the motley assortment comprising 'Working Class B' – 'agricultural labourers, other low-paid nonfactory urban labourers, domestic servants, urban poor, most working-class women whether from Working Class A or B households'?[6] Why not, for the sake of greater precision, assign each of these groups a pool of its own, with its own streams, sluices, barriers, and all the rest?

Neale is undoubtedly right to be dissatisfied with the conventional class trinity, especially with the category of the middle class. (George Kitson Clark put the matter well when he said that the concept of the middle class has 'done more to stultify thought about Victorian England than anything else'.[7]) And there is much in his article that is suggestive and valuable. The question is whether the model helps or hurts his case, whether it does not, for all its curves rather than straight lines and arrows pointing in both directions, make for new crudities and rigidities, whether a misplaced or spurious precision is better that an avowed imprecision. A five-class (or seven- or eight- or 'n'-class) pool-model is not, after all, the only alternative to a three-class box-model. Another alternative is a well-reasoned, well-documented argument in which the nuances of language, rather than the number and thickness of lines, bear the burden of conveying the complexities and subtleties of the social reality.

[6] *Ibid.*, p. 23.
[7] G. Kitson Clark, *The Making of Victorian England* (Cambridge, Mass., 1962), p. 5.

To the sociological historian, however, language is a 'burden' in the worst sense. Having made a great virtue of precise and explicit definitions, he often proceeds to formulate definitions that are either so obtruse as to be incomprehensible or so tautological as to be useless. For the sociologist, there may be some meaning or utility in the definition of social classes as 'conflict groups arising out of the authority structure of imperatively coordinated associations';[8] its abstractness may be appropriate to his purpose, which is to describe the phenomenon of class in its most general, universal, abstract sense. But for the historian, interested in the particularity of a historical situation (or in the particularities of a number of related situations), such a definition can hardly be helpful. At best it plays no part in his research; at worst it distracts him from attending to the actualities of the historical situation. What it does do is give him the illusion that by virtue of some such definition, he has 'objectively identified'[9] the concept of class. It is this illusion, this claim of objectivity, that is the driving force behind the enterprise of sociological history.

The historian, any historian, may properly be accused of hubris, of professing to know more about a historical event, to understand it better, more objectively, than those contemporaries who lived through it. It is an inescapable occupational hazard. For all his wariness of the 'Whig fallacy' – the history of hindsight in which the past is read in terms of the present – for all his attempts to avoid that fallacy by immersing himself in contemporary sources, it remains his eternal temptation and besetting sin. But where the traditional historian is abashed by his presumptuousness, the sociological historian flaunts it; it is his pride and distinction. He invents a language that he claims conveys the social reality better than the language of contemporaries; he freely reorders and remodels the experiences of contemporaries; he abstracts, generalizes, theorizes for whatever purposes he deems proper, to elicit whatever categories or postulates he deems important. At every point he is asserting his independence of and his superiority over those contemporaries who provide his material. In the currently fashionable phrase, they are his 'objects'; he alone can see them 'objectively', scientifically.

Yet even as objects contemporaries have a limited interest for the sociological historian, whole dimensions of their experiences being denied or belittled by him. The only parts of their experience he can recognize, because they are the only parts he can use, are those that

---

[8] Neale, *op. cit.*, p. 9.
[9] *Ibid.*, p. 10.

manifest themselves externally, that are visible, measurable, quantifiable. Their ideas, attitudes, beliefs, perceptions enter into his tables and models only when they express themselves behaviourally – in riots, or elections, or church attendance, or production and consumption.

It is often said that this kind of sociological history is the only democratic form of history; it is the history of the 'anonymous' masses instead of 'great men', the politicians, writers, leaders of one sort or another who emerged in their own time as identifiable individuals. There is no question but that sociological history has had the effect of suppressing these notable individuals. The question is whether it has succeeded in bringing to life the anonymous masses, whether it has not 'upstaged' the masses just as it has the leaders, whether it does not display towards the masses the same condescension, the same sense of superiority, it does towards all contemporaries.

It is true, of course, that individual contemporaries, contemporaries who distinguished themselves in one fashion or another, cannot be presumed to speak for the anonymous masses. But if distinguished contemporaries are thus disqualified, surely a historian, generations removed from those masses, familiar with them only through certain kinds of records that happen to have been preserved, must be immodest indeed to think that he can understand them better than the wisest men of their time. Surely, he cannot afford to ignore the considered judgments of these contemporaries. Nor can he afford to confine himself to their private letters and memoirs in preference to their essays and books, on the assumption that truth is best revealed – exposed, 'given away' – at the level of least consciousness, that greater consciousness brings with it more of the delusions of 'false consciousness'. There is something slanderous about this assumption. It implies that a great contemporary, precisely when he is at his greatest, expressing himself most carefully and deliberately, is least to be trused to tell the truth. And if the great men of the time are thus defamed, so also are all those anonymous people who bought their books, listened to their speeches, or otherwise accorded them the title of greatness. What purports to be democratic history may well prove to be the most insidious kind of 'elitist' history.

When the discussion of class is retured to contemporaries, one discovers quite different conceptions from those found in the tables and models of the 'new' historians. One also discovers why these historians cannot readily incorporate the contemporary concepts into their own models. Contemporaries, it appears, were not only acutely class-conscious; their class-consciousness was a highly charged moral affair. Over and above all those economic, legal, and social distinctions that can be quantified and diagrammed, there is an order of facts that defies the sociological imagination: men's perceptions of themselves in relation to others, and their conceptions of what is proper and improper, just and unjust, right and wrong about those relations. The most ingenious sociologist cannot translate these perceptions and conceptions into the language – the models, abstractions, and quantifications – or sociology. They were rendered at the time, and they are still only intelligible, in literary language, the discourse of ordinary people as well as the learned, a language thoroughly, ineradicably penetrated by moral nuances.

If we refuse to indulge the current prejudice against greatness, we may choose to consult, on the subject of class, one of the great commentators on Victorian England, Thomas Carlyle. Carlyle was great not only in himself but in his influence, and in his influence not only upon readers of all classes but also upon some of the greatest and most influential of his own contemporaries – Mill, Arnold, Dickens, Eliot, Disraeli, Kingsley, Ruskin, Swinburne, Thackeray.[10] Some of these, Mill most notably, were eventually put off by the blatantly undemocratic tone of Carlyle's later writings. But the younger Carlyle helped shape the moral, intellectual, and social consciousness of early Victorian England as perhaps no other single figure did. And even when he provoked criticism, he confronted his critics with an alternative vision of society they could not ignore.

What is remarkable is that Carlyle had the effect he did in spite of a rhetoric so extraordinary that today it tends to repel all but the staunchest devotee. We think of the nineteenth century as an age of great conformity, repressive of all individuality, enthusiasm, passion. We also think of it as an age of great complacency and hypocrisy, in which the realities of life were obscured by polite euphemisms and a mindless adherence to convention. If anything could put such myths to rest, a reading of Carlyle would do so.

He was the most individualistic, indeed eccentric of writers, and the

[10] A typical testimonial to Carlyle's influence was expressed by George Eliot in 1855: 'It is an idle question to ask whether his books will be read a century hence: if they were all burnt as the grandest suttees on his funeral pyre, it would only be like cutting down an oak after its acorns have sewn a forest. For there is hardly a superior or active mind of this generation that has not been modified by Carlyle's writings; there has hardly been an English book written for the last ten or twelve years that would not have been different if Carlyle had not lived. The character of his influence is best seen in the fact that many of the men who have the least agreement with his opinions are those to whom the reading of "Sartor Resartus" was an epoch in the history of their minds.' (*The Leader,* Oct. 1855, quoted by John Mander, *Our German Cousins* (London, 1974), p. 84.)

most outspoken. He denounced the false 'gospels' of the age, the 'foul and vile and soul-murdering Mud-gods', with all the fervour of a Jeremiah.[11] His invectives are famous: utilitarianism was 'pig philosophy'; laissez-fairism was the freedom of apes; parliamentary reform was 'constitution-mongering'; material progress was 'mammonism'; rationalism was 'dilettantism'. And the more he denounced these false idols, and the more intemperately and idiosyncratically he did so, presenting his ideas in the guise of a newly published work of German philosophy or the chronicle of a twelfth-century monk, using elaborate metaphors and obscure references, the more attentively he was read. It is perhaps just as well that much of his audience did not understand all his allusions; Professor Teufelsdröckh, the hero, or anti-hero, of *Sartor Resartus*, translates, in its most refined version, as Professor Devil's Dung. But those who did know German, including Mill and Arnold, were not disconcerted by his pungent language, perhaps because they respected the moral passion inspiring it.

It is ironic – but only because of what historians have since made of it – that Carlyle should have coined the phrase, 'Condition-of-England Question'. Today this is generally interpreted as the 'standard-of-living question', which is taken as an invitation to quantification, the amassing of statistics relating to wages and prices, production and consumption, birth and death rates. Carlyle understood it quite otherwise. Having opened his book, *Chartism*, with the 'Condition-of-England Question', he followed it with an extremely sceptical chapter on 'Statistics'.

Tables are like cobwebs, like the sieve of the Danaides; beautifully reticulated, orderly to look upon, but which will hold no conclusion. Tables are abstractions, and the object a most concrete one, so difficult to read the essence of. There are innumerable circumstances; and one circumstance left out may be the vital one on which all turned. Statistics is a science which ought to be honourable, the basis of many most important sciences; but it is not to be carried on by steam, this science, any more that others are; a wise head is requisite for carrying it on. Conclusive facts are inseparable from inconclusive except by a head that already understands and knows.[12]

To 'understand' and to 'know', Carlyle said, was to ask the right questions, questions that could not be answered with the most comprehensive figures and charts. The opening sentence of his book defined the condition-of-England question as the 'condition and disposition of the Working Classes'. If we are inclined to forget the

[11] Thomas Carlyle, *Reminiscences*, ed. J. A. Froude (New York, 1881), p. 226.
[12] T. Carlyle, 'Chartism', in *English and Other Critical Essays* (Everyman's edn.), p. 170.

second of these terms, Carlyle never was. What gave Chartism its enduring strength, he explained, was the fact that it was only a new name for an age-old phenomenon: it meant 'the bitter discontent grown fierce and mad, the wrong condition therefore, or the wrong disposition, of the Working Classes of England'. The question 'What is the condition of the working classes?' had as its corollary: 'Is the condition of the English working people wrong; so wrong that rational working men cannot, will not, and even should not rest quiet under it?' And this raised the further question: 'Is the discontent itself mad, like the shape it took? Not the condition of the working people that is wrong; but their disposition, their own thoughts, beliefs and feelings that are wrong?' The answers to these questions were not quantifiable because the condition of people depended not upon their material goods but upon their moral disposition. 'It is not what a man outwardly has or wants that constitutes the happiness or misery of him. Nakedness, hunger, distress of all kinds, death itself have been cheerfully suffered, when the heart was right. It is the feeling of *injustice* that is insupportable to all men.'[13]

Carlyle's other famous invention, the phrase 'cash payment the sole nexus', derived from the same moral impulse.[14] He attributed to the economists the deplorable idea that men were subject to the principle of supply and demand as surely as material goods were, that human relations were best left to the impersonal forces of the marketplace, that cash payment was the sole nexus between man and man. What outraged him was not only that men were reduced to this inhuman condition – although that would be outrage enough – but that this condition should be represented as perfectly natural, a God-given law of nature. This was blasphemous as well as inhuman, a mockery of God and of man.

If the relations of individual men were tainted by this modern heresy, so were the relations of classes. Like most of his contemporaries, Carlyle had a simple view of the class structure of England: there was an upper class and a lower class, a class of the rich and a class of the poor. Generally, again like most of his contemporaries, he pluralised each of these, making them the 'upper classes' and 'lower classes'; sometimes he gave them a special Carlylean twist, as when he spoke of the 'Under Class'. But his special contribution to the nomenclature – and to the conception – of classes was his distinction between the 'Toiling Classes' and the 'Untoiling'.[15] It was here that the two

[13] *Ibid.*, pp. 165–67, 188. (Carlyle's italics.)
[14] *Ibid.*, p. 208.   [15] *Ibid.*

classes, so far from being simple descriptive terms, became morally charged.

And it was here that Carlyle parted company from Marx and Engels, who were happy to borrow his aphorism about the cash nexus and to quote him on the condition of the lower classes. For what Carlyle meant by Toiling and Untoiling was not at all what Marx or Engels meant by what might seem to be their equivalents: Labour and Capital. His Toiling Classes included those members of the upper classes who did in fact work; and his Untoiling Classes included those of the working who did not work. Thus the rich comprised 'rich master-workers' and 'rich master-idlers' (or Master Unworkers').[16] And among the poor too there were 'Unworkers', made so by the monstrous Poor Law which created 'houses for idling' under the euphemism of 'workhouses'.

The implications of Carlyle's distinctions were momentous, for they made him something very different from the primitive or crypto-socialist that some present-day socialists would make of him. Socialists can share Carlyle's outrage at the condition of the poor, his condemnation of the idle rich, his detestation of laissez-faire economics. They can find in him premonitions of the evils of dehumanization, desocialization, and alienation. They can even share his respect for work, under certain ideal conditions; the young Marx might have said, as Carlyle did: 'Labour is not a devil, even while encased in Mammonism; Labour is ever an imprisoned god, writhing unconsciously or consciously to escape out of Mammonism!'[17]

What the Marxist cannot do, however, and what Carlyle insisted upon doing, was to make of work an ennobling quality for the capitalist as well as the labourer – provided only that the capitalist was a 'master-worker' rather than a 'master-idler'. *'Laborare est orare'*: this was the true gospel according to Carlyle.[18] 'All work . . . is noble; work is alone noble.'[19] And this dictum redeemed the capitalist, the working capitalist, the 'Mill-ocracy', as Carlyle put it, as much as the working-man.[20] Just as in the Marxist schema the concept of surplus value, or exploitation, illegitimized, so to speak, the capitalist, made him the villain of that particular morality play, so the concept of work legitimized him for Carlyle – made of him a 'Captain of Industry', a natural leader and a true hero.

This is why the struggle between rich and poor, between the upper and lower classes, was not, for Carlyle, the same inexorable, fatal

---

[16] *Past and Present* (Everyman's edn.), pp. 1, 5.
[17] *Ibid.*, p. 199.   [18] *Ibid.*, p. 193.
[19] *Ibid.*, p. 147.   [20] *Ibid.*, p. 166.

war-to-the-death that the class struggle was for Marx. Indeed for Carlyle, a symptom and also a cause of the prevailing misery and discontent was the fact that there was such a struggle. The idle aristocracy, abdicating its natural political role, made the process of government seem artificial, the fortuitous product of competition and struggle. This was the true perversion of political economy. Denying the proper function of government, the laissez-fairists also subverted the proper relationship of the governed and the governors. And without this relationship, cash payment became the sole nexus connecting the rich and the poor.

After reading the reviews of *Chartism*, Carlyle remarked: 'The people are beginning to discover that I am not a Tory. Ah, no! but one of the deepest, though perhaps the quietest, of all the Radicals now extant in the world.'[21] Carlyle's radicalism may not be ours. Nor was it that of all radicals at the time.[22] But it was a form of radicalism that most contemporaries recognized as such. One reader of *Past and Present* quipped that the book would be very dangerous if it were ever 'turned into the vernacular'.[23]

Carlyle's radicalism consisted not in the answers he gave to the condition-of-England question but in putting the question itself, and in putting it in such a form that it raised the most fundamental doubts about the legitimacy of prevailing doctrines and class relations. Nothing is more banal than the idea that England, that any country, is divided into an upper and a lower class, into rich and poor. What Carlyle did was to raise the idea of class to a new level of consciousness by giving it a new moral urgency. In Victorian England the idea of work was a powerful moral concept, a cogent instrument of legitimization and illegitimization. By associating it with the idea of class, Carlyle made problematic – 'dangerous', as one reader said – what had

[21] James Anthony Froude, *Thomas Carlyle: A History of His Life in London, 1834–1881* (London, 1884), 1: p. 174, Feb. 11, 1840.

[22] In his review of *Past and Present* in the *Deutsch-Französische Jarhbücher* in 1844, Engels opened on a kindly note: Of all the books published in England the preceding year, *Past and Present* was the only one 'worth reading'; and of all the learned men in England, Carlyle was the only one to be concerned with the 'social condition of England'. But the review became progressively sterner, with Engels taking Calyle to task for not realizing that the cause of the social evil was private property. The bulk of the review, however, consisted of a critique of Carlyle's relgious views, which Engels characterized as a form of 'pantheism'. The old question, 'What is God?' Engels reported (paraphrasing Feuerbach), had finally been answered by German philosophy: 'God is Man'. (*Marx-Engels Gesamtausgabe,* ed. D. Riazanov (Berlin, 1930), Part 1, vol. II, pp. 405–31.) The following year, in *The Condition of the Working Class in England*, Engels quoted approvingly the 'cash nexus' statement. (He used the expression twice, the first time without attribution.) (Ed. W. O. Henderson and W. H. Chaloner (Oxford, 1958), pp. 138, 312.

[23] James Pope-Hennessy, *Monckton Milnes: The Years of Promise, 1809–1851* (London, 1949), p. 184. Milnes was passing off as his own a comment Harrier Martineau had earlier made in a letter to him.

previously been the most natural and innocent of propositions, that England was divided into two classes.

In *Sartor Resartus*, Carlyle described the extremes to which those two classes were being pushed. The book is an elaborate play upon a treatise, *Die Kleider, ihr Werden and Wirken*, by the ubiquitous Herr Teufelsdröckh, Professor of Allerlei Wissenschaft at the University of Weissnichtwo. The clothes metaphor inspired Carlyle to invent two sects, Dandies and Drudges, the first worshipping money and the trappings of gentlemanliness, the second slaving to keep barely clothed and fed.

Such are the two Sects which, at this moment, divide the more unsettled portion of the British People, and agitate that evervexed country. . . . In their roots and subterranean ramifications, they extend through the entire structure of Society, and work unweariedly in the secret depths of English national Existence, striving to separate and isolate it into two contradictory, uncommunicating masses. . . . To me is seems probable that the two Sects will one day part England between them, each recruiting itself from the intermediate ranks, till there be none left to enlist on either side.[24]

If Carlyle's final words remind us of Marx, with his predictions of the polarization of classes – the increasing concentration of wealth on the one hand, the increasing proletarianization and pauperization on the other – the rest of the passage recalls Disraeli's famous phrase, 'the two nations'. I would not go so far as some historians who have claimed that Disraeli made of that expression a 'houschold word'.[25] Nor would I make too much of the fact that others used it before him.[26] It is enough to say that Disraeli dramatized and popularized a concept that was, as we say, 'in the air'.

Disraeli also dramatized, perhaps romanticized as well, the condition-of-England question. In *Coningsby*, published in 1844, five years after Carlyle's *Chartism*, Disraeli referred to the 'Condition-of-England Question of which our generation hears so much'.[27] A few months later, in an address to his constituents, he claimed some priority for that concept: 'Long before what is called the "condition of the people

---

[24] *Sartor Resartus* (Everyman edn.), pp. 214–15.

[25] Kathlene Tillotson, *Novels of the Eighteen-Forties* (Oxford, 1965), p. 80; Robery Blake, *Disraeli* (London, 1966), p. 210.

[26] Asa Briggs quotes one of several such usages. In 1841, the famous American preacher William Channing wrote: 'In most large cities there may be said to be two nations, understanding as little of one another, having as little intercourse, as if they lived in different lands.' (Briggs, 'The Language of "Class" in Early Nineteenth-Century England', in *Essays in Labor History*, ed. A. Briggs and J. Saville (New York, 1960), p. 48.)

[27] Benjamin Disraeli, *Coningsby: or The New Generation* (London, 1948), p. 78.

question" was discussed in the House of Commons, I had employed my pen on the subject.'[28] He had already begun writing *Sybil* and was evidently anticipating a criticism that was to be leveled against that book: that parts of it sound like a transcript of Royal Commission reports and parliamentary debates. Since he had in fact been listening to those debates (a Factory Bill had been introduced in that very session of parliament) and was actually inserting verbatim into his novel portions of one of those reports (the second report of the Children's Employment Commission which had been released in 1842), Disraeli had reason to be sensitive on this account.[29]

The message of *Sybil* is too familiar to require much discussion. It is also perfectly clear and explicit. Unlike Carlyle, with his extended metaphors and heavy irony, Disraeli, even when writing fiction, was engaged in a not very subtle form of political indoctrination. If parts of *Sybil* read like transcripts of the blue books (which they were), other parts sound like extracts from a *Short Course in the History of England, by a Young Englander*, or from penny pamphlets on 'the social problem'. In the novel the crucial passages announced themselves, so to speak, by the presence of capitals. Thus the first mention of the two nations theme appeared in a dialogue between Egremont, the good aristocrat (one is tempted to capitalize these identifications, as in a morality play), and 'the stranger', later identified as Stephen Morley, an Owenite who has joined forces with the Chartists.

'Say what you like, our Queen reigns over the greatest nation that ever existed'.

'Which nation?' asked the younger stranger, 'for she reigns over two'.

The stranger paused; Egremont was silent, but looked inquiringly.

'Yes', resumed the stranger. 'Two nations; between whom there is no intercourse and no sympathy; who are as ignorant of each other's habits, thoughts, and feelings, as if they were dwellers in different zones, or inhabitants of different planets; who are as formed by a different breeding, are fed by a different food, are ordered by different manners, and are not governed by the same laws'.

'You speak of – ' said Egremont, hesitatingly.

'THE RICH AND THE POOR.'

[28] W. F. Monypenny and G. E. Buckle, *The Life of Benjamin Disraeli Earl of Beaconsfield* (London, 1929), I, p. 629. The allusion, his biographers tells us, was to his novel, *The Voyage of Captain Popanilla*, published in 1828. But neither the term nor the subject in the usual sense appears in that novel.

[29] For an analysis of his indebtedness to the Commission Report, see Sheila M. Smith, 'Willenhall and Woodgate; Disraeli's Use of Blue Book Evidence', *Review of English Studies* (1962).

This final line of bold type was followed by a fade-out scene worthy of a grade C movie: The grey ruins were suffused by a 'sudden flush of rosy light', and the voice of Sybil was heard singing the evening hymn to the Virgin – 'a single voice; but tones of almost supernatural sweetness; tender and solemn, yet flexible and thrilling'.[30]

This was Disraeli prose at its worst, blatantly tendentious and mawkishly romantic. Most of it was very much better – tendentious, to be sure, but cleverly so – sharp, acerbic, witty, and surprisingly often conveying some provocative thought. And even the romantic interludes were redeemed by a latent irony that made for a slightly off-beat, campy effect. *Sybil* was, in fact, an eminently readable book, and although the literary strategy was obvious enough – the contrast between high society and the life of the lowliest poor, between parliamentary intrigue and Chartist conspiracy – there were memorable episodes satirizing the upper classes and dramatizing the lower. The opening scene, for example, in the fashionable club, found a group of rich, blasé, and rather effete young men chatting idly about the forthcoming Derby races, with one man confessing that he rather liked bad wine because, you know, 'one gets so bored with good wine.'[31] In the same mood were scenes featuring the ladies of the great houses who thought they were wielding political power (perhaps they were wielding power – Disraeli left the matter ambiguous) by extending or withholding invitations to their dinner parties; they vainly attempted to extract information from dim-witted lords who did not know that they were being pumped, for the very good reason that they knew nothing at all.

On the other side of the social spectrum was the reality that these fashionable men and women were so abysmally ignorant of: the reality of THE PEOPLE, or THE POOR – terms which Disraeli used interchangeably. Disraeli has been criticized, and properly so, for overdramatizing the condition of England in the nineteenth century and over idealizing the condition of England in the good old days.

When I remember [says Sybil, as if she were recalling her own youth in pre-Reformation times] what this English people once was; the truest, the freest, and the bravest, the best-natured and the best-looking, the happiest and most religious race upon the surface of this globe; and think of them now, with all their crimes and all their slavish sufferings, their soured spirits and their stunted forms; their lives without enjoyment, and their deaths without hope; I may well feel for them, even if I were not the daughter of their blood.[32]

[30] B. Disraeli, *Sybil, or The Two Nations* (Penguin edn., 1954), pp. 72–3.
[31] *Ibid.*, p. 15.   [32] *Ibid.*, p. 126.

Even if the extravagant rhetoric, with all those superlatives – the truest, the freest, the bravest – did not forewarn us that Disraeli intended us to take this mythically and allegorically, the last sentence should surely alert us to that possibility; for at this point in the story we know that Sybil was not, in fact, 'the daughter of their blood', far from being one of the people, whe was the purest descendant of one of the oldest and noblest families.

But apart from such mythicized representations of past and present (intentionally mythicized, as I read Disraeli), there were scenes which, however exaggerated, revealed important and frequently ignored aspects of social reality. For all his fantasies and extravagances, Disraeli had a clear perception of different varieties of conditions and different kinds of poverty. He distinguished, for example, between rural and industrial poverty, between manufacturing and mining towns, between the ordinary working poor and an underclass that was almost a race apart, brutalized, uncivilized, living in a virtual state of nature. There was a precision in these distinctions the historian may well respect.

The historian may also profitably read the exchange between the good aristocrat Egremont and the Chartist Gerard in which each cited statistics about the condition of England, the one proving that it was much better, the other much worse, than ever before, with Gerard concluding (like Carlyle before him) that in any event it was not so much material conditions that were at issue as the relations of men with each other.[33] Earlier the Owenite Morley had made the same point: 'There is no community in England; there is aggregation, but aggregation under circumstances which make it rather a dissociating than a uniting principle.'[34]

When sociologists make this distinction, under the labels of *gemeinschaft* and *gesellschaft*, historians listen respectfully. When Disraeli did it, he was dismissed as a medievalist and romantic. Yet Disraeli was careful to assign this speech about community not to Sybil, who *was* a medievalist and romantic, but to the Owenite, who believed that 'the railways will do as much for mankind as the monasteries ever did.'[35] Neither Morley nor Gerard had any hankering for a pre-industrial age; both wanted only to humanize and socialize relations under the con-

---

[33] *Ibid.*, p. 171.

[34] *Ibid.*, 71. On one occasion Morley goes so far in urging the principle of 'association' as to declare the home to be 'obsolete'. 'Home is a barbarous idea; the method of a rude age; home is isolation; therefore antisocial. What we want is Community.' Gerrard, the Chartist, benignly but firmly puts him down: 'It is all very fine, . . . and I dare say you are right, Stephen; but I like stretching my feet on my own hearth.' (p. 190).

[35] *Ibid.*, p. 88.

ditions of industrialism. The one character in the novel whose occupation it was to exalt and perpetuate the past was a fraud, if a kindly one; this was the antiquarian Hatton, who made his fortune by tracing – inventing, if need be – the lineage of noble and would-be-noble families, and who himself turned out to be the brother of the vilest and lowest of the rabble.

If Disraeli's cast of characters included good aristocrats as well as bad, so it also included good factory owners as well as bad ones. To be sure, the best of these factory owners happened to be a younger son of an old, impoverished landed family. And it was this heritage that made his so exemplary a character: 'With gentle blood in his veins, and old English feelings, he imbibed, at an early period of his career, a correct conception of the relations which should subsist between the employer and the employed. He felt that between them there should be other ties than the payment and the receipt of wages.'[36] (If the last sentence was not a conscious echo of Carlyles's 'cash nexus', it testified to the prevalence of that sentiment at the time.) Disraeli's account of this model factory town was more than a little idyllic; everyone was happy, healthy, moral, and content. But it is also noteworthy that what Disraeli was idealizing, contrary to the conventional image of him, was a *factory* town. (In the same spirit, in his earlier novel *Coningsby*, he had Sidonia interrupt Coningsby's reveries about the glories of Athens. 'The Age of Ruins is past,' Sidonia reminded him. 'Have you seen Manchester?')[37]

Disraeli's two nations, like Carlyle's two classes, were more complicated than they appear at first sight – and again, because they were moral as well as descriptive categories. Just as Carlyle's upper classes contained a toiling and an idle class, so Disraeli's rich contained a responsible and an irresponsible element. For the indolent club–lounger titillated by the idea of drinking bad wine, or the ladies of the salons who looked upon politics, like matrimony, as a game devised for the exercise of their female wiles, Disraeli had nothing but contempt. Riches, position, power had 'only one duty – to secure the social welfare of the PEOPLE.'[38] Just as work was the legitimizing principle for Carlyle, so duty was the legitimizing principle for Disraeli. Where Carlyle, putting a premium upon work, found most of his heroes among the 'Mill-ocracy', the 'Captains of Industry', Disraeli looked primarily to the landed aristocracy who, in his mythical rendition of English history, traditionally functioned in this responsible, moral fashion.

[36] *Ibid.*, p. 179.
[37] B. Disraeli, *Coningsby*, p. 116.
[38] B. Disraeli, *Sybil*, p. 264.

If Carlyle and Disraeli chose to eulogize and mythicize different groups among the upper classes, they were in agreement that it was the responsibility of the upper class to rule – humanely, justly, compassionately, but rule – and the obligation of the lower classes to be ruled. The main plot of *Sybil* centred about the attempt of the lower classes to find salvation in themselves, to try to cure their condition with their own resources, by developing leaders of their own and seeking power on their own behalf. This was the aspiration of the Chartists and, according to Disraeli, the lesson of its failure. In spite of the fact that Gerard was the purest, noblest, wisest of men, the movement degenerated into an illegal conspiracy and finally into a wild, bloody, pointless rampage, as a result of which both Morley and Gerard died and Sybil was disabused of her illusions – her 'phantoms', as Egremont delicately put it. These phantoms included her faith in the people as the means of their own salvation, her belief that the poor could do no wrong and the rich no right, and her conviction that between the two 'the gulf is impassable.'[39]

Sybil has generally been taken as the heroine of the book. But if so she was a distinctly flawed character – the heroine, perhaps, but not the hero. Even her final aggrandizement came not from her being the true heir to Mowbray – with her father's death the title went to another claimant – but from her marriage to Egremont, who had just come into his own title and whose fortune, as the gossiping ladies noted, was equaled by only 'three peers in the kingdom'.[40] It was Egremont, the good aristocrat, who bore the moral burden of the book. It was he who wanted to obtain, as he said, 'the results of the Charter without the intervention of its machinery', a somewhat cryptic statement that bewildered some characters in the novel and that others interpreted as 'sheer Radicalism', 'the most really democratic speech that I ever read'.[41] What Egremont meant, of course, was that the welfare of the people could best be ensured not by transferring power to them, as the Chartists advised, but by exercising power on their behalf. Elsewhere, less cryptically, Egremont declared that 'the rights of labour were as sacred as those of property; that if a difference were to be established, the interests of the living wealth ought to be preferred; . . . that the social happiness of the millions should be the first object of a statesman, and that, if this were not achieved, thrones and dominions, the pomp and power of courts and empires, were alike worthless.'[42]

Contemporaries did not always know what to make of Disraeli, and historians know still less. The distinguished historian, G. M. Young,

[39] *Ibid.*, p. 270.   [40] *Ibid.*, p. 398.
[41] *Ibid.*, p. 272.   [42] *Ibid.*, p. 281.

who was old-fashioned enough (and old enough) to draw upon his own memories and those of his acquaintances, asked one elderly Gladstonian why his generation had been so profoundly distrustful of Disraeli. The answer surprised Young. It was, the old man said, because of 'his early Radicalism'.[43] Whatever one may think of the practicality of Disraeli's kind of radicalism, or of its desirability, or whether it was radical at all, or even whether Disraeli was entirely serious in propounding it, one cannot deny that it did colour his own thinking and the thinking of contemporaries about him.

More important, however, than Disraeli's solution of the social problem – the nation unified under the direction of a 'natural' aristocracy dedicated to the 'social welfare' – was his conception of the problem itself: a society in which the two classes were diverging so rapidly that they were perilously close to becoming 'two nations'. Many contemporaries who did not subscribe to his ideology, who found him too radical or insufficiently radical, shared his view of the social condition. And it was this view – this class model, so to speak – that was enormously influential, that made the 'two nations' a graphic image of the social reality and a powerful symbol of discontent.

Disraeli and Carlyle are only two of the many Victorians whose vision of the social reality helped shape that reality as well as reflect it. If one is looking for class models, surely their two-nation and two-sect models are as worthy of consideration as any the historian may devise. Or one might contemplate the three-class model reluctantly advanced by James Mill – reluctantly because utilitarianism was a profoundly individualistic theory loath to assign any reality to such 'fictions' as society or class. Yet even Mill could not entirely dispense with some idea of class, although he did shun the word; in his schema the people were divided into an 'aristocratical body', a 'democratical body', and a 'middle rank', the latter being the repository of virtue, intelligence, and leadership. Matthew Arnold's three classes were substantively the same as James Mill's, but his characterizations of them made for a radically different conception of society. Positing an aristocracy of 'barbarians', a middle class of 'philistines', and a populace combining the worst features of both, he obviously had to look elsewhere for virtue, intelligence, and leadership – to a state capable of transcending these classes. Without his class 'model', one cannot begin to comprehend either his idea of the state or his analysis of the social reality.

There are obviously other ways of drawing upon the contemporary

[43] G. M. Young, *Victorian Essays* (London, 1962), p. 163.

consciousness of class, not only by inquiring into all the eminent and not so eminent men who had occasion, in books, articles, speeches, or memoirs, to reflect upon their times and experiences, but also by consulting a variety of other sources that dealt with the same issue more obliquely, less self-consciously: novels, tracts, newspaper accounts, parliamentary debates, Royal Commission reports, legislative acts, and administrative measures. A few obvious models emerge from these sources – two or three classes, for the most part, often with each class pluralized ('working classes', for example), suggesting an acute sense of the fluidity and complexity of social relations. But whatever the model, it almost invariably contained a strong moral component. The classes themselves were described in moral terms, and the relations among them were presumed to have a moral character (or criticized for failing to exhibit the proper moral character, which was itself a moral judgment). Just as we would not today (or most of us would not, even today) define familial relations in purely behavioural terms – age, sex, physical condition, economic circumstances, social status – so the Victorians would have found inadequate any purely behavioural description of social relations that did not take into account men's sense of duty and obligation, propriety and responsibility, right and wrong.

This is where much of recent social history goes grievously astray. Even those works that avoid the more egregious fallacies of misplaced precision, excessive abstraction, and obfuscatory language are insufficiently attentive to the quality of mind that permeated nineteenth-century England. It may seem odd that historians should fail to avail themselves of such obvious sources of evidence as the ideas and beliefs of contemporaries, of the great men of the time as well as the ordinary men – until one realizes that to take seriously that evidence would be to jeopardize the enterprise of social history as it is generally conceived. Intent upon creating a scientific, objective history, these historians think it necessary to purge the social reality of the values that interfere with this 'value free' ideal.

It is not only this ideal of a positivist science that is inimical to the moral imagination. It is also a distaste for the particular kind of moral imagination that prevailed in nineteenth-century England. Today all moral concepts are to some degree suspect; they strike the modern ear as condescending, subjective, arbitrary. And they are all the more disagreeable applied to classes – where the poor were described, as they habitually were in the nineteenth-century, as 'deserving' or 'undeserving', or when the working classes were divided into the 'respectable' and the 'unrespectable', or when reformers announced their intention of fostering among the lower classes the virtues of thrift, temperance, cleanliness, and good character.

To the latter-day historian this moral temper suggests a failure not only of compassion but also of understanding. One recent author characterized it as an ideological 'deformation' produced by the 'distorting lens' of the middle class, a deformation so pervasive it even affected the consciousness of the working classes themselves.[44] From this perspective the moral imagination of the Victorians is not something to be understood and described as an essential part of the social reality, but something to be exposed and criticized from the vantage point of the historian's superior understanding of the reality. And the reality itself is assumed to be best understood in 'objective' – which is to say, economic – terms without reference to such subjective ideas as moral character.

To call for a restoration of moral imagination in the writing of social history – in the writing of all history, indeed, but it is in the realm of social history that it is most sadly lacking – is not to give license to the historian to impose his own moral conceptions upon history. This has been the impulse behind yet another fashionable school of thought, that of the 'engaged' or 'committed' historian. In this view, all pretensions of objectivity are suspect, the only honest history being that which candidly expresses the moral, political, and personal beliefs of the historian. At the opposite pole, in one sense, from the sociological mode, this kind of 'engaged' history shares with sociological history a contempt for the experiences and beliefs of contemporaries and an overweening regard for the superior wisdom and judgment of the historian.

What is wanted is not so much the exercise of the historian's moral imagination as a proper respect for the moral imagination of those contemporaries he is professing to describe. This, to be sure, takes an exercise of imagination on the historian's part – a sensitivity to moral ideas, a tolerance for ideas that may not be his own, above all a respect for moral principles as such, so that he will not dismiss them too readily as rationalizations of interest, or deformations of vision, or evidence of an intellectual obtuseness that conceals from contemporaries those simple economic facts which are so obvious to the historian.

It is a modest undertaking that is called for, indeed an exercise in modesty. It asks for nothing more than that moral data – the ideas, beliefs, principles, perceptions, and opinions of contemporaries – be taken as seriously, be assigned the same reality, as facts about the

[44] Gareth Stedman Jones, *Outcast London: A Study in the Relationship between Classes in Victorian Society* (Oxford, 1971), pp. 16, 196, 344.

distribution of income, consumption of meat, or growth of population. The historian is in the fortunate position of being able to do what the sociologist cannot do; he can transcend the fact-value dichotomy that has so plagued sociological thought. The values of the past are the historian's facts. He should make the most of them, as the great Victorians did.

13

Afterword

R. S. NEALE

I

I ended the introduction to *Class in English History* with the words, 'History must become theoretical or it will become irrelevant.' Since I closed that sentence, everything I have heard from historians or read in their writings about the impropriety of theoretically based historiography, has reinforced by belief that a theoretical path *is* the only path to historical knowledge. I do not mean by this that a theoretical path guarantees historical knowledge; merely that some theoretical paths point in the right direction, and that approaches to the writing of history which are explicitly non-theoretical or atheoretical can only lead to a historiography in which, it seems, anything goes. And this, as Karel Williams observes, celebrates the failure of empiricism as serendipity. Yet because empirical historians necessarily use a non-neutral language already saturated in points of view, they cannot escape their theoretical and ideological historicity, and neither can their work be value or theory free – which means that only some things go. (And this celebrates empiricism's success as ideology with which it epigones bludgeon sceptically serious undergraduates into tears and into silence.) Occasionally awareness of the limitations of empiricism forces itself into the consciousness of empirical historians, leading to a certain uneasiness of mind and to a drift away from the merely empiricist position.

To illustrate this drift I begin by chronicling five instances of the atheoretical stance of historians, each of which may be taken as illustrating one of five stages in the increasing mystification of an unsophisticated theory of how historians gain historical knowledge; but a theory nevertheless. As each instance is unfolded it will be seen to reveal aspects of the inadequacy of the empirical theory of historical knowledge. Also I hope to suggest how historians, who seek to fend off the theoretical by using everyday language, generally fail in their endeavours.

In place of the seven ages of man, I give you the five ages of empirical historiography! The sixth age, the age of theory, has yet to arrive, when it does, afterwards, in the seventh age, we may all rest.

The practising historian. A postgraduate student in an essay writes, 'When I first started this course, I asked one of our "practising" historians (he works in a College of Advanced Education) what was the point in studying a course entitled, "Theory and Method in Economic and Social History"? He said "None!" So I then asked how he wrote history. He replied, "You select one event and off you go".' This answer, reminiscent of Christian's cry of, 'Life! life! eternal life!' as he single-mindedly pursued his personal salvation, embodies the simplest and most vulgar form of a merely empirical theory of historical knowledge. It is a celebration of history as serendipity and the basic building block of all narrative history.

The university lecturer. At a recent conference on the preparation of the 1888 volume of Australia's bi-centennial history, I mentioned, as a possible orgainizing framework, the structure of the Australian economy, and, as a starting point, the economy in its international setting. I was firmly put in my place by one of the university lecturers present who said, 'We should assume the economy, and the book should be a history of interesting bits in 1888.' This assertion embodies a slightly more sophisticated version of the empirical theory, because if does recognize that some assumptions have to be made, even though, in this instance, the content of the assumptions was not specified, and the assumptions made would have had little effect on the search for knowledge. Nevertheless, the university lecturer's recognition of the need for assumptions does reveal the possibility of doubting the certainty offered by my student's colleague.

The reviewer. In a review of my Book on Bath – my attempt to practise what I preach – Peter Borsay writes, 'For the traditional view of the town, with its emphasis on architecture, manners, anecdote, and elegance, is here replaced by a radical argument (rather than a history), dense and complex, detailed yet abstract, at times cynical and pessimistic, always serious – almost evangelically so.'[1] 'A radical argu-

---

[1] Review of *Bath 1680–1850: A Social History*, by Peter Borsay, *Social History Society Newsletter* (Autumn, 1981), p. 9.

ment (rather than a history)' – this statement lifts the discussion about historical knowledge to a higher level. What Borsay does is to imply tht history, whatever it is, is counterposed to argument – that an argument is not history – and that it is unusual for history to be serious. He does not advocate or defend such a position, it is true, but his words indicate his preference; history should describe. And what should it describe? In this case, it should describe, happily and supposedly without purpose, the outward show of the rich and elegant. Borsay's response to my history of Bath is typical of responses to it. Thus, whatever history is, it is not an argument. (How then I wonder can any PhD student write a thesis?) But this is a view which Lawrence Stone, for all his wish to revive narrative history, could not support. Narrative for Stone is an argument. Indeed, does not all historiographical description, by its very selection and structure and use of language, contain argument? If this is the case, there remains the question, what structures the narrative and the argument it contains, but something one might call theory?

The historian without theory. An historian, writing on class, goes out of his way to assert his atheoretical, down-to-earth use of ordinary language. Arthur Marwick writes, 'I prefer the "ordinary language". I prefer "class" to mean that people in everyday life mean by it, rather than what Runciman or Weber tell me I should mean by it . . . Class, perhaps, is too serious a subject to leave to the social scientist.'[2] Fortunately for history and for the argument in his book, Marwick's practice is distant from his pronouncements; he uses a concept, class awareness, which is similar to my own class perception, and he writes about caste society, status society, and classless society. Also, he discusses a variety of images of class and, somewhat naively, criticizes Marx on class and on historical development. All of this is remote from the 'ordinary language' of the ordinary people, at least as I know them. Which is to say that noisily atheoretical historians are very like ordinary people, they frequently profess one thing while doing something else; they profess their atheoretical, down-to-earthness, but actually think and write theoretically, and necessarily, use a conceptual language. In this instance Marwick uses a language of class, which is beyond the power of ordinary language in the mouths of ordinary people. What is disturbing, as far as knowledge is concerned, is that atheoretical historians do not understand what it is they do. Thus, Marwick, having explicitly rejected all theory, even though using

[2] Arthur Marwick, *Class: Image and Reality in Britain, France, and the USA since 1930* (London, 1981), p. 15.

theory all the time, does claim to advance an 'hypothesis' and a
'fundamental thesis'. Notwithstanding this fundamental thesis, 'that
the exact forms of class . . . are determined by the historical evolution
of the particular country',[3] has negligible content, he does attempt to
correct what he refers to as the muddled history of other historians.
Yet I cannot see how the issues he raises can be settled without
recourse to far more rigorous conceptual and theoretical discussion
than he allows for.

   Marwick is characteristic of those empirical historians, who cannot
recognize their own theory when they see it – and they use theories all
the time – but who are vaguely aware that they do theorize as they seek
to 'prove' their own loosely knit hypotheses. Nevertheless this, too, *is*
an advance on the most vulgar form of the empirical theory of historical knowledge. Not only does Marwick make assumptions, he
admits to constructing hypotheses and, despite his protestations to the
contrary, he uses conceptual language; historians may be innocent, the
language they use never is. Perhaps we should conlcude that history is
too serious a subject to leave to historians!

Isaiah Berlin. Twenty years ago Isaiah Berlin published an essay which
might well be the wellspring of recent historians' rejection of theoretical history. Certainly they can always turn to his essay for a
sustained, ready-made argument that history, in its search after the
unique, is *sui generis.* Yet in that essay, Berlin also took historians'
practice light years away from the merely empirical theory of historical knowledge. Read what he writes:

Historical explanation is to a large degree arrangement of the discovered facts
in patterns which satisfy us because they accord with life as we know it and
can imagine it. . . . When these patterns employ concepts or categories that
are ephemeral, or confined to trivial or unfamiliar aspects of human experience, we speak of such explanations as shallow, or inadequate, or eccentric,
and find them unsatisfactory on those grounds. When these concepts are of
wide implication, familiar, common to many men and many civilizations,
we experience a sense of reality and dependability that derives from this very
fact, and regard the explanations as well founded, serious, satisfactory. On
some occasions, seldom enough, the explanation not only involves, but
reveals, basic categories of universal import, which, once they are forced
upon consciousness, we recognize as underlying all our experience; yet so
closely interwoven are they with all that we are and feel, and therefore so
totally taken for granted, that to touch them at all is to communicate shock to
the entire system; the shock is one of recognition and one that may upset us,

[3] *Ibid.,* p. 361.

as is liable to happen when something deep-set and fundamental that has lain unquestioned and in darkness, is suddenly illuminated or prised out of its frame for closer inspection. When this occurs we call such explanations profound, fundamental, revolutionary, and those who proffer them – Vico, Marx, Freud – men of depth or insight or genius.[4]

The rhetoric of this passage is persuasive – yet what does it say? Does it say that some explanations, grounded on the organization of data with the help of universal categories and concepts, stated within a general pattern of thought and tested by current experience, are better than others? Does it say that Marx, along with Vico and Freud, has offered a profound, fundamental and revolutionary explanation? Does it? And when Berlin writes, 'The sense of the general structure of experience – that is the pattern, understanding of which may indeed be useful to scientists but which is absolutely indispensable to historians, without it, they remain chroniclers or technical specialists. They may achieve accuracy, objectivity, lucidity, literary quality, breadth of knowledge, but unless they convey a vision of life, and exhibit a semi-intuitive sense of what fits what . . . the result is not recognized by us as an account of reality'[5] does he not write of Collingwood's *a priori* imagination or of Popper's intuitive leap towards theory in science, and, maybe, of praxis in Marxist sense? Does he not write of something one might call theory? Again Berlin writes, 'Historians cannot ply their trade without a considerable capacity for thinking in general terms; but they need, in addition, peculiar attributes of their own: a capaicty for integration, for perceiving qualitative similarities and differences, a sense of the unique fashion in which various factors combine in the particular concrete situation . . . The gifts needed are those of association, not dissociation, of perceiving the relation of parts to wholes.'[6] If he is saying anything at all, is he not saying we need a whole battey of intellectual tools: theories, general ideas, and concepts all as sharp as razors? For how else *do* we relate parts to wholes – provided of course that we know what is a part and what a whole? And when Berlin writes that scientists must 'construct bold hypotheses unrelated to empirical procedures'[7] does he not also write

---

[4] Isaiah Berlin, 'The Concept of Scientific History', *History and Theory*, 1, (1961), p. 24. The most recent version of this debate was sparked by Lawrence Stone, 'The Revival of Narrative', *Past and Present* (November 1979). Two subsequent contributions, both in *Past and Present*, are: E. J. Hobsbawn, 'The Revival of Narrative: Some Comments', (February 1980) and Philip Abrams, 'History, Sociology, Historical Sociology', (May 1980). Abrams writes, 'History must be theoretical because that is how structuring is apprehended. History has no privileged access to the empirical evidence relevant to the common explanatory project. And sociology has no privileged theoretical access.' (p. 5).

[5] *Ibid.*, p. 29.   [6] *Ibid.*, p. 30.   [7] *Ibid.*, p. 31.

of Popper's intuitive leap towards theory at the same time as he misrepresents the subsequent practice of scientists and the dependence of science upon analogy? And when he writes of the gifts of both scientists and historians, rather than of the language, concepts, theories and methods they need in order to practise at all, especially if they seek to produce knowledge and to claim for that knowledge the utility which Berlin believes it to have, does he not mystify the practices of both?

Berlin seems to recognize the necessity for theory, indeed, like Marwick, he cannot escape that necessity, but he balks at its language and does not squarely face the theoretical implications of his own rhetoric. Thus the difference between us, I think, is both slight and profound. Whereas Berlin seems willing to settle for the notion that the historian works through his gifts, especially his intuitive capacity to perceive relationships (which is a form of theorizing) and test them against his experiences, I also press the next, much harder stage of his practice. This is the stage of clarification and coherent exposition of what might well derive from a flash of insight not shared by others. And then to test that exposition through experience, not merely as personally experienced but as understood in all its density and complexity, which is to say, conceptually and theoretically. Without such a test there *is* only personal experience expressed in a language that can never mimic reality. Language, with all its image reservoirs, is too weak and malleable to bear the weight Berlin would place upon it – experience of commonsense, only partly represented in language, is never the same as experience of reality.

This leads us to my case for theorizing, which is very simple. Explicit theorizing is an attempt to be intellectually honest. It is a way of penetrating the structure of language and the habits of thought – the image-reservoirs and shimmer of words – which drown our understanding. It is the only path to knowledge, because to theorize covertly and implicitly, while pretending to an objectivity that is demonstrably unattainable, howsoever strong the will, is either dishonest, lacking in that intellectual integrity, supposedly the hallmark of disinterested inquiry, or perverse, showing uncritical commitment to historically, and therefore, ideologically determined modes of thought, in the face of overwhelming evidence and argument. So, in the language of ordinary people, much admired by historians, I merely ask historians to cut their gamon and pater as dimber dambers and become bob culls; to come clean, to lay their intellectual and ideo-logical cards on the table, to be honest, to drop the pretence, in relation to marxist history, of being holier than thou, and to join R. J. Morris and E. P. Thompson as penitents, conscious perhaps of the images trapped in every sentence they close off and the narratives they construct. And in the language of history, I ask historians to accept the fact and implications of their own historicity. A simple request, I would have thought, to make of historians. And not a novel one.

That I may be seen to practise what I preach (and because it is important for my argument) let me try to be more conceptually and theoretically explicit than in *Class in English History*. Before commenting upon the essays in this collection and upon several recent books, relevant to the argument in *Class*, let me state as concisely as I can the essence of my position on the social structural articulation of English society, as it may be constructed for the early eighteenth century and as it may be seen to have changed over a period of about one hundred and fifty years.

II

Social structure in England in the first half of the eighteenth century was a product of the articulation of its several modes of production, some of which were sub-sets of the dominant agrarian–capitalist mode of production. Each mode of production had distinctive forms of property relationships and distinctive methods whereby those with property appropriated surplus value and distributed the total product and, thereby set boundaries to the realization of the production potential of the forces of production. The agrarian–capitalist mode of production had at its economic centre the legally enforceable, complex and flexible, contractual relationships characteristic of a society built on private property in land, which had evolved from the property relationships of feudal society. Thus, these contractual relations were a modern set of legal relations bearing, paradoxically, the hallmark of the benefit of England's legal and political backwardness in the seventeenth century. The economic and social structure of this mode of production consisted of rentier landlords, capitalist tenant farmers, and wage labourers; a very distinctive set of relations of production and of appropriation relations in Europe at the time. These property and appropriation relations, and the ways they affected and intermeshed with other modes of production, were central to the process of economic and social structural change in our period.

The agrarian–capitalist mode of production was the dominant mode of production. Historically, its actors had turned land into capital and productive work into wage labour – a key element in its legal relations was the wage contract. However, the agricultural sector was not wholly agrarian–capitalist; in many regions capitalist landowners and farmers, and their wage labourers, lived cheek by jowl with copyholders, lifeholders and small freeholders, whose tenures signified the tenacity of relations of production characteristic of pre-capitalist modes of production. However, it is also true to say, that in the immediate hinterland of some towns these pre-capitalist tenancies had come into the hands of people already integrated into the dominant mode of production.

Within the agrarian–capitalist mode of production, economic and political advantage sometimes lay with the beneficiaries of entailed estates who were able to augment their share of the agricultural surplus through winning property rights in place at court and gaining appointments as functionaries in the growing administrative branches of the crown, mainly in London. In these circumstances political rights, such as those held by closed corporations and the proprietors of rotten boroughs, also stood out as property rights.[8] Thus many agrarian-capitalists were also parasitic on the crown and dependent on residual but resilient pre-capitalist relations of production for their ability to appropriate an even greater share of surplus value. Competition structured by this melange of pre-capitalist property relations was to be a source of division within the ranks of the propertied classes throughout the eighteenth and early nineteenth centuries, although these divisions declined in intensity as capitalist relations of production, including those of industrial capitalism, spread.

Next, there was the rural/urban manufacturing mode of production. This, too, had two elements. First, the capitalist sector characteristic of the putting-out industries. In these industries capitalist entrepreneurs controlled raw materials, stocks of goods, warehouses and assorted tools and machines, and employed wage labour, as in great segments of the west country woollen industry. Secondly there was the sector characterized by petty production. In this sector artisans, owning tools, frequently worked on their own account or in small workshops, as in shoemaking, tailoring and building. In these trades there was a

---

[8] Wade's *Black Book*, first published in periodical parts, is a detailed account of the material gains made by those able to supplement revenues from property with incomes derived from place at court and the exploitation of political property rights. Wade's account of the activities of Lord Huntingtower in Ilchester, between 1802 and 1820, shows the extent to which contemporaries failed to distinguish political from property rights. *The Black Book: A New Edition* (London, 1828), Vol. I. pp. 12–91, Vol. II, pp. 172–3. See also Norbert Elias, *The Civilizing Process* (Basel, 1939) for what, one might call, the deferential rights of the landowning élites, and their role in the development of manners.

blurring of distinction between masters and journeymen. However, even in these trades, whenever market conditions were favourable, capitalist relations tended to oust pre-capitalist relations of production.

In some industries, in the early decades of the eighteenth century, relations of production characteristic of developed industrial capitalism could be found; in mining, in the metal, glass and fulling industries, and in shipbuilding. Nevertheless, the industrial capitalist mode of production did not become dominant in England until the second half of the nineteenth century – uneven economic development remained a major characteristic of the economy.

In cities such as Bristol and Norwich, but especially in London, where international as well as local market conditions were favourable, the urban manufacturing mode of production was embedded in a mercantile mode of production characterized by large capitals, frequently of a joint stock nature. In this mode of production merchant capitalists generated surpluses through the exploitation of price and cost differences as well as through the appropriation of surplus labour in the production process.

Then there was the monied-interest, also concentrated in London. Its members were the finance capitalists of their day. As products of the military role of the state, which served the interests of the oligarchy at the head of the agrarian-capitalist mode of production, they were a sub-set of that mode of production. The key instruments in their appropriation of a substantial portion of the domestic agricultural surplus were: the national debt, intricate networks of international and national credit, and taxation, behind which lay the coercive power of the state. These coercive powers also protected the links between the dominant mode of production and the world economic system; additional sources of surplus for the oligarchy of agrarian capitalists and the monied interest were colonialism and slavery. In terms of personnel the monied-interest was not easily distinguished, either from the great agrarian-capitalists, or from those with place at court, or from those engaged in the mercantile mode of production. A fact which highlights the problem contemporaries had in comprehending the significance and desirability of this financial mode of production.

It was, perhaps, this financial aspect of the capitalist mode of production in England, spanning agrarian and mercantile capitalism, yet dependent upon the military and administrative role of the state, in a country surrounded by a predominantly politically absolutist and economically feudal world, that gave England its edge in the race to accumulate the wealth of the nation. In *Class in English History*, I refer to this period as, the heroic age of primitive accumulation; it should also be emphasized that it was a period of uneven economic development. Therefore, as I wrote in *Class in English History*, English society may be characterized as 'neither pre-industrial nor industrial, neither feudal nor industrial capitalist, neither classless nor multi-class, neither order-based nor class-based, neither one thing nor another although dialectically it was both. . . . Consequently, the late seventeenth and early eighteenth centuries were socially complicated. It is not to be wondered at that men were confused and uncertain.'[9]

Not until there were significant developments in technology, notably in the application of steam power to production and transport, was it possible for the industrial capitalist mode of production to become dominant; but it grew to dominance slowly and unevenly. Furthermore, because the key to productivity increases, even with the new technology, still rested with skilled manpower, industrial capitalism in England in the early nineteenth century, was marked by relations characteristic of pre-industrial capitalist modes of production. Thus, in the first four or five decades of the nineteenth century, when England's economy was overwhelmingly capitalist, it was not industrial; the articulation of the various modes of production was still complex. The significance of this complexity for class consciousness was immense.

My views about the order and class perceptions of social groups as they developed and changed over a period of one hundred and fifty years, and my views about other historians' assessments of those perceptions, which I discuss in *Class in English History*, derive from my conception of the articulation of the several modes of production as I have sketched it here. And all the papers included in this present volume, which I comment upon in *Class in English History*, may also be seen to refer to some element in that conception. Thus, authors of the papers in the section entitled Theory raise questions of a theoretical or conceptual kind – I have already commented upon their significance. And authors of the papers in the part entitled Interpretation all use a particular theoretical/conceptual framework with which to knit together descriptions of key aspects of English history in the period. Since these authors all use theoretical frameworks different from mine they generally appear to challenge or deny some component in my own description of the development of class and class consciousness. Nevertheless, I claim, that if one examines the theoretical/conceptual assumptions on which these accounts are based, and if one brings to the fore central elements in the structure of the arguments used, they

[9] R. S. Neale, *Class in English History 1680–1850* (Oxford, 1981), pp. 94 and 99.

may all be seen to be encompassed by the conception I have outlined here – this in undoubtedly true of the contributions from Laslett, Perkin, Thompson and Calhoun. I also believe this to be true of the contributions from Foster, Himmelfarb and myself; each writes about a particular fragment of the larger whole I have attempted to outline. In fact each of these authors writes about a different element in the articulation of modes production I have described, and about the relationships of those elements to economic change in the latter part of our period; because none of them can really mimic reality, each account is only partially true. Moreover, the authors represented in this collection collectively direct attention to the nature and importance of class perceptions across the whole spectrum of English social structure: the ruling elites (Laslett, Perkin, Himmelfarb); the labouring masses (Perkin, Thompson); the pre-industrial manufacturing classes (Thompson, Calhoun); the industrial working class (Foster); the class of industrial capitalists (Foster); the urban petty producers, the middling class (Neale). At the same time several contributors, in exploring relationships between classes, have much to say about each and every class listed above. This is to say that the writings in this collection, and the linguistic signs their authors use, should be read in relation to each other, and that they amplify, sometimes in the 'everyday language' of empirical historiography, the conception of the articulation of modes of production I claim to be central to my own work. I believe, therefore, that read in conjunction with my commentary upon them in *Class in English History*, these essays provide students with a coherent and comprehensive historical perspective on social structure in the period under discussion. However, I do not doubt that many students (and their teachers) will wish to move outwards (or inwards) from that perspective towards what they will undoubtedly regard as 'the real past'. And from that notion I will not deflect them (or their teachers) provided that they remember always that the real past is a construct, not a natural reality, and that if they use a different language to construct it, they will produce a different reality – hence the importance of the language of class and, as Calhoun reminds us, of community.

III

With all this in mind I come back now to the recently published books to which I referred in the introduction. The first of these books, H. T. Dickinson, *Liberty and Property: Political Ideology in Eighteenth Century Britain*, is important for my argument because it enlarges what I say about the role of perceptions about relationships between property and liberty for the growth of class consciousness throughout the whole of our period. Although Dickinson's book is not explicitly structured by my conception of the articulation of modes of production, it does take up some of the themes identified in *Class in English History*. What *Liberty and Property* does is bring a clearly formulated political/ideological superstructure to the conception I have outlined.

Dickinson's account of the development of a coherent, radical, oppositional, utopian mode of thought (Ideology in Dickinson's terminology) out of the resentment and frustration felt by those members of the agrarian–capitalist orders excluded from a share in the perquisites and status of office, and denied what they felt should be their proper share of the available agricultural surplus, is persuasive. Although the argument is similar to that of J. G. A. Pocock in *Feudalism, Capitalism and Beyond*, Dickinson takes it further. He suggests a lineage linking Tory opposition early in the eighteenth century with Wilkeite radicalism in the 1760s, the Association movement in the 1780s, the Constitutional Corresponding Societies of the 1790s, and urban radicalism in the early nineteenth century. And it is here, I think, that he and I would part company. Dickinson's argument is more than a little touched with idealism.

Ideas there undoubtedly were, and the lineage of ideas can always be traced, and ideas were and are of crucial importance. But, more important, in my view, were the developments in the articulation of modes of production that intensified old conflicts or generated new ones, and led to the creation of stronger or newer social groups whose members had good reasons, either of feeling or reason, to adapt some of the stock of existing ideas for their own radical purposes. For example, the emergence of spokesmen who perceived that property *was* inimical to liberty, and the increasing use of Lockeian natural rights arguments in the fact of the presumptuous power and privilege of property, depended more on the existence of social groups and on the emergence of new ones, and on their spokesmen, than on any lineage of Lockeian ideas, especially as received opinion about Locke allowed natural rights arguments to lapse. And Dickinson is aware of this. Just as he is also aware that most men of property came to see that they had a common interest opposed to all those without property, and that this perception generated a conservative and organicist ideology of order. Even so, Dickinson does see the parliamentary, political moment, serving rather like an act of God, as the key element in the lineal march of radical, oppositional politics.

In my view Dickinson sidesteps the issue I now raise. He glosses over the social basis for the burgeoning demands for political reform when he writes,

A book on ideology and political argument is not the place for a detailed treatment of those social and economic changes which created an urban and commercial middle class that was increasingly interested in gaining political representation, or for an examination of the practical means by which support for parliamentary reform was mobilized. Clearly the growth of London and other urban centres, the increased wealth of the middling ranks in society, the steady expansion of the Press, and the mobilization of public opinion through clubs and extra parliamentary organizations all helped to create pressure for a reform of the system of representation.[10]

Instead he emphasizes the role of what he refers to as ideology.

This emphasis by Dickenson on ideology and his minimilist position in regard to context also lead him to misconstrue the social meaning of the arcadian, agrarian message of many late eighteenth-century radicals. According to Dickinson, the failure of these radicals to develop solutions relevant to the social and political problems confronting the urban labouring population (the working classes in Dickinson's terminology) was a result of their middle-classness, which blocked their capacity to perceive the industrial capitalist world in which they lived. Whereas I attribute this spate of radical writing, much of it predicated on the notion that labour had a right to the whole of its product, to these radicals' true perception of their actual place in the predominantly agrarian-capitalist, non urban, non-industrial mode of production, in which they lived, and to the hegemony of ideas about property, still predominantly landed property, generated from that mode of production. In *Bath, 1680–1850*, I argue that these ideas could never have been a rallying cry for any member of the labouring population, except the gardeners of Bath. Further, using the terminology of the five-class model, I doubt whether most of these radical writers, such as Spence and Hall, could properly be categorized as middle class.

The extent to which Dickinson misconstrues the social meaning of late eighteenth- and early nineteenth-century radical writing, and over-emphasizes the part played by ideological lineage in their dissemination, is shown, I think, in my own work on Bath. It is also brought sharply into focus by I. J. Prothero in *Artisans and Politics in Early Nineteenth-Century London: John Gast and his Times*, published in 1979.

[10] H. T. Dickinson, *Liberty and Property: Political Ideology in Eighteenth Century Britain* (London, 1977), p. 205.

I was able to notice it only briefly in *Class in English History*, but would like to say more about it now.

Prothero's book has a greater significance than its title suggests. The central character, John Gast of the Shipwrights Union, actually remains a shadowy, and oftentimes a peripheral figure. But the behaviour of the London artisans he exemplifies is used by Prothero as a model for the behaviour of artisans throughout England and Western Europe. And this is because Prothero locates them firmly within the urban manufacturing mode of production as it was embedded in the mercantile mode of production in London; not that Prothero says so in so many words. Nevertheless, the model of economic growth and development implicit in the book is one in which both occurred through the proliferation of trades and small workshops and the expansion of existing enterprises, rather than through any great technological or organizational innovations. Furthermore, the economy of London, as it affected the shipwrights, was one in which the state (the late eighteenth-century version of the financial mode of production above), through its wartime naval policies, played a crucial role in stimulating economic activity in a highly capitalistic industry in which the control of productivity – and the appropriation of the product of labour – still rested, at least in part, with skilled men, such as shipwrights. In these circumstances there was a multitude of trades all with their traditional organizations and practices. The shipwrights and the artisans generally were conscious of the value of their skills and of the product of their labour. Accordingly they esteemed themselves for their freedom from charity and poor relief, and for the schemes of self-help and cooperation they developed; as the core of their self-perception, they developed the idea of respectability.

Within such a set of relations of production, with its associated level of consciousness, artisans did not see themselves opposed as a class to their employers, nor to the middle-classes generally. Rather they measured and valued themselves as against an autocratic government and its hordes of parasitic non-producers, and against big monopolistic merchants and middlemen. As Prothero writes, 'the anti-capitalist ideas which evolved in this period were those appropriate to artisans, not opposing all masters but condemning "merchant capitalism", the monopolist middlemen. It was a theory, not of exploitation within production, but of unequal exchange. And for most of those who held it, this was no "false consciousness" but an accurate analysis of the situation.'[11]

[11] Iowerth Prothero, *Artisans and Politics in Early Nineteenth Century London: John Gast and his Times* (Baton Rouge, 1979), p. 336.

This consciousness owed little to the influence of outsiders. Although Gast's radicalism fed on the available stock of ideas, including those of Cartwright and Paine, it sprang from the immediate experience and assumptions of artisans themselves.[12] Indeed, the absence of an homogenous body of ideas among London artisans and the degree to which they spent as much effort opposing each other as they did opposing their perceived opponents, is itself evidence of the importance of immediate experience for the development of consciousness, and a demonstration of the secondary role of ideas, whatever their lineage.

The experience of John Gast and the shipwrights sprang from their work situation in the mercantile mode of production. It involved them in campaigns to preserve the apprenticeship system, to establish a general union, to support Hunt and the Spencean revolutionaries during militant phases of post-war radicalism, to support the abolition of the Combination Laws, the taxes on knowledge, and 'Old Corruption', and to oppose the government over Queen Caroline. As they took part in all these campaigns they became an extremely militant fraction of the population of London. As Prothero points out this militancy lasted well into the 1840s; thus the militant Chartists of the East London Democratic Association, such as Harney and Vincent, before he became a temperance lecturer, were probably more characteristic of London Chartists than those of the London Working Men's Association. On the other hand, the failure of Gast and the London artisans to generate a critique of a society based on private property, more coherent and penetrating than those of Spence and Hodgskin, which might have been capable of uniting the trades for concerted class action, is also a demonstration of the intellectual constraints placed on them by the uneven and isolating economic development characteristic of the urban, manufacturing and mercantile mode of production and its medley of trades. Gast and his friends, for all their self-generated, militant respectability, perhaps, because of it, were in a sort of revolutionary limbo. Their experience did not arise from the urban, factory conditions conducive to the generation of a class consciousness one might associate with the industrial capitalist mode of production, nor from community, which as we shall see, conditioned the populist and riotous responses of the labouring population in the capitalist but pre-industrial manufacturing mode of production characteristic of eighteenth- and early nineteenth-century England, at least according to Calhoun. Consequently, the activists among these artisans were always too few. The rank and file of artisans were not really like Gast and the five hundred who regularly turned up to lectures at

[12] *Ibid.*, p. 97.

the Rotunda; perhaps the rank and file did drink too much and never did understand what was happening to them! In any event, the mere lineage of radical ideas did not help them. Further, their experience of the mode of production which created them also made them respectable, and in the end, politically impotent.

In *The Question of Class Struggle* (1982), C. J. Calhoun uses his concept, community, (see chapter 6) in an attempt to tie some aspects of the lineage of oppositional ideas, as described by Dickinson, to economic and social structures, and to interpret the activities of London artisans as described by Prothero. In doing so Calhoun adds an important conceptual and analytic dimension to our reading of these descriptions, and also develops one aspect of the argument in *Class in English History*.

Calhoun begins his book with the assertion that, 'The most widespread, powerful, and radical social movements in the modern world have been of a type we may call "populist".'[13] And the question he considers is, should historians cast popular, radical political and industrial action before 1820 in England, in the mould of Marx's *class* consciousness, or should they conceptualize it as populist, having its roots in community rather than in class? (In this Afterword, as in *Class in English History*, italics distinguish Marx's notions of class from those of others.)

As his opening sentence shows, Calhoun has no doubt about his own answer. But he wants to persuade the rest of us to see the world as he does. In the act of persuasion he sometimes refers critically to Marx on *class*, but his interrogation is mainly directed at E. P. Thompson's notion of class. In fact Calhoun's *The Question of Class Struggle* is a critique of Thompson's *The Making of the English Working Class* which could have the effect of appropriating and neutralizing the empirical detail of *The Making* (see chapter 7).

According to Calhoun, Thompson, in adding political oppression as a new dimension to Marx's notion of *class*, distanced himself from all other Marxists such that Thompson is not really a Marxist. But Calhoun finds some good in this distancing because it helps Thompson escape from the Marxian constraints of category and structure, and allows him to emphasize the consciousness and experience in the identification of *class*. Nevertheless, this emphasis on *class* consciousness also traps Thompson into making a fundamental error; it leads him to see a lineage of *class* consciousness in pre-class society, i.e., in

[13] C. J. Calhoun, *The Question of Class Struggle: Social Foundations of Popular Radicalism during the Industrial Revolution* (Oxford, 1982), p. vii. Calhoun's language of community should be compared with Raymond Williams' language of community in *Culture and Society* and *Keywords*. See also chapter 6, above.

late eighteenth- and early nineteenth-century England. The problem is that Thompson reads the present in the past and is unaware that he thereby imposes a spurious continuity in the making of the English working-class; at least at the level of consciousness. This emphasis on the language of *class* consciousness, by Thompson, and his search for a lineage of *class* consciousness also lead him to ignore or neglect the social bases of collective action.[14] Therefore he 'fails to confront the community-based populist movement which he has, in part, empirically described.'[15] Instead, Thompson merely adds conceptual confusion to the complexity of the real past and obscures the true significance of the empirical work on the eighteenth- and early nineteenth-centuries reported in *The Making of the English Working Class*.

Calhoun claims that the true significance for the real past of Thompson's empirical work may only be grasped if we change our theoretical stand-point; if we relegate consciousness to its secondary role and concentrate on identifying those social organizations which determine the conditions or boundaries for social action. Then we would discover that 'traditional communities were the crucial social foundation for radical collective action,' and that 'In the early part of the industrial revolution, community was the crucial bond unifying workers for collective action.'[16] In the pre-1820 period these radical communities were traditional communities, mainly consisting of artisans in the towns and workers in a variety of manufacturing industries. As yet untouched by the industrial mode of production, but threatened by incorporation into it, both types of community were vigorously engaged in resisting the destructive effects of industrialization upon them. While these community based responses were often radical and insurrectionary, as in Luddism and the Pentridge Rising, and sometimes oddly feminist and loyalist, as in the affair of Queen Caroline, the movements and ideas emanating from these communities always sprang from a sense of outrage as their members were threatened by loss of occupation, identity, and community. Furthermore, these communities also sensed a loss of a proper and traditional moral and political order. As they did so they became the bearers of the 'moral economy' of the eighteenth century. Their apparent capacity to resist these threats to their traditional existence was made possible by the still existing bonds of community. Thus the objectives of these community-based movements and ideas were not those characteristic of a class society; everywhere they were populist. These threatened communities had either to resist, in radical and

---

[14] *Ibid.*, p. x. [15] *Ibid.*, p. ix. [16] *Ibid.*, p. xii and p. 7.

insurrectionary ways, or die – frequently they did both. It is Calhoun's view that once we understand the community/populist basis of radical action we will see more clearly that 'There is a real and problematical sense in which (Thompson) chronicles not the making of the English working class but the rise and fall of the radical English artisanate.'[17]

Compared with such radical artisanal communities, workers in a developed class society, such as those in post Chartist England, were likely to be much less radical and insurrectionary and more reformist.

Calhoun attributes the reformist tendencies of workers in a class society to three factors; loss of community consequent upon industrialization, difficulties of creating substitute formal organization, and possibilities of achieving real material and status gains within the industrial mode of production. Thus, workers in the newer factory industries and rapidly expanding industrial towns were left without either the community basis to support or the traditional interests to motivate collective action: they might build community, or they might pursue reform, but factory workers were not of a piece with the reactionary radicals who had dominated popular movements before the 1820s. Thus the new working classes were typically reformist.[18]

Where radical action did persist within the industrial mode of production it was still largely conditioned by community, and only latterly by formal organization. Calhoun's evidence for his claim that the most radical, working-class action was still conditioned by community is presented in a series of tables showing that centres of radical working-class activity, such as Oldham and Stockport, were more adult, more male, better paid, more evenly divided between spinning and weaving, and characterized industrially by small factories, than other, less radical towns such as Manchester and Bolton (see chapter 11).

Finally, he claims, it was not until ideas based on the labour theory of value, ideas more suited to an industrial labour force than to artisans, had a wide circulation, that anything akin to *class* consciousness could be thought to exist.

I have given this much space to an account of Calhoun's argument because I believe that he has identified a basic conceptual/theoretical weakness in Thompson's history, a weakness also noted in *Class in English History*, hinted at, almost in passing, by Prothero in *Artisans and Politics*, and touched upon by Genovese. Calhoun has also added a language of community and populism to the languages of order and of class.

But, the weight of argument is not all on Calhoun's side. He is weak on Marx on *class* and wrong about the novelty of *class* consciousness in

[17] *Ibid.*, p. 14.   [18] *Ibid.*, p. 231.

Thompson's treatment of *class*. Where Thompson drifts away from Marx is not in bringin political oppression as a new dimension to *class*, it was there all along, but in severing connection between *class* and structure, as shaped by modes of production, and *class* consciousness, and in conflating class perception or awareness (experience) and *class* consciousness. Thompson in spite of his protestations to the contrary, also has a cavalier attitude to theory, particularly to a theory of the historical development of societies at the core of which lies the concept, mode of production. This is the sort of theory which I believe Stedman Jones argues for as internal to history,[19] and which I have outlined earlier in this Afterword as it applied to England in the eighteenth and early nineteenth centuries. But Thompson remains much closer to such a theory than Calhoun.

Calhoun's own procedure, to import into history aspects of social-structural theories of collective action, however refreshing and intuitively valuable, tends to produce the same kind of rigid determinism he claims was characteristic of marxist historiography before Thompson. The thrust of much of his argument is that men may *only* act as their existing social organization permits them to act. Yet social organization is not free floating, it *is* tied to the mode of production and, presumably, only changes with changes in the mode of production. In any case social organization must surely be thought of as fixed and determining for any cohort of people. This seems to deny people an active life; for example, since community is something given to any cohort of people, it cannot be their product. Moreover, except that social organization (community) changes, it seems there can be no development in consciousness. Thus Calhoun's book is deficient in the lineage of ideas, however tenuous that lineage might be, and his model seems to allow little room for relations between one social organization and another, or for interplay between structure (organization) and consciousness. One might say that he allows no place for history itself. Applied to the pre-1820 period, this model suggests that people could only act as members of communities, as conceptualized by Calhoun, and that as members of such communities, they could only act within a framework of ideas called populist. The end result is a replacement of one set of categories by another; position in the production process by social organization, and a re-ified *class* consciousness by a re-ified populism. Since social organization seems to be a

[19] Gareth Stedman Jones, 'From Historical Sociology to Theoretical History', *British Journal of Sociology* (1970), pp. 295–305; and see chapter 5 above. For the relationship between E. P. Thompson and Marx, see Perry Anderson, *Arguments within English Marxism* (London, 1980), *New Statesman*, May–June 1980, and R. S. Neale, 'Theory and History: A Note on the Anderson/Thompson Debate', *Thesis Eleven*, 2 (1981), pp. 23–9.

function of the mode of production the model also makes it difficult to see how change might occur, other than through changes in the mode of production, for example, through the growth of larger factories employing more male labour in more densely settled urban regions. Is it only my imagination, or is there a remarkable symmetry between Calhoun on community and Althusser on eternities?

Calhoun seems aware of this problem: plainly consciousness did change, from radical populism to reformist class consciousness, according to Calhoun. But his explanation of the alleged change in consciousness lacks conviction. He writes, 'On a sociological level, the critical shift in the transition to "class" action came with the development of formal organizations which could mobilize workers for national action. On an ideological level, the key to the transition was the development of an argument of exploitation based on the labour theory of value.'[20] There are two reasons why this explanation is unsatisfactory. The first is, in seeming to make workers' action contingent on formal organization, the explanation prompts the question, why the development of new formal organization? If the answer to this question is that the development of formal organization was contingent on experience, then formal organization was itself determined, presumably by the mode of production and changes in it. If the answer is that formal organization was contingent on some prior development in consciousness, such as an awareness of a need for and possibility of such organization, where were the seeds of that consciousness to be found other than in those communities held by Calhoun to have determined another kind of consciousness? In short, how and why, in Calhoun's model, do formal organizations as mediators of class consciousness come into being? Does consciousness have a role?

The second reason is that, while Calhoun's claim about the significance of the labour theory of value tells us that consciousness was important, his claim is not demonstrated, merely asserted. But that is how the claim generally appears in historiography (see chapter 1). The labour theory of value seems to be allowed no lineage, no history; it simply enters the system rather like Marx's 'lightning of thought'. Yet as I suggest in *Class in English History*, notions about labour's right to the whole of its product pre-dated Ricardo and were frequently used as a basis for reactionary, populist writing with a strong basis in and appeal to community. Thus Calhoun's 'key' opens for us a Pandora's box of unsolved questions about interrelations between modes of production, social organization, and consciousness.

[20] Calhoun, *The Question of Class Struggle*, p. 115.

Calhoun's work is also disappointing at the point where he endeavours to translate the concept community into some kind of empirical reality. In his theory Calhoun tells us that community is not a place, not a population, but a cluster of variables based on familiarity, specific obligations and diffuse obligations, all worked out in a great network of social relationships. But in his history, the radical communities surviving within the industrial mode of production are little more than places; more adult, more male, better paid, more evenly divided between spinning and weaving, and with more small factories that other places – there are remarkably few people in Calhoun's communities – and I doubt that they can bear the weight of theory placed upon them!

It seems to me that community in Calhoun is more elusive than *class* in Marx and that populism is just as problematic as *class* consciousness in Thompson. Certainly the problem of inferring populist consciousness from behaviour is as great as that of inferring *class* consciousness from behaviour. In the end the question of which language to use is a question of judgement about whether the concepts used serve to conceal or reveal more about the past we attempt to construct, or mask the messages we seek to signal to people in our own time. And while I agree with Calhoun, that thought, whether ideological or utopian, should not be regarded as free-floating, that *class* and *class* consciousness are inappropriate as general category and concept for the pre-1820 period, and that there are advantages in adding the concept populism to highlight certain aspects of the history of the labouring population in England in the eighteenth century, I reserve the right to use the categories, order and class, and the concept class perception for some aspects of eighteenth- and early nineteenth-century history; and to carry the category *class* and the concept *class* consciousness around with me all the time for use when appropriate. I do so not only because of the historical appropriateness of the category and concept on some occasions, but because the language we use is never neutral. The language of class carries with it the idea of conflict, of a conscious and positive striving for change and improvement, and the possibility of self-making. The sociological language of community connotes resistance only, and, generally, failure at that. (As Raymond Williams observes, nobody uses 'community' in a hostile sense.) In the language of class, men and women are subjects. They are objects in the language of community. To the extent that we uncritically adopt the sociological language of community we carry our own dilemmas to our construction of the past; we make it a mirror of and a justification for our own loss of nerve.

My agreement with Calhoun on some issues does no harm to my outline of the articulation of modes of production above.

My next historians take our discussion of class back to the early years of the eighteenth century, to a part of England more commonly associated with Tess Durbeyfield, the Mayor of Casterbridge, and Bathsheba Everdene, than with the grubbier, urban and industrial aspects of class, even in the nineteenth century. They are C. R. Dobson and R. W. Malcolmson. Dobson is author of *Masters and Journeymen: A Prehistory of Industrial Relations 1717–1800* (1980), Malcolmson of 'A set of ungovernable people': the Kingswood colliers in the eighteenth century', published in J. Brewer and J. Styles (eds), *An Ungovernable People*, (1980).

Dobson's book is a modest one. Its aim, to enlarge the statistical coverage of industrial disputes in the eighteenth century. Although his list is not exhaustive, for example, Dobson has not identified any industrial disputes in eighteenth-century Bath, his coverage is comprehensive, in all, 383 industrial disputes between 1717 and 1800, of which 60 took place in the period 1717–40. Twelve of these 60 disputes occurred in London compared with only four in the whole of the midlands and the northern parts of the country. However, seventeen disputes, nearly one third of the total, occurred in the industrial regions of south-west England. Of these seventeen disputes, fifteen took place in the textile industry. A majority of disputes (twelve) were about wages, the remaining five were about legislative proposals to restrict the capacity of weavers to organize.

Of the sixty disputes in the period 1717–40, twenty-one were in the textile industry and forty-three of them were about wages or hours of work.

Some places in the industrial south-west, including Bristol, Taunton, Tiverton and Cullompton, were particularly militant in these disputes. The worst years were 1724–29 and 1736–38, and 1741.[21] For example, at Taunton, in 1725, 500 weavers who broke looms in a dispute over wages were in a bloody conflict with an equal number of townspeople and tradesmen. In 1729, in Bristol, Fetcham, a master clothier defending his house against hundreds of weavers demanding a wage increase, opened fire, killing seven weavers and the sergeant in charge of a detachment of soldiers called in to keep the peace. A decade later, in 1738, weavers throughout Wiltshire struck for an increase of

[21] C. R. Dobson, *Masters and Journeymen: A Prehistory of Industrial Relations 1717–1800* (London, 1980), pp. 15–29. See also, J. de L. Mann, 'Clothiers and Weavers in Wiltshire during the Eighteenth Century', in L. S. Pressnell (ed.), *Studies in the Industrial Revolution* (London, 1960).

one penny on the prevailing price of fourteen pence per yard. When one of their leaders was arrested, 1500 weavers marched on Melksham, demanding his release. In the town they destroyed nine houses and several workshops and fulling mills belonging to Coulthurst, the leading clothier opposing their claims. The military was called in, the Riot Act read, and three weavers were tried and hanged at Salisbury.

Dobson's comments on these disputes in the west country are brief but striking. Contrasing the peacefulness of disputes elsewhere in the country with the turbulence of those in the west, he writes, 'In the Wiltshire, Somerset and Devon woollen trade, disputes involved whole towns and villages, turning almost to civil war. . . . Such riots were not spontaneous, but carefully planned.'[22] So planned were they, that in the Wiltshire strike and riots of 1726, it was reported that some of the weavers had been 'sent to invite the Kingswood colliers to their assistance'.[23] Malcolmson reveals the significance of this invitation, the Kingswood people were then the most ungovernable people in England, their assisance would have been invaluable.

My question is, which language should we use to interpret these disputes, the language of order, the language of class, or the language of community?

And my answer is that the choice of language by the historian should not be arbitrary, but should flow from perceptions about the mode of production within which these disputes arose. Thus these weavers were wage labourers employed in the capitalist sector of the rural/urban manufacturing mode of production. They should be placed towards the lower end of the labouring population rather than among the ranks of artisans and handicraftsmen; their wages were low, a gross return of less than £20 a year, their trade, easy to enter, was subject to unrestricted competition, and in some towns they worked in workshops little different from small factories. Their employers were all master clothiers, themselves struggling to extract surplus value (profit) in the face of intense foreign competition. Seized of a belief in the economy of low wages and high prices, they confronted their wage labourers with wage cuts, the brutal economies of truck, and refusals to pay higher money wages.[24] In these circumstances weavers organized themselves across the region in concerted

[22] *Ibid.*, pp. 30–1.

[23] R. W. Malcolmson, '"A Set of Ungovernable People"': The Kingswood Colliers in the Eighteenth Century', in J. Brewer and J. Styles (eds.), *An Ungovernable People* (London, 1980), p. 93.

[24] C. R. Dobson, *Master and Journeymen*, pp. 15–29 and Appendix A; J. de L. Mann, *The Cloth Industry in the West of England from 1640–1880* (Oxford, 1971), pp. 103–8, and in L. S. Pressnell (ed.), *Studies in the Industrial Revolution.*

movements against their capitalist employers. It is true that these movements were regionally based and not nation-wide, that the weavers appear to have acted without benefit of the labour theory of value, and it is probably true that they derived their strength from community links and relationships. Nevertheless, it is pertinent to note that although they sometimes sought advice from the gentry and intervention by JP's, weavers were not concerned about prices, either of food or of products, nor, it seems, about the 'moral economy' referred to by Calhoun. Their struggles were always against their employers for a greater share of the product. Moreover, within the framework of self-generated formal organizations they crossed the boundaries of community and occupation, and set groups within communities, at least as places and populations, against each other to the point at which property was extensively damaged or destroyed, much blood shed, and people killed and executed. These movements in the industrial west country have a remarkably class-like, if not *class* look about them, so much so that Dobson finds these weavers comparable to certain strike-prone occuptaional groups within twentieth century class society!

Other evidence in Dobson's book about the London society of journeymen tailors, which had a formal London-wide, and, therefore, regional organization as early as 1720, when taken in conjunction with what is known about the circumstances in which journeymen tailors in Bath first organized themselves into a union in 1763, as well as the evidence offered by Thompson in *The Making* and by Morris in *Class and Class Consciousness in the Industrial Revolution*, and Dobson's evidence about west-country weavers,[25] persuades me that any impending imperialism of the language of community should be resisted – hence my already stated reservations about it.

Such a resistance would not mean, as I believe Calhoun might have it mean, that one must concede what sometimes appears as the established imperialism of Thompson's views on *class* consciousness. There are alternatives. I have argued elsewhere that one might prefer a language of order, or of class perception, or of class consciousness, taking care all the while to distinguish the latter from the italicized Marxian version, *class* consciousness. I suggest now that we should carefully select our language according to an understanding of the articulation of modes of production in our period. Thus we should

[25] R. S. Neale, *Bath, 1680–1850*, pp. 69–70, 76, 91, 225, 269, 324; E. P. Thompson, *The Making of the English Working Class* (London, 1963), *passim*; R. J. Morris, *Class and Class Consciousness in the Industrial Revolution 1780–1850* (London, 1979), *passim* but esp. pp. 12–20; Dobson, *Masters and Journeymen*, pp. 60–73.

distinguish various manifestations of consciousness by social groups generated by these modes of production and their articulation. This means that we should avoid making an assumption about a linear progression from one mode of production to another – an assumption which seems to me to underpin most accounts of industrialization in this period – and accept the fact that the uneven economic development of England and the accompanying rise and fall of social groups or classes has significance for all description and discussion of class consciousness. Consequently, the evidence we use and the conclusions we arrive at should be regionally and chronologically specific. Yet it must also be understood that modes of production are not regions and that regions may contain their own peculiar mix of modes of production, as for example, in London and the west country. To this understanding we must add an appreciation of the fact that ideas rarely pass from mode of production to mode of production or from class to class like olympic torches. Therefore, to change the metaphor in mid-run, we may have to accept the fact that the axe of nineteenth- and twentieth-century class consciousness, like that belonging to George Washington, may have had seven different handles and five heads; and that *class* consciousness and populism were only two of them.

Therefore, while I am persuaded that the response of the west-country weavers to their position in the production process may be though of as class-like, I am equally persuaded by Malcolmson's argument, that the response of the Kingswood colliers, described as probably, 'the most rebellious group of labouring men in the country between the 1720s and 1750s',[26] in a place almost surrounded by the west country weaving industry, is best encapsulated in Calhoun's language of community; their contribution to the consciousness of subsequent generations of the labouring population was not the militant trade unionism of the west country weavers nor the formal organization of the London tailors, nor their own militancy, it was Methodism in all its guises. And next door to Kingswood was Bath. Bath was a mass of contradictions. In the 1730s, when the weavers and colliers in surrounding areas were doing their best – or their worst – to protect themselves, the city was run by a closed corporation struggling to preserve itself against the disruptive effects of the modernizing process. For a time the corporation met with some success. But, infiltrated by dynamic entrepreneurs, surrounded by agrarian-capitalist landowners, and attractive to men of the London based monied interest, it succumbed. In the 1760s the corporation joined the race to get rich.

[26] R. W. Malcolmson, 'A Set of Ungovernable People', p. 89.

Bath grew. It attracted an immigrant labour force of uprooted men
and women, yet to create for themselves an identifiable community,
but able to establish formal organizations as early as the mid-1760s.
When it came, that community, in the lower part of the town, it
generated support for a set of forward looking politcal ideas more
threatening to established authority than either those of Kingswood
colliers or of the west country weavers, even at their most militant.
But these ideas did have roots in a 'utopian' past, in a lineage of
oppositional ideas as described by Dickinson – in memory the radicals
of 1812 looked back to the Revolution of 1688 – and they had roots in
experience as described by Prothero, and in community as analysed by
Calhoun, except that the artisanal community in Bath was new, not
much more than seventy years old in the 1830s. By that time the body
of ideas in the community transcended community. Through their
support for Roebuck and the Philosophic Radicals they embraced the
discontents of the Irish and the Canadian rebels and the wider principles of American democracy; they were the middling class, built on
community no doubt, but a class nevertheless (see chapter 8). Whether
they were ripe for revolution in 1832 we shall never know. Then,
when the Charter came, some of the artisans, from the same community, were a class in another sense. Which is to say that while we do
need a language of *class* and of order, and a language of community
and of populism, we also need a language that encapsulates the richness and density in the period 1680–1850, a language that is 'dense and
complex, detailed yet abstract', a language through which to express a
radical argument which is also history, such as that which is only to be
found in the Materialist Conception of History and its key concept,
the mode of production.

But there's the rub, say my critics, or some of them. The materialist
conception of history has, can have and should have no privileged
status; it is certainly not history and is poor theory, no better and
probably worse than most others.

IV

And that brings me to *history* and Barthes' reflection upon it.

For Barthes, *history* is a limp word; vague, yet important and
insistent, taking the place of several signifieds. '*History* is a moral
notion,'[27] says Barthes. And so it is. And there are as many moralities
as there are historians. In my five ages of empirical historiography I

[27] Roland Barthes, *Roland Barthes by Roland Barthes* (London, 1977), p. 126.

notice some of them; Peter Borsay chides me with writing an argument in place of *history*; and I am sure that the University lecturer
would chastise me for denying the masses their interesting *history*. But
there are others even more wrathful; Gertrude Himmelfarb, whose
paper I include in this collection for its moralistic energy (see chapter
12), and Pat Rogers and Adam Fergusson. Pat Rogers charges me with
anger and a natural-born grumpiness. He derides my unfamiliar *Bath
1680–1850* for its 'grandiloquent polemical expressions (which) float
upon a froth of loosely handled documentation',[28] only to reveal his
own nominalist familiars; an impulse to count words and list names,
and to attribute the act of writing solely to individual psychological
processes. But Adam Fergusson, another reader, reads no anger in my
Bath, only dullness. It does not match, he says, the reality of Dickens'
description of the plight of Mr Winkle shut out from his lodgings in
the Royal Crescent in his night shirt.[29]

The limpness of *history*.

Because I acknowledge limpness in my own work I find it difficult
to respond to Morris's interrogation of *Class in English History*, at least
in a form he might find persuasive. In his review of the book Morris
writes, 'Neale rightly rejects the possibility of an empirical value free
and particularistic social history, but what basis can he offer for the
explicit theorizing which he advocates? His answer, the materialist
conception of history, is no less ideological and value laden than
alternatives like political economy, 1950s sociology and the use of
contemporary perceptions. . . . I prefer the more "broad church"
approach of Raphael Samuel's *People's History and Socialist Theory*.'[30]

Although I am reluctant to accept Morris's appropriation of the
word 'ideology', for reasons I will refer to later, and notwithstanding
that his interrogation of *Class in English History* is the very mirror of
the book itself, I take his point. Just as I have tried to make explicit the
outlines of the model of the articulation of modes of production
hidden in *Class in English History*, I should remove my case for the
materialist conception of history from the discourse of that book and
be as plain as I can; although plainness like facts can rarely answer the
questions we ask of each other and the world around us. But I
comment first on Morris's contraposing of *Class in English History* and
People's History and Socialist Theory, a contraposition, perhaps, which
Morris sees linked to the present political climate in England.

[28] Review of *Bath, 1680–1850: A Social History*, in *Times Literary Supplement*, August, 1981.
[29] Review of *Bath, 1680–1850: A Social History*, in *The Times*, 6 June, 1981.
[30] Review of *Class in English History 1680–1850*, in *The Economic History Review*, 34(4) (1982),
pp. 648–9.

It is true that I see the problems of the empirical theory of historical knowledge as much in *people's history* as in *history* – the limpness of the object is unchanged by the addition of an adjective. Indeed, I sense an anti-intellectual moral stridency in the work of some of the practitioners of *people's history*, and it may be this that is signified by the choice of title. Most of all I see little gain in confronting an empirical *history* with an empirical *people's history*. Nevertheless, as I worked in my Australian study (with the kookaburras mocking every word I wrote) I was struck by the matching of my words with the Ruskin-writing of Raphael Samuel. After all it *is* Samuel who writes,

A socialist history isn't, or shouldn't be, simply a question of a different subject matter, but rather a different way of looking at society as a whole. It needs to be theoretically informed if it is to resist the scholastic fragmentation of the subject matter, and to escape those territorial sub-divisions which corral historical inquiry within professionally-defined fiefs. It needs theory if it is to bring about the reunification of history with other forms of knowledge; if it is to engage in comparative inquiry; and if it is to bring the interpretation of the past and the understanding of the present into dialogue with one another. . . . In short, the book has taken the occasion of the current debate on theory to ask historians to consider the conditions of existence of their work, and the possibilities of a different kind of knowledge.[31]

And I can endorse all that Samuel says in this passage and much more besides, and I thought that I had voiced similar sentiments in *Class in English History*, adding only a discourse on aspects of appropriate theory for a socialist *history*, and some description of eighteenth and early nineteenth century England. I was struck, too, on listening to the kookaburras while reading *People's History and Socialist Theory*, by the realization that I must have been 'teaching' and writing *people's history* all my adult life without signifying it as such. (I certainly do not see myself as contraposed to Raphael Samuel.) Yet I am not sure what I would gain by adopting the limp and moral signification of *people's history* for my practice – as M. J. Morris should know, 'broad churches' have a habit of becoming narrowly sectarian. I really don't like churches of any kind.

So, why do I argue for the materialist conception of history?

In brief. The materialist conception of history is; coherent, comprehensive – with high content, critical, optimistic, consciousness-raising, and useful – it works. Above all it speaks to me in the words used by Isaiah Berlin writing on great *history*, I will quote them again, 'On some occasions, seldom enough, the explanation not only involves,

[31] Raphael Samuel (ed.), *People's History and Socialist Theory* (London, 1980), pp. L and LII.

but reveals, basic categories of universal import, which, once they are forced upon consciousness, we recognize as underlying all our experience; yet so closely interwoven are they with all that we are and feel, and therefore so totally taken for granted, that to touch them at all is to communicate shock to the entire system, the shock is one of recognition and one that may upset us, as is liable to happen when something deep-set and fundamental that has lain unquestioned and in darkness, is suddenly illuminated or prised out of its frame for closer inspection. When this occurs we call such explanations profound, fundamental, revolutionary, and those who offer them . . . men of depth or insight or genius.' So I find the materialist conception of history intellectually exciting, disturbing, and matched by experience. I realize, too, that to say this is to speak to no-one who is not already persuaded and, probably, to convince Morris that he was right to pass off my work as 'ideological', just like political economy and 1950s sociology.

Yet there is here a moment to pause. There may be a sense in which Morris's statement, that my position is *just* as 'ideological' as others, reflects some gain. If the materialist conception of history is *just* as 'ideological' as other *history*, then the claim that it alone is ideological seems to have been relinquished. And if I add to this concession from Morris, Thompson's belated moment of self-criticism, in which he concedes, 'that the historian, in every moment of his or her work, is a value formed being, who cannot, when proposing problems or interrogating evidence, in fact operate in this value-free way'[32] – and knocks the bottom out of his argument in *The Poverty of Theory* – it may be possible to say that some of us, at least (Morris, Thompson, Neale), agree that we are *all* in the same bottom. If this is the case, then it is all gain, but a small advance; the big battalions, led by the men of Mont Pélèrin, the cliometricians, and the 'university lecturers in history', have yet to realize that they are in the same bottom with us. Only when they do so will it be possible for all of us to examine our sailing orders. In the meantime there seems to be no reason for secrecy.

Coherence. A logically coherent theory, interpretation if you prefer that word, is, surely, preferable to one that is inconsistent and internally contradictory; in spite of Barthes. Because this seems to many to be the case, recent theorists of Marxism and theoretically minded marxist historians have sought to clarify and refine the materialistic conception of history. Among theorists I include Althusser, Amin, Avineri, Balibar, Cohen, Lukács, Rader and Shaw: among historians; Anderson,

[32] *Ibid.*, p. 407.

Barrington-Moore, Brenner, Dobb, Hobsbawm and Hilton. To follow these writers in their texts, as they search for coherence and illumination in the materialist conception of history, is an exhilarating experience. While they may not agree with one another, and while the reader may be stimulated to open a discourse with every one of them, their contributions are rich with criticism and analysis and with the relation of theory to practice, all informed by a theory built around the concept of the mode of production and the notion of contradiction. Therefore, for me to state the materialist conception of history in all its coherent complexity, in answer to Morris, would be to write a book bigger even than Kolakowski's. And were I competent to write such a book, its writing would occupy the rest of my life. Yet, were I competent, and were I to attempt such a book, it could in no sense be definitive in the way an empiricist historian would comprehend that term; even to claim to be able to write such a definitive text, is to make a claim running counter to the materialist conception of history itself.

Because I seem to evade Morris's interrogation I add now that I stand by my own small contribution to the clarification of the materialist conception of history; my account of the transition from feudalism to capitalism, my analysis of *class*, my brief statement on modes of production in eighteenth century England, and, what perceptive readers of *Bath, 1680–1850* will have read, my criticism of Crouzet's critique of the secondary aspect of Marx's notion of primitive accumulation. (This is my account of the financial relations linking Chandos, Wood and Theobald in their work towards building a pleasure resort for successful agrarian and commercial capitalists.) And it would be up to my critics to show that the materialist conception of history, and my contribution to it, *is* incoherent. Of course, this would require a deal of reading on their part, particularly if they dispensed with the confusions and distortions of Popper, Acton and the men of Mont Pélèrin. Since, in the process, they would acquire another language, that, too, would be all gain, for they would learn that the measuring of one set of signifieds and signifiers against another is a formidable task. (Some might even come to agree with my alternative reading of Isaiah Berlin.)

Comprehensiveness. A theory that can encompass and account for more of the information about the world, which comes to us through experience, yet which, at the same time, enlarges that stock of information by directing our attention to structural aspects of reality unapproachable by mere empiricism, and which points to the limitations of empiricism while retaining high content, is surely preferable to one with high content but limited range. Thus, in art, analytical cubism represented reality more completely than earlier perspectival painting; it generated a revolution in ways of seeing and representing reality that has still not worked itself out. And I have observed on at least two earlier occasions that we need something like an analytical cubist revolution in our ways of comprehending and representing the past.

In *Class in English History* I referred readers to Karl Mannheim's contribution to this question and the problem of comprehensiveness. At that time (1976–78) I was too dismissive of Mannheim's concept of relational knowledge. Mannheim was on to something. I believe now that the clue to understanding Mannheim's concept is his injunction to historians to follow the methods of philology, and I have a hunch that his advice was to read Saussure and to understand something of semiology. This means I think, that for Mannheim, the concept/ signifier 'Utopia', and what, it signified, can *only* be understood in relation to the concept/signifier 'Ideology', and what it signified. Further, that these concepts change in content over time. Therefore, the only knowledge we can have about what is signified is relational, and absolute knowledge as sought by all historians, tarred with the empiricist brush steeped in a correspondence theory of language and of historical knowledge, is impossible.

Because I prefer Mannheim's concepts, 'Ideology' and 'Utopia', I reject Morris's appropriation of 'Ideology' to describe my work, his usage drowns difference in its image reservoir.

What is ideology, asks Barthes. He replies, 'It is precisely the idea *insofar as it dominates*: ideology can only be dominant. Correct as it is to speak of an "ideology of the dominant class", because there is certainly a dominated class, it is quite inconsistent to speak of a "dominant ideology", because there is no dominated ideology: where the "dominated" are concerned, there is nothing, no ideology, unless it is precisely – and this is the last degree of alienation – the ideology they are forced (in order to make symbols, hence in order to live) to borrow from the class that dominates them.'[33] Therefore, when I write, in Mannheim's sense, I write 'utopia' and seek truth (in Marx, *class* consciousness).

I also comprehend 'utopia' as consisting of many strands, some of which historians have attempted to subsume in the languages of order, classlessness, and community, as well as of *class*. And I see a place for all these languages when linked to the articulation of modes of production as I have described it. I believe that this process shows the

[33] Roland Barthes, *The Pleasure of the Text* (New York, 1975), p. 32.

materialist conception of history to be more comprehensive in its handling of the eighteenth and early nineteenth centuries than other conceptions of *history* currently available. The Afterword is in fact an exercise in comprehensiveness. In it I try to show that the materialist conception of history, on the question of *class*, can accommodate its critics. This accommodation can be extended to other areas of criticism.

The materialist conception of history can also embrace other critical theories, such as structuralism (it *is* structuralist) and it can live with, and enjoy, semiology. Empiricism cannot. Neither can political economy, nor 1950s sociology. As for the merely empirical use of contemporary perception, it is a procedural method revealing little about reality, only certain perceptions of it signified in a language itself arbitrary, displayed by historians using a language sharing their subjects' imagery and the thought processes structured by it. As a method, this *history*-as-ideology, clearly lacks the comprehensiveness of the materialist conception of history.

Critical. It was once put to my by one of my students, that 'debunking' is a central characteristic of the materialist conception of history. It is. A similar characteristic is plain enough in my own writing, so I am told. But *critical* is brother and sister to 'Utopia'. I need say no more about it.

Optimistic. Consciousness-raising. These two characteristics are children of 'Utopia'. The materialist conception of history places women and men where they belong, as actors shaping their lives in their own image, changing their image on the way. Therefore, changing the way they shape their lives. And it reaches out to all people. But it shows, too, how they are locked in a world and images not of their own making. In this contradiction it gives to those who suffer the condescension of the present, ways of constructing the past so that they may shrug off those who condescend. In *Class in English History* I wrote, 'It is through *class* that the pessimism of Pope's observation, "Man Never is, but always To be blest," is to be proved false.' Barthes, for all the pleasure of his text, has yet to change my mind.

Usefulness. By now it should be clear what I mean. It is that in the social sciences and the humanities – if not in natural science itself, the concept of utility – usefulness – workability, as the final or ultimate test of a theory, is always subjective. Thus, the utility of neo-classical political economy is measured by the material and social gains alleged to accrue to all members of society (at least on average) from its application. The utility of the materialist conception of history is that it challenges in theory and in practice, which is to say historiographically, the reality of these alleged gains; it shows that what is useful may not be true, and it generates action. It does so within a conceptual framework which is: coherent, comprehensive, critical, optimistic and consciousness-raising.

Yet the fact that the materialist conception of history happens to be optimistic, consciousness-raising and useful, at least for some people and some groups of people, is not its justification as historiography. This justification is that its theory, its approaches and methods, its language and concepts facilitate the production of true knowledge, recognizable as such because it is predicated on what Agnes Heller has called the one empirically universal value in our historical consciousness, '*the value-idea of freedom*'.[34] (Which I take to be comparable with, if not the same as, Marx's notion of humankind as '*gattungswesen*'.) It is this value-idea that renders useful historiographical works based on the materialist conception of history – but they *are* historiographical works subject to critical-value interrogation such that they may be seen to be true knowledge. Consequently, the materialist conception of history also works as historiography. And this is to say that it works for students of history like Margaret Setter, and for their historiography; they, too, are part of my argument. Asked to reply to any one of Voltaire's *Letters Concerning the English Nation*, Margaret wrote:

Dear Monsieur Voltaire,

More than two hundred years separate your life from mine, and examined superficially, the world about which you write looks totally different from the one I know, whether it be customs, manners, level of technology, or any other thing we might care to consider. Yet, on closer inspection, it turns out to be not so different after all, for the problems which you defined as individual and moral, and which we define as social and political are with us still.

And the evils you denounced so passionately; war, arbitrary punishment, torture and other forms of injustice are here today and defy solution. The extremes of wealth and poverty have widened and the great majority of the world's population still live out their lives in a miserable thraldom to poverty and ignorance. In one of your most memorable phrases you refer to 'those miserable physicians of souls'; those men who in your day were the priests of the Catholic Church, who exclaim interminably about the trivial offences men might commit, yet are silent concerning the real causes of suffering in our world. These 'physicians' abound in our world, confining men's minds in the closed, sterile systems of thought you so detested, and thereby blinding men's eyes to the real possibilities and alternatives open to them.

[34] Agnes Heller, *A Theory of History* (London, 1982), p. 114.

For the fact that there are real alternatives available marks the essential difference between your age and mine. I read your words, and can imagine you speculating about the future, trying to make sense of all the changes impinging on you, not knowing where you are being taken, just as I am doing in my own time. You are aware you are on the threshold of a progressive period, just how progressive you cannot imagine. At the same time you are apprehensive, imagining the problems that lie ahead. The forces set in motion in your lifetime are creating the means whereby it will become possible, for the first time in history, to eliminate poverty for all mankind. At the same time these forces are generating institutional forms which in time will act as a fetter on further progress; which will perpetuate and extend the discrepancies of wealth in the world. And that brings me to the subject of my letter to you; my reply to your letter concerning Mr Locke.

Mr Locke, instead of speculating about the nature of the soul, a problem occupying men's minds since the days of the ancient Greeks, and singularly unproductive of any real knowledge, wisely dares to doubt. He disputes Descartes' contention that the soul is identical to thought; able to grasp in some kind of intuitive manner such metaphysical notions as for example, God, space, the infinite. Not so, says Locke, it is from the organs of our five senses we derive knowledge of the world. Man and animals all share this capacity. What distinguishes man from the animals is his capacity to reflect on the mind's activities, for man knows that he knows. This is a very dangerous doctrine, for until now man has been separated from the animals by an unbridgeable gulf, from the moment of God's creation. If it is a proven fact that animals have similar sensory organs of thought and feeling to man, then the difference becomes simply one of degree. This raises a problem for which you do not have an explanation, undermining as it does the Genesis account of the Creation, for if animals have no soul yet move, the same could be said for humans.

This leads to the consideration of the nature of knowledge, a question still inspiring many theories. Man's brain has been studied, reduced to its simplest elements, but that still does not tell us how it works, how it manufactures knowledge. No wonder you are forced to return to God as a first principle to surmount this difficulty. But there are other, more important implications to be drawn from Locke's theory. Locke asks whether the soul, whose existence may be coterminous with the body and likewise consisting of matter, may be capable of thought (and is unable to answer). If it is, then this could also be conceptualized as a variety of matter, capable of being set in motion without God's intervention. This implies that man can pursue his activities unimpeded and without any laws to guide his behaviour. Another philosopher, Thomas Hobbes, had also considered this problem of man conceived as matter in motion and concluded that men must make, or act as if they had made 'a social contract' putting absolute power into the hands of the sovereign for the good of all. This reasoning recognized a distinction between positive law, which determines distribution of property, and natural law, ascertainable by reason, which asserts as an absolute law the right to the preservation of the individual and of the society of which he is a part. Locke undermined this principle by substituting the idea of a social contract provisional upon the performance of the King of his proper function, that of protecting property rights. He exercises a trusteeship, which if betrayed, renders his position forfeit, and justifies revolution. Locke based property rights on natural law, but by assuming that men had given tacit consent to the introduction of money, removed all the natural law limitations on the property right.

It is not surprising that you defend Locke by claiming his ideas do not contradict the tenets of revealed religion, for you are otherwise at a loss to contain the forces at work within your society, threatening it with chaos. You are aware that an entire conception of culture is in retreat and you have nothing to put in its place, apart from the exhortation to man to exercise tolerance, compassion and care for his fellow creatures. You are aware of the 'potentially socially disruptive forces of a society recognizable based on private property'. Such a society cannot be made to cohere by appeals to pursue Virtue, as Mandeville was quick to point out in his attack on Shaftesbury. Shaftesbury had counted on the natural benevolence of human beings to produce harmony among mankind.

You cannot be blamed for this lack of understanding for you are attempting to understand a new phenomenon, a stage in society witnessing the last heroic phase of primitive accumulation. By this I mean the vast accumulation of money and systems of credit which will make it possible for England to introduce complex machinery into manufacturing, to transform its economic and social structure. This process is popularly referred to as the Industrial Revolution, a term that will seem strange to you. You live in a world of scarcity, so it will be impossible for me to convey to you a sense of the abundance that is about to be created but perhaps one example will suffice. I am a descendent of that 'mob' you see around you as a vague, amorphous, threatening mass, yet the wealth that has been created allows me, and a woman at that, to attend a university, something you would consider Utopian. But that is only because I am fortunate to have been born in one of the wealthy countries. In the meantime, the intervening period between your time and mine will be brutal and dehumanizing for most people. There will be ceaseless argument and struggle and John Locke's theory of property rights will be used in ways he would not have approved. It will be asserted by men like Adam Smith that what really distinguishes property is the fact that it gives some men the right to appropriate the product of the labour of others. Labour is therefore not simply necessary to maintain property, but is the source of all wealth. But you say that it is trade which has enriched English citizens, helping make them free. By this I take you to mean the middle ranks of society, although you note that trade is not despised by the aristocracy with whom you compare the French nobility, to the latter's disadvantage. Since Government is controlled by landowners it is really this which acts as an economic force in accumulating wealth. Your middle ranks share in this freedom, or extended privilege, call it what you will, but your praise rings rather hollow when it is considered just what lengths these men of property will go to protect their interests, adding fifty new capital offences to the laws. You are forced to tacitly acquiesce in this for if God has become superfluous, and the King no longer rules by Divine Right but is liable to be dismissed, and if self-interest alone appears to legitimize the accumulation of wealth and power in your society, how do you justify this? What do you say to the vast majority of people in your society who are miserably poor, who have nothing to exist with but by selling their labour?

It is obvious you are a man showing great sensitivity to the sufferings of others but this problem is incapable of resolution for you. You are forced to justify the existence of great extremes of wealth and poverty on three related, but logically unconnected grounds. First, you rationalize the existence of poverty on the grounds that the poor, having been born in that state, are not absolutely unhappy, and that their need to constantly labour for the necessities of life prevents them from too closely considering their situation. Second, it is your perception that society as you know it can only exist on the basis of such inequality, for otherwise no one would make himself available to labour for another and therefore society could not be perpetuated. Third, you assume that every man is born with the innate desire to dominate and possess the fortunes of another. From these assumptions it follows that human equality is impossible since to attempt to attain it would lead to disorder, therefore rigorous property laws are legitimate because they preserve the existing situation, that is, order. They keep the poor working to preserve that property, and this ceaseless toil prevents them considering their situation too closely and, as a result, attempting to usurp the property rights of others. Mandeville was far more honest when he phrased it thus: 'Vice is beneficial found when it's by Justice lopt, and bound.'

You understand perfectly well that Locke's theories, though potentially subversive in the wrong hands, are safe so long as philosophers 'do not write for the people and are devoid of emotional fire.' But emotional fire is exactly the thing that will inspire many of them as the century proceeds. Various radical theories will emerge, formulated by men advocating the Rights of Man as opposed to property, or, using Locke's argument based on natural law in a way he would not have approved, claim for the labourer the right to the toal product of his labour, there being no other tangible property to which he can lay claim. One philosopher, who will be the very epitome of 'emotional fire' will proclaim to the poor that they do not have to bear their condition, it is not inevitable, that they will make a revolution!

The name of this man is Karl Marx, and different though you are, I think in time you would have understood him, for you both share, each in your own way, a passionate concern for liberty and humanity. After Marx, the world will never be the same, for there will be revolutions, not in the way Marx would have liked, but revolutions nonetheless. His ideas will appeal to men and women of widely differing experiences, but having in common the one central conviction, that the world can be changed by conscious human activity. Between you and Marx lies a century of economic and social development, and a corresponding development in social thought. Marx will announce his departure from the approach of other philosophers by announcing 'the chief defect of all materialism up to now . . . is that the object, reality, what we apprehend through our sense is understood only in the form of the object or contemplation; but not as sensuous human activity, as practice, not subjectively!' By this he means that the social reality we know is not directly ordained by God, nor is it simply an object impinging on our senses, and it certainly is not the objective realization of consciousness. It is the result of men and women engaged in an endless dialectic with nature to produce their means of subsistence. You will no doubt be asking how man, whom you see as innately greedy, hungering for power over others and driven to work only by necessity can change the world without bloodshed, destruction of property and disorder. You will say it is not right that one man should compel another to surrender what is rightfully his. The answer is of course, that Marx was looking at society in a different way. His conception of man was that of a species-being, innately creative and productive, who could only fulfil his true nature in and through society, but at the same time it was society itself as presently constituted which prevented that fulfilment. Man being a social being, would act in concert with other men having interests in common with him but antagonistic to the common interests of other groups of men. These antagonistic relations centred around the institution of property and the relations of domination and subordination preceding them, Marx called them class relations. At first only the ruling class, that is those men standing in positions of authority in relation to production would act self-consciously, in their own class interest, but gradually, in practice, working men and women would realize the fact that capital, property, was only accumulated labour. When they did so they would overturn the existing property relations so that labour, instead of serving the interests of accumulated labour, would be served by it. People acting in accordance with their social being, would organize production in a rational manner, finally appropriating to themselves the entire product of their labour. At this moment, Marx believed, pre-history would cease and real, human history begin. So far this has not occurred anywhere in the world, although many countries have abolished what Marx called capitalist property relations. Many revolutions have been deformed or reversed, either from the weight of their own past, or from having to survive in a hostile world, or both. But the struggle for political and social renewal never ends and your writings reveal that you, too, are part of that struggle.[35]

Historiography (true knowledge)? Ideology? History?

[35] Margaret Setter, an essay written for the course, 'The Development of Capitalism in England, 1680–1850' at the University of New England, NSW. I have omitted the footnotes normally required for student essays.

Suggested Reading

MAINLY THEORY WITH SOME HISTORY

Abrams, Philip, 'History, Sociology, Historical Sociology', *Past and Present*, 87 (1980).

Althusser, Louis and Balibar, Étienne, *Reading Capital* (London, 1970).

Anderson, Perry, *Arguments within English Marxism* (London, 1980).

Barthes, Roland, *Writing Degree Zero* (London, 1967).

Barthes, Roland, *The Pleasure of the Text* (New York, 1975).

Bechhofer, F. and Elliott, B., 'Persistence and Change: The Petite Bourgeoisie in Industrial Society', *European Journal of Sociology*, XVII (1976).

Berlin, Isaiah, 'The Concept of Scientific History', *History and Theory*, I (1961).

Calhoun, Craig, *The Question of Class Struggle: Social Foundations of Popular Radicalism during the Industrial Revolution* (Oxford, 1982).

Cohen, G. A., *Marx's Theory of History* (London, 1979).

Culler, Jonathan, *Ferdinand de Saussure* (Harmondsworth, 1977).

Danto, Arthur C., *Analytical Philosophy of History* (Cambridge, 1976).

Dahrendorf, Ralf, *Class and Class Conflict in Industrial Society* (London, 1959).

Elias, Norbert, *The Civilizing Process*, Vol. I (New York and Oxford, 1978, original edition 1939).

Eagleton, Terry, *Criticism and Ideology* (London, 1976).

Fox, Elizabeth and Genovese, E. D., 'The Political Crisis of Social History: A Marxian Perspective', *Journal of Social History*, 10 (1976/77). See also other contributors to this Symposium.

Gerth, H. H. and Mills, C. Wright (eds.), *From Max Weber: Essays in Sociology* (London, 1948).

Giddens, Anthony, *The Class Structure of Advanced Societies* (London, 1973).

Goldmann, Lucien, *The Human Sciences and Philosophy* (London, 1969).

Heller, Agnes, *A Theory of History* (London, 1982).

Hobsbawm, E. J., 'From Social History to the History of Society', *Daedalus*, 100 (Winter, 1971).

Hobsbawm, E. J., 'The Revival of Narrative, Some Comments', *Past and Present*, 86 (1980).

Kamenka, Eugene and Neale, R. S. (eds.), *Feudalism, Capitalism and Beyond* (London, 1975).

Kolakowski, Leslek, *Positivist Philosophy: From Hume to the Vienna Circle* (London, 1972).

Lakatos, Imre, 'Falsification and the Methodology of Scientific Research Programmes', in Lakatos, I. and Musgrove, A., *Criticism and the Growth of Knowledge* (Cambridge, 1970).

Macpherson, C. B., *The Political Theory of Possessive Individualism* (Oxford, 1962).

Mandelbaum, Maurice, *History, Man and Reason* (Baltimore and London, 1971).

Mannheim, Karl, *Ideology and Utopia* (London, 1936).

Marx, Karl, *Capital*, especially Vol. I (various editions).

Marx, Karl, *The Economic and Philosophic Manuscripts of 1844*, ed. by D. J. Struik (New York, 1964).

Marx, Karl, *Communist Manifesto*, in *Selected Works in Two Volumes* (Moscow, 1950).

Marx, Karl, *Critique of Hegel's 'Philosophy of Right'*, ed. by J. O'Malley (Cambridge, 1970), especially pp. 131–42.

Marx, Karl, *The German Ideology* (Moscow, 1964).

Marx, Karl, 'Preface to a Contribution to a Critique of Political Economy', in *Selected Works in Two Volumes* (Moscow, 1950).

Marx, Karl, *Critique of the Gotha Programme*, in *Selected Works in One Volume* (Moscow, 1968).

Moore, Barrington, Jr., *Social Origins of Dictatorship and Democracy* (London, 1967).

Moorhouse, H. F., 'The Marxist Theory of the Labour Aristocracy', *Social History*, 4 (1978).

Mousnier, Roland, *Social Hierarchies, 1450 to the Present* (London, 1973).

Neale, R. S., *Class in English History, 1680–1850* (Oxford, 1981).

Parkin, Frank, *Class Inequality and Political Order* (London, 1957).

Popper, K. R., *The Poverty of Historicism* (London, 1957).

Rader, Melvin, *Marx's Interpretation of History* (Oxford, 1979).

Samuel, Raphael (ed.), *People's History and Socialist Theory* (London, 1981).

Shapiro, Gilbert, 'Prospects for a Scientific Social History', *Journal of Social History*, 10 (1976/77).

Shaw, William H., *Marx's Theory of History* (London, 1978).

Stedman Jones, Gareth, 'Class Struggle and the Industrial Revolution', *New Left Review*, 90 (1975).

Stone, Lawrence, 'The Revival of Narrative', *Past and Present*, 85 (1979).

Stuart, Hughes, H., *Consciousness and Society* (London, 1959).

Thompson, E. P., 'Eighteenth-century English Society: Class Struggle without Class?', *Social History*, 3(2) (May, 1978).

Thompson, E. P., *The Poverty of Theory* (London, 1978).
Timpanaro, Sebastian, *On Materialism* (London, 1975).
Vološinov, V. N. *Marxism and the Philosophy of Language* (New York, 1973).
Williams, Raymond, *Keywords* (London, 1976).
Williams, Raymond, *Marxism and Literature* (Oxford, 1977).
Williams, Raymond, *Politics and Letters* (London, 1981).

MAINLY HISTORY WITH SOME THEORY

Antal, F., *Hogarth and his Place in European Art* (London, 1962).
Beer, Max, *History of British Socialism* (London, 1920).
Brewer, J., *Party Ideology and Popular Politics at the Accession of George III* (Cambridge, 1976).
Brewer, J. and Styles, E. (eds.), *Un Ungovernable People* (London, 1980).
Briggs, Asa, 'Middle-Class Consciousness in English Politics, 1780–1846', *Past and Present*, 9 (1956).
Briggs, Asa, *Chartist Studies* (London, 1958).
Bythel, D., *The Hand-Loom Weavers: A Study in the English Cotton Industry During the Industrial Revolution* (Cambridge, 1969).
Church, R. A. and Chapman, S. D., 'Gravenor Henson and the Making of the English Working Class', in E. L. Jones and G. E. Mingay (eds.), *Land, Labour and Population in the Industrial Revolution* (London, 1967).
Clarke, J., Critcher, C., Johnson, R., *Working Class Culture* (London, 1979).
Currie, R. and Hartwell, R. M., 'The Making of the English Working Class?', *Economic History Review*, XVIII (1965).
Davidoff, Leonore, 'Class and Gender in Victorian England: The Diaries of Arthur J. Munby and Hannah Cullwick', *Feminist Studies*, 5(1) (1979).
Dickinson, H. T., *Liberty and Property, Political Ideology in Eighteenth Century Britain* (London, 1972).
Dinwiddy, John, 'Luddism and Politics in the Northern Counties', *Social History*, 4 (1979).
Dobson, C. R., *Masters and Journeymen, A Prehistory of Industrial Relations 1717–1800* (London, 1980).
Donnelly F. R., 'Ideology and Early English Working Class History: Edward Thompson and His Critics', *Social History*, 1 (1976).
Donnelly, F. R. and Baxter, J. L., 'Sheffield and the English Revolutionary Tradition, 1791–1820', *International Review of Social History*, XX (1975).
Engels, Frederick, *The Condition of the Working Class in England in 1844*, edited by W. O. Henderson and W. H. Chaloner (Oxford, 1958).
Foster, John, *Class Struggle and the Industrial Revolution: Early Industrial Capitalism in Three English Towns* (London, 1974). See also *Social History*, 1 (1976); *Socialist Register* (1974); and *New Left Review* (1975).
Gammage, R. G., *History of the Chartist Movement* (London, 1854).
Halévy, Elie, *The Growth of Philosophic Radicalism* (London, 1972, original edition 1928).

Hall, Charles, *The Effects of Civilisation on the People of European States* (London, 1805).

Hamburger, J., *James Mill and The Art of Revolution* (New Haven, 1963).

Hamburger, J., *Intellectuals in Politics: John Stuart Mill and the Philosophic Radicals* (New Haven, 1965).

Harrison, B. and Hollis, P., 'Chartism, Liberalism and Robert Lowery', *English Historical Review*, LXXXII (1967).

Hay, D., Linebaugh, P. and Thompson, E. P., *Albion's Fatal Tree: Crime and Society in Eighteenth-Century England* (London, 1975).

Hobsbawm, E. J., *Primitive Rebels* (Manchester, 1959).

Hobsbawm, E. J., *Labouring Men: Studies in the History of Labour* (London, 1964).

Hobsbawm, E. J. and Rudé, G., *Captain Swing* (London, 1969).

Hollis, P., *The Pauper Press: A Study in Working Class Radicalism in the 1830s* (Oxford, 1970).

Hudson, Derek (ed.), *Munby, Man of Two Worlds* (Cambridge, 1972).

Jones, David, *Chartism and the Chartists* (London, 1975).

Kovalev, I. V., *Anthology of Chartist Literature* (Moscow, 1956).

Laslett, Peter, *The World we have Lost* (London, 1971).

Lukács, G., *History and Class Consciousness* (London, 1971).

Maccoby, S., *English Radicalism, 1786–1832* (London, 1955).

Mavor, Elizabeth, *The Ladies of Llangollen* (Harmondsworth, 1971).

Menger, Anton, *The Right to the Whole Produce of Labour* (London, 1899).

Morris, R. J., *Class and Class Consciousness in the Industrial Revolution 1780–1830* (London, 1979).

Musson, A. E., 'Class Struggle and the Labour Aristocracy', *Social History*, 1 (1976).

Neale, R. S., *Class and Ideology in the Nineteenth Century* (London, 1972).

Neale, R. S., *Bath, 1680–1850: A Social History* (London, 1981).

Ögilvie, William, *An Essay on the Right of Property in Land* (London, 1782).

Paulson, R., *Hogarth: His Life, Art and Times* (New Haven, 1971).

Perkin, H. J., *The Origins of Modern English Society, 1780–1880* (London, 1969).

Pinchbeck, Ivy, *Women Workers in the Industrial Revolution 1750–1850* (London, 1930).

Prothero, Iowerth, *Artisans and Politics in Early Nineteenth Century London: John Gast and his Times* (Baton Rouge, 1979).

Rudé, G., *The Crowd in History: A Study of Popular Disturbances in France and England, 1730–1848* (New York, 1964).

Rudkin, Olive, *Thomas Spence and his Connections* (London, 1927).

Schoyen, A. R., *The Chartist Challenge: A Portrait of George Julian Harney* (London, 1958).

Simon, Brian, *Studies in the History of Education, 1780–1870* (London, 1960).

Smith, F. B., *Radical Artisan, William James Linton 1812–1897* (Manchester, 1973).

Stedman Jones, Gareth, *Outcast London: A Study in the Relationships between Classes in Victorian England* (Oxford, 1971).

Thomis, M. V., *The Luddites: Machine-Breaking in Regency England* (Newton Abbot, 1970).

Thompson, E. P., *The Making of the English Working Class* (London, 1963).

Thompson, E. P., 'The Moral Economy of the English Crowd in the Eighteenth Century', *Past and Present*, 50 (1971).

Thompson, E. P., 'Patrician Society, Plebeian Culture', *Journal of Social History*, 7 (1974).

Thompson, E. P., *Whigs and Hunters: The Origins of the Black Act* (London, 1975).

Vincent, John, *Pollbooks: How Victorians Voted* (Cambridge, 1967).

Ward, J. T., *Chartism* (London, 1973).

Williams, Karel, *From Pauperism to Poverty* (London, 1981).

Wilson, Alexander, *The Chartist Movement in Scotland* (Manchester, 1970).

Index